# A THEOLOGY OF LOVE

# A THEOLOGY OF LOVE

WERNER G. JEANROND

Published by T&T Clark International
*A Continuum Imprint*
The Tower Building, 11 York Road, London SE1 7NX
80 Maiden Lane, Suite 704, New York, NY 10038

www.continuumbooks.com



British Library Cataloguing-in-Publication Data
A catalogue record for this book is available from the British Library

ISBN: 978-0-567-13037-2 (Hardback)
978-0-567-64692-7 (Paperback)

Typeset by Fakenham Photosetting, Fakenham, Norfolk
Printed and bound in Great Britain by CPI Antony Rowe Ltd, Chippenham, Wiltshire

In memoriam
**Gerhard Riehm**
1956–2009

Cousin, friend, *duine le Dia*

# *CONTENTS*

# *PREFACE*

Love is at the centre of Christian faith. God loves this universe in which human love as a gift of God is able to transform lives. God's love and human love are of primary importance for theological reflection. However, Christian thinkers have developed often radically different approaches to the relationship between divine and human love and to the significance of body, desire, gender and sexuality for human love. Moreover, while reflecting on love led some Christians to hope for the restoration of a paradise once lost as a consequence of original sin, others expect the fulfilment of life through the transformative power of love in accordance with God's creative and reconciling project.

In the present volume I shall explore the potential and ambiguities of Christian approaches to the praxis of love – always aware that love is not a Christian invention or possession. Discussions of biblical and post-biblical theologies of love and of their respective agendas, motivations and problems shall provide a context for developing a critical and self-critical theology of love today.

This book is the result of a longer journey of learning and teaching. It has been researched and written in three countries, and I am deeply indebted to my family and a great number of colleagues and students in Sweden, Denmark, and Scotland for their generous support, patient encouragement and constructive criticism.

I began working on this book at Lund University in Sweden. A previous research project, funded by the Swedish Research Council, on the concept of God in global dialogue led me to see afresh the significance of the concept of love for theological thinking. Together with Björn Larsson, professor of French at Lund University, I have been exploring concepts of love in literature and religion for a number of years. I am most grateful to him for our ongoing conversations and discussions, not least with regard to the intricate relationship between love and freedom. We have also taught a course together on love, literature and religion at the Centre for Theology and Religious Studies in Lund University and have learned a lot from the participants in this multidisciplinary venture. This research on love has attracted much interest even outside the academy, and I am happy to acknowledge how much I have benefited from lectures, meetings and conversations in churches, public libraries, discussion groups, conferences and seminars throughout Sweden. I also wish to thank the journalists who have made aspects of this research available to a wider audience and thus supported a public conversation on the development, potential, and ambiguities of love.

Work on this book has been interrupted by a number of heavy administrative duties both in Lund University and in the Swedish and Nordic Research Councils. The challenges associated with academic administration have deepened my insights into the connection between respect for otherness, love, reconciliation, and peace.

My Danish colleague Arne Grøn has accompanied this project from the start with unfailing encouragement and critical perspectives. A fellowship at the Danish Institute for Advanced Studies in the Humanities at Copenhagen in 2002-3 allowed me to begin this work in a creative multidisciplinary environment. I wish to thank Birgitte Possing, then director of this unique research institution, and my fellow researchers at this Institute very warmly for an exciting and rich year. A fellowship at the Center for Subjectivity Research at the University of Copenhagen in the autumn of 2007 offered me the space to devote myself again fully to this project. I wish to thank its directors Dan Zahavi, Josef Parnas and Arne Grøn as well as its administrator Pia Kirkemann for all their kind support. During my time at this Center I also benefited from regular conversations on the theology of love with Arne Grøn, Niels Grønkjær and Claudia Welz. Lectures at the Theological Faculties of the Universities of Copenhagen and Aarhus, at the Danish School of Education in Copenhagen, at the Royal Library in Copenhagen, and at the Danish Kierkegaard Society offered me welcome occasions to present some of my thoughts to receptive and responsive audiences. I am very grateful to all my Danish friends and colleagues and their institutions for their kind and generous support of my research.

In January 2008 I moved to the University of Glasgow. My new colleagues and students in Scotland have welcomed me and encouraged my work with proverbial Glasgow warmth and hospitality.

In addition to those already mentioned, the following institutions kindly invited me to present aspects of my research on the theology of love in lectures and conferences and thus offered me valuable opportunities for discussion and learning: The University of Chicago, the University of Texas at Austin, Saint Michael's College (Vermont), the Catholic University of America, University College Dublin, the Einstein Forum in Potsdam, the Elijah Interfaith Institute in Jerusalem, the University of Oslo, the Norwegian Søren Kierkegaard Society, the European Society for Philosophy of Religion (ESPR), the Stockholm School of Theology, the University of Leuven, Institut Catholique de Paris, the Centre Pompidou in Paris, *ad fontes* Denkwochen at Château d'Orion, the University of Tilburg, the Istituto di Scienze Religiose di Trento, the University of Aberdeen, the University of Edinburgh, and the University of Glasgow.

Many people have supported my research through generous conversation, important bibliographical information and pertinent criticism. I am particularly indebted to Regina Ammicht Quinn, Antonio Autiero, Göran Bexell, Ward Blanton, Jeffrey Bloechl, Lieven Boeve, Tomas Bokedal, Philippe Bordeyne, Johannes Bur, William R. Burrows, James M. Byrne, Kari Børresen, Svein Aage Christoffersen, Cecelia Clegg, Pádraic Conway, Ingolf U. Dalferth, Bernard Durel, Lis Engel, Henrik Vase Frandsen, Seán V. Freyne, David Fergusson, Doug Gay, Alon Goshen-Gottstein, Jean Greisch, Cristina Grenholm, Johanna Gustafsson, Kjetil Hafstad, Gösta Hallonsten, Susanne Heine, Jan-Olav Henriksen, Antje Jackelén, David Jasper, Elke Jeanrond-Premauer, Joseph Komonchak, Mikael Lindfelt, Barbro Matzols, Dietmar Mieth, Marius Timmann Mjaaland, Susan Neiman, George Newlands, Sarah Nicholson, Troels Nørager, Michael S. Northcott, Martha C. Nussbaum, Perry Schmidt-Leukel, Birger Olsson, Sverre Raffnsøe, Eckhart Reinmuth, Richard Rosengarten, Christopher Roussel, Joeri Schrijvers, Yvonne Sherwood, Mona Siddiqui, Wilfrid Stinissen, Sturla J. Stålsett, Jesper Svartvik, Jayne Svenungsson, Pia Søltoft, David Tracy, Marina Vidas, Heather Walton, Graham H. Whitaker, Peter Widmann, and Lynn R. Wilkinson.

I happily acknowledge Paul Holloway's and Ian Hazlett's valuable comments on chapters 2 and 7 respectively. Julie Clague, Ola Sigurdson, and Jakob Wirén read the entire manuscript and helped me to improve it in many ways. In addition, Julie Clague offered me collegial and stylistic support. All remaining errors are, of course, my own.

I warmly thank Thomas Kraft and Anna Turton from T&T Clark/ Continuum as well as Nick Fawcett and David Defew for their interest in this book and their work on its production.

This theology of love is dedicated to my cousin Gerhard. Ever since our common childhood he has shown me that the love of God transcends even the greatest handicap and invites us all to participate in an inclusive and transformative community of friends. Gerhard died suddenly while I was completing this book.

Glasgow, 8 September 2009
Werner G. Jeanrond

## *NOTES FOR THE READER*

All translations of quotations from foreign languages are my own if not stated otherwise. Italics in quotations are original if not stated otherwise. All biblical quotations are from the *The Holy Bible: New Revised Standard Version* (New York/Oxford: Oxford University Press, 1989).

# Chapter 1

# *HORIZONS OF LOVE*

## All You Need is Love!

All we need is love. God is love. Love is all that matters. Love is stronger than death. Love is divine ... There seems to be no shortage of poignant phrases praising the power of love in our lives. Singing and writing about love has been at the centre of our cultural expression as long as we can remember. The wonder of love has inspired our best poets, artists and composers. The attraction to write about love has been unshaken even when the cultural forms and manifestations of love have been changing.

There is a consensus in the popular mind as well as in science that we human beings need love in order to live. Although there is widespread disagreement as to the origin of love — is it divine, human, evolutionary, biological, or cultural? — nobody questions the fact that we need love to develop our personalities, our relational capacities, and our outlook on life. Having experienced love seems to create in us an urge to love. We feel part of a miraculous dynamics of love. We experience a call to love, a vocation to relate to others in love. We long to be loved and to be able to love.

We share this desire with women, men and children from other cultures, present and past, and we feel that we can directly relate to their longing for love. We understand their desire; we can compare notes on love in spite of the often dramatic differences between their expressions of love and our own. Love stories excite our imagination across linguistic, cultural and religious divides. Verdi's *La Traviata* touches our hearts, although the social circumstances of Violetta's love story might appear strange to us. The love of Tristan and Iseult still speaks to us, although their cultural background and linguistic expression differ so much from ours. There seems to be a universal dimension in love that transcends all its particular shapes and expressions. Love communicates through differences in time, place and language.

We speak of our love for and of our parents, our children, our partners, spouses and friends, God, our enemies and strangers, and sometimes even ourselves. Love involves many different levels of relationships, yet still seems to be one. Love involves our bodies in different ways — it might find expression in a warm handshake, in a friendly look, in an encouraging eye contact, in a stormy sexual encounter. It seems that our radically different physical expressions do not hinder us from identifying the underlying experience as one of love.

We seem to know when love is in the air notwithstanding its particular appearance, shape and genre. But what is it what we so easily identify as love?

## What is Love?

Love seeks the other. Love desires to relate to the other, to get to know the other, to admire the other, to experience the other's life, to spend time with the other. Nobody else can love in my place. There is no vicarious love. Love requires a concrete agent, a loving subject. Love can be accompanied by much joy and much pain; it can give rise to great emotional turmoil and heavenly bliss. Hence, love always includes emotion, yet it is more than emotion. It has the potential to affect the entire fabric of our human relationships.

In spite of all the differences in detail, human experience, wisdom and knowledge lead us to approach love as a summary concept for certain kinds of human relationships: relationships that affirm some subject or object, acknowledge its value and are motivated further to explore the subject or object of their attention. Moreover, this kind of relationship is often inspired by an intense desire to seek some sort of union with the other, to enter into deeper community with the other, to form a common body, to become one.

We can love objects and we can love subjects. We sometimes say that we love a car, a movie, music, money, sunshine, snow and sublime colours. We can love conditions and values, such as freedom, truth, beauty, justice, power and virtue. We can also say that we love our parents, children, teachers, siblings, friends and fellow workers; we can say that we love the poor, the needy, the happy and the sad; we can say that we love God. We claim to love our dogs, cats, cows and gardens. Whatever we claim to love, we always experience love as transitive: it makes no sense to exclaim just that 'we love'; we must always say whom or what we love.[1] Not only grammatically, love needs the other.

We can distinguish between personal love relationships in terms of their respective intensity and exclusivity. The love between two persons brings together the personal, the erotic and, possibly, even the sexual attraction and energy of human beings and thus changes the partners' way of being in the world as well as their experience and understanding of their body and its extension.

It makes good sense to state that we love subjects that are not even or no longer physically present. Love does not always require full or immediate physical presence. Everybody somewhat familiar with the technical possibilities in our cyber age will appreciate that personal relationships can be initiated and fostered via the internet, with the help of particular forms of communicative techniques.[2] Language, understood in its wider sense as symbolic action, is a primary carrier of love's expression, extension and development.[3]

We can say that we love our dead relatives and friends, perhaps we may claim to love Mother Theresa or Napoleon. As Søren Kierkegaard reminds us in his *Works of Love,* we can love the dead. 'The work of love in recollecting one who is dead is a work of the most unselfish love.'[4] Thus, we can feel being part of larger bodies of love, not only of the intimate and sexual body of love as created and enjoyed by a loving couple, but also as part of a family, a circle of friends, a people, or a religious body, such as the 'body of Christ' or the 'community of saints'. Already at this point we must conclude that the experience of love has implications for our understanding of our own body and its possible extension.

[1] Cf. Augustine's reflections on the transitive verb *to love* in his *De Trinitate* VIII,11; Augustine, *Later Works,* trans. and ed. John Burnaby, The Library of Christian Classics, Ichthus edition, Philadelphia: Westminster Press, 1955, p. 52.

[2] See here, for example, Brett Lunceford, 'The Body and the Sacred in the Digital Age: Thoughts on Posthuman Sexuality', *Theology & Sexuality* 15:1 (2009), pp. 77–96.

[3] See ibid., p. 84, for challenging reflections on language, media, and extensions of the body in our technological age.

[4] Søren Kierkegaard, *Works of Love,* ed. and trans. Howard V. Hong and Edna H. Hong, Princeton, NJ: Princeton University Press, 1995, p. 349.

### Love and Difference

No experience of love — however intense, emotionally charged and sweet it may be — removes the powerful experience of difference. Human desire for community or union with other persons, or with God, originates not only in the recognition of likeness and mutuality, but also in the awareness and actual experience of difference and otherness. Difference provides necessary energy for all forms of love.[5] Human desire for the other subject arises then also out of the experience of difference or radical difference. No experience of love can ever remove from us our individuality, including our always personal journey towards death, though it can make that journey through life towards our always personal death different. Love has the potential to transform our lives. Love makes a difference.

This potential is often experienced as ambiguous. When people declare that love has destroyed their lives, that love lies at the bottom of their particular misery, that love has given them more pain than death ever will, and so on, they point to the experience of unfulfilled love, of rejected or frustrated love, to the pain of having opened oneself to another person who then might have taken advantage of this situation by exploiting rather than loving the other. Love, we must conclude, is a risky business[6]: there is no guarantee that our desire for the other, our investment of feelings and body, our care for the other and our risking of our own self in this new and mysterious relationship with the other will ever result in a new and united 'body' of blissful experience.

Love cannot be *made.* Sex can be made, but not love. Love is and remains a creative mystery. When we say in English, I can 'fall in love', this means that I can be drawn into the transformative and revolutionary experience of love by the power of love. I can be taken into a new experience of another person or a community of persons and in this dynamics I may encounter my own self in a new and different way. I can be invited to become part of a new body which transcends my own body. No amount of practical preparation or intellectual consideration can ever prepare me fully for the actual experience of

[5] Cf. Ola Sigurdson, *Kärlekens skillnad: Att gestalta kristen tro i vår tid,* Stockholm: Verbum, 1998, p. 93.

[6] Cf. Vincent Brümmer, *The Model of Love: A Study in Philosophical Theology,* Cambridge, UK: Cambridge University Press, 1993, pp. 170 and 229. See also Dietmar Mieth, *Das gläserne Glück der Liebe,* Freiburg i. B.: Herder, 1992, p. 39.

encountering the otherness of the other and the otherness of my own self. Love is not a principle, but praxis.

I use the word *praxis* in order to combine attention to the actual encounter with the other and ongoing critical and self-critical reflection.[7] The decision of how to approach the status of love in our lives and thoughts is crucial: if we treat of love in terms of a given theory or doctrine that only needs to be applied to specific situations and encounters, we miss the dynamics of the actual encounter and risk subordinating the other (and the self) to preconceived notions, prejudices and ideologies. If we treat of love in terms of total spontaneity of encounter without benefiting from education, convention, guidance, wisdom and tradition we will not know how to appreciate love's power to transform our lives and visions, and we will risk romanticizing, demonizing or idolizing any momentary sensation, encounter or experience. Therefore, we need an approach that is attentive both to the phenomenon and to the critical and self-critical reflection on its different and shifting manifestations in human life.

Erich Fromm proposed that we should approach love as an art which needs to be learned just as we need to learn the art of living. '[I]f we want to learn how to love we must proceed in the same way we have to proceed if we want to learn any other art, say music, painting, carpentry, or the art of medicine or engineering.'[8] Fromm then divides this process of learning into two parts: the mastery of the theory and the mastery of the practice. While I of course agree with him that we need to know all the relevant facts and embark on a committed journey of lifelong practice in which both theory and the results of my practice are to be blended into one,[9] I consider Fromm's approach still lacking in one important respect. The dynamics of love might challenge any existing knowledge of both facts and performance in the very act of loving. Thus, our theoretical knowledge about the potential of love will need to be submitted to actual love if love is to remain free to rediscover the other, the self and the transforming encounter between both. While the analogy with an art is certainly useful and stretching for many popular notions

[7] For a philosophical discussion of the Greek roots, the development, and the philosophical potential of this term see Alfred Schmidt, 'Praxis', in Hermann Krings, Hans Michael Baumgartner and Christoph Wild, eds, *Handbuch philosophischer Grundbegriffe*, vol. 4, Studienausgabe, Munich: Kösel, 1973, pp. 1107–38.

[8] Erich Fromm, *The Art of Loving*, London: Allen & Unwin, (1957) 1975, p. 5.

[9] Ibid.

of love, a deeper appreciation of love requires a more dialectical approach that will try to safeguard the dynamics of both the rich and complex experience of love and the insights emerging from actual acts of loving.[10]

Approaching love as praxis is my attempt to open all alleys of attention, experience, reflection, and critical research on the way towards a multifaceted understanding of this mysterious and dynamic phenomenon in our lives — of its nature, history, development and potential.

Reflecting on love can never be as good, as rewarding or as confusing than actually to love. But reflecting on love might help us better to understand what we are doing when we love or when we think that we love. The critical and self-critical reflection upon this praxis and its different and shifting expressions may help us better to appreciate the promises and ambiguities of love both in the past and in our own time. It might also help us to sharpen our eyes for detecting instances of pseudo-love, distortions of love, or unrealistic expectations of love and resulting disappointments. It might make us more aware of the close connection between love and power. It may confront us with the shadows and sufferings of love.

For example, suspicions of projection have been voiced in psychoanalysis with reference to assumed love relationships whose incapacity to allow for personal transformation has been interpreted as a sign of the lack of genuine love.[11] Neurotic love relationships may be caused by dysfunctional family structures, one-sided dependencies on the mother or father, and may lead to a wide spectrum of relational distortions, including narcissism, projection and idolization.[12] Sociologists have described how — especially in our culture — many love relationships have been overburdened with particularly unrealistic expectations. They have alerted us to the need to discuss tendencies of reducing love to a couple's insular pursuit of happiness in or even against a threatening environment. The couple's inability to appreciate the interconnectedness of all forms of love may eventually lead

[10] Martha C. Nussbaum, *Love's Knowledge: Essays on Philosophy and Literature*, New York and Oxford: Oxford University Press, 1990, pp. 7 and 261–85, widens the perspective on love by exploring the interrelationship between philosophy and literature. This approach allows also emotional knowledge to regain proper attention.

[11] See, for instance, Jean-Richard Freymann, *L'Amer amour*, Strasbourg: Arcane, 2002.

[12] See, for instance, Fromm, *The Art of Loving*, pp. 83–106, on the disintegration of love in contemporary Western society.

to an implosion of their own inward-looking love relationship.[13] The love of a couple that is isolated from other relationships is in acute danger of suffocating. Hence, the circumstances and horizons of love relationships are deserving of closer attention.

## A Theology of Love

Also the theological treatment of love needs to be analysed with some measure of suspicion and critique. Why has there been a strong tendency to propagate 'pure Christian love' over against the blending of love with eroticism, often interpreted as 'impure love'? Would it not be more appropriate to appreciate the erotic dimension in *all* forms of love? To be sure, not all expressions of love are sexual, but there does not seem to be any expression of love that is not in some sense erotic. I shall return to this observation below in this chapter. Stressing the erotic nature of all human love may make us more sensitive towards rediscovering the aspect of desire operating in all forms of love.[14]

Moreover, some Christian thinkers have promoted the theory that real love was somehow detached from the human body, i.e. purely spiritual. Against such voices it would seem to be important to emphasize that all human love is always embodied, gendered and historically conditioned.[15] Human love can escape the human conditions of time, space and language only at the price of death.

More than forty years have passed since the last major vogue of more comprehensive theological treatments of love. The works by Anders Nygren, Paul Tillich, Karl Rahner, Hans Urs von Balthasar, C. S. Lewis and Daniel Day Williams and others all contained important insights, but have also added new problems to the theological reflection on love.[16] The contrast between true 'Christian love' as

[13] See Ulrich Beck and Elisabeth Beck-Gernsheim, *The Normal Chaos of Love*, trans. Mark Ritter and Jane Wiebel, Cambridge, UK: Polity Press, 1995.

[14] On the broad spectrum and development of the concept of desire see Camille Dumoulié, *Le désir*, Collection Cursus, Paris: Armand Colin, 1999.

[15] For an in-depth study of the history and significance of Christian approaches to body and bodiliness see Ola Sigurdson, *Himmelska kroppar: Inkarnation, blick, kroppslighet*, Logos, Pathos Nr 6, Göteborg: Glänta, 2006.

[16] Anders Nygren, *Agape and Eros: The Christian Idea of Love*, trans. Philip S. Watson, Chicago: University of Chicago Press, 1982 (1930–6); Paul Tillich, *Love, Power, and Justice: Ontological Analyses and Ethical Applications*, Oxford: Oxford University Press, 1954; Karl Rahner, *Schriften zur Theologie*, vol. 5, Zurich and Cologne: Benziger, 1962, pp. 494–517, and *Schriften zur Theologie*, vol. 6, Zurich and Cologne: Benziger, 1965,

*agape* and worldly or misunderstood love as *eros*, the problematic evaluation of the human desire in love, and the role of love in the constitution of the human self are some of the more prominent issues that require further theological clarification today.

In the meantime, a number of books, essays and articles, mostly in theological dictionaries and handbooks, have restated the tradition and its developments, but have rarely attempted an original consideration of the possibilities and ambiguities of a contemporary theology of love.[17] However, in the last few years, interest in love and in the theology of love is rapidly increasing everywhere in Western culture and in respective academic disciplines. When I begun my work on this book I quickly noticed that I was not alone engaged in rethinking the theology of love, its development and its potential. I have tried to keep up as well as I could with the sudden flood of publications within my linguistic reach, although I am afraid that not everything important may have come to my attention. Moreover, I decided from the outset to limit my focus to theological approaches to love in a more narrow sense. Thus, I am not attempting any kind of comprehensive discussion of important contributions by ethicists and moral theologians,[18] exegetes,[19] philosophers and philosophers of religion.[20]

---

pp. 277–98; John McIntyre, *On the Love of God*, London: Collins, 1962; Hans Urs von Balthasar, *Love Alone Is Credible* (1963), trans. D. C. Schindler, San Francisco: Ignatius Press, 2004. C. S. Lewis, *The Four Loves* (1960), Glasgow: Collins, 1977; Daniel Day Williams, *The Spirit and the Forms of Love*, Digswell Place: James Nisbet, 1968; Josef Pieper, *Über die Liebe* (1972), in Pieper, *Werke in acht Bänden*, vol. 4, ed. Berthold Wald, Hamburg: Felix Meiner Verlag, 1996, pp. 296–414.

[17] See, for example, Helmut Kuhn, *'Liebe': Geschichte eines Begriffs*, Munich: Kösel, 1975; Bernard V. Brady, *Christian Love*, Washington, DC: Georgetown University Press, 2003; Carter Lindberg, *Love: A Brief History Through Western Christianity*, Malden, MA and Oxford: Blackwell, 2008; 'Liebe', in *Lexikon für Theologie und Kirche*, 3rd edn, vol. 6, Freiburg i. B.: Herder, 1997, pp. 908–24; 'Liebe', in *Theologische Realenzyklopädie*, vol. 21, Berlin and New York: de Gruyter, 1991, pp. 121–91; 'Liebe', in *Religion in Geschichte und Gegenwart*, 4th edn, vol. 5, Tübingen: Mohr Siebeck, 2002, pp. 335–49; 'Amour', in *Dictionnaire Critique de Théologie*, ed. Jean-Yves Lacoste, Paris: Presses Universitaires de France, 1998, pp. 33–9; 'Love', in *Christianity: The Complete Guide*, ed. John Bowden, London: Continuum, 2005, pp. 714–16.

[18] See, for example, Gene Outka, *AGAPE: An Ethical Analysis*, New Haven and London: Yale University Press, 1972; and Margaret A. Farley, *Just Love: A Framework for Christian Sexual Ethics*, New York and London: Continuum, 2006.

[19] For bibliographical information see chapter 2 below.

[20] Irving Singer, *The Nature of Love*, 3 vols, Chicago and London: University of Chicago Press, 1966–87; Vincent Brümmer, *The Model of Love*; Adriano Fabris, *I paradossi dell'amore fra grecità, ebraismo e cristianismo*, Brescia: Morcelliana, 2001; Troels Nørager, *Hjertets længsel: Kærlighed og Gud religionsfilosofisk belyst*, Copenhagen:

However, the contributions by previous generations of theologians and philosophers and, more recently, by philosophers, psychologists, sociologists, literary scholars, historians, ethnologists, gender scholars, and feminist thinkers to rethinking the theology of love will be discussed in this study in as much as my limited knowledge and competence allow.

My ambition in this book is not to retrace the history of love in Western theology and culture; rather I wish to engage with selected, though significant approaches — past and present — to the Christian praxis of love in order to advance our understanding of this praxis and of its demands on our lives today. Although I am not offering a comprehensive history of the Christian praxis of love, I am very much aware of the fact that all love — and every theology of love — has a history.

## Love Has a History

Neither the praxis of love nor any reflection upon this praxis ever occurs in a vacuum. Rather all experiences of and reflections on love are embedded in a particular space, time and language. Any longing to retrieve the one and only authentic understanding of love would be as naïve as the search for the one and only valid interpretation of a complex literary text. Even though a great many cultures and religions have developed discourses, praises, defences and practices of love, love cannot therefore be automatically approached as a trans-cultural phenomenon. Rather every form or expression of love is rooted in a specific culture, even when it occurs as a radically transformative force within that culture. Respect for the plurality of expressions must be part of any effort to conceptualize love.

Already a cursory look at the career of love in the Christian tradition discloses the historical nature of its different and varied manifestations. At times love has been used or invoked in order to commit what we today would consider to be more or less atrocious crimes: in the name of love corporal punishment was inflicted on children until not so long ago. Proverbs 13.24 was cited as biblical foundation for this practice. 'Those who spare the rod hate their children, but those who love them are diligent to discipline them.' Infidels have

Anis, 2003; Jean-Luc Marion, *The Erotic Phenomenon* (2003), trans. Stephen E. Lewis, Chicago and London: University of Chicago Press, 2007; Zygmunt Bauman, *Liquid Love: On the Frailty of Human Bonds*, Cambridge, UK: Polity Press, 2003; Harry G. Frankfurt, *The Reasons of Love*, Princeton, NJ: Princeton University Press, 2004.

been persecuted and killed for the love of truth. 'Witches' have been burned out of love for their souls.

It is important to pay particular attention to this shift of object within the Christian discourse on love: a person's soul may have been loved while the same person's body was being tortured or destroyed. Many persons have perished in the shadow of 'Christian love'.

Changes in the understanding of personhood require changes in the understanding of love and vice versa. The dialectics of love and self, on the one hand, and of love and community, on the other hand, will be a central concern of this book. Moreover, love has been appealed to by conflicting parties in church and society — all pointing to love as their ultimate motive behind their attempts to justify their actions against the respective other group. Therefore, we need to be prepared to identify and expose sectarian invocations and uses of love in the Christian tradition.

## Love Has a Social Location

Particularly blissful experiences of love have been enjoyed by people who then have claimed that they have entered heaven, yet sooner or later the same people have discovered that they still live on earth although now with an eye open to heaven. The transformative potential of love points to the social location of every experience and expectation of love. As we are going to see in greater detail in chapter 2 when discussing biblical discourses on love, all biblical theologies of love, as indeed all discourses on love, also reflect particular social locations. In the Johannine community, for instance, love among Christians from within this particular community is praised as the highest form of love and defended as the primary means of constructing the 'identity' of this local community against the outside threat of other religions and the inside threat of conflicting orthodoxies and forms of deviation.

## Love and the Embodied Self

All loving relations into which we humans are capable of entering are made possible, but are also limited, by our physical existence. Human love does not happen outside of the human body. There is no human love without the body. Moreover, love requires attention to the bodily limits and limitations of the other as well as of the self. Thinking about love forces us to reflect on our bodies and their nature as well as on their possible extensions into larger bodies opened by love. As we have seen already, through acts of love we can participate even in larger 'bodies', such as the body of Christ.[21]

Moreover, we have already alluded to the interconnectedness of our understanding of love and our understanding of the construction of corporeality in our thinking. Accordingly, it would be wrong to posit some firm understanding of the body prior to any exploration of love. Rather, body and love and the human self constitute each other.[22] Hence, I do not agree here with Pamela Sue Anderson's claim that 'an account of love must begin prior to human relationships with an account of selves who are capable of relating. Thus a rightful conception of self(hood) must be able to account for a most basic capacity to love.'[23]

The Christian discourse of love has always referred to the Incarnation of God in Jesus Christ as the manifestation of divine love on earth, thus defending the significance of the human body for God's love of humanity and of this divinely created universe. However, belief in the Incarnation has not always protected Christianity from belittling the body.[24] Far from it, as we shall see in the subsequent chapters. Rather an ascetic trend, visible also in parts of Graeco-Roman culture, manifested and established itself firmly in early Christian approaches to love and has been present in all Western Christian traditions ever since. Thus, we shall have to consider how an adequate Christian theology of love today might be able to retrieve the positive significance of the body as the necessary place for the praxis of love in this universe.

However, contemporary attempts to reconstruct the human body do not make such a retrieval of the body's significance any easier. We are confronted today both with a public commodification of the (young) body and a repression of the (fragile and old) body. The body is threatened in many ways. Not only does Christian tradition approach

[21] Cf. Sigurdson, *Himmelska kroppar*, pp. 289–590, discusses different bodies implied in the Christian faith in the incarnation, e.g. the individual body, the ascetic body, the erotic body, the sacramental body, the resurrected body.

[22] See my discussion of Jean-Luc Marion's analysis of flesh and body below in chapter 6.

[23] Pamela Sue Anderson, 'Unselfing in Love: A Contradiction in Terms', in Lieven Boeve and others, eds, *Faith in the Enlightenment? The Critique of Enlightenment Revisited*, Amsterdam and New York: Rodopi, 2006, pp. 243–67, here p. 248.

[24] See Alison Jasper, 'Recollecting Religion in the Realm of the Body (or Body ©)', in Pamela Sue Anderson and Beverly Clack, eds, *Feminist Philosophy of Religion: Critical Readings*, London: Routledge, 2004, pp. 170–82.

the body as the bearer of sin and corruption and therefore recommend a strict moral control of all bodily utterances, fluids and extensions, but also considerable trends within post-Christian or non-Christian secular culture spread negative attitudes towards the human body.

Fasting, painful sporting activities, beauty operations, all sorts of medicines and remedies are recommended in order to reach a higher level of control over the body. A new and perfect body is longed for — a kind of secular object of salvation. The desire for the perfect body seems to have replaced the desire for the perfect soul in many quarters of Western society. This fight against the present and imperfect body and for the new and perfect body can, of course, never end. Asceticism, once the hallmark of religious aspirations, has made a comeback in the secular cult of the body. This cult of the body has seemingly reached eschatological proportions.[25] Moreover, this desire for perfect bodies has become an inexhaustible source of wealth generation for those market forces that have offered their mediating remedies to meet this desire, fully conscious of the fact that this desire never can be stilled. Love cannot be made through the production of perfect bodies.

The tasks of a contemporary theology of love, therefore, ought to include the demythologization of the ongoing cult of the body and the reconstruction of possibilities for Christian respect and care for the body.[26] Christian expectations of salvation in the Gospels witness to the great respect for the body among the disciples of Jesus. Jesus is portrayed as showing great care for the physical integrity of the persons whom he met on his way. The healing accounts in the Gospels strongly emphasize the bodily reality of Jesus' praxis of love.[27]

## Human Love is Gendered

When we talk of the human body, we must note that there is no such thing as the human body as such. Rather every human body is a sexed body, female or male. But even the insight into the fact that the body is gendered has a history and a rather perplexing one.

[25] For a detailed discussion of the relationship between religion, body and sexuality see Regina Ammicht Quinn, *Körper — Religion — Sexualität: Theologische Reflexionen zur Ethik der Geschlechter*, Mainz: Grünewald, 1999.

[26] For important theological contributions see Regina Ammicht Quinn and Elsa Tamez, eds, *Body and Religion, Concilium* 2002:2, London: SCM, 2002.

[27] See Helmut Jaschke, *Heilende Berührungen: Körpertherapeutische Aspekte des Wirkens Jesu*, Mainz: Grünewald, 2004.

Thomas Laqueur and others, who have examined the history of body and gender in the West, remind us that the image of the human body as male and female, which we assume today, is neither self-evident nor particularly old.[28] Moreover, the images of the human body which we have come to entertain tend to be rather resistant to challenges because their alteration would require considerable changes in our image of the self and considerable renegotiations of the structure of social power. This can be shown with regard to modern challenges to the traditional image of the body which has dominated body discourse for nearly two thousand years.

This traditional image saw the body as a one-sex body: 'the standard of the human body and its representations is the male body'.[29] Women have been understood as less perfect men. The matrix in which this insight was reached was not biology but gender. Gender discourse has structured the view of our biological considerations. Hence, the nature of sex is a function of our acts and demands of representation, rather than the result of biology.[30] Yet these needs are changing, albeit slowly. In this context Laqueur reminds us of the intimate interplay, biological and rhetorical, between our images of the body and the world beyond it.[31] It is this subtle interplay which has been changing since the eighteenth century when sex as we know it was invented.[32]

The recognition of difference between the sexes does not yet settle the way in which these differences are handled.[33] The cultural setting and the language through which we construct difference change over time. '[B]asically the content of talk about sexual difference is unfettered by fact, and is as free as mind's play.'[34]

[28] Thomas Laqueur, *Making Sex: Body and Gender from the Greeks to Freud*, Cambridge, MA and London: Harvard University Press (1990), 1992, pp. 8–24. See also the contributions and discussion on gender in *Kön, Res Publica: Symposions teoretiska och litterära tidskrift* 35/36 (1997); and Gerard Loughlin, ed., *Queer Theology: Rethinking the Western Body*, Oxford: Blackwell, 2007.

[29] Laqueur, p. 62.

[30] Ibid., p. 115.

[31] Ibid., p. 122.

[32] Ibid., p. 149.

[33] Ibid., p. 222: 'Sex and sexual difference are not simply there, any more than gender is.'

[34] Ibid., p. 243. For some critical comments on Laqueur's findings see Arne Jarrick, *Kärlekens makt och tårar: En evig historia*, Stockholm: Pan–Norstedts Förlag, 1997, pp. 105–29. For a critique of Laqueur's constructivist approach to natural science and gender see esp. pp. 261–3.

Laqueur's account stresses the contingent nature of our constructions of bodies, sexual differences and gender. Our symbolic expressions of 'body realities' need critical and self-critical interpretation. One line of interpretation has suggested that there is no 'really real' reality there to back up our symbolic constructions, thus leading to a new ignorance of factual bodies. Such an idealistic discourse frees our discussion of gender and sex from all 'natural' ingredients, i.e. from everything that has to do with bodies. The consequences of such a view for the understanding of love are deconstructive indeed.[35]

Rather than embarking on a totally naturalistic theory of body or on a totally culturalistic theory of body, it seems appropriate to acknowledge the actual interconnection between nature and culture as the place where love can be considered.[36]

## Love is Erotic

Eroticism (or the erotic) can mean a number of things in today's parlance. It may refer to the spiritual and psychological side of the experience of love over against a mere sensually and physically experienced sexuality. It may refer to the overall role that love and sexuality play in a particular culture. Or it may refer simply to sexual love.[37]

The word itself goes back to the Greek *Eros*, the god of love, and has a rich and varied history. Part of the original Greek perception of Eros was his uniting force that brings together previously separated beings.

In Plato's dialogue *The Symposium* Aristophanes praises Eros for he 'loves human beings more than any other god; he is their helper and the doctor of those sicknesses whose cure constitutes the greatest happiness for the human race'.[38] Aristophanes tells the myth of how Zeus had separated the once whole and round human beings into halves in order to hinder them from climbing up to heaven to attack the gods.[39] Ever since, human beings are

[35] Cf. Ammicht Quinn, *Körper*, p. 65.

[36] Cf. ibid., p. 66.

[37] Cf. Regina Ammicht Quinn, 'Erotik/Eros', in Peter Eicher, ed., *Neues Handbuch theologischer Grundbegriffe*, vol. 1, Neuausgabe 2005, Munich: Kösel, 2005, pp. 253–9, here p. 253.

[38] Plato, *The Symposium*, trans. Christopher Gill, London: Penguin, 1999, p. 22 (189d).

[39] Cf. ibid., pp. 22–7 (189d–193d).

looking to become whole again. Thus 'love' is 'the name for the desire and pursuit of wholeness'.[40] And Aristophanes leaves no doubt here that this desire transcends mere sexual attraction. It is a desire for human wholeness intimately bound to proper behaviour towards the gods. However, it is desire that wishes to overcome the punishment by Zeus so that 'each of us finds his loved one and restores his original nature'.[41] Not unlike the biblical myth of paradise, this vision of erotic love is looking back to a once-existing wholeness before the 'Fall' as a result of divine punishment. The future of this love desires the wholeness of the past.

In the same dialogue Socrates, recalling a conversation with Diotima, describes love's status between the mortal and the immortal. Eros appears as a mediator between the gods and the humans in charge of promoting and maintaining the relationality of the whole. Eros loves wisdom and the beautiful.[42] Love desires the good things and happiness.[43] Moreover, love desires these 'for ever'.[44] Immortality thus emerges as the ultimate object of love.[45] Diotima refers to pregnancy not only in body, but also in mind, both of them present in the desire to give birth and reproduce. 'Because he's pregnant, he's attracted to beautiful bodies rather than ugly ones; if he's also lucky enough to find a mind that is beautiful, noble and naturally gifted, he is strongly drawn to this combination.'[46] This desire for and the pursuit of beauty call for education and a step-by-step approach. Like in Greek culture in general, the erotic power is understood here with reference to men and their specific physical and intellectual aspirations.

In Plato's dialogue *Phaedrus*, eros appears also as madness, though as one coming from the gods.[47] Eros needs to be tamed in order to unfold his cognitive power.[48] In this dialogue Plato also describes

[40] Ibid., p. 26 (193a).

[41] Ibid., p. 27 (193c).

[42] Ibid., p. 40 (204b).

[43] Ibid., p. 42 (205d–e).

[44] Ibid., p. 43 (206a).

[45] Ibid., p. 46 (208e).

[46] Ibid., pp. 46–7 (209b).

[47] Plato, *Phaedrus*, trans. R. Heckforth, in *The Collected Dialogues of Plato*, ed. Edith Hamilton and Huntington Cairns, Bollington Series LXXI, Princeton, NJ: Princeton University Press, 1961, pp. 475–525, here p. 492 (245a–c).

[48] Ibid., pp. 499–500 (253d–254e).

the ascent of the immortal soul to the place beyond heavens of which 'none of our earthly poets has yet sung, and none shall sing worthily'.[49] Such is the life of the gods:

> It is there that true being dwells, without color or shape, that cannot be touched; reason alone, the soul's pilot, can behold it, and all true knowledge is knowledge thereof. Now even as the mind of a god is nourished by reason and knowledge, so also is it with every soul that has a care to receive her proper food; wherefore when at last she has beheld being she is well content, and contemplating truth she is nourished and prospers, until the heaven's revolution brings her back full circle.[50]

For the other souls the ascent is much tougher and needs a number of rebirths. 'Now in all these incarnations he who lives righteously has a better lot for his portion, and he who lives unrighteously a worse.'[51]

Here is not the place to discuss Plato's doctrine of the soul in any detail. However, his notion of ascent, his concept of memory, and his understanding of eros and desire have strongly influenced Western notions of love. Eros shows the way to a life on earth in 'happiness and concord, for the power of evil in the soul has been subjected, and the power of goodness liberated; they have won self-mastery and inward peace'.[52]

The erotic realm includes here sexual desire, cognitive desire, and the longing for union with the divine. It has entered the Christian tradition in two forms. Either the erotic realm is judged to stand in contradiction to the transcendent spirit of religion and therefore has to be excluded as sinful from divinely inspired relations; or the erotic realm is considered vital for the relationship between the believer and God and thus becomes an important object for theological reflection.

The first and negative assessment of the erotic has identified eros with contingent realities that are obstacles to the spiritual vocation of the human being. In the theology of Anders Nygren, for instance, *eros* is the competitor of the genuinely 'Christian love', *agape. Eros* and *agape* are not compatible. *Eros* is self-centred and possessive, while *agape* is self-giving and divine. In spite of his critique of later Augustinianism, Nygren shares Augustine's distinction between worldly love, characterized by self-love (*eros*), and heavenly love,

[49] Ibid., p. 494 (247c).
[50] Ibid., p. 494 (247c–d).
[51] Ibid., p. 495 (248e).
[52] Ibid., p. 501 (256b). See also Ammicht Quinn, 'Erotik/Eros', p. 254.

characterized by self-giving love (*agape*).[53] We shall have to return both to Augustine's and to Nygren's theology of love at a number of occasions in this book and in greater detail below in chapters 3 and 5 respectively. However, already at this point of our reflections, it might be useful to underline that Nygren was not critical as such of the sexual expression of human love. Instead his critique was directed against the erotic conviction that human beings could ever reach God through their own desire, mystical contemplation, ascent or action.

A different and positive reception of the erotic can be found in the mystical tradition. In Christian (as well as in Jewish and Islamic) mysticism the unity of love is explored and defended, and the erotic dimension is understood to be part of this unity.[54] The presence of the erotic in the discourse of mystical love found inspiration firstly in the Song of Songs;[55] secondly in the light which this text has thrown over the reading of the creation accounts in the Hebrew Scriptures; and thirdly in a positive evaluation of the human desire for union with God.[56] The works of Pseudo-Dionysius (around AD 500) have helped to establish the mystical genre within Christian theology.[57]

[53] Cf. Augustine, *De civitate Dei* XIV, 28; *The City of God*, trans. Henry Bettenson, London: Penguin, 2003, pp. 593–4. See Anders Nygren, *Agape and Eros: The Christian Idea of Love*, trans. Philip S. Watson (1953), Chicago: University of Chicago Press, 1982, pp. 532–48.

[54] Annemarie Schimmel, *Wie universal ist die Mystik: Die Seelenreise in den großen Religionen der Welt*, Freiburg i. B.: Herder, 1996, p. 116: 'Sehnsucht nach der Heimat, von der das Herz getrennt ist — das ist ein allen Mystikern gemeinsames Thema.'

[55] See Ulrich Köpf, 'Hoheliedauslegung als Quelle einer Theologie der Mystik', in Margot Schmidt together with Dieter R. Bauer, eds, *Grundfragen christlicher Mystik*, Stuttgart-Bad Cannstatt: Frommann-Holzboog, 1987, pp. 50–72.

[56] For an in-depth discussion of the development of Christian mysticism in the West and of its different roots and inspirations see Bernard McGinn, *The Foundations of Mysticism: Origins to the Fifth Century*, London: SCM, 1992. See McGinn's critique of Nygren, ibid., p. 27: It is clear from Plato's *Symposium* 'that Plato's notion of love is not purely egotistical and self-serving, as Anders Nygren claimed; rather true *eros* is love for the Good that seeks to beget the good, either the good of human offspring or of virtue'.

[57] See McGinn, *The Foundations of Mysticism*, pp. 157–82. – Pseudo-Dionysius, *The Complete Works*, trans. Colm Luibheid, The Classics of Western Spirituality, New York and Mahwah: Paulist Press, 1987. However, Denys Turner, *The Darkness of God: Negativity in Christian Mysticism*, Cambridge, UK: Cambridge University Press, 1995, p. 47, emphasizes that Pseudo-Dionysius' (= Denys the Areopagite's) theology, though employing a richly erotic imagery, is concerned with

> the ascent of the *mind* up the scale of negations which draws it into the cloud of unknowing, where, led by its own *eros* of knowing, it passes through to the darkness of union with the

The mystics do not understand the bodily passion of love in terms of a heteronomous or anti-divine attitude; rather genuine love for God takes hold of the entire human self. Mystical love for God and its positive evaluation of the body by no means exclude a necessary decision in favour of an ascetic and chaste lifestyle. Many men and women have adopted a monastic or eremitic lifestyle in order to be more fully able to devote themselves to the love of God and the love of neighbour. Thus, asceticism can be also appreciated as a training of the body and not necessarily as a submission or an exclusion of it.[58]

The mystical tradition does not represent a separate way from the religious culture of its time. Rather it has always also reacted to the culture of the day in creative ways and offered its own vision of the dynamics of love.[59] This vision can take the form of a more direct, more personal, and more poetic discourse on God; it may develop a subtle spirituality in contrast to the at times rather strong expression of hierarchical order in the Catholic Church of the West. The counter-cultural potential of Christian mysticism can even manifest itself within a particular monastic tradition, e.g. John of the Cross and his vision of Carmelite reform. Moreover, women mystics, such as Hildegard of Bingen, Hadewijch of Brabant,[60] and Mechthild of Magdeburg, express a new erotic language that differs considerably from the male rhetoric and power of the day in whose institutions women were not allowed to participate.

The mystical discourse of love thus shows that the erotic and the sacred need not be understood in terms of radical opposition. Rather they have been experienced to be closely connected. However, mystical theology does include its own ambiguities. Although the erotic may be affirmed, this does not necessarily lead to an affirmation of an embodied self as we are going to see in more detail below in chapter 4.

---

light. It is therefore the *eros* of knowing, the passion and yearning for the vision of the One, which projects the mind up the scale; it is the dialectics of 'knowing and unknowing' which govern that progress, and it is not in the traditional metaphors of affectivity, touch, taste and smell, but in the visual metaphors of light and dark, seeing and unseeing, that that progress is described.

[58] Cf. David Jasper, *The Sacred Desert: Religion, Literature, Art, and Culture*, Oxford: Blackwell, 2004, pp. 25–55.

[59] See Arnaud de la Croix, *Lebenskunst und Lebenslust: Sinnlichkeit im Mittelalter*, trans. Gritje Hartmann, Darmstadt: Wissenschaftliche Buchgesellschaft, 2003, pp. 110–23. See also Saskia Murk-Jansen, *Brides in the Desert: The Spirituality of the Beguines*, London: Darton, Longman and Todd, 1998, pp. 114–16.

[60] See below, chapter 4.

## Networks of Love

The human desire for love always develops within larger networks of relationships. Many of these relationships are not at all symmetrical in the sense that Western imagination wishes the love of a couple to be. The relationship between parents and children are rarely symmetrical: newborn babies cannot extend their love to their parents in the way the parents are able to show to them in so many ways. Hence, the activity of one subject of love does not need to be matched by other subjects in order for love to flow. Children love their parents in different ways than parents love their children. The parental vocation to love children into freedom, away from physical and emotional dependence on their parents, in order to allow the children to become mature subjects of love, does not necessarily correspond to the desires of the children themselves. Often children wish to remain within an unchanging union of love with their parents.[61]

More recently, maternal love has received more academic attention. Gender-conscious studies, for instance in history and theology, have examined the specific nature of the mother's love for the child and its changes since the advent of modernity.[62] Cristina Grenholm analyses the different shapes of motherly and fatherly love. Fatherly love tolerates more distance from the child than motherly love. Thus, fatherly love is able to transcend more easily the necessarily more private orientation of motherly love in the direction of the public realm.[63] Also differences between the mother's love relationship to her child and her love relationship to her partner are of interest here: sexuality is not constitutive for motherly love. However, in the parental network of love, all loves are united in their recognition of the vulnerability of both mother and child. From the beginning of pregnancy motherly love participates in a process which, if accepted, neither the father nor the mother can control.[64] Thus, the vulnerability of the child confronts us with an insight into the necessity of love if life is to continue.[65]

[61] See also Erich Fromm, *The Art of Loving*, pp. 38–46.

[62] See Elisabeth Badinter, *L'amour en plus: Histoire de l'amour maternel (XVIIe-XXe siècle)*, Paris: Flammarion, 1980; and Cristina Grenholm, *Moderskap och kärlek: Schabloner och tankeutrymme i feministteologisk livsåskådningsreflektion*, Nora: Nya Doxa, 2005.

[63] Cf. Grenholm, p. 65.

[64] Ibid., pp. 154 and 165.

[65] Cf. ibid., p. 188. See also Fromm, *The Art of Loving*, p. 50: 'It seems, however, that the real achievement of motherly love lies not in the mother's love for the small infant, but in her love for the growing child.'

There has been a tendency — not only in Christian tradition — to prioritize the giving of love over the receiving of love. A problematic image of God has suggested that God is the infinite giver of love who never needs or longs to receive love from her creatures. Accordingly giving love was considered more virtuous than receiving love. However, some Christian thinkers in the Reformation tradition have argued that the human attitude towards divine love ought to be characterized by a humble attitude of reception. We shall have to return to this debate on giving and receiving love in Christian thinking later on in our investigation.

Notwithstanding this debate on the virtues of love, nobody doubts that an experience of love is always prior to my loving. I have to develop first into an agent or a subject of love. This process of growth differs from one person to another. It varies from culture to culture and depends on cultural, social and religious circumstances as well as on collective and personal expectations. The networks of love that make my own growth as lover possible comprise not only parents. Depending on my circumstances I might have been fortunate enough to experience also the love of siblings, grandparents, a larger family, friends, parish communities and religious leaders, teachers and many other people that in one way or the other have had an impact on my childhood and youth. It is in such networks of love that I can grow into a person able to receive and to give love.[66]

Love demands mutuality, but not symmetry. Love is a relationship between persons that desire to be with one another, to find out more about the other, to experience the other as subject in view of her own personal potential and limitations, to accept the other even then when a fuller understanding for the other is lacking. Even friendship between two persons does not always depend on symmetry of experience, emotion and expression.[67] Rather friendship is first of all marked by commitment to one another. Human love for God can by definition not be symmetrical, though it too demands mutuality.

Rather than looking for symmetry in love, it might be more appropriate to reflect on the conditions of maturity in love. However, this reflection depends on the prior discussion of whether we understand love first and foremost in terms of an attitude, an emotion or a relation.

[66] See Irving Singer, *The Pursuit of Love*, Baltimore and London: Johns Hopkins University Press, 1995, pp. 6–8.

[67] I shall discuss friendship in more detail below in chapter 8.

## Love as Attitude, Emotion and Relation

Nobody will seriously question the presence of emotions in human experiences of love. Nor will anybody doubt that loving and being loved both have to do with attitudes towards the other and the self. The question at stake at this point of our investigation, however, is whether emotion and attitude offer sufficient explanatory power for a comprehensive theology of love.

It is interesting to note with Vincent Brümmer that 'most of the comprehensive concepts of love developed within it [the Christian tradition] have been attitudinal rather than relational. Love has generally been taken to be an attitude of one person towards another, rather than as a relation between persons.'[68] Brümmer blames this reductionist understanding of love on the ontological prejudice of our intellectual tradition 'that there are only two sorts of reality: substances and attributes'.[69] Against this background Brümmer defines love as 'not merely a feeling or emotion but also a purposive commitment to adopt a complex pattern of actions and attitudes to the beloved'.[70]

I agree with Brümmer that any reduction of love to the level of mere emotion would withdraw love from the horizon of commitment and responsibility and instead locate it in a horizon of arbitrariness and transience. '[A]lthough we cannot be held responsible for our feelings, we can be held responsible for keeping our commitments. The sincerity of the commitments (and of expressions of the feelings which gives rise to them) are [sic] therefore tested by the faithfulness of the lover. If he fails to keep his commitments we say that his love is not true.'[71]

In both Jewish and Christian religion love is understood as a commandment: 'Hear, O Israel: The Lord is our God, the Lord alone. You shall love the Lord your God with all your heart, and with all your soul, and with all you might' (Deut. 6.4–5). 'You shall also love the stranger, for you were strangers in the land of Egypt' (Deut. 10.19). 'You shall love your neighbour as yourself: I am the Lord' (Lev. 19.18). In the New Testament these commandments are combined by Jesus, for instance, in Matthew's Gospel:

[68] Brümmer, *The Model of Love*, p. 33.

[69] Ibid.

[70] Ibid., p. 153. Cf. here also Pamela Sue Anderson, 'Unselfing Love', pp. 243–6.

[71] Ibid., p. 154.

> 'You shall love the Lord your God with all your heart, and with all your soul, and with all your mind.' This is the greatest and first commandment. And a second is like it: 'You shall love your neighbour as yourself.' On these two commandments hang all the law and the prophets. (Matt. 22.37–40)

Can love be commanded? While our postmodern sensitivity might react negatively to any suggestion to combine commandment and love, it might be interesting to review the age-old relationship between love and law in this context. Both love and law aim at ordering human relationships and are themselves inspired by relational traditions and experiences.[72] Hence, our study will have to consider both within the larger horizon of the dynamics of love.

Attitudes and emotions, attention and commitment, commandment and law, beneficence and gifts, devotion and admiration, and respect are among the ingredients that may enter into our experience of love. But neither of them alone nor all of them together can exhaust the dynamics of love. 'Rather than looking on love as an attitude which might issue in a relationship, we could also look on love as a relationship which involves partners adopting a complex set of attitudes towards each other.'[73] Only understood as a relationship does love disclose its complex dynamics. The aim of our study is to explore the complexity of this specific sort of relationship.

## The Complexity of Love

The overwhelmingly rich and multifaceted attention to the phenomenon of love, not only in the traditions of the West, makes it impossible for a single researcher to offer a comprehensive account of the different discourses on this phenomenon. No individual possesses a complete picture of all the treatments of love in philosophy, theology, religious studies, literary science, history, sociology, psychology, gender studies, natural sciences, medicine, cultural studies, art history, media science, legal science, etc. Who can claim to have read all the poems on love, listened to all the songs of love, looked at all the paintings and photographs depicting love, seen all the films portraying the dynamics and tensions of love, or have experienced all the shades, forms, and dimensions of love?

[72] Cf. Paul Tillich, *Love, Power, and Justice*; and Paul Ricœur, 'Love and Justice', trans. David Pellauer, in Werner G. Jeanrond and Jennifer L. Rike, eds, *Radical Pluralism and Truth: David Tracy and the Hermeneutics of Religion*, New York: Crossroad, 1991, pp. 187–202.

[73] Brümmer, *The Model of Love*, p. 156.

Hence, the purpose of this study cannot be comprehensive. Rather the aim of this book is to reflect upon the potential of love from within a theological horizon. Both significant traditions and ruptures in the development of Christian discourses on love and contemporary contributions to the theological discussion of love shall be studied and explored here. I do not intend to simplify or harmonize the theological study of love. Yet I do wish to present what I consider to be significant features of a relational understanding of the Christian praxis of love. My investigations of selected historical contributions to the debate on love are therefore intended to provide constructive and critical challenges to contemporary theological thinking on love, though not exhaustive studies in historical theology. Moreover, a critical understanding of such important developments may both enrich the reader's horizon and challenge any possible conviction that our selective conceptions of love in the twenty-first century might automatically deserve dogmatic priority.

Here I have chosen to discuss only a few among the many Christian 'schools' of love. I devote three chapters to this historical exploration of developments, influences, resources, and major problems in past traditions of love: In chapter 2, I shall discuss biblical challenges to a theology of love. In chapter 3, I offer a critical reading of Augustine's theology of love, and in chapter 4, I analyse new models of love which have been emerging from the twelfth to the sixteenth century.

In chapters 5 and 6, I examine modern theological approaches to the Christian praxis of love: first prominent defenders of a sharp separation between agape-love and eros-love, and then Christian thinkers trying to fuse anew both aspects.

In chapter 7, I explore some of the institutions of love in our time. Chapter 8 analyses the interdependence between personal, local and global spheres for an adequate understanding of the politics of love in our universe.

In the final chapter of this book I approach the love of God in which all aspects of the Christian praxis of love culminate. Here I consider divine and human love and approach salvation, sexuality, and forgiveness in the light of love.

## Chapter 2

---

# *BIBLICAL CHALLENGES TO A THEOLOGY OF LOVE*

### Love at the Centre

All Christian thinkers agree that love is the central focus of Christian faith in God. The double love commandment proclaimed by Jesus according to the Gospels of Matthew, Mark and Luke has been deeply engrained in Christian belief and praxis:

> 'You shall love the Lord your God with all your heart, and with all your soul, and with all your mind.' This is the greatest and first commandment. And a second is like it: 'You shall love your neighbour as yourself.' (Matt. 22.37–9; cf. Mark 12.29–31; Luke 10.27–8)

Love refers both to the nature of God (1 John 4.8 and 16: 'God is love') and to the divinely ordered nature of relationships. Thus it concerns a broad network of interdependent relationships: between God and God's creation; God and human beings; God and the Church; between human beings and God; between one human being and another; between human beings and the universe, between human beings and their diverse cultural and religious traditions and expectations; and between every human being and her or his own emerging self.

In this chapter I shall explore some of the biblical voices on love and assess their potential for a theology of love today. However, I would like to begin by commenting briefly on the complex task of a critical retrieval of biblical discourses on love.

### A Hermeneutics of Love

Today a theology of love faces serious questions and suspicions: first, since expressions and theories of love have changed over the centuries, how can we continue to speak of the one and same 'love' as the centre of Christian praxis?

Secondly, the study of religions, recent interreligious encounter and dialogues, and the study of the Graeco-Roman world, have made abundantly clear that love is not an exclusively Christian concern and domain. Love is not a uniquely Christian possession. Rather, love is practised and propagated by many religious and humanist movements, both ancient and modern. Does love differ from movement to movement?[1] Is there a natural cross-fertilization of all of these manifestations of and discourses on love? Moreover, God's love cannot be restricted to the realm of the Christian churches. To what extent, then, can love be understood as the ultimate feature of *Christian* identity? Can love ever be free from ambiguities?

Thirdly, within the Christian movement, love has had a tainted history. Love has been invoked in order to punish children, to persecute non-believers, heretics, and revolutionaries, to exclude and even burn women who dared to challenge the patriarchal order in church and society. Any critical historical investigation into the career of love in the Christian movement must be prepared to apply not only a hermeneutics of retrieval, but also a hermeneutics of suspicion that is attentive to the shadows of *Christian* love. From the very beginning of Christian self-awareness and self-construction through narratives, letters, pseudepigraphy, prayers, liturgies and other forms of communication, patriarchal approaches fought for dominance. A Feminist theological reconstruction of Christian origins is necessary in order to free the emancipatory dynamics of the Christian praxis of love for women, men and children today from a long and debilitating history of Christian patriarchalism.[2]

Thus, talking meaningfully and constructively about love today is not without problems. However, becoming aware of the complexity and ambiguity of the development of Christian approaches to love

[1] For a discussion of love in different religious traditions and of freedom as the necessary corrective of love, see Reinhold Bernhardt, 'Die Polarität von Freiheit und Liebe. Überlegungen zur interreligiösen Urteilsbildung aus dogmatischer Perspektive', in Reinhold Bernhardt and Perry Schmidt-Leukel, eds, *Kriterien religiöser Urteilsbildung*, Beiträge zu einer Theologie der Religionen 1, Zurich: Theologischer Verlag, 2005, pp. 71–101.

[2] See Elisabeth Schüssler Fiorenza's important contributions to this task and to the methodology necessary for this task in her seminal study *In Memory of Her: A Feminist Theological Reconstruction of Christian Origins*, London: SCM, 1983.

does not make it impossible to explore the potential of Christian forms and expressions of love. Since many contemporary Christian discourses on love, in the academy, in church, and in society at large, claim to stand in the tradition of love supported by the Christian movement's foundational experiences, it seems important to investigate the treatment of love in the biblical traditions that have inspired the Christian movement and its pluriform praxis of love.

Traditionally, Christian theologians were particularly keen to ascertain the differences between the Jewish and Graeco-Roman approaches to love, on the one hand, and the Christian understanding of love, on the other, in order to argue for the superiority of Christian religion. In the 1930s, the Swedish theologian Anders Nygren, for instance, argued in his magnum opus *Agape and Eros: The Christian Idea of Love* for the singularity of Christian love:

> One of the most striking differences between the Commandment of Love, as it is interpreted in the Old Testament and in Christianity, is that in the latter it is universal in its scope. In Judaism love is exclusive and particularistic: it is directed to one's 'neighbour' in the original and more restricted sense of the word, and it is directed to 'neighbours only' ... Christian love, on the other hand, overleaps all such limits; it is universal and all-embracing.[3]

Moreover, Nygren sharply contrasted agape-love with 'the egocentric character of Eros-love'. 'It is not too much to say that self-love is the basic form of all love that bears the stamp of Eros.'[4] For Nygren, eros-love is in the Greek heritage so often and wrongly fused with Christian agape-love, although the latter 'excludes all self-love'.[5]

More recent biblical studies, however, have developed more critical approaches to love by profiling its respective development within particular biblical contexts. The shift in exegetical interest from Christian apologetics to a critical and self-critical discussion of the biblical texts has paved the way also for a review of the treatment of love in both the Hebrew Scriptures and the New Testament. This change in hermeneutical consciousness has allowed more nuances in the development of love to emerge which in turn are challenging some of the classical theological convictions on the unique, universal and a priori superior scope of 'Christian love'.[6]

[3] Anders Nygren, *Agape and Eros: The Christian Idea of Love*, trans. Philip S. Watson, Chicago: University of Chicago Press, 1982 (1930–6), p. 63.

[4] Ibid., p. 216.

[5] Ibid., p. 217.

[6] In spite of helpful comments on specific issues of the Christian praxis of love, Francis Watson, *Agape, Eros, Gender: Towards a Pauline Sexual Ethic*, Cambridge, UK:

Recently, the Danish exegete Troels Engberg-Pedersen has reminded both exegetes and theologians again of the continuing presence of Nygren's dogmatic approach to love in the respective collective subconscious of many scholars.[7] Nygren's sharp distinction between Christian agape-love, understood in terms of self-giving love, and Greek eros-love, understood in terms of searching and longing for what is desired and considered to be beautiful and desirable, was a *theological* distinction and not a distinction based on an adequate reading of the Greek text of the Bible or on a unique biblical use of language. Thus, it is not correct to state that all uses of *agape* in the Septuagint and the New Testament, in fact, signify the kind of love prioritized as 'agape' by Nygren.[8] Rather the Greek words *agape* and *philia* have often been selected for reasons of style, rather than for reasons of semantic distinction or contrast.[9] No theological case on the uniqueness of Christian love can thus be constructed on linguistic or terminological observation. 'On the contrary, there is basic agreement on the understanding of love's central nature in the Jewish, Christian and Greek texts.'[10]

One of the most significant insights into the nature of biblical texts has been the understanding of biblical texts as *texts*. That means biblical texts ought not to be reduced to collections of individual propositions or pillaged in search for quotes that might support one or the other doctrinal conviction; instead they ought to be approached as complex communicative entities. As such they are able both to refer back to their particular contexts and to open their semantic potential to readers within always changing social, religious

---

Cambridge University Press, 2000, overall remains fully committed to a renewed apologetic version of the traditional scheme of *agape* and *eros* for his development of a Trinitarian sexual ethics.

[7] Troels Engberg-Pedersen, 'Fra "Eros och Agape" til Venskab: Antikkens forestillning om kærlighed i forhold til kroppen, selvet og det gode (frelsen)', in Henrik Rydell Johnsén and Per Rönnegård, eds, *Eros and Agape: Barmhärtighet, kärlek och mystik i den tidiga kyrkan*, Skellefteå: Artos & Norma, 2009, pp. 11–27, here p. 12.

[8] Engberg-Pedersen agrees with James Barr's critical remarks in Barr, 'Words for Love in Biblical Greek', in L. D. Hurst and N. T. Wright, eds, *The Glory of Christ in the New Testament: Studies in Christology in Memory of George Bradford Caird*, Oxford: Clarendon Press, 1987, pp. 3–18. Moreover, the Swedish exegete Birger Olsson also points to the considerable overlap between the different Greek words for love. Cf. Birger Olsson, *Johannesbreven*. Kommentar till Nya Testamentet (KNT) 19, Stockholm: ESF-förlaget, 2008, p. 232.

[9] Engberg-Pedersen, pp. 15–17. The use of both terms as synonyms can also be documented in Philo's writings. (Ibid., p. 16.)

[10] Ibid., p. 18.

and linguistic contexts.[11] Moreover, as texts they always already participate in a communicative system that is marked by changing conventions and styles. Hence, the fact that biblical texts always appear in particular literary forms (e.g. hymns, laws and regulations, prayers, lamentations, narratives, etc.), are received with the help of particular reading genres and reading styles, and are always interpreted contextually in particular functions has challenged any naïve use of biblical texts for the sake of providing building material for ambitious and unambiguous theological doctrines.[12]

As a result, hermeneutical developments have sharpened the theologian's perception of the phenomenon that all discussions and descriptions of love in the Bible witness to particular experiences, circumstances, expectations and desires. Biblical discourses on love have a rich and varied history. Therefore any effort to converse with biblical texts on the understanding and development of love draws the contemporary reader and thinker into a conversation, at times even a struggle, with this historical flow of experiences, ideas, desires, ideologies, ambiguities and expectations.

Love is neither a Christian invention nor a Christian possession.[13] Rather the Christian development of love is firmly rooted in the Jewish religious tradition and in the encounter of both traditions with their Graeco-Roman cultural context for their respective development. According to both Christian and Jewish praxis, love of God, love of neighbour, love of self, and love of God's creation are intimately related. The different attentions in love must, of course, be distinguished, but ought never to be separated. Ultimately, the divine love command concerns the development of right relationships between persons and communities and the various *others*: God as the

[11] Cf. Werner G. Jeanrond, 'Text/Textuality', in Kevin J. Vanhoozer, ed., *Dictionary for Theological Interpretation of the Bible*, Grand Rapids: Baker Academics, 2005, pp. 782–4.

[12] See Werner G. Jeanrond, *Text and Interpretation as Categories of Theological Thinking*, trans. Thomas J. Wilson, Dublin: Gill and Macmillan, and New York: Crossroad, 1988; reprint: Eugene, Oregon: Wipf and Stock, 2005, pp. 73–128; and Jeanrond, *Theological Hermeneutics: Development and Significance*, London: SCM, 1994, pp. 78–92.

[13] For a brief overview of the significance of love in different religious traditions see J. Bruce Long, 'Love', in Mircea Eliade, ed., *The Encyclopedia of Religion*, vol. 9, New York: Macmillan, 1987, pp. 31–40, here p. 31: 'The concept of love, in one form or another, has informed the definition and development of almost every human culture in the history of the world — past and present, East and West, primitive and complex.'

radically other, the human other, God's mysterious creation project, and the otherness within my own self.

While biblical Hebrew has a number of linguistic expressions for the different experiences and challenges of love (e.g. intimate relationship, desire, loyalty, solidarity, charity, commitment, concern, attention, appreciation, friendship, sympathy), the English language combines a great variety of experiences under the overlapping terms of 'love' and 'charity'.[14] The advantage of this linguistic reduction consists in the implicit acknowledgement of the deeper connection between all forms and expressions of love. Its disadvantage lies in the loss of differentiation between the many forms and expressions.

In any case, there is not *the* Christian praxis of love. Rather the Christian praxis of love has always been a pluriform phenomenon. There have always been tensions and shifts in emphasis from one Christian experience and conceptualization of love to another. I would like to illustrate this point with regard to both the double love commandment, i.e. the love of God and the love of neighbour, and the shifting horizon of love.

## Love of God and Love of Neighbour

There is great unanimity in the different biblical texts about the origin of love.[15] Love comes from God. It emerges from God's creative and reconciling presence in the universe. This divine love makes human love first of all possible. God's love manifests itself both through the divinely granted covenant with God's people, Israel, and through God's acts as creator of the universe. Within the covenant, therefore, the love of God is the greatest commandment.

> Hear, O Israel: The Lord is our God, the Lord alone. You shall love the Lord your God with all your heart, and with all your soul, and with all your might. Keep these words that I am commanding you today in your heart. (Deut. 6.4–6)

In these verses, known as the *Shema Israel* (Deut. 6.4–5), as well as in their communicative context, the love relationship between God and

[14] For a recent reassessment of the semantic potential of 'charity' as distinct from 'love' see Rowan Williams, *Lost Icons: Reflections on Cultural Bereavement*, London and New York: Continuum, 2000, pp. 65–115.

[15] In this section I make use of some reflections previously published in my article 'Biblical Challenges to a Theology of Love', *Biblical Interpretation* 11 (2003), pp. 640–53.

his people is based on the Sinai covenant. It is important to note that here the expression of love of God is not so much a matter of intimate affection as a matter of 'obedience to God's commandments, serving God, showing reverence for God, and being loyal to God alone'.[16]

Depending on which Hebrew word is used to express the nature of the relationship between God and God's people, different nuances are emphasized in the texts. Hence, there are many meanings of love in the Hebrew Scriptures and a number of prominent terms that give expression to them (e.g., *dôd, ra'yâ, yādîd, hāšaq, 'āhēb,* and *hesed*). The single English term *love* has contributed to the widespread illusion that we here are dealing with a well-defined phenomenon and its unambiguous expression. All of the different Hebrew expressions translated as 'love' nevertheless refer to experiences of close relationship, although not all of them denote (sexual) intimacy.

The expression of God's relationship through the verb *'āhēb,* for example, enjoys a significant development over time and context. The prophet Hosea uses this same term when likening God's relationship with Israel to the relationship of the (patriarchal) husband to his wife (Hos. 3.1). In spite of this enlargement of association into the area of marital intimacy, there is no question that all the founding activity and energy of this relationship originate in God's will. God makes Israel's love possible.[17]

Even the expression of God's relationship through the noun *hesed* undergoes a development. This term 'compactly incorporates all three of these dimensions (commitment, provision for need, freedom) in a single word'.[18] The Mosaic covenant tradition 'stretches the meaning of the term beyond its usual secular usage to incorporate the possibility of forgiveness as an act of divine *hesed*'.[19] Hence, the close connection between love and forgiveness is an integral part of the biblical heritage.

The communicative possibilities of dealing with the different dimensions of God's love for Israel and Israel's love for God were somewhat restricted in the process of the Septuagint translation, where the hitherto not too common Greek term *agape* was chosen to lend expression to nearly all of the Hebrew terms for love. The verb *phileo* is used only very rarely. The verb *erao,* which can refer to sexual

[16] Katherine Doob Sakenfeld, 'Love (OT)', in *The Anchor Bible Dictionary,* vol. 4, New York: Doubleday, 1992, pp. 375–81, here p. 376. See also A. D. H. Mayes, *Deuteronomy,* New Century Bible, London: Oliphants, 1979, pp. 176–7.

[17] Katherine Doob Sakenfeld, 'Love (OT)', p. 377.

[18] Ibid., p. 378.

[19] Ibid., p. 379.

love, was avoided altogether in the Pentateuch as a translation of the Hebrew *'āhēb* (which can have the same connotations).[20]

The price for this restriction of connotations has been high, especially for later Christian readers of the Hebrew Bible through Greek. The reduction of a wider imagination of religious love that includes the erotic dimension of human relationality to a narrower imagination that wishes to understand religious references to love to be free from eros has contributed to the problematic rupture between eros and agape in the Christian theology of love. We shall have to return to this problem below and in the following chapters.

Of course, we can appreciate the Greek translators' problem of finding words that would not lead to a false identification between Yahweh and Eros, the Greek god of love whose veneration was widespread and popular at the time. Nevertheless, avoiding one problem in *translation* has led to other problems in the *reception* of the text. Translations rarely reduce ambiguities. The New Testament writers do not use the term *eros* either. Their preferred verbs for talking about love were *agapan* and *philein*. The early Christians were afraid of confusing their understanding of God's love with either profane or philosophical concepts in Greek love and friendship.[21]

In spite of the shifts in language, there is agreement throughout the Hebrew Bible on the faithfulness of God's love and on God's mercifulness and willingness to forgive the breaches of the relationship which God has offered to the people. The divine offer of love embraces all aspects of reality. To love God implies accepting and respecting the creative power of God's love and presence, but also loving the other human being and one's own emerging self.

> For the Lord your God is God of gods and Lord of lords, the great God, mighty and awesome, who is not partial and takes no bribe, who executes justice for the orphan and the widow, and who loves the strangers, providing them food and clothing. You shall also love the stranger, for you were strangers in the land of Egypt. You shall fear the Lord your God; him alone you shall worship; to him you shall hold fast,[22] and by his name you shall swear. (Deut. 10.17–20)

[20] Cf. William Klassen, 'Love (NT and Early Jewish)', in *The Anchor Bible Dictionary*, vol. 4, op. cit., pp. 381–96, here p. 381.

[21] Cf. T. Spidlik, 'Love of God and Neighbour', in Angelo Di Berardino, ed., *Encyclopedia of the Early Church*, trans. Adrian Walford, Cambridge: James Clarke & Co., 1992, pp. 506–7.

[22] Mayes, *Deuteronomy*, p. 211, interprets this phrase as 'synonymous with love'.

Love of God and love of neighbour thus belong together. Although they need to be distinguished, they must not be separated. For women, men, and children to love God demands openness to God's creative project, letting oneself be drawn into this project and to follow its rules and wisdom, respecting God's divinity, accepting God's otherness, desiring to know more about God, and longing for an always intensifying closeness to God.

According to the Synoptic Gospels, Jesus' praxis of love is also naturally anchored in this covenantal understanding. The covenant and its laws provide the framework for the successful divine-human relationship. Jesus never abandoned the covenantal order. Rather he re-emphasized the love commandment from Deuteronomy when provoked to identify the greatest commandment within the Torah. The Synoptic portrayal of Jesus' famous restatement of the double love commandment ('You shall love the Lord your God with all your heart, and with all your soul, and with all your mind.' And 'You shall love your neighbour as yourself.' Matt. 22.37–40 and par. in Mark and Luke) is based on citations both from Deut. 6.5 (see above) and from Lev. 19.18 and 34 and thus highlights the Hebrew tradition (though in its Greek Septuagint translation) in which the Christian love commandment is thus firmly rooted.[23] Theologically speaking, it is not of great importance to know whether or not Jesus was the first to have introduced the combination of both love commandments.[24] It is more important to appreciate the significance of this double commandment for the proclamation of God's reign in the Synoptic Gospels.[25] Love is the central focus of the

[23] Cf. Klassen, 'Love (NT and Early Jewish)', p. 385.

[24] Birger Gerhardsson does 'not think that Jesus was the first in Israel to make this combination': Gerhardsson, *The Schema in the New Testament*, Lund: Novapress, 1996, p. 276. Franz Mussner, *Was hat Jesus Neues in die Welt gebracht?*, Stuttgart: Katholisches Bibelwerk, 2001, p. 49, also affirms that, as far as the double love command is concerned, Jesus has not brought anything new into the world. However, Mussner considers the correlation between Deut. 6.5 and Lev. 19.18 to be new. Moreover, he sees in Matt. 5.43–8 a very important radicalization of the double command when in the sermon on the Mount Jesus demands the love of enemies and contrasts this command expressively with Lev. 19.18.

[25] See also Ulrich Luz, *Studies in Matthew*, trans. Rosemary Selle, Grand Rapids: Eerdmans, 2005, p. 205: 'For Matthew, Jesus' authoritative interpretation of the Law is decisive, making the commandment to love the greatest commandment under all circumstances and the one on which the rest depends (22:40).' See also Luz, ibid., p. 210: 'Here Matthew is in line with Hellenistic Judaism which focused on the commandment to love and the Decalogue, subordinating the others … The main difference between Matthew and rabbinic Judaism is that his interpretation of the Law rests on the absolute authority of one teacher, Jesus.'

human–divine and the human–human relationship. However, for the Jesus of the Synoptic Gospels this focus calls for concrete action rather than emotion or for a lengthy theological or legal deliberation.[26]

This fact is most clearly expressed in Luke's Gospel where the story of the Good Samaritan (Luke 10.25–37) is told immediately after the citation of the double love commandment. Moreover, by redefining the meaning of 'neighbour', the Lukan Jesus establishes a principle of moral obligation.[27] The point of the parable is not to *have* neighbours, but to *become* a neighbour to others.[28] The praxis of love which Jesus proclaimed and lived through his actions reaches out to all sorts of people: the friends, the needy, women, children, the poor, the suffering, the sick, the sinners, the foreigners, and the enemies. This praxis reflects God's goodness to all and gathers all people around God's creative and reconciling presence.

> But I say to you that listen, Love your enemies, do good to those who hate you, bless those who curse you, pray for those who abuse you ... Your reward will be great, and you will be children of the Most High; for he is kind to the ungrateful and the wicked. Be merciful, just as your Father is merciful. (Luke 6.27–8 and 35b–36)

The constructive and charitable relationship to all people that characterizes this understanding of love is an important theological

[26] Cf. Ulrich Luz, *Das Evangelium nach Matthäus: 3. Teilband: Mt 18–25*. EKK I/3, Zurich and Düsseldorf: Benziger and Neukirchen-Vluyn: Neukirchener Verlag, 1997, p. 273.

[27] Philip Esler, 'Jesus and the Reduction of Intergroup Conflict: The Parable of the Good Samaritan in the Light of Social Identity Theory', *Biblical Interpretation* 8 (2000), pp. 325–57, here p. 345: 'In the context of the group-oriented ethics of first-century Palestine this was indeed a radical step.' Esler (p. 351) draws attention also to the related passage in Acts 10.34–5 where Peter says, 'I truly understand that God shows no partiality, but in every nation anyone who fears him and does what is right is acceptable to him.' Søren Kierkegaard, *Works of Love*, ed. and trans. Howard V. Hong and Edna H. Hong, Princeton, NJ: Princeton University Press, 1995, p. 32, sees in the commandment to love one's neighbour an *eternal* transformation of human love. 'Consequently, *only when it is a duty to love, only then is love eternally secured.*' For a discussion of Kierkegaard's theology of love see below, chapter 5.

[28] Cf. François Bovon, *Das Evangelium nach Lukas: 2. Teilband: Lk 9,51–14,35*. EKK III/2, Zurich and Düsseldorf: Benziger and Neukirchen-Vluyn: Neukirchener Verlag, 1996, p. 99. 'Indem wir andern Nächste werden, erfüllen wir das Gesetz, also den Willen Gottes, und nehmen unsererseits das Anliegen und die Haltung Christi an. So zu verstehen ist die Dynamik der Bewegung auf die andern zu, und so zu verstehen ist der Realismus einer Gebärde, die unseren Kräften entspricht und den Wahn von karitativer Allmacht aufhebt' (ibid).

event — notwithstanding whether or not it is dominical. Rather its centrality in the Synoptic Gospels provokes disciples and theologians alike to widen the horizon of love so as to include the enemy, the foreigner, and the sinner.[29]

Parallel with this widening of the horizon, the Gospels reveal a relativization of traditional family bonds.[30] Jesus is reported to have redefined the question of identity in his community now in terms of belonging to God and active participation in God's reign: 'My mother and my brothers are those who hear the word of God and do it' (Luke 8.21). Jesus does not question the potential usefulness of the traditional pillars of Jewish religious life and identity, i.e. family, Temple, Torah, and the land, but he relativizes their significance for the emergence of God's reign by subordinating these pillars of tradition to the transformative praxis of love.[31] The coming of God's reign will be promoted through love, not through the preservation of established religious tradition.

## The Changing Horizon of Love

The Johannine community also stresses the close connection between love of God and love of the other, but in its writings, i.e. the Gospel of John and the three Letters of John, the 'others' refer to members of this particular Christian community.

> God is love, and those who abide in love abide in God, and God abides in them ... We love because he first loved us. Those who say, 'I love God', and hate their brothers or sisters, are liars; for those who do not love a brother whom they have seen, cannot love God whom they have not seen. The commandment we have from him is this: those who love God must love their brothers also. (1 John 4.16b, 19–21)

The Johannine understanding of Christian love includes two further dimensions: the love of God is related, first, to oneness or harmony within the Christian community, and second, to Jesus' own example of self-sacrifice for his friends. Overall, the Johannine reflection on

[29] Cf. Gerd Theißen, *Die Religion der ersten Christen: Eine Theorie des Urchristentums*, 3rd edn, Darmstadt: Wissenschaftliche Buchgesellschaft, 2003, p. 106.

[30] The texts in the Synoptic Gospels on the family of Jesus are complex and difficult. Upon closer inspection, they reveal many layers including the interests of respective communities to profile different approaches to Christian mission and leadership. For a more detailed discussion see Michael Goulder, *St. Paul versus St. Peter: A Tale of Two Missions*, Louisville, KY: Westminster/John Knox Press, 1995, pp. 8–15.

[31] Cf. Jeanrond, *Theological Hermeneutics*, p. 178.

love is intimately linked with the faith in God's sending of his Son to the world.[32]

With regard to the first dimension, it is striking to see how much the Gospel of John focuses on the issue of abiding in the love of God.[33] 'As the Father has loved me, so I have loved you; abide in my love. If you keep my commandments, you will abide in my love, just as I kept my Father's commandments and abide in his love' (John 15.9–10). It is obvious that love characterizes the network of relationships between God, the Son, and the community against the very real threat of hatred, i.e. that which destroys the inner-Christian bond, from outside and, in particular, from inside the community.[34] Love, then, is a commandment to work for unity and harmony within the parameters of this community.

With regard to the second dimension, it is important for the author to show that love has to do with self-sacrifice on behalf of the others within the same community.

> We know love by this, that he laid down his life for us — and we ought to lay down our lives for one another. How does God's love abide in anyone who has the world's goods and sees a brother in need and yet refuses help? (1 John 3.16–17)

The Johannine approach to love evolves around an intensification of love that aims to strengthen the community from within. 'I give you a new commandment, that you love one another. Just as I have loved you, you also should love one another. By this everyone will know that you are my disciples, if you have love for one another' (John 13.34–5). It is interesting to note that this restatement of the biblical love command is understood here to be a new (*kainos*) commandment.[35]

[32] Cf. Olsson, *Johannesbreven*, pp. 232–4 and 286; and Hans-Josef Klauck, *Der erste Johannesbrief*. EKK XXIII/1, Zurich: Benziger, and Neukirchen-Vluyn: Neukirchener Verlag, 1991, p. 261.

[33] On the use, significance and possible interpretation of the Greek verb *menein* (to remain) in the Johannine literature see Birger Olsson, *Johannesbreven*, pp. 228–9. Olsson proposes to interpret these passages in terms of an interiorization of older concepts through a renewal of God's covenant. Cf. also ibid., p. 233.

[34] Olsson reads the Letters of John from the perspective of an inner-Jewish struggle according to which some of the Christians in the Johannine community have returned to their Jewish faith. The conflict between Jewish Christians and lapsed Jewish Christians was related to the issue of the messianic nature of Jesus. Cf. Olsson, pp. 279–81.

[35] For an in-depth analysis of the Johannine love commandment see Enno Edzard Popkes, *Die Theologie der Liebe Gottes in den johanneischen Schriften*, Wissenschaftliche Untersuchungen zum Neuen Testament. 2. Reihe 197, Tübingen: Mohr Siebeck, 2005, pp. 249–72.

Thus, according to John, there is no doubt that love is central to Christian discipleship, although the scope of love in John's community differs considerably from other New Testament writings. The Johannine discourse on love centres on a particular Christian community's own inner life — including the call to pay attention to those 'brothers' who require help and assistance. The equality of the (male?) members of the Christian community may thus be stressed.[36] However, the shift from a love that is actively concerned about all the others now to a love that is primarily directed towards the inner circle of a particular Christian church cannot be overlooked.[37] In this community love functions first of all in terms of internal loyalty over against a societal context experienced as threatening.[38] The fact that the Johannine community celebrates God's universal love for the world in the sending of the Son should not mask this narrowing of the community's overall horizon of love.[39] Moreover, love and oneness are linked here in such a manner as to suggest that love is not so much the way to handle difference, conflict and otherness as a way of avoiding — if not perpetuating — all three. Here, John clearly differs from, for example, Luke, and from Paul to whom I now turn.

All New Testament discourses on love witness to the divine origin of love, but they draw different conclusions from this insight. To acknowledge God as the author of love and to reflect upon God's nature as love does not necessarily lead to the same kind of theological conviction or indeed to the same kind of praxis of love in church and world.[40]

[36] Cf. Theißen, pp. 108–9.

[37] Cf. here also Birger Olsson, *Johannesbreven*, p. 194; cf. p. 224: 'The passage in the Bible that speaks most of love thus has a clear limitation', and p. 233. Klauck, pp. 278–80, also stresses this inward-looking horizon in the theology of love in 1 John, but warns against over-interpreting this phenomenon as purely negative.

[38] See Bruce J. Malina and Richard L. Rohrbaugh, *Social-Science Commentary on the Gospel of John*, Minneapolis: Fortress Press, 1998, pp. 59–61 and 233. See also Popkes, p. 328.

[39] Cf. Popkes, pp. 192–248. Popkes stresses the Johannine texts' universal aspirations, but fails to appreciate how these aspirations are compromised by the inward-looking perspective on love in the community.

[40] With regard to the vogue of Trinitarian approaches to church and society in contemporary theology one might wish to add a cautionary remark here: references to the inner-Trinitarian love do not automatically lead to an adequate Christian praxis of love. Insights into the divine mystery do not necessarily provide guarantees for adequate Christian action. Cf. Werner G. Jeanrond, 'Revelation and the Trinitarian Concept of God: Are they Key Concepts for Theological Thought?', in Werner G. Jeanrond and Christoph Theobald, eds, *God: Experience and Mystery, Concilium* 2001:1, pp. 120–30.

For John love is an instrument of unity for those who belong narrowly to the Johannine church, whereas for Paul love can also be a means of resolving conflict, difference and otherness in a more diverse Christian community. References to love are many in Paul's Letters. First I wish to highlight Paul's approach to love in his First Letter to the Corinthians; then I shall problematize Paul's radicalization and spiritualization of Christian love.

To the disunited community at Corinth Paul wishes to suggest an unusual, extraordinary way of approaching one another in everyday life. Here Paul approaches love from the perspective that all members of this Christian community belong to the body of Christ (1 Cor. 12.27–31). In his famous praise of love (1 Cor. 13.1–13) Paul neither moralizes, nor sentimentalizes, nor psychologizes. Instead he demonstrates a praxis inspired by the goal of God's creation. Love is not an idea or abstraction.[41] Rather Paul points to concrete attitudes:

> Love is patient; love is kind; love is not envious or boastful or arrogant or rude. It does not insist on its own way; it is not irritable or resentful; it does not rejoice in wrongdoing, but rejoices in the truth. It bears all things, believes all things, hopes all things, endures all things. Love never ends. (1 Cor. 13.4–8a)

Moreover, for Paul love is the central dimension of Christian discipleship and existence (cf. Gal. 5.6). Love draws the Christian into the truth. As such it unfolds an eschatological dynamics (1 Cor. 13.12–13). But it also has a personal dynamics, for love invites the Christian disciple into union with Christ. 'Who will separate us from the love of Christ? Will hardship, or distress, or persecution, or famine, or nakedness, or peril, or sword?' (Rom 8.35). Paul answers himself:

> No, in all these things we are more than conquerors through him who loved us. For I am convinced that neither death, nor life, nor angels, nor rulers, nor things present, nor things to come, nor powers, nor height, nor depth, nor anything else in all creation, will be able to separate us from the love of God in Christ Jesus our Lord. (Rom 8.37–9)

Not even death can separate the Christian from the love of Christ. That means that this love not only is unlimited, rather it has the quality of eternity, namely of God's own realm. God's presence, love, and respect for creation will never end. This in turn means that the love relation that God offers to the human being in Christ both respects God's divinity and the humanity of the human being without

[41] Cf. Wolfgang Schrage, *Der Erste Brief an die Korinther, 3. Teilband: 1 Kor 11,17–14,40*, EKK VII/3, Zurich and Düsseldorf: Benziger and Neukirchen-Vluyn: Neukirchener Verlag, 1999, p. 294.

dissolving the one into the other. God's love respects the difference between the human being and God and thus invites all through the praxis of love into a process of disclosure of the mystery of both — of God's divinity and the humanity of the human being.

Yet for Paul, this understanding of love is not confined to the limits of the human subject. Rather every genuine love comes from God and extends to the entire community, which God has called into existence through Christ (cf. Rom 5.5). It is interesting to note that 'Paul seems most comfortable speaking about the love of God/Christ in the first person plural.'[42] For Paul, the love of God is a gift of the Holy Spirit who *possesses* the believer. One does not simply accept the gospel, but is handed over to it (6.17), arrested by it, compelled to serve as God's slave by the Spirit (7.6).[43]

Without discussing further New Testament communities and their respective references to love, already at this point we can conclude that the Bible offers important aspects and initiatives for a theology of love. However, this theology is characterized by a plurality of different contextual insights and expressions. There is agreement on the divine origin of the gift of love and on the potential that love has for the development of a Jewish and a Christian praxis. Although the Christian understanding of God's relationship to the world in Christ opens up an ethos marked by attention to love, there is a shifting horizon within this attention to love that raises pressing questions and concerns. Is love to inspire only the relationship between the Christian community and God or does it even concern the relationship between Christians and non-Christians? To what extent does the focus on love include enemies and outsiders? How does a Christian praxis of love approach otherness inside and outside the Christian community?

## Biblical Challenges to a Theology of Love

Concluding this chapter I wish to emphasize some central biblical challenges to our present discussion of adequate theologies of love.

First of all, biblical love has a history. Tracing the development of a theology of love throughout different biblical contexts and traditions

[42] Klassen, 'Love (NT and Early Jewish)', op. cit., p. 392.

[43] On Paul's understanding of living transformed by the Spirit, see Ulrich Wilckens, *Der Brief an die Römer, 2. Teilband: Röm 6–11*, EKK VI/2, Zurich, Einsiedeln and Cologne: Benziger, and Neukirchen-Vluyn: Neukirchener Verlag, 1980, pp. 68–72.

can make the contemporary reader aware of the variety of communal and personal expressions of love as well as of the connection between the commandments to love God, to love the other human being, and to love oneself in the right way.

Secondly, both in the Hebrew Scriptures and the New Testament we detect trends of including and of excluding 'others' from the horizon of love. The universal horizon of God's love to which the various creation accounts and some of the covenant narratives witness is at times narrowed down by concerns for communal identity both in Israel[44] and in the Church. The Bible does not contain any pure or original passage on love to which we could return for any timeless and unambiguous understanding of love. Both the *Shema Israel* in Deut. 6.4–6 and the understanding of God as love in 1 John 4 are embedded in concrete community contexts, religious concerns and group-identity issues.

Thirdly, a combination of linguistic, semantic, communicative, philosophical and cultural developments has promoted the reduction of the degree of passion in biblical considerations of love. Desire and passion are present in a number of texts in the Hebrew Bible, but strikingly absent in the texts of the New Testament. In Exodus 20.5 God is described as a 'jealous God'. In Jeremiah 2–3 we read of God's passionate love for his people, but also of God's disappointment over Israel's failure to love God. Emotions are evoked when God contemplates his love for Israel (see Isaiah 49.15–16). Likewise, human love for God is expressed in images portraying deep emotions:

> As a deer longs for flowing streams,
> so my soul longs for you, O God.
> My soul thirsts for God, for the living God.
> When shall I come and behold the face of God?
> My tears have been my food day and night,
> while people say to me continually,
> 'Where is your God?' (Psalm 42.1–3)

Body and soul are involved in this love relationship between human beings and God. The entire human person loves God. In such texts the separation between eroticism and piety that later on was to permeate the development of some forms of Christian spirituality is not yet visible. Rather, the whole human person desires God's presence.[45]

[44] See, for example, the book of Ezra, esp. Ezra 9–10.

[45] Cf. Othmar Keel, 'Erotisches im Ersten Testament', *Meditation: Zeitschrift für christliche Spiritualität und Lebensgestaltung* 26:2 (2000), pp. 6–11.

Notwithstanding later allegorical interpretations and theological reconstructions,[46] the rich imagination of the love poetics in the Song of Songs offers the reader a beautiful hymn to love in all its erotic splendour and shapes. Moreover, this text and its desires and imagination are not infiltrated by patriarchal concerns.[47] The hymn begins with these verses:

> Let him kiss me with the kisses of his mouth! For your love is better than wine, your anointing oils are fragrant, your name is perfume poured out; therefore the maidens love you. Draw me after you, let us make haste. The king has brought me into his chambers. We will exult and rejoice in you; we will extol your love more than wine; rightly do they love you. (Song 1.2–4)

The presence of this text in the biblical canon might serve as a promising reminder that human sexuality and erotic desire ought to be well integrated into a theology contemplating the network of the divine–human love relationship.[48]

Fourthly, many of the biblical texts display a certain amount of ambiguity with regard to the question that occupies so many of today's readers. How can I relate to my own emerging self within the network of interdependent love relationships? Does love enhance or reduce my freedom as a person?[49] Feminist thinkers have often stressed that one needs first some measure of selfhood in order to be able to invest it into the network of love relationships.[50] While many biblical texts, the Gospels in particular, point to Jesus' regard for the entire human person — including her bodily integrity,[51] the process of personal maturing in love is only referred to in passing.

[46] Among the immense literature see, for example, Franz Dünzl, *Braut und Bräutigam: Die Auslegung des Canticum durch Gregor von Nyssa*, Tübingen: J. C. B. Mohr (Paul Siebeck), 1993; and Samuel Rubenson, 'Himmelsk åtrå: Höga Visan i tidigkristen tolkning', in Henrik Rydell Johnsén and Per Rönnegård, eds, *Eros and Agape: Barmhärtighet, kärlek och mystik i den tidiga kyrkan*, Skellefteå: Artos & Norma, 2009, pp. 105–27.

[47] Keel, p. 8.

[48] See Carey Ellen Walsh, *Exquisite Desire: Religion, the Erotic, and the Song of Songs*, Minneapolis: Fortress Press, 2000.

[49] Cf. Björn Larsson, *Besoin de liberté*, Paris: Seuil, 2006, pp. 97–113.

[50] See, for instance, Elizabeth A. Johnson, *She Who Is: The Mystery of God in Feminist Theological Discourse*, New York: Crossroad, 1993, p. 265; and Margaret A. Farley, *Just Love: A Framework for Christian Sexual Ethics*, New York and London: Continuum, 2006, pp. 200–4.

[51] For a discussion of Jesus' respect for the bodily integrity of human beings see, for instance, Helmut Jaschke, *Heilende Berührungen: Körpertherapeutische Aspekte des Wirkens Jesu*, Mainz: Grünewald, 2004.

Paul, in line with his understanding of love as a form of Spirit possession (cf. Rom 8.15 and Phil 3.8–11; see also above) which is to be actively cultivated, goes so far as to speak of a radical transformation of the self as a result of the power of Christ's love: 'I have been crucified with Christ; and it is no longer I who live, but it is Christ who lives in me. And the life I now live in the flesh I live by faith in the Son of God, who loved me and gave himself for me' (Gal. 2.19b–21). What does such a view of intimate unity between Christ's love and the human person mean for the human person's self-understanding as a subject of love? In view of the general agreement between the Jewish, Christian and Greek understanding of love (see above), the question remains: why this repression of desire, body, and self in some of the New Testament approaches to human love?

Troels Engberg-Pedersen sees an answer to this question in the problem of asceticism in antiquity.[52] For the Apostle Paul, ultimately, body and self (in the sense in which we understand both today) have no role to play in the cognitive realm in which one loves God and is loved by God.[53] Even with regard to the Christian praxis of love between human beings, body and individual self are to be renounced (cf. Phil. 2.3–4). Thus, there is a tension in Pauline theology between the human person's actual contribution to the body of Christ, on the one hand, and the radical spiritualization of love beyond any concern for body and self (cf. Gal. 5.5–6). While Paul recognizes the demands of human physical existence, at the same time he locates the praxis of genuine love beyond this realm of existence.

Why this radicalization and radical spiritualization of love which characterizes Paul's, and, as we have seen already, John's approaches to love? Engberg-Pedersen focuses here on a social function: this radical concept of love serves to maintain a clear distinction between those who are part and those who are not part of the realm in which love rules. Group identity is constructed and maintained with reference to its superior love. 'The radical concept of love represents a sectarian strategy.'[54] Love has become the key to Christian self-identification (see Rom. 12–13) and demarcation from others.[55] The

[52] Engberg-Pedersen, 'Fra "Eros och Agape" til Venskap', p. 19.

[53] Ibid., p. 21.

[54] Ibid., p. 25.

[55] James D. G. Dunn, *The Theology of Paul the Apostle*, Grand Rapids: Eerdmans (1998), 2006, p. 733, praises Paul without exposing the ambiguities in his theology of love:

> Among the most innovative features which shaped Christian theology for all time are the key terms which Paul introduced. Above all we should think of 'gospel,' 'grace,' and 'love' –

friends (*philoi*) in John and the beloved brothers (*agapetoi adelphoi*) in Paul are special — not because of their bodiliness or individuality, but because of their communal confession of and adherence to 'Christian love'.

The Christian praxis of love has been ambiguous from its beginning. The sectarian tendencies in some of the theologies of love in New Testament, however, are not the whole story. Rather the praxis of love reported in the Gospels is often much richer and challenging. The spiritualizing concepts of love are thus in tension with alternative anthropologies and theologies according to which the human person is created as a subject capable of loving God, other human beings, herself, and God's entire creation. Human sexuality is not an obstacle to the human vocation to become an agent of love. On the contrary, God meets the human being in God's *incarnate* Son (cf. John 1.14). The belief in God's assumption of a human body does not only present a challenge to any thought of human love without a body, but stresses the participation of the very body in all acts of eternal love. The story of the woman with the alabaster jar, which we find in all the Gospels, illustrates the respect for and appreciation of Jesus' body (Matt. 26.6–13; Mark 14.3–9; Luke 7.36–50; John 12.1–8). At the same time it inspires the reader's erotic imagination (especially in Luke and John where she anoints Jesus' feet and wipes them with her hair — in Luke she also kisses Jesus' feet) and thus might help in overcoming the contemptuous attitude of many Christians towards the body, an attitude that sharply separates between pure (i.e. non-physical) and impure (i.e. physical) expressions of love.[56] At times eroticism has been demonized and erotic expressions of love in the Bible have been explained away with reference to deeper spiritual senses and concepts, at times in support of social cohesion. Bodily love was often considered ambiguous, whereas spiritual love, tendentiously identified and proclaimed as *agape*, was considered to be above suspicion. However, in our reading of the Bible there is no unambiguous expression of love. The crucial question, then, is not the one between pure and impure love, but between love on earth

---

gospel as the good news of Christ focusing in his death and resurrection, grace as epitomizing the character of God's dealings with humankind, love as the motive of divine giving and in turn the motive for human giving. Between them, in their specialist Christian usage, these words sum up and define the scope and character of Christianity as no other three words can. And that specialist Christian usage, in each case, we owe entirely to Paul.

[56] See Elisabeth Schüssler Fiorenza, *In Memory of Her*, pp. 128–30 and 330–1, for a wider consideration of this narrative's different versions in the Gospels and for its theological meaning and significance.

affected by eternity and love on earth not wishing to be affected by eternity.[57]

Fifthly, a theology of love would need to attend to the question of criteria of adequacy for the Christian praxis of love. If all true love comes from God, all expressions of love must be tested against this their eternal vocation. Following Paul's and the Synoptic Gospels' line of argument, we may ask to what extent any praxis of love represents an adequate response to God's always prior love for us, a love that is creative, embodied, erotic, faithful, respectful and eternal. Or with reference to John's community it would seem appropriate to ask: does the Christian praxis of love reflect Christ's invitation to follow him on his way to God, a way that does not know either status or hierarchy, but heeds the call to be one another's *servants* (cf. John 13)?

A more comprehensive theology of love is needed. But already at this point the danger of reducing either a Jewish or a Christian praxis of love to a mere object of faith or a principle of confession has become clear. This danger has been facing the Christian praxis of love from its very beginning. In view of this narrowing of love and its accompanying spiritualization, I wish to approach love as a way of life, as praxis. Rather than attempting to lift all human differences and forms of otherness to a higher spiritual level in the name of love, the praxis of love is firmly rooted in the everyday encounter of belonging and difference, conflict and otherness. It seeks a new world order where all human beings can respect God's otherness as well as each other's otherness and actively explore God's gifts of creation, reconciliation and community.

In chapters 3 and 4, I shall explore central developments in the post-biblical theology of love. First I shall examine Augustine's theology of love. In his thinking both the biblical heritage and aspects of Greek philosophy and culture merge into a grand scheme of love that came to influence all subsequent approaches to love in Western Christian thinking.

[57] See the discussion of Kierkegaard's *Works of Love* below in chapter 5.

## Chapter 3

# *AUGUSTINE'S THEOLOGY OF GOD'S LOVE*

### Approaching Augustine's Theology of Love

When we today think of love we usually think first of intimate relationship and sex; when Augustine (354–430) thought of love, he thought first of all of God.[1] When we consider human love, we focus on what we can do in and through love; when Augustine considered human love, his perspective was what God is doing in and through human love. When we think of sex and sexual desire, we see potential for a meaningful life; when Augustine thought of sex and sexual desire, he was reminded of sin and death, i.e. the consequences of the Fall of Adam and Eve. Hence it seems as if great differences of interest and approach between this once highly influential Church Father and us today would render any effort to understand the old bishop's theology of love either meaningless or very problematic: meaningless for how could we benefit from his radically different approach, and problematic for why should we bother to reconstruct an outdated view of love that owed everything to his theological *Überbau* and nothing much to human experience and agency, as we now understand them. Would it not be best simply to hand Augustine's theology of love over to the historians of theology and of ideas rather than trying to reopen a dialogue on love with such an unattractive dialogue partner?

My reading of Augustine on love both confirms and challenges this view. Augustine's radical separation between a theology of love and a theology of sexuality and marriage certainly appears

[1] In this chapter I have reworked and expanded my article 'Augustinus teologi om kärlek', in Henrik Rydell Johnsén and Per Rönnegård, eds, *Eros och agape: Barmhärtighet, kärlek och mystik i den tidiga kyrkan*, Skellefteå: Artos & Norma, 2009, pp. 128–48.

alien to us today who are so used to considering love and sex in one breath. Moreover, his views on agency and subjectivity in love are repulsive to most of us on first sight: God is everything and the human being nothing. How then are we to love God, one another and ourselves, if in reality we are unable to love? Have our sexuality, our bodiliness, our erotic inclination, our complex desire for union with the other nothing to do with that love with which we are to love God?

Yet a struggle with such a radically different approach to love and sexuality might help us in the twenty-first century to trace the rich, complex and problematic history of effects of Augustine's understanding of love, sex and marriage. Moreover, a closer study of Augustine's approach might lead us to question any self-assured starting points in our own discourses on love and sex and to regain a deeper and more critical sense of our own framework of references for contemporary theologies of love.

Augustine has been the most influential thinker in the Western Christian tradition. Here it is not possible to discuss his interesting life and impressive work against the background of the ancient world.[2] Rather I shall concentrate on his approach to love. However, it is important to recall that this towering figure in Christian thought only spent five years of his life (383–8) in what today is called Europe. His home was in North Africa. After his brief European interlude he returned to North Africa and spent the remainder of his active life there in the service of the Church as pastor, teacher, writer and spiritual leader. In 395 he was consecrated Bishop of Hippo. Although he never visited Europe again, Augustine has helped shaping the development of 'Europe' like few other thinkers in history.

I shall first discuss Augustine's approach to human sexuality and marriage against his dual background in Graeco-Roman and Christian convictions. Secondly, I shall review his theology of love, paying particular attention to the question of divine and human agency. Thirdly, I shall consider the implications of Augustine's understanding of love for human subjectivity, agency, and community.

[2] For a longer biography see Peter Brown, *Augustine of Hippo: A Biography*, London: Faber & Faber, 1967; and James J. O'Donnell, *Augustine, Sinner & Saint: A New Biography*, London: Profile Books, 2005. For more concise books on Augustine see Henry Chadwick, *Augustine*, Past Masters, Oxford and New York: Oxford University Press, 1986; and Richard Price, *Augustine*, Fount Christian Thinkers, London: Fount, 1996.

Finally, I shall try to explore the potential of Augustine's theology of love for reflecting on the Christian praxis of love today.

Obviously, I must limit my discussion to some key texts. The main texts consulted here were written or reworked and concluded during Augustine's mature period as theologian and church leader: *On Christian Doctrine* (*De doctrina Christiana*), a work begun already in the late 390s, but completed only in 426; *On the Good of Marriage* (*De bono coniugali*) of 401; his book on *The Trinity* (*De Trinitate*) completed around 417; *The Homilies on St John* (*Tractatus in Epistolam Iohannis*) of 415; and *The City of God* (*De civitate Dei*), especially the second part, books 14–17, written in 418–20.

I have, of course, also consulted other texts by Augustine, e.g. the *Confessions*, but my chief attention will be on the texts just named. They might count as somewhat representative for his later thinking. However, it has been argued that his 'negative evaluation of sexuality is a constant which runs through his entire written corpus, and cannot, therefore, be seen as a characteristic peculiar to the late Augustine alone'.[3]

## Augustine's Approach to Sexuality and Marriage

Augustine's anthropology is firmly based both on a painful awareness of the fact that all human beings partake in the Fall of Adam and Eve and on the faith that in Jesus Christ God has opened up a way of healing and salvation.[4] While the Fall resulted in a basic disorder between flesh and spirit, i.e. a disorder of desires, Christ has initiated the grace and presence that allows the human will to distinguish between good and bad desires and to follow the law of God amidst the pressures of conflicting desires. Sexuality as such is not evil — Adam and Eve were sexual beings even before the Fall[5] — but in us sexual desire (*concupiscentia carnis*) presents a drive towards disorder,

[3] Mathijs Lamberigts, 'A Critical Evaluation of Critiques of Augustine's View of Sexuality', in Robert Dodaro and George Lawless, eds, *Augustine and His Critics: Essays in Honour of Gerald Bonner*, London and New York: Routledge, 2002, pp. 176–97, here p. 182.

[4] Cf. Tarcicius J. van Bavel, 'Love', in Allan D. Fitzgerald, OSA, ed., *Augustine through the Ages*, Grand Rapids and Cambridge: Eerdmans, 1999, pp. 509–16, esp. p. 510.

[5] Cf. St Augustine, *Concerning the City of God against the Pagans*, trans. Henry Bettenson, London: Penguin, 2003, p. 585 (XIV, 23). Referred to henceforth as *City of God*.

towards chaos and evil, since it is connected with the curse of death, the consequence of the Fall.[6]

Marriage provides the only possible framework for human sexuality to unfold itself in a rational, i.e. ordered and constructive, way. In other words, marriage is the only form in which sexual desire might attain its legitimate goal, namely the orderly and honourable procreation of the human race. Human procreation in turn results in the blood relationship of all men and women and thus in the bonding of all human beings. Here we find the basis for human society. Hence marriage provides an order for sexual desire, for procreation, and for social bonding and stability.

In his reflections on *The Good of Marriage*, Augustine identifies three goods: offspring, fidelity, and sacrament (XXIV.32).[7] Fidelity refers to the lifelong bonding in friendship between husband and wife, and sacrament refers to 'something greater than could arise from our feeble mortality' (VII.7).[8] Once again, we see the close connection between his reflections upon marriage and his painful awareness of human death.

Augustine is fully conscious of the fact that marriage is neither a Christian invention nor possession. Rather, he argues, 'Marriage itself, of course, in all nations exists for the same purpose, the procreation of children. No matter how these children turn out in the end, marriage was instituted in order that they might be born in an ordered and honorable way.' And he adds, 'nevertheless the married people of our day are not to be compared to the married people of ancient times' (XVII.19),[9] explaining immediately what he means here:

> Married people today have something that is granted to them as *a concession* because of the honorable state of marriage, although this concession does not pertain to the essence of marriage itself; I am referring to the use of intercourse beyond the need of procreation, something that was not conceded to the ancients. (XVII.19)[10]

Hence Augustine admits here that marriage in practice, though not in idea, has evolved and changed throughout history; and he introduces

[6] Cf. Beverley Clack, *Sex and Death: A Reappraisal of Human Mortality*, Cambridge, UK: Polity Press, 2002, p. 35.

[7] Important passages from Augustine's *The Good of Marriage*, trans. David G. Hunter, are reprinted in Eugene F. Rogers, Jr, ed., *Theology and Sexuality: Classic and Contemporary Readings*, Oxford: Blackwell, 2002, pp. 71–86, here p. 86.

[8] Ibid., p. 77.

[9] Ibid., p. 83.

[10] Ibid.

the thought that the institution of marriage is to provide a space in which carnal desire could be forgiven. For this aim he establishes a kind of hierarchy of forms of sexual intercourse which illustrates his point on the concessionary dimension of marriage most clearly:

> Conjugal intercourse for the sake of procreation carries no fault; intercourse for the sake of satisfying lust, provided that it takes place with a spouse, carries a forgivable fault (*venialis culpa*) because of marital fidelity; but adultery or fornication carries a mortal fault. Therefore, abstention from all intercourse is better even than marital intercourse that takes place for the sake of procreation. (VI.6)[11]

It is important to recall that Augustine pursues a double task in this text: on the one hand, he tries to defend marriage against those who have argued that virginity and continence were more in line with the vision of the gospel and the Apostle Paul. On the other hand, Augustine tries to defend the gospel and the apostle's recommendation of a chaste life (1 Cor. 7). Hence, he demonstrates that nothing is wrong with the institution of marriage as such, but that the chief point of Christian discipleship is to have one's will formed in such a way that it controls all evil desires and develops all good desires. Although sexuality and marriage as such are good, abstention is better for Christians. 'Marriage and fornication, therefore, are not two evils, one of which is worse, but marriage and continence are two goods, one of which is better' (VIII.8).[12] Sexuality apart from procreation does not belong to the essence of marriage.[13] The framework for Augustine's consideration of marriage is clearly linked to his theology of creation, to his hermeneutics of the Fall, and to his eschatology, yet not specifically to his theology of love.

It is interesting to observe how Augustine quotes generously from 1 Corinthians in order to argue in favour of marriage and continence without one single time referring to Paul's praise of love in that same text, i.e. 1 Corinthians 13. Love does not really enter into Augustine's discourse on marriage and sexuality.[14] Rather, he remains very much in the tradition of Graeco-Roman attempts at developing an order of desire that could tame the otherwise chaotic forces present in sexual

[11] Ibid., p. 76.

[12] Ibid., p. 77.

[13] Cf. Lamberigts, p. 183.

[14] Only friendship between the spouses is praised by Augustine in this context. Cf. Bernard V. Brady, *Christian Love*, Washington, DC: Georgetown University Press, 2003, p. 95.

desire.[15] Peter Brown sums up Augustine's position in the following way:

> This view of marriage deliberately looked past the physicality of married intercourse. Sexual desire still disquieted Augustine. In mankind's present state, the sexual drive was a disruptive force. Augustine never found a way, any more than did any of his Christian contemporaries, of articulating the possibility that sexual pleasure might, in itself, enrich the relations between husband and wife.[16]

Rather, Augustine developed a spiritual framework in which sexuality could be subjected to the higher order of reason. Conversely, if a couple engages in sex purely for pleasure, then it is no longer subject to reason, but to lust.[17] To put it the other way around: if Adam and Eve had not fallen, they still would have made love and had children in Paradise, though this would have taken place without lust.[18]

There has been much speculation over the extent to which Augustine's own experiences of lack of self-control in his youth and early manhood might have contributed to the development of his views on sexuality, especially on the uncontrollable nature of sex. Moreover, his accounts in the *Confessions* have provided much food for speculation as to his desire to overcome painful experiences of loss, such as the loss of a dear friend who died and the loss of his concubine.[19] I cannot go into such speculations here, although it would be interesting to explore to what extent painful personal experiences have influenced his theology. Such speculation could offer us some biographical background to Augustine's reduction of the body to a secondary position in his theology.[20]

[15] For a reading of the history of sexuality in the Graeco-Roman period see Michel Foucault, *A History of Sexuality* (1976–84), trans. Robert Hurley, 3 vols, London: Penguin, 1990–98, here esp. vol. 2: *The Use of Pleasure* (1992), and vol. 3: *The Care of the Self* (1990).

[16] Peter Brown, *The Body and Society: Men, Women and Sexual Renunciation in Early Christianity*, London and Boston: Faber & Faber, 1990, p. 402.

[17] Cf. Augustine, *De bono coniugali* XI. See also Clack, p. 35; and Lamberigts, p. 181.

[18] Augustine, *De civitate Dei*, XIV. 23. See also Andrew Louth, 'The Body in Western Catholic Christianity', in Sarah Coakley, ed., *Religion and the Body*, Cambridge Studies in Religious Traditions 8, Cambridge, UK: Cambridge University Press, 1997, pp. 111–30, esp. p. 118.

[19] Saint Augustine, *Confessions*, trans. Henry Chadwick, Oxford: Oxford University Press, 1992, p. 61 (IV. ix).

[20] See Carter Lindberg, *Love: A Brief History Through Western Christianity*, Malden and Oxford: Blackwell, 2008, pp. 53–7.

Theologically speaking, Augustine is very clear on the fact that the Fall has caused a dramatic weakening of the will. Human beings have lost control over their bodies. Augustine seems to have suffered from an inability to control or rather to avoid erections of his penis. In Eden, he explains in the *City of God* (XIV, 23), the penis would have been subject to Adam's will, a position reversed by the Fall.[21] Beverley Clack concludes: 'If sin is defined as disobedience, and the penis is characterized by its disobedience to the mind, it is relatively easy to conclude that sex is something sinful in itself.'[22] And she continues:

> The desire to return to the control over the erection possible in Eden haunts Augustine, and ultimately shapes the way in which the spiritual and the sexual are opposed in his theology. If one is to be spiritual, the sexual must be repressed.[23]

Or put in another way, the bodily is exterior, and there is no way to the interior via the exterior. Rather interiority is the chief goal: the soul must be at home in the body and in control.[24]

Andrew Louth has emphasized the connection between this longing for an interiority that 'renders the body "transparent"' and Augustine's view of the eschatological potential of a community of souls that had been cut off from one another by the opacity of the fallen body.[25] Toward the end of the *City of God*, Augustine describes his heavenly vision like this:

> [P]erhaps God will be known to us and visible to us in the sense that he will be spiritually perceived by each one of us in each one of us, perceived in one another, perceived by each in himself; he will be seen in the new heaven and the new earth, in the whole creation as it then will be; he will be seen in every body by means of bodies, wherever the eyes of the spiritual body are directed with their penetrating gaze. (XXII, 29)[26]

This vision that has influenced Augustine's plan for his own religious community already on this side of death (cf. the beginning of his rule: 'The chief motivation for your sharing life together is to live

[21] Augustine, *City of God*, p. 585: 'Then why should we not believe that the sexual organs could have been the obedient servants of mankind, at the bidding of the will, in the same way as the other, if there had been no lust, which came in as the retribution for the sin of disobedience?' (XIV, 23).

[22] Clack, p. 34.

[23] Ibid.

[24] Cf. Andrew Louth, p. 119.

[25] Ibid.

[26] *City of God*, p. 1087.

harmoniously in the house and to have one heart and soul seeking God'[27]), is informed by a theology of union in God, a theology that has shaped Augustine's understanding of love to which we now turn.

## The Logic of Augustine's Theology of Love

For Augustine there exists only one true and lasting form of love, namely the love of God.[28] God alone is immutable and therefore worthy of our true love. Hence, whenever we humans genuinely love, we love God in our acts of love. The meeting with another human person does as such not have a co-constitutive character for me as an emerging spiritual subject. Rather when I love the other person, I love God in her, and the other person loves God in me. Hence, ultimately only God can love or be loved. He is the *summum bonum,* the highest good, which we all desire. Unlike the *concupiscentia carnis,* which is a destructive force, there is a *concupiscentia caritatis,* so to speak, that is the most constructive force operative in us human beings. Only in this love (*caritas*) of the *summum bonum* does the human being properly love himself or herself.[29]

From the idea of God as the highest good it follows that God alone is the true goal of our life, God alone is deserving of our love and attention. In this regard Augustine distinguishes between what human beings can enjoy (*frui*) and use (*uti*). Obviously, God alone as *summum bonum* can be enjoyed, while all other aspects of our reality, created by God, can be loved (*uti*) because of God's love for them.[30]

In *De doctrina Christiana,* Augustine interprets the divinely instituted rule of love — 'you shall love your neighbour as yourself' (Lev. 19.18), and 'you shall love the Lord your God with all your heart, and with all your soul, and with all your might' (Deut. 6.5) — in this way:

[27] Praeceptum I.2, trans. George Lawless, OSA, *Augustine of Hippo and His Monastic Rule,* Oxford: Clarendon, 1987, p. 81. See also Louth, p. 119.

[28] On the difficulties of conceptual distinctions between Augustine's shifting terminology of love see Oliver O'Donovan, *The Problem of Self-Love in St. Augustine,* Eugene: Wipf and Stock (reprint), 1980, p. 11.

[29] Cf. Oliver O'Donovan, ibid., p. 23; and Hannah Arendt, *Love and Saint Augustine,* ed. Joanna Vecchiarelli Scott and Judith Chelius Stark, Chicago: University of Chicago Press, 1996, pp. 26–8.

[30] Cf. T. J. van Bavel, 'Love', p. 511.

> Thus all your thoughts and all your life and all your understanding should be turned toward Him from whom you receive these powers. For when He said, "With thy whole heart, and with thy whole soul, and with thy whole mind," He did not leave any part of life which should be free and find itself room to desire the enjoyment of something else. But whatever else appeals to the mind as being lovable should be directed into that channel into which the whole current of love flows. Whoever, therefore, justly loves his neighbor should so act toward him that he also loves God and with his whole heart, with his whole soul, and with his whole mind. Thus, loving his neighbor as himself, he refers the love of both to that love of God which suffers no stream to be led away from it by which it might be diminished (I, xxii).[31]

Hence it becomes clear that the neighbour is not loved for his or her own sake. Rather we love our neighbour for God's sake. Every genuine love relationship thus becomes an occasion for a relationship with God. And loving the neighbour, and indeed also our own selves, ultimately, becomes a function of our love of God.[32]

In his work on *The Trinity*, Augustine explains: 'It is God, then that causes us to love our brother, when love causes us to do so; and the first object of our love must needs be that very love wherewith we love our brother' (VIII, 11).[33]

The philosophical framework in which Augustine developed his concept of love as the *summum bonum* is Platonic. However, unlike Plato, Augustine identifies the *summum bonum*, i.e. love (*caritas*), with the personal God. For Plato, all human beings love the good, whereas for Augustine, all human beings love God who is love.[34] The Johannine theology of love (*Deus est caritas*[35]) provides the biblical framework for this fusion of the highest good and God who is love. No other New Testament text defends the unity of love in such a dramatic way as John does. No wonder that Augustine feels attracted to John's theology of love, and not only to Paul's as is occasionally argued.[36] As John's Gospel and letters develop a theology of love against any form of communal disunity and against any form of outside pressure on the community, Augustine conceives of the unity of love in terms of

[31] Saint Augustine, *On Christian Doctrine*, trans. D. W. Robertson, Jr, New York: Macmillan, 1958, p. 19.

[32] Cf. O'Donovan, p. 39.

[33] Augustine, 'The Trinity', in John Burnaby, ed. and trans., *Augustine: Later Works.* The Library of Christian Classics: Ichthus Edition, Philadelphia: Westminster Press, 1955, p. 53.

[34] Cf. Irving Singer, *The Nature of Love*, vol. 1: *Plato to Luther*, 2nd edn, Chicago and London: University of Chicago Press, 1984, pp. 163–9.

[35] 1 John 4.8 and 16.

[36] See, for example, Hannah Arendt, *Love and Saint Augustine*, pp. 3–4.

a theological unity. Here, a Platonic heritage, a biblical tradition and a mentality that seeks unity and stability beyond all worldly divisions and conflicts merge. God is love. All human intentions and motivations will have to be measured and judged against this insight.[37]

Augustine's much-quoted dictum 'Love, and do what you will' from his *Homilies on 1 John* has often been misread: It has nothing to do with a general sentiment of the sort 'Love is all you need'.[38] Rather Augustine refers here to the rootedness of all good intentions in love. Since God is love, and love is our origin, Augustine argues 'that the actions of men are discerned only according to their root in charity'.[39]

> The difference in intention makes a difference in the acts. Though the thing is one, yet when we measure it by the difference of intention, the one lovable, the other damnable, we find that one is to be glorified and the other execrated. Such great virtue has charity: you see that it alone divides, it alone distinguishes the actions of men.[40]

For Augustine, proper love is always *amor dei*, never *amor sui*. Proper desire is always directed towards God as the *summum bonum*. This desire is possible only because the Holy Spirit ignited love in us, he himself being love. All we can do is to love God, who is love, for God's sake.

As we know from his *Confessions*, Augustine identifies any desire to find oneself, to find one's neighbour, to find happiness as an in-depth desire to find God.[41] 'Like his Greek antecedents he wished to affirm the erotic dynamism in everything. But for him it had to occur within a theological cosmos that directed all the stirrings of life toward the Christian God.'[42]

Nothing of what is so important in our own contemporary reflections upon love — i.e. embodiment, gender, human subject, relational

[37] See John Rist, 'Augustine of Hippo', in G. R. Evans, ed., *The Medieval Theologians*, Oxford: Blackwell, 2001, pp. 3–23, here p. 9.

[38] Cf. ibid., p. 18:

> "Love and do what you wish," far from being a licence for situation ethics, is nothing less than a call to mankind to want to want [sic!] what God wishes, loves, and commands, and to conform our actual wishes and practices to those second-order wants. Nor does it prevent Augustine from holding to certain moral absolutes: such as the strict prohibition on lying, even in a good cause.

[39] Augustine, 'Ten Homilies on the First Epistle General of St. John', in Augustine, *Later Works*, trans. John Burnaby, The Library of Christian Classics, Philadelphia: Westminster Press, 1955, pp. 251–348, here p. 316 (Seventh Homily, 8).

[40] Ibid., p. 316 (Seventh Homily, 7).

[41] Cf. *Confessions*, 200–2 (X. xxv–xxix). Cf. also Henry Chadwick, *Augustine*, p. 23.

[42] Singer, p. 165.

choice, the desire for and acknowledgement of otherness — has any great significance for Augustine. The emerging subject is of no ultimate concern to him, in spite of him having spent hundreds of pages in his *Confessions* on precisely that: the journey of his own troubled and restless self towards understanding how to reach beatitude, everlasting happiness. Longings, bodies, images of the self, all of these are subjected to change in time, hence they are not eternal.

In *De vera religione* Augustine comments on his position on bodies:

> Let a man love his neighbour as himself. No one is his own father or son or relation or anything of the kind, but simply a human being. Whoever loves another as himself ought to love that in him which is his real self. Our bodies truly are not what we really are. So we are not to desire or set great store by a human body.[43]

Once again, we see that love has to do with human interiority and does not as such relate to exterior things such as bodies. 'Augustine is always calling us within. What we need lies "*intus*", he tells us again and again.'[44]

Augustine's understanding of the human body, however, is not consistent. In his earlier writings he follows Neo-Platonist dualist tendencies by understanding the human being as composed of a mortal, changeable, earthly body and an immortal, unchangeable, divine soul. The soul is more than a mental operator, it also controls processes such as nutrition, metabolism, growth, maturing, and sexuality. The soul, as such belonging to the incorporeal, intelligible realm, is the mover of the body; it is the body's principle of motion. Also the later Augustine still affirms that the ultimate goal of the human soul lies in the intelligible, immaterial world, even if the human being often forgets this in his everyday existence. But at the same time, the Church Father now also accepts the anti-Platonist view that the eternal life which is to begin with the resurrection of the dead is to comprise both body and soul

[43] Augustine, *De vera religione* XLVI, 89, in Avrelii Avgvstini, *Opera* IV,1, Corpus Christianorum, Series Latina 32, Turnhout: Brepols, 1962, p. 245. On Augustine and the Platonists on love see Oliver Davies, *A Theology of Compassion: Metaphysics of Difference and the Renewal of Tradition*, London: SCM, 2001, pp. 75–81. See also Alison Jasper, 'Recollecting Religion in the Realm of the Body (or Body ©)', in Pamela Sue Anderson and Beverley Clack, eds, *Feminist Philosophy of Religion: Critical Readings*, London: Routledge, 2004, pp. 170–82, here p. 172.

[44] Charles Taylor, *Sources of the Self: The Making of the Modern Identity*, Cambridge, MA: Harvard University Press, 1989, p. 129.

of the resurrected.[45] This change in Augustine's attitude to the body must, however, not be taken to be less hostile to the body. Rather, in his later years he is no less convinced of the devastating consequences of the Fall than before. Moreover, Adam's Fall has corrupted the entire human constitution — body and soul. The only possible way towards salvation from this predicament demands turning against the sensual world towards the spiritual or divine realm.[46]

Augustine explains that there are two ways of loving the neighbour: we must care for those in need, but more importantly, we must draw them to God. Caring for the other person and for the self are acts of benevolence.[47] Proper love, however, is always directed to God.

> Man, then, as viewed by his fellow-man, is a rational soul with a mortal and earthly body in its service. Therefore he who loves his neighbor does good partly to the man's body, and partly to his soul. What benefits the body is called medicine; what benefits the soul, discipline.[48]

Augustine very much recommends compassion for the other person in need. Everybody needs food, shelter and clothing. But these bodily concerns are never sufficient in themselves. Without the medicine of the mind, i.e. discipline, there is no salvation.

> He, then who loves his neighbor endeavors all he can to procure his safety in body and in soul, making the health of the mind the standard in his treatment of the body. And as regards the mind, his endeavors are in this order, that he should first fear and then love God. This is true excellence of conduct, and thus the knowledge of truth is acquired which we are ever in the pursuit of.[49]

Moreover, Augustine treats even of the love of enemies within this logic of love. In *De doctrina Christiana* he writes

> Thus it is that we also love our enemies. For we do not fear them, since they cannot take away that which we love. Rather are we sorry for them, for the more they hate us, the further removed are they from that which we love. If they were

[45] Cf. Christoph Horn, 'C.II.6 Anthropologie', in Volker Henning Drecoll, *Augustin Handbuch*, Tübingen: Mohr Siebeck, 2007, pp. 479–87, here, pp. 479–80.

[46] Cf. ibid., pp. 483–7.

[47] For a discussion of these different forms of love see O'Donovan, pp. 32–41.

[48] On the Morals of the Catholic Church XXVII, trans. Richard Stothert and Albert Newman, in *St. Augustine: The Writings against Manicheans and against the Donatists – The Nicene and Post-Nicene Fathers of the Christian Church*, vol. 4, ed. Philip Schaff, Edinburgh: T&T Clark (1887) 1996, p. 55.

[49] On the Morals of the Catholic Church XXVIII, ibid., p. 56. On the fear of God and the relationship to loving God see James J. O'Donnell, *Augustine, Sinner & Saint*, pp. 157–9.

> to turn to Him and love Him as the source of all blessedness, they would necessarily love us also as companions in a great good. (I, 29)[50]

Thus, all forms of love are related to each other in the love of God.[51]

In his *De Trinitate* (*On the Trinity*) Augustine sums up his theology of love once more by answering the question: how much charity ought we to give to our brother and how much to God?

> The answer is, To God incomparably more than to ourselves, and to our brother as much as to ourselves; ourselves we love the more, the more we love God. It is, then, out of one and the same charity that we love God and our neighbour: but we love God for God's sake, and for God's sake ourselves and our neighbour. (VIII, 11)[52]

## Subjectivity, Agency, and Community

The young Hannah Arendt (1906–75) devoted her doctoral dissertation to a study of Augustine's concept of love.[53] She points out in this that Augustine distinguishes between true and false love, i.e. true and false *amor*. False love has the wrong object, one that continuously disappoints its craving (*appetitus*).

> Augustine's term for this wrong, mundane love that clings to, and thus at the same time constitutes, the world is *cupiditas*. In contrast, the right love seeks eternity and the absolute future. Augustine calls this right love *caritas*: the 'root of all evils is *cupiditas*, the root of all goods is *caritas*'.[54]

Both right and wrong love (*caritas* and *cupiditas*) have this craving desire (*appetitus*) in common. Hence, Augustine warns in his *Commentaries on the Psalms*: 'Love, but be careful what you love.'[55]

Of course, only true love reconnects human beings with their own interior roots, the *summum bonum*, God. Trying to find oneself, to find

[50] *On Christian Doctrine*, p. 25.

[51] See also O'Donovan, pp. 112–20.

[52] Augustine, *Later Works*, trans. John Burnaby, p. 53.

[53] Hannah Arendt, *Der Liebesbegriff bei Augustin: Versuch einer philosophischen Interpretation*, Berlin: Julius Springer, 1929. For a recent English edition of this work with an Interpretative Essay, see Joanna Vecchiarelli Scott and Judith Chelius Stark, eds, *Love and Saint Augustine*, op. cit. I shall refer here to this more recent and enlarged English edition, but, where appropriate, also provide references to the original German edition (G).

[54] Arendt, p. 17 (cf. G, p. 13). The quotation refers to Augustine's *Commentaries on the Psalms*. See *Enarrationes in Psalmos* XC, s. I, 8, in Avrelii Avgvstini, *Opera* X, 2, Corpus Christianorum, Series Latina 39, Turnhout: Brepols, 1956, p. 1260.

[55] Augustine, *Enarrationes in Psalmos* XXXI, II 5, in Avrelii Avgvstini, *Opera* X, 1, Corpus Christianorum, Series Latina 38, Turnhout: Brepols, 1956, p. 228.

the neighbour and to find God — all these searches are in fact one and the same search: the search for the good, the immutable, the eternal, God. It is interesting to note with Hannah Arendt, that love for Augustine is always related to the future, never to this present and passable world. Hence, this love never affirms the present, it remains radically eschatological.

In what follows I shall not examine Arendt's overall negative view of the potential of love for political thinking.[56] Rather I am interested in her discussion and critique of Augustine's approach to love. I agree with a number of scholars that her study of Augustine represents a significant contribution both to the understanding of Augustine and his theology of love.[57]

Arendt demonstrates to what extent Augustine differs from Paul's understanding of love in this respect. 'The crucial importance that love of neighbor had for Paul as the possibility of "perfection" even in this world is not shared by Augustine, at least not in this conceptual context in which love is understood as desire (*appetitus*).'[58] Augustine can put it bluntly and write 'if you love God you are in heaven even though you still are on earth'.[59]

Arendt diagnoses here a relativization of the world and a removal of neighbourly love from the conditions of this world. In *De doctrina Christiana* Augustine had written: 'Among those who are able to enjoy God with us, we love some whom we help, some by whom we are helped, some whose help we need and whose wants we supply, and some on whom we bestow no benefits and from whom we await none ourselves' (I, xxix).[60] Arendt concludes from this that the emphasis in this neighbourly love 'is on mutual help, and this insistence is the clearest sign that love remains harnessed to the "for the sake of" category, which rules out meeting my fellow men (in their concrete worldly reality and relation to me) in their own right'.[61]

In view of Arendt's remarks we might want to say today: For Augustine the human subject becomes a subject when she loves,

[56] For a discussion of Arendt's view of love as political vice see Eric Gregory, *Politics and the Order of Love: An Augustinian Ethic of Democratic Citizenship*, Chicago and London: University of Chicago Press, 2008, pp. 197–240.

[57] Cf. ibid., pp. 219–20.

[58] Arendt, p. 32.

[59] Augustine, *Enarrationes in Psalmos* LXXXV, 6, in Avrelii Avgvstini, *Opera* X, 2, Corpus Christianorum, Series Latina 39, p. 1181.

[60] *On Christian Doctrine*, p. 24.

[61] Arendt, p. 42.

or rather when God loves in her, whereas we today base our understanding of love on our prior understanding of human subjectivity. We shall have to come back to these distinctions. But let us first consider the remainder of Arendt's important analysis of Augustine's logic of love.

Hannah Arendt reminds us that Augustine allots being to human persons only in so far as they are participating in the being to which they stand in relation because of the Creator's act. Our human being is not immutable, only the true being, God, who is love, is. That implies that only by relating to this true being does the created being receive knowledge, insight, revelation about her own call to being. For Augustine, in Arendt's words, '[o]nly in referring back from mortal existence to the immortal source of this existence does created man find the determinant of his being'.[62] Living in this universe that has been created by God as heaven and earth, mortal being is related to the world she inhabits: Either through *concupiscentia* (*amor mundi*) she loves her world, i.e. the created instead of the creator, or through *caritas* (*amor dei*) she loves God. Loving God implies self-denial and world-denial. What does that mean for the love of neighbour? Arendt explains:

> Man's absolute isolation in God's presence, which actualizes the return, explains how divinely ordained love serves to realize self-denial. The reason is that love amounts to renouncing any independent choice and any originally established relation with the world.[63]

This consideration of the logic of Augustine's understanding of love prompts Arendt to question the social horizon of Augustine's love. 'However, what we cannot understand is how, through this love by which we deny both ourselves and the world, another person can still be considered our neighbor, that is, as someone specifically connected to us.'[64]

Nevertheless, Augustine does not forget the neighbours, although he approaches them in respect to that which lives in them as their interior source. The same source is loved in each individual human being. No individual means anything in comparison with this source. Arendt concludes:

> The Christian can thus love all people because each one is only an occasion, and that occasion can be everyone. Love proves its strength precisely in considering even the enemy and even the sinner as mere occasions for love. It is not

[62] Ibid., p. 50 (G, p. 37).

[63] Ibid., p. 95.

[64] Ibid.

> really the neighbor who is loved in this love of neighbor – it is love itself. Thus the neighbor's relevance as neighbor … is overcome and the individual is left in isolation.[65]

Hence, love is not the foundation for the fellowship of Christians, the Church. Rather it is the common faith that makes us fellow Christians with each other, as Augustine explains in the first of his *Homilies on 1 John* (I, 3).[66] Hannah Arendt also reflects upon this connection between faith and Christian community. Christian social life for Augustine emerges from faith in a common destiny — a destiny that all human beings share with Adam and Eve and their Fall. We are all biological relatives of them, marked by original sin, death and the conflict of desires. 'Humanity's common descent is its common share in original sin. This sinfulness, conferred with birth, necessarily attaches to everyone. There is no escape from it. It is the same in all people. The equality of the situation means that all are sinful.'[67] In this society founded on Adam human beings have made themselves independent of their Creator and built their own world. 'The world's sinfulness derives from its origin independent of God.'[68] The world is a community marked by death, the result of original sin, 'in other words this community is historical'.[69] Nevertheless, the world is still relevant both as the arena in which salvation appears in Jesus Christ and because of the 'constant tie to the past and thereby to original kinship, which consists of an equal share in original sin and thus in death'.[70] In Jesus Christ the possibility of relating anew to the Creator has been made possible. Divine grace gives a new meaning to human togetherness, namely defence against the world.

> This defense is the foundation of the new city, the city of God. Estrangement itself gives rise to a new togetherness, that is, to a new being with and for each other that exists beside and against the old society. This new social life, which is grounded in Christ, is defined by mutual love (*diligere invicem*), which replaces mutual dependence. Faith dissolves the bonds that tied men to the world in the original sense of the earthly city, and so faith dissolves men's dependence on one another. Therefore, one individual's relationship to another also ceases to be a matter of course, as it was in interdependence. The fact that it is no longer

[65] Ibid., p. 97.
[66] *Homilies on 1 John*, p. 261.
[67] Arendt, p. 102.
[68] Ibid., p. 103.
[69] Ibid.
[70] Ibid., p. 107.

a matter of course is expressed, on the one hand, by the commandment of love, and, on the other hand, by the specific indirectness of this love.[71]

Here Arendt confronts us with a great dilemma when dealing with Augustine's theology of love. In his logic of love the human subject either disappears amidst the concern for the true being of the human race or becomes insignificant because of what he or she might represent for me, namely the reminder that she and I ought to love God. Hence, the community of believers is not built on love, but on a biologically mediated common destiny into which God sends his revelation of grace.[72] To put it bluntly: Augustine's theology of love does not help us to form human community. Rather, forms of human community are grounded in the necessities of the human condition marked by original sin. Marriage is a way of ordering procreation; the Church is a community of believers that have been called to see their destiny, to face their innermost *memoria*,[73] to unmask their common dangers of being trapped by their own world (*mundus*), and to be united in their belief that their common sinful past has been disclosed by God. Original sin determines the framework of this community, and not love for each other in any genuinely constituting sense. The human subject is created, recreated and thus ultimately constituted by God's love alone. There can be no talk about any form of co-constituting creativity in human love.

## Insights From Augustine's Theology of Love

Should we abandon Augustine's theology at this point or is there anything in it that still could assist us today in our particular attempts to develop theologies of love? I think Augustine's approach to love provokes at least four insights of importance for any future theology of love.

First, every theology of love is developed against the background of philosophical anthropology, cosmology, and concrete human experiences. In other words, love has a history and any critical approach to love must become aware of this history as much as possible. Neo-Platonist influences provided a starting point for Augustine's

[71] Ibid., p. 108.

[72] Gregory, *Politics and the Order of Love*, p. 198: Arendt 'challenges the political implications of both divine love and the goodness of love itself — finding in neither the capacity for action nor mutual respect.'

[73] Cf. Charles Taylor, *Sources of the Self*, p. 135.

theology of love that a priori located true love onto a level different from this world. His mythological interpretation of the Fall and the resulting cosmology provide the dynamic that ultimately aims at moving human beings away from their world (*mundus*) to their real home in God's love. Augustine's personal experiences of loss, mortality, and lack of rational control over his body provide gripping illustrations of his place in this cosmological drama and its eschatological density.

Second, every theology of love is informed by a particular biblical hermeneutics. Both the Johannine understanding of love and a careful selection of Pauline perspectives on love inform the mature Augustine's theological foundation of a concept of love that was developed firmly within a Neo-Platonist anthropological framework.[74] Moreover, Augustine's relation to Greek traditions of approaching human sexuality suggests a clear separation between forms of sexual conduct and reflections upon love. Love, as presented and demanded by the Johannine texts in the New Testament, suggests a bifurcation between the Christian praxis of love and bodily expression of love. Augustine follows Pauline thoughts on sexual abstention, though not the apostle's thoughts on the pluriformity of Christian existence and the potential of love to promote a reconciled understanding of Christian difference and community.[75] Thus, Augustine fuses Johannine ideas on love with Pauline ideas on sexuality while neglecting alternative biblical visions of love.

Third, every theology of love has implications for our understanding of human subjectivity and agency and vice versa. Augustine's theology of love has, as we have seen, severe implications for any assessment of human subjectivity and human agency. Augustine's logic of love is both informed by an anthropology of original sin and by a theology of spiritual love. As a result, the human person combines an exterior body and an interior soul seeking control over this body on the way to love. Hence, love demands the subjection of the body to the soul. Sexuality's own dynamics presents a heavy challenge to the determination of good and bad desires, so heavy in fact that a life beyond bodily relations is to be preferred even to the

[74] See Volker Henning Drecoll, 'B. II.4. Neuplatonismus', in Drecoll, *Augustin Handbuch*, pp. 72–85. Here I cannot discuss the influences of North-African Manichean traditions on the younger Augustine's thinking on body, sexuality and love.

[75] See above, chapter 2.

ordered sexual intercourse within marriage. In this theology the body pays the prize of the logic of love.

Also our contemporary postmodern approaches to love presuppose, of course, particular concepts of human subjectivity and agency. At times, and often with direct and critical reference to Augustine, particular conceptions of the body are hailed as suitable starting points for an understanding of love.[76] Sexual desire is praised in terms of an unambiguous desire, fully fit to lead us to a happy self-realization in the meeting with others. Augustine's doctrine of original sin is rejected as an enslaving and oppressing mythology, and human love is considered as a soteriological force in its own right.[77] Here love assumes the status not only of an experience of ultimacy, but as the primary location of divine revelation and divine sanction both of sexuality and of specific human relational projects.

Paul Ricœur has reminded us not to throw out the baby with the bathwater when considering Augustine's doctrine of original sin. Ricœur joins the critics of Augustine's doctrine of original sin, yet invites us to approach this doctrine in terms of a symbol and thus to reconsider the potential of its insights.

> In one sense, it does take up one fundamental aspect of the experience of evil, namely, the both individual and communal sense of human impotence in the face of the demonic power of evil already there, long before any bad initiative may be assigned to some deliberate intention. However, [in Augustine] this enigma of the power of evil already there is set within the false clarity of an apparently rational explanation.[78]

Ricœur calls Augustine's concept of original sin a 'quasi-concept that we may assign to an antignostic gnosis'.[79] However, this is not to abandon the symbolic content of Augustine's concept, namely the fact that any theology of love will have to be constructed against the background of the existence of sin and evil and of their social

[76] Cf. Regina Ammicht Quinn's enlightening discussion of the relationship between sexual desire and God's punishment in Christian tradition in her book *Körper-Religion-Sexualität: Theologische Reflexionen zur Ethik der Geschlechter*, Mainz: Grünewald, 1999, pp. 239–41.

[77] For a discussion of contemporary trends to make love into a religion see Troels Nørager, *Hjertets længsel: Kærlighed og Gud religionsfilosofisk belyst*, Copenhagen: ANIS, 2003, p. 15.

[78] Paul Ricœur, *Figuring the Sacred: Religion, Narrative, and Imagination*, trans. David Pellauer, ed. Mark I. Wallace, Minneapolis: Fortress Press, 1995, p. 254.

[79] Ibid. See also Ricœur's article '"Original Sin": A Study in Meaning', trans. Peter McCormick, in Paul Ricœur, *The Conflict of Interpretations*, ed. Don Ihde, Evanston: Northwestern University Press, 1974, pp. 269–86.

consequences. Illusions of pure sexuality, pure love and pure human relationships are not helpful for a critical evaluation of the potential of love, of subjectivity and of human agency.

Fourth, every theology of love has implications for our understanding of community and transformation. Hannah Arendt helped us to focus on the impossibility of building an embodied community of love on Augustine's theology of love. The social price of Augustine's thinking on love is high indeed. For him love lives in heaven and not on earth.[80] Clearly, such a theology and its world-denying features are dangerous and ought to be resisted. But once again, Augustine's insight into the inner connectedness of all love relationships is too valuable to be discarded in the flow of the critique of his Neo-Platonist geography of love. Love is one and love has an eschatological character. Here Augustine is right, although we have good reason to think differently about what this oneness and its eschatological character might mean for a theology of love today.

Ultimately, we are faced with the following theological challenges when considering Augustine's concept of love today: Have human beings been graced with the transformative power of love and, as a result, can they themselves be genuine subjects and agents of love? Has the human being as a sexed subject in baptism been endowed with a new heart in order to love God, the neighbours and enemies and her own self in a variety of imaginative ways — all of which need constant review and revision in the light of God's creative and reconciling Spirit? Is the Eucharistic community of Christ's disciples gathered and transformed in *this* universe and as a sacrament for *this* world?[81] Our way of meeting these challenges will reveal to what extent we consider ourselves to be capable of loving.

The next chapter of our investigation of paradigmatic theologies of love will lead us to consider different ways of approaching the issues of subjectivity, on the one hand, and of the created universe as the location for both divine and human love, on the other hand, in the first half of the second millennium. In spite of the very different perception of the world and of human agency, of theology and anthropology, of biblical hermeneutics and the organization of

[80] Eric Gregory, *Politics and the Order of Love*, p. 206, cites Ronald Beiner's assessment of Arendt and Augustine with regard to their respective view of the world: 'For Augustine, we are more "at home" in the world than we ought to be; for Arendt, we are more estranged from the world than we ought to be.'

[81] Cf. Werner G. Jeanrond, *Guds närvaro: Teologiska reflexioner I,* 2nd edn, Lund Arcus, 2006, pp. 154–69.

monastic life and church, we shall be confronted everywhere with Augustine's massive, though shifting, influence on Christian spiritualities and theologies in general and on approaches to love, marriage and sexuality in particular.[82]

[82] On Augustine's towering status in Christian life and thought see Henry Chadwick, *Augustine*, pp. 1–4.

# Chapter 4

## *REDISCOVERING THE LOVING SUBJECT*

### Love and Subjectivity in Context

Medieval theologies of love carry on the biblical and Augustinian tradition, yet also radically renew it. A first glance at medieval treatments of love would suggest that some of our own contemporary preoccupations and concerns were already shared by our medieval forerunners. Unlike Augustine's strong focus on *divine* love, medieval authors reflect more on the God-given *human* capacity to love and they explore the journey to authentic love in a number of ways. Thus, not only God is understood as a loving subject, but also women and men. Moreover, the medieval authors were not afraid of a certain measure of difference in approaching love.

The twelfth century is not only known for the cultivation of love in Western Europe; rather it has been a great century for the spirituality of love in many of the world's religions.[1] This spirituality manifested itself in major works, such as the emergence of the *Kabbalah* in France and Spain, the texts by great Sufi writers, such as 'Aṭṭār, Ahmad al-Ghazāllī, Ibn 'Arabī, Ramanuja's writings in India and the composition of the *Gita Govinda,* the establishment of the school of Pure Land Buddhism by Honen in Japan, and Bernard of Clairvaux's theology of love. This global attention to love also prepared the way for significant works on love in the subsequent century, such as Rumi's love poetry, the book of Zohar, and Thomas Aquinas' theology of love.

[1] Cf. Ewert H. Cousins, 'Preface', in *Bernard of Clairvaux: Selected Works,* trans. G. R. Evans, The Classics of Western Spirituality, New York and Mahwah: Paulist Press, 1987, pp. 5–11.

Among the major shifts that occurred in twelfth-century theological thinking in Western Europe, M.-D. Chenu identified a new attitude towards nature as an independent object of study and an increasing desire to live the gospel in this world and not in a way that implied flight from it.[2] This new orientation in Christian faith praxis and thinking provided a changed matrix also for the theology of love in the High Middle Ages. Moreover, this new matrix appears to be much closer to our own theological horizon than the rather negative and world-denying ethos of Augustine.

However, we ought to be careful not to read our modern and postmodern preoccupations with issues of individual subjectivity and pluralism into medieval European mentality. After all, the framework of reference for the medieval Christian thinkers differs significantly from our own. With regard to twelfth-century religion, Caroline Walker Bynum has alerted us to the fact that it was not concerned with the individual self at the expense of corporate awareness.

> Rather twelfth-century religious writing and behaviour show a great concern with how groups are formed and differentiated from each other, how roles are defined and evaluated, how behaviour is conformed to models. If the religious writing, the religious practice, and the religious orders of the twelfth century are characterized by a new concern for the 'inner man', it is *because* of a new concern for the group, for types and examples, for the 'outer man'.[3]

Nevertheless, there seems to be a closer relationship between medieval and contemporary understandings of love than between Augustine's approach to love and our own. We today continue to be influenced both by the mystics' rediscovery and refiguration of the loving relationship between self and God, by the systematic study of love in Thomas Aquinas, and by the manifestations of romantic love at the medieval courts in Southern France. All of these strands within the development of love have helped to shape subsequent approaches to love until today.

For many theological voices of the twelfth and thirteenth century, the human being was capable of love after all, thanks to her likeness to God. God has created men and women in His image. All human beings carry this *imago Dei* within themselves. Once again, even the medieval thinkers acknowledge the divine origin of love, but they

[2] M.-D. Chenu, OP, *Nature, Man, and Society in the Twelfth Century: Essays on New Theological Perspectives in the Latin West*, selected, ed. and trans. Jerome Taylor and Lester K. Little, Chicago and London: University of Chicago Press, 1979.

[3] Caroline Walker Bynum, *Jesus as Mother: Studies in the Spirituality of the High Middle Ages*, Berkeley, Los Angeles and London: University of California Press, 1982, p. 85.

draw new and different conclusions from this fact: God has allowed us to love because we bear God's image within ourselves. Hence, compared to Augustine, here we can see the beginnings of a changed anthropology that affirms the human capacity to love and that is keen to explore how this capacity works and how it can be developed and improved in the respective orders of life.

In the Western world we are so used to taking the individual's needs, desires and longings as the sole starting point for any consideration of the self that we may miss the fact that our medieval ancestors always already located the individual within specific social contexts and frames of vocations. 'A quite particular sense of the relationship between inner and outer, between motive and model, characterizes twelfth-century discussions of belonging to groups.'[4] Thus, our medieval ancestors did not attempt to embark on a loving journey inspired by uniquely individual aspirations which by necessity included freedom from any social or group constraints. Rather they searched for appropriate patterns and forms that located the development of a loving self within particular social groups and their place in God's cosmos. To be sure, we today share with them the pain of choice and the urge to choose a life, but they would not want to share our conviction that a course of life must be chosen at the expense of social bonds, patterns and aspirations. Moreover, they considered the differences between social roles, talents, groups and patterns in terms of complementary contributions to the whole of the group (e.g. a religious order, a family, a guild, etc.) and to Christian society as a whole.[5]

For our purpose of examining selected contributions to a theology of love it is therefore of great importance to pay heed to the fact that the writers on love to be considered in this chapter all treat of ways of love within particular models of life. This social imagination was the home for their discourses on love. Models contemplated by these authors include the primitive church, the apostolic life, the desert Fathers, the garden of Eden, Christ himself, Christian martyrdom, etc. Models developed by these authors included the priestly life, the monastic life, the Beguine life, the secular life.[6] Hence, this dialectics between model and love rules out any quick translation between medieval and contemporary discourses of love. However, it might be

[4] Walker Bynum, op. cit., p. 89.
[5] Ibid., p. 95.
[6] Ibid., pp. 102–3.

precisely this dialectical understanding of love and social imagination that could provide a significant contribution to a theology of love today.

The rediscovery of the loving subject from the Middle Ages up to the Reformation is intimately linked to monastic developments. The courtly love traditions, the Beguine mystics, and the Reformation are important instances on the way to broaden the social location of love beyond the traditional monastic model. In this chapter I invite the reader to join me in discussing this complex development on love which, together with Augustine's legacy, has proved to be of crucial significance for all subsequent development of theologies of love. I shall first examine Bernard of Clairvaux's (1090–1153) mystical approach to love and then discuss the systematic approach to love in the theology of Thomas Aquinas (1225–74). Before considering distinctive female voices on love related to new patterns of apostolic life in and at the margins of the Church,[7] I shall trace the origins of romantic love in medieval culture. Finally, I shall turn to Martin Luther (1483–1546). His theology of love combines Augustinian, medieval and emerging modern perspectives on love and thus forms an important link between past and present.

## Bernard of Clairvaux's Love Mysticism

Bernard's theological development is closely related to the emerging Cistercian model of life.[8] His approach to love must thus be understood first in connection with this particular model of monastic vocation before its wider implications can be considered. Bernard did not embrace this model of existence in solitude; rather he joined the new monastic foundation at Citeaux in the year 1113 together with thirty friends and relatives.[9]

[7] Bernard McGinn distinguishes three strands of medieval theology: the monastic, the scholastic, and the vernacular. He calls the third strand 'vernacular' in order 'to indicate its primary distinguishing mark – linguistic expression in the medieval vernacular tongues'. Bernard McGinn, 'Introduction', in B. McGinn, ed., *Meister Eckhart and the Beguine Mystics: Hadewijch of Brabant, Mechthild of Magdeburg, and Marguerite Porete*, New York: Continuum, 1994, pp. 1–14, here p. 6.

[8] For a comprehensive study of Bernard's life and work see Peter Dinzelbacher, *Bernhard von Clairvaux: Leben und Werk des berühmten Zisterziensers*, Darmstadt: Wissenschaftliche Buchgesellschaft, 1998.

[9] Immo Eberl, *Die Zisterzienser: Geschichte eines europäischen Ordens*, Darmstadt: Wissenschaftliche Buchgesellschaft, 2002, p. 37.

The monastery at Citeaux had been formally established in 1098 by reform-minded monks from the monastery at Molesme, a place founded in the spirit of the Cluny reform movement. Thus, Bernard and his fellow novices made a conscious decision to choose this ascetic monastic reform model as their form for developing their inner and outer life. The main orientation of the Cistercian community and of its quickly increasing network of monasteries throughout Europe was contained in the *Carta Caritatis*, i.e. the new order's guiding constitution. Hence, even programmatically, love (*caritas*) was at the centre of the Cistercian movement.

This new religious order had founded the monastery at Clairvaux in 1115 around Bernard as abbot and a number of his own relatives who went along with him from Citeaux to Clairvaux.[10] Reform monasticism, family bonds and the gift of mystical contemplation all contributed to the particular horizon of Bernard's theology of love.

The different attempts to reform and renew Christianity in medieval Europe were all motivated by demonstrations of a sincere will to return to ancient Christian order.[11] Both the Cistercian way and Bernard's own journey within it were guided by such an aspiration. Notwithstanding this, both the order and its most famous monk participated in a larger process of theological rediscovery that not only involved acts of biblical interpretation but also a reassessment of the potential of human knowledge and experience.

Bernard saw love as the overarching concern of Christian life and thinking, though in a way that differed from Augustine's. For Bernard, the relationship between love and knowledge came into closer focus. Moreover, love itself was seen as a form of knowledge. He agreed with Augustine that only love can attain God in this life, not knowledge. But for the abbot 'knowledge has an important, even a necessary, role to play in our ascension to God, both at the beginning of the process, where Christ enlightens the soul through his saving mysteries, gradually illuminating the intellect that has humbly recognized its fallen state, and also at the end, where knowing is lifted up into love'.[12]

[10] Ibid., p. 40.

[11] Cf. Bernard McGinn, *The Growth of Mysticism: Gregory the Great through the 12th Century*, The Presence of God: A History of Western Christian Mysticism, vol. 2, New York: Crossroad, 1994, p. 150; and Immo Eberl, *Die Zisterzienser*, pp. 11–19.

[12] McGinn, *The Growth of Mysticism*, p. 202. See also Dinzelbacher, pp. 51–2, on the role of human reason in Bernard's mystical theology.

For Bernard, love was no longer separated from the body, but properly linked to the body. The body was the original place of contact between the human and the divine, and it remained so in spite of its corruption as a consequence of the Fall. Bernard's chief interest concerned 'the transition from carnal to spiritual love achieved in Christ risen and ascended'.[13] Jesus Christ was thus understood as the firstborn human being that showed us how we through *imitatio Christi* might follow him to spiritual love. Hence, the map is clear: from carnal love to a mature spiritual love, in this life and in this world. The way to spiritual love does involve practising Christ's virtues, especially humility and unselfish love.

The reader of Bernard's sermons on the Song of Song will observe the dynamic and transformative nature of Christian love.[14] Bernard discusses steps, ways and states of progress on the road to the fullness of love. Moreover, he frequently appeals to his listeners' own experience. On the way to the supernatural goal of human life three books, so to speak, are at our disposal: the book of creation, the book of scripture, and the book of experience.

Whereas for Augustine purified desire remained the only human activity on the way to divine love, Bernard clearly links human desire and human love as the pair that moves the soul to the fullness of God's love. Of course, like Augustine, Bernard leaves no doubt as to the absolute priority of divine love over human love.[15] However, God's love must meet with the fallen human being where it factually is, in its struggle with selfish carnal love,[16] hence the rationality of the Incarnation. According to Bernard, there is genuine human love, however much this human love is in need of transformation. Moreover, any form of contemplation of God's love will be authentic only when it leads to an intensification of the praxis of love. The interplay between action and contemplation is the hallmark of Bernard's monastic vision of the Christian praxis of love.[17]

In his text *De Diligendo Deo* (On Loving God), Bernard offers a concise theology of love. This text, written for his friend Aimeric,

[13] Ibid., p. 177.

[14] Bernard of Clairvaux, *Song of Songs*, 4 vols, Kalamazoo: Cistercian Publications, 1971–80.

[15] McGinn, *The Growth of Mysticism*, p. 194.

[16] Cf. ibid., p. 195.

[17] Cf. Jean Leclercq, 'Introduction', in *Bernard of Clairvaux: Selected Works*, trans. G. R. Evans, pp. 13–57, here p. 27.

cardinal deacon of the Church of Rome, contains as an appendix also a letter to the monks of the Grande Chartreuse, written earlier by Bernard upon their request.[18]

The reason why God should be loved is God himself. He first loved us (1 John 4.9–10). To love God is a natural law. 'And so God deserves to be loved for himself, even by the unbeliever (Rom. 3.2), for even if he does not know Christ, he knows himself' (p. 178). Anybody of clear insight into himself will acknowledge the higher goods of the soul, i.e. dignity, knowledge, and virtue. All are gifts of God and therefore point to God (p. 176). Hence, '[n]o one, not even an unbeliever, can be excused, if he does not love God with all his heart, all his mind, and all his strength' (p. 178).

Bernard does not refer to an atheist when he speaks of an unbeliever, but to one who does not know Christ. For the Christian, God's love has been most deeply expressed in 'Jesus and him crucified' (p. 179). And Bernard turns to the Song of Songs in order to express his passionate love for Christ,[19] the bridegroom of the Church, his bride, who 'is sick with love' (Song 3.11) (p. 179). Using sensory images from the Song of Songs and interpreting them allegorically in order to illustrate the sweetness of the bridegroom's visits to the chamber of the heart, the abbot concludes that it 'befits us, too, to fortify our own hearts with the testimony of faith, if we want Christ to be a frequent guest' (Eph 3.17) (p. 181). Moreover, we share a duty to love (p. 184), because we have received the love of God gratuitously, in fact the love of the whole Trinity (p. 184). Faith and love are here intimately linked.

Like Augustine before him, Bernard explains the two sides of human desire: either we desire to have our longings fulfilled — an impossible thing that leads to a meandering and hopeless search — or we desire that which leaves nothing further to be desired. Then we have no need to bother with these other things (p. 189). God himself has created the longing in us. 'He himself fulfils the desire' (p. 191).

But unlike Augustine, Bernard then goes on to differentiate between *four degrees of love.* The *first degree* acknowledges bodily love

[18] Bernard of Clairvaux, 'On Loving God', in Bernard of Clairvaux, *Selected Works,* trans. G. R. Evans, pp. 173–205. The page numbers in the text refer to this edition.

[19] Cf. Antoon Geels, *Kristen mystik: Ur psykologisk synvinkel,* Part I, Skellefteå: Norma, 2000, p. 91: 'For Bernard the love poetry of the Song of Songs offers the best way to describe the union of the human soul with God.'

as a natural drive, though a drive that can receive proper orientation only if it is directed to and shared with the neighbour and thus extended to the community. 'This is righteousness, to share what is common to your nature with him who has the same gift of nature' (p. 193). However, only in God can we love our neighbour with purity. Hence, we turn to God and love him — still — for our own good. This is the *second degree* of love. This encounter with God motivated by our own needs will awaken in us a true taste for God himself. We can then say to our flesh, 'Now we love God not because he meets your needs; but we have tasted and we know how sweet the Lord is' (Ps. 33.9) (p. 194). Loving God for God's sake is the *third degree* of love. Interestingly, the *fourth* and ultimate *degree* of love concerns human love for the self, i.e. when man loves himself only for God's sake. Bernard says that he 'should call him blessed and holy to whom it is given to experience even for a single instant something which is rare indeed in this life. To lose yourself as though you did not exist and to have no sense of yourself, to be emptied out of yourself (Phil. 2.7) and almost annihilated, belongs to heavenly not to human love' (p. 195). In the light of this union between God and God's creature Bernard expresses his frustration about the heaviness of the world that draws us from this momentous rapture down to the circle of life's desires.

> And if indeed any mortal is rapt for a moment or is, so to speak, admitted for a moment to this union, at once the world presses itself on him (Gal 1:4), the day's wickedness troubles him, the mortal body weighs him down, bodily needs distract him, he fails because of the weakness of his corruption and – more powerfully than these – brotherly love calls him back. Alas, he is forced to come back to himself, to fall again into his affairs, and to cry out wretchedly, 'Lord, I endure violence; fight back for me' (Is 38:14), and, 'Unhappy man that I am, who will free me from the body of this death?' (Rom. 7:24) (p. 195)

Yet this frustrated experience that the loving union with God cannot endure under the conditions of this body is comforted by the eschatological prospect of faith: there will be a time when God will be all in all. When will that be? For the time being, 'it is impossible to draw together all that is in you and turn towards the face of God as long as the care of the weak and miserable body demands one's attention. So it is in a spiritual and immortal body, a perfect body, beautiful and at peace and subject to the spirit in all things, that the soul hopes to attain the fourth degree of love, or rather, to be caught up to it' (p. 196). However, this state of the soul is the result of God's action. Human effort cannot produce this union. Rather, it presupposes freedom from the mortal body (p. 197). Once again (cf. above in chapter 1), we observe a longing for the 'perfect body'.

Bernard's vision of a loving union with God, however, does not share in the contempt for the human body found in most of Augustine's writings. Rather Bernard acknowledges the flesh as a good and faithful companion to the good spirit. 'Truly the soul does not want to be perfected without that which it feels has served it well in every condition' (p. 198). Body and soul together are on their way to eternal glorification. Bernard paints a sumptuous picture of the eternal banquet: 'Here is fullness without disgust, insatiable curiosity which is not restless, an eternal and endless desire which knows no lack, and lastly, that sober intoxication (Acts 2:15) which does not come from drinking too much, which is no reeking of wine, but a burning for God' (p. 199).

Human desire and love must begin with the mortal body. They are then directed through the stages of love[20] 'until the spirit is fulfilled (Gal 3:3)' (p. 204). Bernard defends our fleshly existence as part of the journey on the way to fulfilment in the love of God where 'every need of the flesh will vanish and fleshly love will be absorbed in the love of the spirit, and the weak human affections we have now will be changed into divine affections' (p. 205).

McGinn has stressed the fact that for the Abbot of Clairvaux the union between God and the human person is always understood in terms of a union of love, never of substance. 'The human being is in God through *caritas* (1 John 4:16), not in any consubstantial way.'[21] In Sermon 71 on the Song of Songs, Bernard of Clairvaux contrasts the unity between God Father and Son with the union between God and the human being:

> But we think of God and man as dwelling in each other in a very different way, because their wills, and their substances are distinct and different; that is, their substances are not intermingled, yet their wills are in agreement; and this union is for them a communion of wills and an agreement in charity. Happy is this union if you experience it, but compared with the other, it is no union at all. (71.10)[22]

Bernard does not suggest that the glimpses of such a blissful union with God are the overarching or ultimate goal of Christian love on

[20] Geels, *Kristen Mystik*, p. 90, notes that at different points in his writings Bernard distinguishes between three, four, seven or even twelve stages of love.

[21] McGinn, *The Growth of Mysticism*, p. 215.

[22] Bernard of Clairvaux, *On the Song of Songs IV*, trans. Irene Edmonds, Kalamazoo: Cistercian Publications, 1980, p. 56.

this side of death. Rather he links this form of love with the concrete demands of neighbourly love. Contemplative love must not be played out against active love. In this life, both belong together. In his allegorical interpretation of the Song of Songs he acknowledges that the bride always wants to enjoy the delights of contemplation, but cannot refuse to see the needs of their neighbours.

> After a good work one rests more securely in contemplation, and the more a man is conscious that he has not failed in works of charity through love of his own ease, the more faithfully will he contemplate things sublime and make bold to study them. (47.4)[23]

Bernard distinguishes clearly between heavenly and worldly love. On this side of death, all forms of love complement one another. On the other side of death, human love is completely transfigured by God. Brief contemplative experiences of that transfiguration on this side of death help strengthen our active love for our neighbours.

Here is not the place for an overarching assessment of Bernard's theology. Rather my intention has been to demonstrate both the continuity and differences between Bernard's and Augustine's approaches to love. However, neither Augustine nor Bernard must be read as a systematic theologian. Both attended to the pastoral needs of their respective audiences and communities. Bernard addressed a monastic audience at a time when the new Cistercian combination of contemplation and action promoted the development of a unique European monastic network and thus helped in spreading the abbot's ideas throughout the continent: 'no mystic of the whole Middle Ages was more read and more often cited than the abbot of Clairvaux'.[24]

Among Bernard's mystical theological achievements are the appeal to human experience and the invitation to his monastic audience to read afresh in the book of their hearts.[25] Caroline Walker Bynum reminds us of the monastic interests and male limitations that directed Bernard's theological reflection and preaching.[26] Bernard's theology of love was written for fellow monks, not for a general audience. This is not to suggest that the reception of his theology of love must therefore be restricted to monastic readers. However, the abbot's thoughts on the praxis of love and on the unity of love are

[23] Bernard of Clairvaux, *On the Song of Songs III,* trans. Kilian Walsh, OCSO, and Irene Edmonds, Kalamazoo: Cistercian Publications, 1979, p. 6.

[24] McGinn, *The Growth of Mysticism,* p. 223.

[25] Ibid., p. 224.

[26] Walker Bynum, *Jesus as Mother,* pp. 145–6.

primarily concerned with the development of the monastic model of life. Yet from within this context Bernard has been able to offer important challenges to later theologies of love. These include his exploration of the inner human being, though always in connection with the direction of the outer self. The loving union is also a union of will. Bernard called the human will the 'face' of the inner person.[27] In this monastic theology of love, subject and embodiment are rediscovered, of course not in any modern or postmodern sense, but human beings are invited to love God, each other and their own divinely transfigured selves.

## Thomas Aquinas' Systematic Theology of Love

The Dominican friar Thomas Aquinas offers a comprehensive discussion of love within the framework of his magnum opus, the *Summa Theologiae.*[28] This work was composed for students of theology, and, therefore, has an academic, pedagogical, and — related to both — systematic character. Of course, like everybody else in medieval theology, even Thomas explicitly claims to stand firmly in the biblical and Augustinian tradition. However, his sources transcend these classical influences. It is not only his frequent use of Aristotle's thinking that makes him differ from Bernard of Clairvaux, but also his self-conscious systematic approach to all of theology in the *Summa.*

Referring to and making use of human experience, Thomas casts the net much wider than Bernard. He shares the abbot's overall conviction that any form of genuine love must relate to God, who is the ultimate origin and aim of love, and that we human beings are capable of loving since we are created in God's image. However, Thomas offers a more sophisticated approach to the complexity of love and he develops a set of important distinctions and categories in order to grasp the various dimensions and aspects of divine and human love. Moreover, his still more positive understanding of the human faculty of loving God leads him to suggest that human beings are created to become friends with God. Aristotle's concept of *philia,*

[27] Cf. Theo Kobusch, *Christliche Philosophie: Die Entdeckung der Subjektivität,* Darmstadt: Wissenschaftliche Buchgesellschaft, 2006, p. 71.

[28] For Thomas' other work on love, not discussed here partly because of the lack of a critical edition of the text and partly because of the very considerable overlap of both works, see Saint Thomas Aquinas, *On Charity* (*De Caritate*), trans. Lottie H. Kendzierski, Milwaukee: Marquette University Press, 1997.

friendship (*amicitia* in Latin),[29] receives here its theological baptism, however, in close connection with all the other concepts brought into play during Thomas's great discourse on love in the second part of his *Summa*.

In the first part of this second part, Thomas considers the movement from human beings to God. Within the context of his discussions of emotions (*passiones*), Thomas describes love (*amor*) as first among the passions, i.e. as a natural dimension of human life. It propels us to seek union with the desired object. 'Love therefore is not the union itself, union is a result of love. Hence Dionysius calls love a force that leads to union, and Aristotle says that union is an effect of love' (1a.2æ. 26, 2).[30] Thomas then introduces a number of distinctions: 'There are four words whose meanings are very much alike: *amor*, *dilectio*, *caritas*, and *amicitia*; still they are not interchangeable. For *amicitia*, as Aristotle remarks, is dispositional, whereas *amor* and *dilectio* are episodic; and *caritas* may be either' (26, 3).[31] Moreover, the last three refer to human acts in different ways. For Thomas, *amor* has the widest reference, whereas every instance of both *dilectio* and *caritas* is an instance of *amor*. *Dilectio* contains an element of choice and hence has to do with the will, while *caritas* implies certain perfection in so far as the object loved is highly valued.[32] However, Thomas explains that *amor*, the most basic term, implies a certain passivity, a receptiveness for God who draws the human person towards him, whereas *dilectio* implies human activity. Hence, *amor* 'refers to something more God-like than does the word *dilectio*' (26, 3).[33]

Thomas moves on to distinguish between grades of love: love that wants good things for someone is love in a primary sense, i.e. friendship-love. Love that loves a thing because it contributes to someone else's welfare is love in a secondary sense, i.e. love-of-desire. The first love attends to the other for the other's sake, for who he is; hence it is more perfect than the second (26, 4).[34]

[29] See Aristotle, *The Nicomachean Ethics*, trans. Hippocrates G. Apostle, Dordrecht and Boston: D. Reidel, 1975, esp. pp. 140–80, books 8–9.

[30] St Thomas Aquinas, *Summa Theologiæ*, vol. 19: *The Emotions*, trans. Eric d'Arcy, London: Eyre & Spottiswoode, 1967, p. 67. In the text itself I also give chapter references to Thomas' *Summa* in order to facilitate the reader's possible use of other editions of the *Summa*.

[31] Ibid., p. 69.

[32] Ibid., pp. 69–71.

[33] Ibid., p. 71.

[34] Ibid., p. 73.

The fuller nature of love is then discussed when (in the second part of the *Summa*'s second part) Thomas considers the three theological virtues, i.e. the virtues that are given to us human beings by God, namely faith, hope and love. Love (*caritas*) is the supreme among the three theological virtues that are all infused by God into our hearts (2a.2æ. 24, 2).[35] Without charity, true virtue is not possible (23, 7).[36] 'Charity denotes union with God, whereas faith and hope do not' (24, 12).[37] However, for Thomas this does not imply any sort of denigration of the human will (23, 2).[38] Rather charity is an act of will made possible by God's sharing of himself with us, by God whose essence is love.[39] Therefore, in this life charity can grow in depth or intensity in the human subject. Here, Thomas develops his own categories, not unlike Bernard's attempts, to map out the way of spiritual perfection in love.

Thomas stresses that love is one and, as a result, the Christian praxis of love can distinguish but not separate love of God from love of neighbour: 'Charity means that we love God and our neighbour' (24, 12).[40] And: 'It is then with the same love of charity that we love all our neighbours, seeing them in relation to the one common good, which is God' (25, 2).[41] Charity (*caritas*) is not merely love (*amor*), but friendship (*amicitia*) (25, 2).[42] Here, Aristotle's influence on Thomas becomes visible. Friendship with God and our neighbour is the goal of love.[43]

> God and our neighbour are those with whom we have friendship. But in our love for them (*dilectione*) there is included love for charity itself (*dilectio caritatis*), for loving (*diligimus*) our neighbour and God means that what we love (*amamus*) is that we and our neighbour should love God (*diligamus*), in other words have charity (*caritatem*). (2a.2æ. 25, 3)[44]

Love as the habit infused by God into our soul thus always includes a co-orientation to love's Creator.

[35] St Thomas Aquinas, *Summa Theologiæ*, vol. 34: *Charity*, trans. R. J. Batten, OP, London: Eyre & Spottiswoode, 1975, p. 41.

[36] Ibid., p. 27.

[37] Ibid., p. 77.

[38] Ibid., p. 13.

[39] See ibid., 2a.2æ. 24, 1 (p. 37) and 24, 11 (p. 69).

[40] Ibid., p. 75.

[41] Ibid., pp. 82–5 ('Unde eodem amore caritatis diligimum omnes proximos, inquantum referuntur ad unum bonum commune, quod est Deus').

[42] Ibid., p. 87.

[43] For a detailed study of Thomas' notion of friendship see E. D. H. (Liz) Carmichael, *Friendship: Interpreting Christian Love*, London: T&T Clark, 2004, pp. 105–28.

[44] *Summa Theologiæ*, vol. 34, pp. 86–7.

Our love for God is also the horizon for Thomas's reflection on the commandment to love our enemies. The systematic theologian is very clear about what the precise aim of love for enemies must be: we are not commanded to love our enemies as enemies; that would be absurd. Rather we are called upon to love them as human beings: 'a man who loves God and his neighbour may not exclude his enemies from this general kind of love' (25, 8).[45] Moreover, Thomas realizes that the love of enemies requires a particular attitude of mind. Loving one's enemies for God's sake belongs for Thomas to the perfection of charity. 'For since charity makes us love our neighbour for God's sake, the more we love God, the more love we show our neighbour in spite of his dislike for us' (25, 8).[46] The point thus is not to like our enemies or their evil deeds and intentions, but to love them as fellow human beings who carry God's image in them.

Neighbourly love, however, is not confined to members of our own human species, but it 'includes also those who share the blessings of eternal life', i.e. the angels. Thomas explains, that 'charity's friendship is based on a fellowship of eternal happiness, which we share together with the angels' (25, 10).[47]

Thomas also discusses love of self. First, he distinguishes two ways of considering the body: according to its nature, and according to the corruption that sin and punishment bring with them.

> Now our bodily nature, far from issuing from an evil principle, as the Manichees imagine, is from God. We can therefore use it for God's service ... Accordingly, with the same love of charity by which we love God, we ought also to love our body, though not the taint of sin and the corruption that punishment brings it; on the contrary, charity should make us long for an end to these. (25, 6)[48]

He then affirms self-love in terms of desiring what 'makes for the perfection of reason' (25, 4),[49] and he affirms the body as a necessary part of our person on the way to eternal happiness.[50]

Here we cannot discuss all the intricacies of Thomas' approach to love. We do not need to explore the bizarre logic according to which capital punishment is to be understood as an act of love through

[45] Ibid., p. 105.

[46] Ibid.

[47] Ibid., p. 111.

[48] Ibid., pp. 93–5.

[49] Ibid., p. 93.

[50] On the new concept of the human being in Thomas and on his new approach to body and soul, see Etienne Gilson, *History of Christian Philosophy in the Middle Ages*, London: Sheed and Ward, 1980, pp. 375–83.

which the criminal's soul is freed from his body (25, 6).[51] Nor can we appreciate from our contemporary perspective that the love of one's father ought to take priority over the love of one's mother. However counterintuitive that might be, Thomas argues, that the father plays the more significant part in the process of procreation: human reason comes to us through our fathers, whereas our mothers are responsible for contributing mere matter to our being (26, 11).[52] Here we are back to gender discourse in love and the trend to spiritualize love. For Thomas, after all, the perfection of the human soul, now newly refigured, is and remains the ultimate aim of love.

However, it is worth noting that Thomas defends a unitary concept of love while recognizing love's many dimensions: 'Love has as many different objects as there are different relations between a lover and the various things he loves' (15, 12).[53]

For Thomas, love is even a way of distinguishing the dignity of human beings from that of animals and other 'irrational creatures': 'But irrational creatures can have no share in human life, which of its nature is rational, and therefore no friendship is possible with them except metaphorically speaking' (25, 3).[54]

In Thomas' *Summa* we see a careful effort to retrieve the Augustinian tradition on love and, at the same time, to develop it in accordance with the new scholastic approach to Christian faith. Moreover, we encounter a first thoroughly systematic and comprehensive attempt to order the different dimensions and implications of love (Quaestio 26 is entitled '*de ordine caritatis*'). In this system of love, human agency is appreciated, while the origin of love in God's grace is forcefully acknowledged and praised. The dynamics of love is illustrated through levels of intensity, and the unitary concept of love defended. Love is being explored within both a new discourse of knowledge and a refigured anthropology according to which human beings, in spite of their sinful and imperfect ontological status, can be friends with God thanks to God's grace. Liz Carmichael summarizes this vision of friendship: '*Caritas* as friendship with God touches eternity and the divine and is, in a far more committed and profound manner than natural friendliness or philanthropy, an all-embracing love of

[51] *Summa Theologiæ*, vol. 34, p. 99.

[52] Ibid., p. 149.

[53] Ibid., p. 117.

[54] Ibid., p. 89. For a contemporary discussion of the possibility and impossibility of friendship between human beings and animals, see Eva Österberg, *Vänskap – en lång historia*, Stockholm: Atlantis, 2007, pp. 255–78.

humankind. It cannot be exclusive.'[55] Love concerns the individual person as well as the network of persons. All participate in this divinely granted friendship.

In this view, love as God's gift has the potential to grow in us. It does not increase in a quantitative sense in that one love would be added to another, but in the sense of intensification. It is the human subject that is transformed by the love that God gives. 'This is what God does in fact when he increases charity: he makes it take a deeper hold, and brings it about that the likeness of the Holy Spirit is more perfectly shared in the soul' (24, 5).[56] Thomas distinguishes three degrees of charity. First, we must resist sin and those desires which drive us into the opposite direction of charity. Secondly, we must advance in virtue so that our love can become strong. 'The third stage is when a man applies himself chiefly to the work of cleaving to God and enjoying him, which is characteristic of the perfect *who long to depart and to be with Christ*' (Phil. 1.23) (24, 9).[57]

Thomas also recognizes the intimate relationship between love and peace. 'Peace is an act of charity' (29, 4).[58] It implies two sorts of union: 'one, a bringing of all one's own desires to an ordered unity; the other, union between one's own desires and those of another person. In both cases it is charity that brings it about' (29, 3).[59] Thomas knows, of course, that perfect peace, i.e. the perfect enjoyment of the highest good that causes all of our desires to be united and to rest in one, is not attainable in this world. But imperfect peace is what we can have in this world. It is imperfect 'because, even though the soul's principal movement is to rest in God, still there remain certain obstacles, both within and without, which disturb its peace' (29, 2).[60] It is noteworthy that Thomas understands the contribution of the law in terms of removing those obstacles, though not in terms of creating peace. The ultimate unifying force comes from love and not from the law (29, 3).[61]

Thomas' theology of love opened up a new and wider horizon for the Christian praxis of love: here love has received a universal focus. It is a gift from God that calls for human response, discernment and

[55] Carmichael, *Friendship*, p. 126.
[56] *Summa Theologiæ*, vol. 34, p. 51.
[57] Ibid., p. 63.
[58] Ibid., p. 207.
[59] Ibid., p. 203.
[60] Ibid.
[61] Ibid., p. 205.

moral development. A new social focus is manifest in this approach to love, emerging, to be sure, from within a particular religious movement and imagination and propelled by a striving for moral order, but concerned about all human relationships — in tandem with the new approach to theology and with the universal claims of a strictly hierarchical, fully patriarchal and all embracing church dominance of society and culture.

However, parallel to these universalizing and totalizing ambitions of scholastic theology and high medieval ecclesiastical imagination, generally hostile to the inclusion of erotic elements into their reconfigured theologies of self, love, and church, new approaches to the erotic potential of human love are emerging in the particular culture of the medieval courts, notably in (what we call today) Southern France. Thus, parallel to the ambition of establishing a Christian society in Europe, we observe a secular movement attending afresh to the erotic, though not always sexual, dimensions of love.

## Courtly Love and the Conflicts of Desire

In the twelfth and thirteenth century a new poetry of love appears at Provençal courts and spreads quickly to other European courts. Hence, at this period in time, love is reclaimed as a topic in different social locations, i.e. in monastic life and mystical thought, in academic reflection on theology and church, and in courtly contexts, and it is expressed in different forms of discourse, including mystical contemplation on biblical passages, theoretical reflections on the aims of Christian life, and poetic songs about love and the associated feelings, devotions and desires. The obsession with love seems omnipresent among the learned groups of this period. However, perspective matters here: although all groups are inspired by religious traditions and classical and new motives, not all are interested in exploring a new and creative poetics of desire. The medieval mystics voice their desire for union with God, while the Troubadours express their desire for the object of their love in verse and music.

At the time, marriage is a matter of rational order in society and about to be incorporated even into the ecclesiastical order as one of the sacraments (see below, chapter 7). But marriage is certainly not yet an institution of love. In the feudal milieu, marriage continues to be entangled with dynastic strategy, and in the context of monastic medieval piety, love remains a matter of divine–human relationship. The new cultivation of love as feeling in the feudal milieu of the court is not yet connected with either marriage or religious devotion. Rather the emergence of a new subjectivity among the educated classes of medieval society finds expression in a new poetic imagination of love. Like in the monasteries and in the theological schools, classical sources, in particular Ovid's *Art of Love*, are re-read to inspire this new poetic imagination. The erotic desire, highly spiritualized in medieval church and theology, now returns in secular genres of expression to the world of the noble classes where it unfolds its transformative dynamics.[62]

The Troubadours praise love in word and music. Songs of desire, pain and joy — in always new variations and, significantly, in the vernacular — are directed at the venerated lady in the case of the male Troubadours, or the beloved friend in the case of the female Troubadours.[63] These songs require a holistic interpretation that appreciates the interdependence of words and music.[64] The ongoing and at times heated debate on the origins of the troubadour movement and its songs need not concern us here.[65] More interesting for our topic are the themes of these songs. The joys and disappointments of love, the desire of love, and the very act of love are prominent issues treated in the earlier songs, whereas later songs explore more the feeling of desire and delayed fulfilment in love than the concrete pleasures of actual intercourse.[66] Arnaud de la Croix explains this poetic distanciation from the actual act of love with the increasing concern for the right measure of love between erotic drive and reason. Moreover, concern for this measure represents also an expression of the search for mutuality in love between men and women. De la Croix sees in this development a genuine revolution of

[62] Cf. Arnaud de la Croix, *Liebeskunst und Lebenslust im Mittelalter*, trans. Gritje Hartmann, Darmstadt: Wissenschaftliche Buchgesellschaft, 2003, pp. 7, 22–4, and 110. See also Hugo Kuhn, 'Liebe und Gesellschaft in der Literatur', in Kuhn, *Liebe und Gesellschaft*, ed. Wolfgang Walliczek, Stuttgart: J. B. Metzlersche Verlagsbuchhandlung, 1980, pp. 60–8.

[63] On the female Troubadours see de la Croix, pp. 59–61.

[64] Ibid., p. 32.

[65] See ibid., pp. 34–40 and 48–61, for a the critique of the theories proposed by Denis de Rougemont and other historians. Denis de Rougemont, *Love in the Western World*, trans. Montgomery Belgion, Princeton, NJ: Princeton University Press, 1983. See esp. the Appendix in this edition of the work, entitled 'Inconclusive and Scientifico-Polemical Postscript', trans. Danielle Salti, pp. 325–79. See also Kuhn, pp. 62–3: 'Der Anfang dieser höfischen Literatur ist, wie ich glaube, eine *creatio ex nihilo*.'

[66] De la Croix, pp. 42

the understanding of the sexual act of love. Hitherto it was the man that had taken his wife in the act of love, now the songs sing about the adored lady who commands over the desiring and loving man.[67] Nevertheless, it is still the man who initiates the relationship.[68]

The social system of courtly love was the topic of a book entitled *The Art of Courtly Love* written by Andreas Capellanus (Andrew the Chaplain) late in the twelfth century.[69] Here the priest describes life at the court of Queen Eleanor of Aquitaine. The book, written in Latin, gives Andreas' lengthy account of the practice of love as well as his rather brief refutation of such practice in the name of a higher and spiritualized form of love. Thus, this work contrasts both realms of love, the erotic and the spiritual, however not without deeper — and humorous — insights into the complexities, desires, passions and pleasures of erotic love. But it also considers questions of class and the ability, or inability, of love to overcome such boundaries. Moreover, Capellanus describes the woman's right to choose whether or not she wishes to bestow her love on her self-confessed lover.[70] In general terms he praises the role of the woman in the practice of erotic love in glowing words:

> But although all good things seem to proceed from women, and although God has given them a great privilege and we say that they are the cause and origin of everything good, still they are clearly under the necessity of so conducting themselves toward those who do good deeds that by their approval the good character of these men may seem in every respect to increase from strength to strength.[71]

Although as a clergyman Andreas aspires to live a celibate life, he defends the priest's superior insights into love in the final of eight dialogues, here with a noble woman:

> So if I ask any woman to love me, she cannot refuse me on the pretext that I am a clerk; indeed I shall prove to you by inevitable necessity that in love a clerk is preferable to a layman. We find that a clerk is in every respect more cautious and more prudent than a layman, and conducts himself and his affairs with greater restraint, and is accustomed to keep everything within more proper bounds; that is because a clerk, as the Scripture tells us, has an experienced

[67] Ibid., pp. 43–7.

[68] Ibid., p. 52. De la Croix contrasts the Troubadours with Celtic customs: While in the songs of the Troubadours the woman never initiates a love relationship, in Celtic poetry she enjoys greater freedom in this respect.

[69] Andreas Capellanus, *The Art of Courtly Love*, trans. and ed. John Jay Parry, New York: Columbia University Press, 1990.

[70] Ibid., pp. 50–3.

[71] Ibid., p. 108.

> knowledge of all things [Mal. 2.7]. Therefore in love he is to be preferred to a layman, because it has been found that nothing in the world is so necessary as to be experienced in carrying on all things connected with love.[72]

In the brief 'Rejection of Love' at the end of his book, Andreas lists reasons why love is bad for a man of virtue and for a woman of reputation.[73] Here, the genre of dialogue between man and woman is absent; now alone the cleric speaks and explains the many evils of love in order to dissuade his friend Walter, for whom the entire book is written, to abstain from the pleasures of Venus. Now women are unmasked as true daughters of Eve. For instance, they are said to 'have so much avarice that generous gifts break down all the barriers of their virtue'.[74] Every woman is envious 'because a woman is always consumed with jealousy over another woman's beauty'.[75] 'Woman is also prone to every sort of evil.'[76] Hence, Andreas concludes his diatribe against the love of women by admonishing Walter to be mindful 'to have your lamps always supplied, that is, have the supplies of charity and good works. Be mindful ever to watch, lest the unexpected coming of the Bridegroom find you asleep in sins.'[77]

The reader cannot help wondering if the main concern of this work has not really been to describe the practice of passionate love rather than to refute it. In 1277, about a hundred years after its composition, Capellanus' book was condemned by the Bishop of Paris. The mixing of passionate love and spiritual dimensions, outside of marriage, was not acceptable to church leaders striving after clear distinctions in bodily love: either marital order or licentious disorder.[78] Not only is there a massive disproportion in *The Art of Courtly Love* between the lengthy treatment of love and the brief refutation, but there is also some refutation of the refutation in the discussion of love itself, when a woman of the higher nobility remarks: 'For many people abstain from things that are forbidden and wicked more because of the disgrace in this world than to avoid the torments of the everlasting death.'[79]

Capellanus' work thus presents us with a passionate documentation of the practice of courtly love and a weak rejection of it in the

[72] Ibid., p. 125.
[73] Ibid., pp. 187–212.
[74] Ibid., p. 201.
[75] Ibid., p. 202
[76] Ibid., p. 208.
[77] Ibid., p. 212.
[78] Cf. de la Croix, p. 71.
[79] Capellanus, p. 126.

name of the Church's efforts to purify, order and spiritualize love. The book thus shows that human love is divided into two halves, a passionate and a spiritual. The role of women has been considered radically differently with respect to both loves. While in passionate love women represent all that is good, they risk all that is good in spiritual love when they defile it with their desire-producing bodies.

The love poetry of the Troubadours in the South of (modern) France was complemented by the Arthurian Romance of Celtic origin in Northern France. Chrétien de Troyes (before 1150–before 1190) has given epic form to the traditional love story of Tristan and Iseult, a story that ever since has sung the praise of passionate love in always new adaptations, including Richard Wagner's opera. The Celtic sagas and their refigurations in medieval literature have further upgraded the position of women. The woman is being admired now both as the origin of desire and as the ruler over the heart of men. She herself is understood to initiate the dynamics of love. Hence, the woman becomes the incarnation of eros.

At the same time, we can observe how attention to women, represented as the focus of male desire, shifts from the actual to the projected sphere. Denis de Rougemont thinks that this shift was promoted, in part, by the emergence of a new eros that combines the joy of love with the passion of dying. This new eros, different from the Greek eros, was formulated and disseminated through the Tristan myth. De Rougemont interprets the attraction of this myth, and of subsequent romance influenced by it, in terms of unfulfilled love.

> Unless the course of love is being hindered there is no 'romance'; and it is romance that we revel in – that is to say, the self-consciousness, intensity, variations, and delays of passion, together with its climax rising to disaster – not its sudden flaring.[80]

Such passionate love is opposed to the order of matrimony. Iseult cannot be imagined as Mme Tristan.[81] Rather the passion at work in this myth transcends all structured frameworks for love and hence must culminate in death. 'The tremendous success of the Tristan Romance shows, whether we like it or not, that we have a secret preference for what is unhappy.'[82] Thus, the success of romantic love and its literary refigurations ever since have to do with the pleasures of unfulfilled desire. De Rougemont concludes: 'The

[80] De Rougemont, p. 52.
[81] Ibid., p. 45.
[82] Ibid., p. 51.

happiness of lovers stirs our feelings only on account of the unhappiness which lies in wait for it. We must feel that life is imperilled, and also feel the hostile realities that drive happiness away into some beyond. What moves us is not its presence, but its nostalgia and recollection.'[83]

De la Croix calls this form of erotics an 'erotics of distance'.[84] However, he argues that this form of erotics is not representative of all of the literature in this cultural context. Rather, Chrétien de Troyes, for instance, attempted to develop a new approach to love that aimed at reconciling love with marriage, though not in any ecclesiastical meaning or order.[85] De la Croix is right to underline the enormous changes in the understanding of love that have occurred in a relatively brief period of time. From the discovery of love for the woman in Aquitaine towards the end of the eleventh century, a feeling hitherto reserved for male friendship and which presupposed mutual desire, to the praise of adulterous desire, and now to the project of a new, equal model of love between man and woman in Chrétien's fiction. This new model of love is not dependent on any church law or ritual, but is consummated after the successful passing of all sorts of tests and challenges.[86]

However, we must not confuse the emerging culture of courtly love with the actual sexual practices of ordinary people and of the noble classes.[87] Johan Huizinga reminds us of the need to distinguish two diverging currents in the erotic conceptions of the Middle Ages.

> Extreme indecency showing itself freely in customs, as in literature, contrasts with an excessive formalism, bordering on prudery ... Such customs seem to be absolutely opposed to the constraint and the modesty imposed by courtesy. The

[83] Ibid., p. 52. The last sentence reads in the original French: 'La nostalgie, le souvenir, et non pas la présence, nous émeuvent': Denis de Rougemont, *L'amour et l'occident*, Paris: Plon, 1972, p. 55. Björn Larsson disagrees with de Rougemont. See Larsson, 'À quoi ça sert de lire des romans d'amour ... et de les écrire?', in Centre des Écrivains du Sud – Jean Giono, *Comment j'ai lu des romans d'amour*, Marseilles: transbordeurs, 2008, pp. 14–44, here pp. 31–2: 'Ceux qui, comme Rougemont, identifient la passion à la mort ne sont donc pas à court d'arguments et d'exemples. Cependant, il me semble erroné d'affirmer que la mort est souhaitée ou désirée par les amants ou que la mort est un moyen de sceller l'amour-passion pour l'éternité.'

[84] De la Croix, p. 98.

[85] Ibid., p. 101.

[86] Ibid.

[87] Cf. de la Croix, pp. 124–45; Hans-Werner Goetz, *Leben im Mittelalter vom 7. bis zum 13. Jahrhundert*, Munich: Beck, 1986, pp. 54–61; and Thomas Bein, *Liebe und Erotik im Mittelalter*, Darmstadt: Wissenschaftliche Buchgesellschaft, 2003.

> same circles which showed so much shamelessness in sexual relations professed to venerate the ideal of courtly love.[88]

In spite of the differing forms of attention to and expression of love in the courtly circles of this period we must conclude that the place of love, identified by Augustine with God as the *summum bonum,* has been firmly relocated now to earth. Whereas in the Augustinian tradition love was a divine absolute, in the courtly tradition absolute love has become the focus of human attention. Still the *summum bonum,* love has shifted location: it has become the highest social good.[89] Still mysterious, the exploration of love requires human artists. The masters of love, however, for the time being are to be found only among the aristocracy. The relocation of love in the actual lives of the feudal classes implied a new role for women. Although recognized now as a partner in destiny, this new attention to the presence of women in society, in the arts and in literary representation does not automatically lead to the emancipation of women. Instead the woman is given a new object status: she becomes the highest earthly good, the new object of male desire.[90]

This is not the place to explore further the development of love literature or the complex cultural shifts in the Middle Ages. But we must make reference to the remarkable developments in female self-understanding both in society and church. Among the literary voices challenging continuing suspicion, hatred and fear over against women, Christine de Pizan (c. 1364–c. 1430) occupies a central place. Well educated, she earned her living through her writing. In a number of her works she denounces the widespread misogyny in her culture. However, the fight about the role of women in church and society was to continue. As a result both of the gender clichés in the newly explored Aristotelian thinking and of the reintroduction of Roman law with its traditional patriarchal convictions, the place of women was once again contested.[91] The struggle for full female agency in all dimensions of love is as visible in the Middle Ages as is the philosophical, theological, ecclesiastical and juridical backlash against the emancipation of women.

[88] Johan Huizinga, *The Waning of the Middle Ages,* trans. F. Hopman, London: Penguin, 2001, p. 106.

[89] Cf. Kuhn, 'Liebe und Gesellschaft in der Literatur', p. 62.

[90] Cf. ibid., pp. 63 and 67.

[91] Cf. de la Croix, pp. 108–9.

## Women Mystics

Not only among the Troubadours and the literary circles at the courts can we observe a manifestation of female subjectivity linked with female agency in love, but also in some spheres of religious life. The thirteenth century saw 'the earliest large-scale emergence of women's voices in the history of Christian thought'.[92] Of course, some exceptional Christian women had expressed themselves before that time in the Latin language of Western theology to which, thanks to the educational facilities of their families and of monastic life, they had been granted access.[93] Most prominently, Hildegard of Bingen (1098–1179) and Heloise have left a lasting impression in church and society.[94] However, two developments in the thirteenth century radically altered the position of women in religious life: the shift to the vernacular and the emergence of a new form of religious life in which women themselves took on the roles of active leaders, the Beguine movement.

The Beguines were religious lay women who wanted to live an apostolic life in poverty, chastity and obedience, either alone or in Beguine houses, but outside of established religious orders.[95] Unlike nuns in established religious orders, they did not take vows.

> Beguines followed no authorized rule so the details of their daily lives varied considerably according to when and where they lived. Some women were able to live as Beguines within their families, others lived together in small or large groups, though as the thirteenth century progressed the larger communities became the norm.[96]

[92] Bernard McGinn, 'Introduction: Meister Eckhart and the Beguines in the Context of Vernacular Theology', pp. 1–14, here p. 1.

[93] See Mary T. Malone, *Women and Christianity*, vol. 1: *The First Thousand Years*, Maryknoll: Orbis, 2000.

[94] Here I am not discussing the moving love-story of Abelard and Heloise. It does not offer new perspectives on the Christian praxis of love. Rather it documents the dilemmas of a human love relationship under the pressures of spiritual love. See *The Letters of Abelard and Heloise*, trans. Betty Radice, Harmondsworth: Penguin, 1985. See also Dietmar Mieth, *Das gläserne Glück der Liebe*, Freiburg i. B.: Herder, 1992, pp. 75–81.

[95] Bernard McGinn, *The Flowering of Mysticism: Men and Women in the New Mysticism (1200–1350)*, The Presence of God: A History of Western Christian Mysticism, vol. 3, New York: Crossroad, 1998, p. 6: 'As the twelfth century progressed, more and more laity were attracted to the evangelical rather than to the communal model of apostolic life.'

[96] Saskia Murk-Jansen, 'Beguine Spirituality', in Philip Sheldrake, ed., *The New SCM Dictionary of Christian Spirituality*, London: SCM Press, 2005, pp. 146–8, here pp. 146–7.

They earned their living through handicrafts. In their spiritual life they were dedicated to prayer and contemplation for the sake of attaining a knowledge of God through love; in their active life they engaged in works of charity, such as teaching of girls, attending the sick, the poor, and the dead in death watches. Thus, their acts of charity were directed to life in the world, i.e. outside the walls of traditional religious institutions. While the mendicant orders of Franciscans and Dominicans followed a similar direction of works of love, women were not admitted to their ranks and discipline. The Beguines received papal backing in 1215 and were widely respected for their way of holiness in the Church.

However, this first wave of emancipation of educated Christian women within the sphere of religious life provoked suspicion in the Church and a strong reaction from male theologians wishing to curtail the right of women to express themselves in theological matters. References to the possibility of women to incite lust in men were made, for instance by Henry of Ghent, in order to restrict the audience for any possible teaching by women to only women and girls. Moreover, it was argued, a woman, like any other (male) Christian teacher, needs to possess sound doctrine, but unlike other (male) Christian teachers, women should not teach in public, but only in private.[97] In 1310 Marguerite Porete was burned for not having respected these restrictions and for having departed from 'sound doctrine'. In 1312 the Council of Vienne condemned the entire movement as potentially heretical.[98] One of the effects of this condemnation was that most theological expressions in the vernacular came to an end.[99]

Of particular interest for our reflection on the theology of love is the internal relationship of different aspects of the love practised by these lay religious women. On the one hand, not unlike Franciscan visions of love, the Beguines felt called to practise love in faithful service to suffering fellow human beings at a time of war, Black Death

---

See also Saskia Murk-Jansen, *Brides in the Desert: The Spirituality of the Beguines*, London: Darton, Longman and Todd, 1998.

[97] For Henry of Ghent's views on women teaching at the end of the thirteenth century see McGinn, 'Introduction: Meister Eckhart and the Beguines in the Context of Vernacular Theology', pp. 1–3, and McGinn, *The Flowering of Mysticism*, p. 21.

[98] Heinrich Denzinger and Peter Hünermann, eds, *Enchiridion symbolarum definitionum et declarationum de rebus fidei et morum*, 41st edn, Freiburg: Herder, 2007, nos 891–9 (pp. 388–9).

[99] Cf. Saskia Murk-Jansen, 'Beguine Spirituality', op. cit., p. 147.

and priestly moral decay.[100] On the other hand, this generous self-giving to other people in need was accompanied by a deep desire to be united with God. This mystical desire was expressed in the terms of courtly love.[101] Hence, there is an intimate relationship between attention to the love of God and loving attention to the needs of others. In many ways, the Beguine mysticism moves in the classical furrows of mystical desire for union with God, known since Dionysius the Areopagite (or Pseudo-Dyonysius),[102] and it includes elements of Cistercian spirituality. However, while Bernard's message of loving union was directed to his fellow monks and thus was part of the formation of a male spiritual elite withdrawn from the world, the Beguines directed their message and service of love to the world.[103] Their audience thus differed from the publics of either church theologians or monastic mystics.[104]

This focus on the needs and sufferings of the world were further promoted by the 'popular dichotomy which presented man as Christ's divinity, and woman as his humanity. It is this tension that is reflected in the paradoxes of suffering and love.'[105] This link between female discipleship and suffering supported shaped the particular desire for union with Christ.

What, then, distinguishes this new form of lay spirituality from scholastic theology, on the one hand, and monastic theology, on the other, is not only the use of courtly imagination and of the vernacular for expressing this desire, but also an intensification of union to a much more radical unity of soul and God.[106] Moreover, since the technical tools of both of these theologies — e.g. lectures, disputations, biblical commentaries — were not easily available to these lay women, personal experience (as we have seen above in this chapter, Bernard of Clairvaux had spoken of the 'book of experience') became a central source for their theological thinking. Poetry, sermons, didactic letters, and visionary accounts were the

[100] Cf. Geels, *Kristen mystik*, p. 166.

[101] On the literary context of the Beguine writings, see Murk-Jansen, *Brides in the Desert*, pp. 34–58.

[102] See Pseudo-Dionysius, *The Complete Works*, trans. Colm Luibheid, The Classics of Western Spirituality, New York and Mahwah: Paulist Press, 1987.

[103] Cf. Bernard McGinn, *The Flowering of Mysticism*, p. 12.

[104] Cf. Geels, p. 166.

[105] Saskia Murk-Jansen, *Brides in the Desert*, p. 53.

[106] Cf. Bernard McGinn, 'Introduction: Meister Eckhart and the Beguines in the Context of Vernacular Theology', p. 9.

preferred genres of their approach to the mysteries of faith and the vehicles for sharing their insights with their new and, thanks to the new literacy of this century even among women,[107] shifting audience of lay people.[108]

Bernard McGinn contrasts the two ways of conceiving what came to be called mystical union (*unio mystica*) in the Middle Ages: the first way, emerging in the Latin West and reaching a significant level of sophistication in the twelfth century, held 'that the soul could attain a loving union of wills with God, an *unitas spiritus* whose basic human analogue was to be found in the marriage embrace of the lovers portrayed in the Song of Songs'.[109] The second way, now associated with the emerging women vernacular theologians, pursued a much more radical, and thus also more problematic, understanding which spoke of total union, of union without difference, or what could be described in the later terms of Meister Eckhart as a *unitas indistinctionis,* i.e. 'the insistence that in the ground of reality there is absolute identity between God and the soul'.[110] The way to this total unity required for the Beguine mystics a life of total annihilation. This way was to become of great importance also for Meister Eckhart and his concept of perfect detachment.

This new departure in lay spirituality thus combined a fresh attention to the demands of charity in the world with a massive return to a Platonist concept of loving unity between God and the human soul. A new love of the world and a return to a traditional concept of inner faith shows at the same time the contextual and the counter-cultural sensitivities of these women. The discovery of a new subjectivity in love in the twelfth and thirteenth century continues here, although it now calls for the total surrendering of any human will to the will of God.

For the thirteenth century Beguine Hadewijch of Brabant, for instance, in order to be like God, 'the soul must be impassive, without desires, and this state is the means to union with God'.[111] She goes so far as to demand the painful absence of *minne* (love) in order to attain unity of minne. For her, as the following longer quotation from

[107] Cf. Bernard McGinn, *The Flowering of Mysticism,* p. 4.

[108] Cf. ibid., p. 22.

[109] McGinn, 'Introduction: Meister Eckhart and the Beguines in the Context of Vernacular Theology', p. 12.

[110] Ibid.

[111] Cf. Saskia Murk-Jansen, 'Hadewijch and Eckhart: Amor intellegere est', in Bernard McGinn, ed., *Meister Eckhart and the Beguine Mystics,* pp. 17–30, here p. 27.

one of her poems shows, 'the need to do without the consciousness of the presence of love (God) is associated with union, with being drawn into love'[112]:

> That pleases love most of all, that one should be wholly robbed [devoid] of all pleasure of strangers and of friends and of herself. And that is a fearful life that love demands, that one must do without her fulfilment in order to fulfil her. They who are thus drawn into love and removed [received], and whom she binds, they owe so overly much to love to fulfil her on account of the great power of her strong nature.[113]

Here, the mystical desire for ultimate fulfilment in loving union cannot be stilled; rather the eternal lack of fulfilment must be embraced — in love. Hence, love is a painful journey of desire.[114]

In Hadewijch's mysticism everything circles around *minne*, though not in a theoretical or doctrinal way; rather love needs to be explored and experienced.[115] In our words, we could say that she encouraged the Christian *praxis* of love. This praxis included both contemplation and works of love, and it was located in a wide horizon encompassing universal, Eucharistic, Trinitarian and christological perspectives. Whoever intends to reach God is called to live the virtues present in the God-Man. 'In living the demands of this form of *minne* we actually live the very life of the Trinity.'[116] And this life includes suffering for the sake of likeness to Jesus Christ.[117] *Minne* is for Hadewijch the way of Christian discipleship; it alone is the way to God; it connects the disciple with the inner life of the Trinity. She can speak in colourful erotic terms of her *minne* for Christ.

However, as Barbara Newman and Bernard McGinn have emphasized, the way of *minne* is made possible by a pre-existent relationship between the human soul and God. 'A good Christian Platonist, Hadewijch believed firmly in exemplarism, the doctrine of all creatures' real and eternal existence in the mind of God.'[118] Hence, while the ideal self is already with God, the earthly self still has a long journey ahead of her. 'Hadewijch's exemplary [eternal]

[112] Ibid., p. 28.

[113] Quoted by Murk-Jansen, ibid., p. 28.

[114] See also Murk-Jansen, *Brides in the Desert*, pp. 71–2; and de la Croix, p. 120.

[115] Cf. McGinn, *The Flowering of Mysticism*, p. 201.

[116] Ibid., p. 205.

[117] Cf. Murk-Jansen, *Brides in the Desert*, p. 73.

[118] Barbara Newman, *From Virile Woman to Woman Christ: Studies in Medieval Religion and Literature*, Philadelphia: University of Pennsylvania Press, 1995, p. 146.

self and her historical self are growing together in love to attain the fullness of their primordially given equality with the Beloved.'[119] In this Christian Platonist sense, *minne* is a return to the person's true essence. This motive of return might help us also to relate better to Hadewijch's understanding of a union of indistinction, however difficult and complex, between the human soul and God in *minne*.

Hadewijch's mysticism thus both affirms and dissolves the human subject in love. She sees human love directed both to God and to fellow human beings in need. Moreover, she does not encourage any sweet (or as we would say today romantic) notion of love. *Minne* is hard and life-consuming work for Hadewijch.

At this point it might be helpful to recapture and refine the different understandings of the loving self emerging in the twelfth and thirteenth century. First we have encountered *the bridal self* of monastic mysticism, famously developed by Bernard of Clairvaux in his interpretation of the Song of Songs. This self is conscious of the distance to the beloved, though full of desire for union with the beloved. This self knows the distance between herself as creature and her divine Creator, but their love is so great that in times of bliss, she forgets this difference and behaves as an equal.[120] However, her attitude is not passive, but one of active 'mothering', in the sense of actively pursuing works of charity in the bridegroom's absence.

Secondly, we have examined the scholastic self of Thomas that approaches the way of love in a rational and fully structured manner. Here, too, love is central; however the approach differs from the monastic concern for the self. Now the vision is friendship between the self and God, a relationship made possible by God who is love/friendship. The ultimate goal of this friendship is the perfection of reason in love (*caritas*).

Thirdly, we have investigated the courtly self in the songs of the Troubadours. This self is unfulfilled and consumed by desire for the distant and idealized object of his love. 'In the lover's complaint, moments of adoration and abject submission to the beloved alternate with moods of rebellion and rage, only to issue in renewed if melancholy professions of love.'[121] Faithfulness to this love and courage to

[119] McGinn, *The Flowering of Mysticism*, p. 215.

[120] Cf. Newman, p. 144.

[121] Ibid.

perform the works demanded by this devotion disclose the lover's true dignity. As we have seen above in this chapter, the self of the courtly romance does not, as in the lyrics of the Troubadours, worship an absent love, but is engaged with a concrete love. Moreover, this new self is no longer restricted to male paradigms. Rather women begin to emerge in this movement as loving selves in their own right.

Fourthly, the Beguine mystics, exemplified here by Hadewijch, also make use of bridal mysticism, but further develop the understanding of the bridal self. For Hadewijch, as we have seen above, the bridal self both denotes an empirical self and an ideal self, and the former must grow in *minne*, i.e. in that which she always already ontologically is. Here the desired union in love requires a return of the self to its true origin, Love.

> O Love, were I but love,
> And could I but love you, Love, with love!
> O Love, for love's sake, grant that I,
> Having become love, may know Love wholly as Love![122]

The earthly self is to be emptied or negated. The present self has no future. Here Augustine's theology of love returns with a vengeance. The Beguines

> devised an exquisite form of self-negation that cut to the heart of their identity as lovers. Since a lover can take no joy except in her Beloved, the supreme sacrifice must lie in the willed choice of absence over presence – the same choice that led Isolt and Tristan to their misery and death, and to eternal union beyond death.[123]

The process of rediscovering and doubting the loved and loving self has continued unabated until today. Before discussing modern theological approaches to love, it might be particularly rewarding to examine, however briefly, a major theologian whose work emerged at the interface of medieval and modern conceptions of love and self beyond the monastic order.

## Martin Luther's Approach to Love

Martin Luther (1483–1546) combines in his life and work the struggle with his formation in Augustinian monastic spirituality, with his studies of the Bible and of scholastic theology, and with the demands

[122] Hadewijch, *The Complete Works*, trans. Mother Columba Hart, OSB, New York: Paulist Press, 1980, p. 352. Cf. also Newman, p. 155.

[123] Newman, p. 162.

of an emerging 'modern' subjectivity.[124] This subjectivity transcends traditional ecclesiastical authorities and theological claims in the name of the Christian freedom to respond directly to God's grace and calling. His so-called Reformation breakthrough, i.e. his insight into justification by faith alone,[125] has led to a general understanding that faith and grace were the hallmarks of Luther's theology. Against such a one-sided assessment, the recent Finnish school of Luther research has reclaimed Luther as a theologian of love.[126]

Luther has not specifically treated of love in any systematic way. Rather he reflects on love in the particular contexts that have occasioned his writings, sermons and interventions. Like all the thinkers discussed in this chapter, Luther considers the vocation of the Christian to love God, the neighbour and the self in the right way as central to Christian life. God is love, and the Christian life must be a life of love. What distinguishes Luther from the other thinkers is his emphasis on distinguishing clearly between two kinds of love: God's love (*amor Dei*) and human love (*amor hominis*).

In his Heidelberg Disputation of 1518 (thesis 28) Luther states: 'God's love does not find, but creates its object of love. Human love originates in its object.'[127] Luther thus affirms not only the difference of both loves, but also the genuinely human possibility, however much compromised by sin, to love. While God's love is perfect, human love is deficient. With reference to the cross of Christ, Luther further explains his thesis that God's love, which is present in the

[124] For a recent introduction to Luther's life and work, see Athina Lexutt, *Luther*, UTB Profile, Cologne, Weimar and Vienna: Böhlau, 2008.

[125] This breakthrough occurred sometime between 1513 and 1518. Cf. Marc Lienhard, 'Luther and the Beginnings of the Reformation', in Jill Raitt, ed., *Christian Spirituality*, vol. 2: *High Middle Ages and Reformation*, New York: Crossroad, 1989, pp. 268–99, here p. 270.

[126] See, for instance, Tuomo Mannermaa, 'Liebe VI. Reformation und Orthodoxie', in *Theologische Realenzyklopädie*, vol. 21, Berlin and New York: de Gruyter, 1991, pp. 152–6; Peter Manns and Rainer Vinke, 'Martin Luther als Theologe der Liebe', in Owald Bayer, Robert W. Jenson and Simo Knuuttila, eds, *Caritas Dei: Beiträge zum Verständnis Luthers und der gegenwärtigen Ökumene. Festschrift für Tuomo Mannermaa zum 60. Geburtstag*, Helsinki: Luther-Agricola-Gesellschaft, 1997, pp. 265–86; Carl E. Braaten and Robert W. Jenson, eds, *Union with Christ: The New Finnish Interpretation of Luther*, Grand Rapids: Eerdmans, 1998; Antti Raunio. *Summe des christlichen Lebens: Die 'Goldene Regel' als Gesetz der Liebe in der Theologie Martin Luthers von 1510–27*, Mainz: Philipp von Zabern, 2001; Veli-Matti Kärkkäinen, '"The Christian as Christ to the Neighbour": On Luther's Theology of Love', *International Journal of Systematic Theology* 6 (2004), pp. 101–17.

[127] Martin Luther, *Disputatio Heidelbergae habita. 1518.* In *D. Martin Luthers Werke.* Kritische Gesamtausgabe, vol. 1, Weimar: Hermann Böhlau, 1883, pp. 353–74, here p. 365.

human being, loves what is sinful, bad, foolish, and weak in order to make it just, good, wise and strong. God's love creates the good. 'For the sinners are beautiful, because they are loved; but they are not loved because they are beautiful. That is why human love shuns the sinners, the evil doers.'[128] However, Luther does not condemn human love. Nor does he deny that the objects of human love are part of God's good gifts. Rather, right human love of God acknowledges and praises God for these precious gifts of divine creation.[129]

Human love is real love, but imperfect love, because it always includes egoistic dimensions. Our love always also seeks our own benefits and follows our own desires.[130] However, when God's grace lives in us, when Christ's work works in us (thesis 27),[131] then our perspective is opened to love God as God, and to love the human being as the fellow human being with his real needs and for his own sake.

The ongoing re-reading of Luther's theology of love frees our perspective not only from ideological and instrumentalizing approaches, such as Anders Nygren's reading of Luther's theology of love from a perspective of divine agape versus human eros (see below, chapter 5), but allows us also to appreciate Luther's concern for union between God and human beings, very much in line with the mystical traditions referred to earlier in this chapter. But more importantly than identifying Luther as a mystic, we need to pay attention to the particularly christological nature of his mysticism.[132] Luther is both obliged to the tradition of Christian mystical experience and critical towards any mystical attempt to lift the soul, so to speak, on its own merit. His mysticism aims at conformity with Christ (*conformitas cum Christo*) and humility (*humilitas*).[133]

Luther, like Bernard of Clairvaux whom he appreciated throughout his life,[134] and the men and women mystics in the Christian movement that lived before him, reflected on the possibility of union between

[128] Ibid.

[129] Cf. Mannermaa, p. 153.

[130] Cf. Lexutt, *Luther*, p. 101.

[131] WA 1, p. 364.

[132] Cf. Werner G. Jeanrond, *Gudstro: Teologiska reflexioner II*, Lund: Arcus, 2001, p. 126.

[133] See Gerhard Wehr, ed., *Martin Luther – der Mystiker: Ausgewählte Texte*, Munich: Kösel, 1999, pp. 30–1. For texts and comments on Luther's christological mysticism see ibid., pp. 74–90.

[134] Cf. ibid., p. 32. See also Lexutt, *Luther*, p. 26.

God and the human being. Tuomo Mannermaa has underlined the importance of this *unio*-concept for the relationship between faith and love in Luther's theology.[135] Thanks to God's gift of faith, the process of union between God and the human being, i.e. the process of deification, can begin. Deification as the result of God's love in Christ 'means the "participation" of the believer in Christ which, because Christ is God, is also a participation in God himself'.[136] However, against the scholastic formula that faith is formed through love (*fides caritate formata*), Luther stressed the fact that Christ is the form of faith (*Christus forma fidei*).[137]

One of the crucial distinctions between Luther and his theological predecessors thus concerns the shift of attention from God's gift of love now to God's love in Christ. One of the motives for this shift is Luther's reinterpretation of human love (*caritas*): human love is deficient. While Thomas Aquinas, for instance, saw love as God's gift — together with faith and hope, love is one of the three infused virtues — and thus emphasized the divine origin and unity of love, Luther has split this unity into divine and human love and sees in the work of Christ the only possibility to reunite both loves afresh. Justification by faith is thus related to participation in God's love. Hence, 'it is not love but rather faith that makes our relationship to God possible, namely, faith that is not something that men and women choose for themselves but a gift from God'.[138]

It is certainly correct to point to the centrality of love in Luther's theology, but it is equally important to appreciate the interdependence of love and faith. 'Luther's understanding of love is completely dominated by his faith in the incarnation.'[139]

Faith shaping love offers the appropriate framework for any consideration of good works. Luther's interpretation of the Golden Rule (Matt. 7.12: 'In everything do to others as you would have them do to you') further illustrates his approach both to the love of God and to the love of our fellow human beings. The order here is important: our proper love of God structures the love of our human being.[140] Moreover, within the context of his Lectures on Romans

[135] Mannermaa, p. 154.
[136] Kärkkäinen, p. 105.
[137] Cf. Mannermaa, p. 154.
[138] Kärkkäinen, p. 107.
[139] Ibid., p. 109. See also Raunio, pp. 183–4.
[140] Cf. Raunio, pp. 155–9.

(1515–16),[141] the early Luther wishes to show how the proper love of God is necessary in order to give to God what the human being wrongly has willed for himself, although it is in reality owed to God.[142] Thereafter human beings should will for their neighbours what they too wish from them. Among the things which we have stolen from God Luther lists our own will, our judgement, and the divine honour. Living up to the Golden Rule implies adopting full humility towards both God and our fellow human beings.[143]

Following the Golden Rule thus means for Luther that the human will abandons the striving after its own good and seeks the good for the sake of God and the neighbour.[144] What is at stake here is nothing less than the surrendering of one's own will. Whoever wants to follow the Golden Rule must have his or her own will destroyed.[145] The total annihilation of the self in the mystical tradition is mirrored here in the total destruction of the human will. Only if we love God in Christ can we genuinely love our neighbours. The decision, then, is this: either we love our neighbours because of distorted self-love, or we love our neighbours because of God's love in Christ in us.[146] If the latter is the case, the real needs of our neighbours will become clear to us both rationally and affectively.[147] As Antti Raunio has demonstrated, Luther's understanding of the Golden Rule continues to guide his approach to love also in subsequent years.

In a sermon of 1522 Luther contrasts pagan love (*heidnische Liebe*) with Christian love (*Christliche Liebe*).[148] This move, fully consistent with Luther's overall christological approach to love and to union with Christ in love, has enormous implications for Christian approaches to the theology of love. Here love has lost the character of God's universal gift to humankind. Instead love has been subordinated to Christian confession. Love has been christianized in Luther's thinking. Now christological doctrine defines the matrix for any adequate consid-

[141] Martin Luther, *Der Brief an die Römer*. In *D. Martin Luthers Werke*. Kritische Gesamtausgabe, vol. 56, Weimar: Hermann Böhlaus Nachfolger, 1938. For Raunio's interpretation of Luther's *Lectures on Romans*, see Raunio, pp. 146–220.

[142] Cf. Manns and Vinke, pp. 266 and 284.

[143] Ibid., p. 156.

[144] Cf. ibid., p. 158.

[145] Ibid., p. 188.

[146] Cf. ibid., pp. 204–6.

[147] Cf. ibid., p. 208. For a discussion of the affective aspect of Luther's theology see Birgit Stolt, *Martin Luther, människohjärtat och Bibeln*, Stockholm: Verbum, 1994, esp. pp. 46–55.

[148] Raunio, pp. 248–9. Cf. Luther, *Adventspostille. 1525*. In *D. Martin Luthers Werke*. Kritische Gesamtausgabe, vol. 10.I.2, Weimar: Hermann Böhlaus Nachfolger, 1925, pp. 1–208, here p. 68.

eration of love. In a way, one could say that in Luther's thinking love has become a Christian possession. Luther's aim was not to affirm the praxis of love in light of Christian faith, or a Christian praxis of love; rather it was to distinguish *Christian* love from other forms of love.

Anders Nygren praises Luther's Reformation for the rediscovery of the specificity of Christian love:

> There are times, like those of primitive Christianity and the Reformation, when the specifically Christian conception thrusts itself powerfully to the fore; at other times it has to struggle, often against odds, to maintain itself against alien conceptions of love, but just by contrast with these it is compelled to reveal something of its own unique quality.[149]

I shall have to return to Nygren's own approach to love in the next chapter. Here, however, I have to agree with the Swedish theologian that Luther indeed had succeeded in transforming love into a Christian virtue.

Luther's consideration of the human subject's capacity to love required a firm dogmatic basis. Accepting the divine gift of faith in Christ transforms the fallen and therefore imperfect human subject into a Christian agent of love.[150] Human being and human reason do not disappear in this act of transformation. Rather being in nature (*esse in natura*) must be distinguished from being in grace (*esse in gratia*). In terms of our human nature we are capable of using reason and will to shape our actions. However, in terms of grace the human being is nothing, if without love. For Luther, being in grace means that Christ and the Holy Spirit, i.e. divine love, are present in the human being. All human actions performed without Christ are sinful.[151] Here Luther's polemics against any attempt to perform good works in order to become just and pious leads to the christological conditioning of any genuine work of love.

As in Augustine, Luther refers explicitly to this Church Father, this new will of grace in the human being is love itself.[152] A human

[149] Anders Nygren, *Agape and Eros: The Christian Idea of Love*, trans. Philip S. Watson, Chicago: University of Chicago Press, 1982, p. 29. See also ibid., pp. 242–4, 562, 681–741.

[150] For a discussion of Luther's concept of original sin see Bengt Hägglund, *De Homine: Människouppfattningen i äldre luthersk tradition*, Lund: Gleerup, 1959, pp. 103–28. On Luther's understanding of the corruption of human reason as a result of the Fall of Adam see Brian A. Gerrish, *Grace and Reason: A Study in the Theology of Luther*, Chicago and London: University of Chicago Press, (1962) 1979, p. 30.

[151] Cf. Raunio, p. 299; and Kärkkäinen, p. 112.

[152] Luther, *Decum praecepta Wittenbergensi praedicata populo. 1518.* In *D. Martin Luthers Werke.* Kritische Gesamtausgabe, vol. 1, Weimar: Hermann Böhlau, 1883, pp. 394–521, here p. 437. Cf. Raunio, 300.

will without (Christian) love can only perform evil deeds. And like for Augustine, Luther's anthropological starting point is the fallen human being that must first be transformed by grace before Christ in him or her can perform works of love.[153] Luther's understanding of Christian love thus is fully soteriological:

> The Word of God comes first; after it follows faith, after faith love. Then love does every good work, for love does no wrong, but is the fulfilment of the law [Rom. 13:10]. However, the human being cannot come into agreement with God or act other than through faith. That means that not the human being through any sort of his works, but God brings about salvation through His promise.[154]

I shall return to Luther's approach to love below in chapter 7 when discussing marriage as an institution of love.

## Love and Christian Love

In this chapter we have discussed the re-emergence of the human subject and her desires in theologies of love, on the one hand, and the narrowing down of the horizon of love in theology to a specifically Christian theology of love. Moreover, we have followed the praxis of love in monastic, academic, courtly, and urban contexts and discussed the interplay between the shifting circumstances and emerging forms of expression. The journey of love from monastic and academic milieus beyond the confines of ecclesiastical order reached its climax in the Reformation. Luther's move from a monastic to a political form of Christian existence has freed the theology of love for the world, but, at the same time, subordinated it to the new demands of doctrine and confession. The mystical union of love between God and the human being is still desired, but is journey has now become exclusively christological. Whereas for Thomas Aquinas love was infused by God, in Luther love is essentially linked to the work of Christ and the cross.

We have also seen the difficult beginnings of a new subjectivity in love among educated Christian women. Desire, emotion, and new forms of expression — inspired by the courtly poetics of love — characterize this newly emerging ideal of female discipleship. However, the thus asserted female subject found it necessary to sacrifice her self again on the altar of Christ-like suffering provided

[153] Cf. Raunio, p. 335.

[154] Luther, *De captivitate Babylonica ecclesiae praeludium. 1520.* In *D. Martin Luthers Werke.* Kritische Gesamtausgabe, vol. 6, Weimar: Hermann Böhlau, 1888, pp. 497–573, here p. 516.

by a newly assertive male order of love. Asceticism, suffering, and mystical self-annihilation were ways for women to regain their subjectivity and now to invest it again in order to offer proper care for their souls and their intimate union with the Lord.

Finally, new 'secular' or popular expressions of desire, eroticism, and love have emerged among the feudal elites of the time. The complexity of these cultural, social and literary developments cannot be adequately explored here. But the new literature of love set a cultural dynamics in motion that henceforth provided challenges also to Christian conceptualizations of love. Luther both affirms the joys of love in general, and at the same time spiritualizes Christian approaches to love. Love was no longer a gift from God, but only Christian love.

In the two following chapters I shall discuss how this new dichotomy between Christian love and human love has been received and dealt with by some leading Christian thinkers.

# Chapter 5

# *LOVE AS AGAPE*

## Separating Divine and Human Love

In this chapter I shall explore four different, though related theological approaches to love. In spite of major differences in detail, they all share the conviction that since God is love (1 John 4.8 and 16), divine love must be the sole criterion for any consideration of human love. Thus, here human love is defined from 'above'. Moreover, all four programmes are further motivated by what they oppose, namely any attempt to legitimize human forms of love of self and other. The wish to restore *Christian* love leads these four thinkers to a more or less radical separation between proper, i.e. divine, and improper, i.e. human, manifestations of love. All four stand in the Protestant tradition of thinking, although, as we are going to see, they make use of their common spiritual and theological heritage in different ways.

The Danish philosopher Søren Kierkegaard distinguished sharply between natural or human love, on the one hand, and genuinely Christian love of God and neighbour, on the other hand. He considered the former to be inspired by egoistic intentions, whereas he praised the latter for striving to overcome any self-centred concern by totally attending to the respective other. Although Kierkegaard belongs to the nineteenth century, in recent years his book *Works of Love* has been re-read as a significant contribution to the ongoing discussion of both the nature of Christian love and Christian ethics in general. Therefore I include this publication in this context of important Protestant contributions to the Christian understanding of love.

I shall then analyse the Swedish theologian Anders Nygren's approach to love. His work on the radical separation between human eros and divine agape has influenced the discourse on love in

Christian theology more than any other theological book in modern times. Both Kierkegaard and Nygren devoted a single work to their consideration of love. Both approached love from clearly defined doctrinal perspectives: Kierkegaard offered 'Christian deliberations' about works of love[1] on the basis of selected New Testament treatments of love, and Nygren explored Christian love within the horizon of his restatement of adequate Reformation theology.

The Swiss-German theologian Karl Barth's approach to love follows Nygren's principal dichotomy between human desire and divine love, while, at the same time, also significantly modifying it. Finally, the German theologian Eberhard Jüngel's theology of love offers a more recent, though no less passionate Protestant approach to Christian love 'from above'. Both Barth and Jüngel discuss Christian love within their respective systematic theology project.

All four thinkers continue and further develop Luther's christological concentration of love as well as his doctrinal separation between human love and genuinely Christian love on their way to distil authentically Christian love.

## Søren Kierkegaard's Theology of Universal Neighbourly Love

The Danish philosopher Søren Kierkegaard (1813–55) considers love in a number of his writings. However, it was his book *Works of Love: Some Christian Deliberations in the Form of Discourses* of 1847 that offered a comprehensive theological approach to the phenomenon of love in its two parts.[2] I shall limit my discussion to this book. My aim is not to offer a general reading of Kierkegaard's philosophy. Rather I am interested in his approach to 'Christian love' in this particular publication.

Kierkegaard begins his discourses on love with five observations: Christian love is not concerned with any understanding of love as such, but with the works of love (p. 3); the mystery of love cannot be exhaustively described (pp. 3 and 9); all genuine love comes

[1] Søren Kierkegaard, *Works of Love*, trans. Howard V. Hong and Edna H. Hong, Princeton, NJ: Princeton University Press, 1995, p. 3.

[2] Kierkegaard, *Works of Love*. Page numbers in the text refer to this edition. For the critical edition of this work see *Kjerlighedens Gjerninger, Søren Kierkegaards Skrifter*, vol. 9, ed. Søren Kierkegaard Forskningscenteret, Copenhagen: Gads Forlag, 2004, as well as *Kommentarbind til Kjerlighedens Gjerninger, Søren Kierkegaards Skrifter*, vol. K 9, ed. Søren Kierkegaard Forskningscenteret, Copenhagen: Gads Forlag, 2004.

from God (pp. 3–4 and 10); Christian love is dynamic (p. 10); and Christian love is eternal (p. 8). Kierkegaard's discourses explore the horizon of love disclosed in a number of New Testament texts. He opens every section (and many subsections) of Part I and the first four sections of Part II with a quotation on love from the New Testament. Thus, his approach to love is explicitly related to an interpretation of significant biblical statements on love.

Christian love must be firmly distinguished from ordinary human love. Kierkegaard acknowledges that love may be found in all kinds of traditions. But Christian love differs from natural human love, from any feeling of being or falling in love, from any appeal to lasting friendship, from any romantic love explored in fiction, from any preferential love, in short from any ordinary human endeavour.[3] Only Christian love is eternal. He distinguishes between love (*Kjerlighed*) and erotic love (*Elskov*), between love orientated towards its depth in God and between love rooted in human desires, choices and projects.

> Erotic love (*Elskov*) is still not the eternal; it is the beautiful dizziness of infinity; its highest expression is the foolhardiness of riddles. This explains its attempting an even dizzier expression, 'to love a person more than God.' This foolhardiness pleases the poet beyond measure; it is sweet music to his ears; it inspires him to song. Ah, but Christianity teaches that this is blasphemy. (P. 19)[4]

Christian love demands that God be loved unconditionally. And it distinguishes sharply between love of God and love of neighbour.

> There is only one whom a person can with the truth of eternity love more than himself – that is God. Therefore it does not say, 'You shall love God as yourself' but says, 'You shall love the Lord your God with all your heart and all your soul and all your mind.' (P. 19)

As far as the neighbour is concerned, he must not be confused with any object of preferential love (p. 21). Rather the neighbour is that which is nearest to ourselves. 'The concept "neighbour" is

[3] Ingolf U. Dalferth, '"... der Christ muß alles anders verstehen als der Nicht-Christ ...": Kierkegaards Ethik des Unterscheidens', in Ingolf U. Dalferth, ed., *Ethik der Liebe: Studien zu Kierkegaards "Taten der Liebe"*, Tübingen: Mohr Siebeck, 2002, pp. 19–46, 37: 'Für Kierkegaard markiert das die entscheidende Differenz zwischen *weltlicher* und *christlicher* Liebe: Letztere liebt ohne Ansehen der Person, nicht aus Neigung, sondern *nur aus Pflicht*, und eben deshalb ist allein sie wirklich frei.'

[4] Cf. also: 'But what is it that gives the human being immortality, what else but the love that abides? Erotic love [*Elskov*] is temporality's invention, temporality's most beautiful but nonetheless frail invention' (p. 311).

actually the redoubling of your own self; "the neighbour" is what thinkers call "the other," that by which the selfishness in self-love is to be tested. As far as thought is concerned, the neighbour does not even need to exist' (p. 21). To love God and the neighbour is a commandment, a duty, and only if is recognized as such is love theologically relevant. Only then is its eternal horizon open. The love 'that has undergone the change of eternity by becoming duty does not know jealousy; it does not love only as it is loved, but it loves' (p. 35). This love is independent and is orientated towards the eternal.

Hence, Kierkegaard contrasts two types of love with each other: erotic love and friendship are preferential love, whereas Christian love is the love of self-denial, the love of duty (p. 52).[5] In the first type preferential love is the 'middle term' (*Mellembestemmelse*), in the second type God is the 'middle term' (p. 58). Only if we love God above all else can we love the neighbour and in him every human being. Thus, while the love of God and the love of neighbour need to be clearly distinguished, they are intimately related in Christian love.[6]

At this point it might be helpful to contrast Kierkegaard's approach to Christian love with Augustine's. According to the Church Father it is not possible that a human being truly can love. As we have seen above in chapter 3, only God can love. And all experiences of genuine love are in fact experiences of God's love. Thus, for Augustine, God could not be considered to be a middle term (*Mellembestemmelse*), since He is love's only possible subject or agent. Here Augustine and Kierkegaard differ. For Kierkegaard, human beings can be genuine agents of love, but only in so far as their love is related to divine love. Hence, both thinkers affirm God as the originator and centre of love, while they differ in their assessment of the human potential to love. According to the Danish philosopher, human persons can actively relate to God and their neighbour in love.

Kierkegaard's (like Augustine's) understanding of Christian love is deeply inspired by the Johannine theology of love. He quotes 1 John 4.8 and 16: 'God is love', and, like John, he distinguishes sharply

[5] 'If anyone thinks that by falling in love or by finding a friend a person has learned Christian love, he is in profound error' (p. 57).

[6] On the notion of God as 'middle term' see also M. Jamie Ferreira, *Love's Grateful Striving: A Commentary on Kierkegaard's* Works of Love, Oxford and New York: Oxford University Press, 2001, p. 71: 'For Kierkegaard, what is at stake in this idea is that God should remain the judge of what true love is.'

between the 'world' that does not understand[7] and Christianity that alone understands love in the right way.

> But God is Love, and therefore we can be like God only in loving, just as we also, according to the words of the apostle, can only be *God's co-workers – in love*. Insofar as you love the beloved, you are not like God, because for God there is no preference, something you have reflected on many times to your humiliation, but also many times to your rehabilitation. Insofar as you love your friend, you are not like God, because for God there is no distinction. But when you love the neighbour, then you are like God. (Pp. 62–3)

Once again, we see how much Kierkegaard rejects any form of preferential love.[8] God loves all in the same way. Hence it is logical when Kierkegaard, extending this thought, claims that the work of love in recollecting one who is dead is a work of the most unselfish love (p. 349), the freest love (p. 351), and the most faithful love (p. 355).[9]

Kierkegaard quotes 1 John 4.20 ('If anyone says, "I love God", and hates his brother, he is a liar; for how can he who does not love his brother, whom he has seen, love God, whom he has not seen?') (p. 154), and interprets this Johannine verse claiming that human beings ought to begin with loving the unseen, God, because then they learn what it means to love. That a person actually loves the unseen 'will be known by his loving the brother he sees; the more he loves the unseen, the more he will love the people he sees' (p. 160). However, Kierkegaard hastens to add that the reverse is not true: 'It is not the reverse, that the more he rejects those he sees, the more he loves the unseen, since in that case God is changed into an unreal something, a delusion' (p. 160).

Even linguistically Kierkegaard reveals his discipleship to Johannine thinking on love when he speaks about 'abiding in love' (p. 16), thus taking up the Johannine concept of 'abiding in love' (John

[7] 'There actually is a conflict between what the world understands and what God understands by love' (p. 118).

[8] Cf. here also Ferreira, *Love's Grateful Striving*, pp. 44–7.

[9] Dalferth, op. cit., p. 37: 'Liebe ist keine Funktion gegenseitiger Sympathie, sondern einseitiger Willensbestimmung, die sich – das wird am Verhalten zu Verstorbenen besonders deutlich – in keiner Weise davon abhängig macht, daß der andere sich auch so bestimmt.' – Ferreira, *Love's Grateful Striving*, p. 259, argues that Kierkegaard is not hostile to the specific needs associated with particular instances of care:

> The neighbor love that is commanded in the case of the stranger we meet in physical distress will be a benevolence that will address the stranger's distinctive needs rather than some abstract, formulaic attitude; but it need not have the same tenderness that we would show to an intimate relation. We are not commanded to feel the preference we feel in other cases, but we are commanded not to let the lack of preference militate against the other's equality as a child of God.

15.9–10 and 1 John 4.16b). However, the Danish thinker does not accept the narrow horizon of love that characterizes the Johannine community. While in that community, as we have seen above in chapter 2, the horizon of love was limited to the very community of believers, Kierkegaard universalizes the horizon of love: everybody is my neighbour. Moreover, it is my Christian vocation and duty to become neighbour (*Næste*) to the other. 'Christian love teaches us to love all people, unconditionally all' (p. 49). My neighbour (*Næste*) is the one 'to whom I have a duty' and 'when I fulfill my duty I show that I am a neighbor' (p. 22).[10] 'Christ does not speak about knowing the neighbor but about becoming a neighbor oneself, about showing oneself to be a neighbor just as the Samaritan showed it by his mercy' (p. 22).[11] Thus Kierkegaard combines the Johannine tradition of love both with the universal radicalism of Luke's Good Samaritan narrative (Luke 10.30–7) and with Paul's conviction that love is the fulfilling of the law (Rom. 13.10) (p. 104).

It is important to note that Kierkegaard does not want to get rid of either the human body[12] or its natural desires or emotions. Rather he calls for a change of heart. There is nothing wrong with human desire (p. 67) as such.[13] But it is crucial to examine our desire: is our desire directed towards a particular object or towards loving all?

> In the first case the emphasis is on the exceptionality of the object, in the second case on the essentiality of the need, and only in this latter sense is need an expression of riches, and only in the latter case are the need and the object related equally to each other in the infinite sense, because every human being

[10] 'Den jeg har Pligten mod er min Næste, og naar jeg fuldkommer min Pligt viser jeg, at jeg er Næsten': *Kjerlighedens Gjerninger*, p. 30.

[11] For a detailed analysis of the concept of neighbour in Kierkegaard's *Works of Love*, see Pia Søltoft, 'Den Nächsten kennen heißt der Nächste werden: Über Ethik, Intersubjektivität und Gegenseitigkeit in *Taten der Liebe*', in Ingolf U. Dalferth, ed., *Ethik der Liebe: Studien zu Kierkegaards 'Taten der Liebe'*, Tübingen: Mohr Siebeck, 2002, pp. 89–109.

[12] 'Just as little as the Christian lives or can live without his body, so little can he live without the dissimilarity of earthly life that belongs to every human being in particular by birth, by position, by circumstances, by education etc. – none of us is pure humanity' (p. 70).

[13] M. Jamie Ferreira, 'The Glory of a Long Desire: Need and Commandment in *Works of Love*', in Ingolf U. Dalferth, ed., *Ethik der* Liebe, pp. 139–53, argues that '*Works of Love* is as much about our need to love and our need to be loved by others as it is about our duty to love others' (p. 140). Thus, challenges to need, desire and sacrifice are not to be seen in a one-sided way in terms of an ethics of pure self-denial; rather they must be understood within the larger context of Kierkegaard's promotion of forgiveness and reconciliation (p. 147).

> is the neighbor, the first at hand the best, or because in the sense of *exceptionality* there is no object, although in the infinite sense every human being is the object. (P. 67)

Thus, he can conclude: 'Christianity does not want to make changes in externals; neither does it want to abolish drives or inclination – it wants only to make infinity's change in the inner being' (p. 139).[14] Christianity is concerned about what every human being should become (p. 180), and God is the appropriate educator (p. 377). Christianity knows in fact only one kind of love, namely 'the Spirit's love' (*Aands-Kjerligheden*[15]), and all other distinctions between different kinds of love are therefore meaningless (pp. 143 and 146). Kierkegaard's approach to love is concerned with a new way of seeing.[16] Here he stands firmly in Paul's tradition of the Spirit possession and love, which we have explored above in chapter 2.

So far we have seen to what extent Kierkegaard stresses the radical difference between Christian love and other forms of love — worldly love, Greek love, but also Jewish love: 'Christianity has abolished the Jewish like for like: "An eye for an eye and a tooth for a tooth"; but it has replaced it with the Christian, eternity's, like for like' (p. 376). This radical concentration on Christian originality and uniqueness in matters of love ignores the rich tradition of love of God and of neighbour in the Jewish tradition to which any Christian understanding of love must always be indebted. It is interesting that all four thinkers discussed in this chapter, not unlike the Johannine texts in the New Testament, present Christian love as clearly separated from its Jewish roots.

Kierkegaard approaches the human self with a great measure of suspicion. He urges the Christian to love himself — but in the right way. However he understands this kind of self-love in terms of a love for the other. 'To love yourself in the right way and to love the neighbor correspond perfectly to one another; fundamentally they are one and the same thing' (p. 22). The loving subject must

[14] Arne Grøn characterizes Kierkegaard's approach to love as an ethics of vision: 'We do something *in* seeing: By the way in which we see we are doing something to the other seen': Grøn, 'Ethics of Vision', in Ingolf U. Dalferth, ed., *Ethik der* Liebe, pp. 111–22, here p. 121.

[15] *Kjerlighedens Gjerninger*, op. cit., p. 145.

[16] Cf. Arne Grøn, 'Kierkegaards zweite Ethik', trans. Hermann Schmid, in Niels Jørgen Cappelørn and Hermann Deuser, eds, *Kierkegaard Studies. Yearbook 1998*, Berlin and New York: de Gruyter, 1998, pp. 358–68. Cf. also Dalferth, op. cit., p. 45, who speaks of 'eine neue Sicht dieser Phänomene'.

love without concern for him- or herself. Instead the subject is asked to surrender his or her subjectivity in love and in praise of love for God. The question is not only whether or not the self will get rid of any egoistic or self-centred desires; rather the self is asked to get rid of all self in the act of loving. 'Through self-denial a human being gains the ability to be an instrument by inwardly making himself into nothing before God. Through self-sacrificing unselfishness he outwardly makes himself into nothing, an unworthy servant' (p. 365). The human being 'is nothing'. Here total self-emptying (*kenosis*) is both the way and the goal of Christian love.

Hence, love appears as a function of relating the unworthy creature to the creator and redeemer who Himself has demonstrated his kenotic love on the cross. Although Kierkegaard separates sharply between human beings and God, he nevertheless demands from the human subject nothing less than to love through the love which only God can properly give.

As we are seeing throughout this chapter, it is one of the paradoxes of this strand of Protestant theology to separate the human being radically from God, while at the same time measuring human love totally according to divine love. Human love — and human life — has no dignity on its own. Human beings seem not to be loveable in terms of being creatures bearing God's image. Rather the human self is nothing before God.

Thus, although Kierkegaard formally defends human agency in love (cf. p. 301), theologically this agency is called to accept its emptiness in order to begin the education in divine love.[17] Moreover, this education is restricted to the individual self. Kierkegaard does not discuss the Christian community in social or ecclesial terms. He knows of no institutions of love. Instead all love flows from God, through God and to God.[18] There remains an unresolved tension between

[17] In her compelling discussion of Kierkegaard's approach to love Claudia Welz offers the following summary of Kierkegaard's suspicion of human love: 'In the performance of love, God and human beings are co-workers; the origin and effect of love, however, lies beyond the human action and ability': Claudia Welz, *Love's Transcendence and the Problem of Theodicy*, Tübingen: Mohr Siebeck, 2008, p. 155.

[18] See Arne Grøn, 'Kierkegaards zweite Ethik', p. 368: 'Die Liebe ist schon im voraus gegeben, als Liebe Gottes. Auch die Liebe, welche man fühlt und gibt, ist einem gegeben. Man schafft diese Liebe nicht selbst, sie ist immer schon "im Grunde".' Cf. also Arne Grøn, 'Kærlighedens gerninger og anerkendelsens dialektik', *Dansk Teologisk Tidsskrift* 54 (1991), pp. 261–70, esp. p. 269, on love as gift: 'Kærligheden – den, man selv skal vise – er en gave, en medgift.'

the Spirit's love and human preferential love which Kierkegaard condemns.[19] He just cannot imagine that any form of human love might already be inspired by the Holy Spirit. His approach to love is from above, and in that perspective the human person appears first of all as marked by sin, guilt and misguided desires.

However much Kierkegaard's approach to love follows his Christian doctrinal convictions and assesses all forms of human love accordingly, he insists throughout his book and in its very title that love is not principle or theory, but work. Hence, he stresses the praxis character of love. Love 'is everywhere present where there is one who loves' (p. 301). Thus, the point of Christian faith is not just to proclaim love, but to love.[20]

## Anders Nygren's Theology of Christian Love

*Agape and Eros: The Christian Idea of Love* was the most successful and influential theological book on love in the twentieth century. It was authored by the Swedish theologian Anders Nygren (1890–1978) and originally appeared in two parts in Stockholm in 1930 and 1936. It went through many editions and has been translated into many languages.[21] Throughout the world, countless students of theology and related disciplines have learned from Nygren's book that Christian love stands in radical opposition to both the Greek concept of *eros* and the Jewish treatment of love in law (*nomos*). The uniqueness of Christian love as *agape* as affirmed by this Swedish scholar was widely accepted by theologians and church people throughout the world.[22]

[19] Cf. Welz, ibid., p. 172.

[20] For a discussion of the concept of works of faith in Luther and works of love in Kierkegaard, see Ferrreira, *Love's Grateful Striving*, pp. 248–53.

[21] Anders Nygren, *Agape and Eros: The Christian Idea of Love*, trans. Philip S. Watson, Chicago: University of Chicago Press, 1982. The Swedish original appeared in 1930 (first part) and 1936 (second part): *Den kristna kärlekstanken genom tiderna: Eros och Agape*, första delen, 3rd edn, Stockholm: Svenska Kyrkans Diakonistyrelsens Bokförlag, 1947 and *Den kristna kärlekstanken genom tiderna: Eros och Agape*, senare delen, 2nd edn, Stockholm: Svenska Kyrkans Diakonistyrelsens Bokförlag, 1947. Page numbers in the text refer to the above-listed American edition.

[22] For a sense of how influential Nygren's theology of love has been, see Charles W. Kegley, ed., *The Philosophy and Theology of Anders Nygren*, Carbondale. IL: Southern Illinois University Press, 1970; Walter H. Capps, 'Lundensian Theology in the United States', *Svensk Teologisk Kvartalskrift* 72 (1996), pp. 59–63; Konrad Stock, *Gottes wahre Liebe: Theologische Phänomenologie der Liebe*, Tübingen: Mohr Siebeck, 2000, p. 82; and

Martin Luther King's understanding of love, for instance, was clearly influenced by Nygren's distinctions between eros and agape. When discussing Jesus' command to love one's enemies, Martin Luther King, Jr, explaining that Jesus could not have meant that we should like our enemies and that love was greater than like, writes:

> When Jesus bids us to love our enemies, he is speaking neither of *eros* nor *philia*, he is speaking of *agape*, understanding and creative, redemptive goodwill for all men. Only by following this way and responding with this type of love are we able to be children of our Father who is in heaven.[23]

Anders Nygren was one of the theologians who had formed the so-called Lundensian School of Theology. Other important figures belonging to that School were Gustav Aulén (1879–1977) and Ragnar Bring (1895–1988). They all shared a keen interest in rediscovering major motifs of Reformation theology. They were engaged in motif research: identifying and studying the developments of major motifs of Christian faith through history.[24] In this context Nygren had chosen the Christian motif of love.

It is striking that in his discussion of love Nygren never refered to the debates on love and marriage in early twentieth-century Sweden or Europe. Rather than relating his theological thinking explicitly to the cultural and intellectual developments of his time, he chose to present a theological discussion apart from any such context, although his work was, of course, received against the background of such developments.[25]

Nygren distinguishes sharply between two irreconcilable concepts of love, namely the Platonic and the Christian. He identifies the Platonic understanding of love in terms of *eros* and the Christian in

---

Udo Kern, *Liebe als Erkenntnis und Konstruktion von Wirklichkeit: 'Erinnerung' an ein stets aktuales Erkenntnispotential*, Berlin and New York: de Gruyter, 2001, pp. 96–8.

[23] Martin Luther King, Jr, *Strength to Love*, New York, Evanston and London: Harper & Row, 1963, p. 37. Cf. Bernard V. Brady, *Christian Love*, Washington, DC: Georgetown University Press, 2003, p. 215.

[24] For a more recent affirmative discussion of this approach to theology see Bernard Erling, 'Motif Theology, a Neglected Option', *Svensk Teologisk Kvartalskrift* 77 (2001), pp. 126–35.

[25] For a discussion of these developments see Inga Sanner, *Den segrande eros: Kärleksföreställningar från Emanuel Swedenborg till Poul Bjerre*, Nora: Nya Doxa, 2003; and Werner G. Jeanrond, 'Liebe in Schweden: Per Olov Enquists "Gestürzter Engel"', in Christoph Gellner and Georg Langenhorst, eds, *Herzstücke: Texte, die das Leben ändern. Ein Lesebuch zu Ehren von Karl-Josef Kuschel zum 60. Geburtstag*, Düsseldorf: Patmos, 2008, pp. 193–202.

terms of *agape.* Agape, the word most frequently used in both the New Testament and the Greek translation of the Old Testament, is charged here with a different, particularly Christian meaning, namely the belief that Christian love comes from God.[26] Nygren's pursues a twofold aim: he wishes to expose eros as that human form of egocentric and desiring love which strives to reach the divine sphere by its own strength, and he recommends agape as that form of love which originates in God and therefore requires a human attitude of receptivity and passivity. An erotic attitude focuses on something that is of great attraction and value to us human beings and thus causes desires in us, whereas agape is addressed to every human being and as such creates a value in that being (p. 78). Agape is God's way to humankind (p. 81). For Nygren, there 'cannot actually be any doubt that Eros and Agape belong originally to two entirely separate spiritual worlds, between which no direct communication is possible' (p. 31).

In the development of Christianity, Nygren perceives a problematic mixture, or synthesis, of eros-religion and Christian agape-religion. Therefore he embarks on identifying and restoring the purified Christian understanding of love. The tool for this task was supplied by the Lundensian project of motif-research. 'The purpose of the scientific study of religion is not merely to record the actual conceptions, attitudes, and so forth, that are found in a particular religious *milieu,* but more especially to find out what is characteristic and typical of them all. That is what motif-research deliberately and consistently seeks to do, and is indeed fully capable of doing' (p. 37). Agape and eros are contrasted as major Christian and non-Christian religious motifs. Nygren concludes that agape

> is the centre of Christianity, the Christian fundamental motif *par excellence,* the answer to both the religious and the ethical question. Agape comes to us as a quite new creation of Christianity. It sets its mark on everything in Christianity. Without it nothing that is Christian would be Christian. Agape is Christianity's own original basic conception. (P. 48)

Nygren also contrasts the Christian agape-religion with the Jewish religion of the law. In spite of the many affinities and connections between Judaism and Christianity, Christianity is for him 'a fundamentally different thing from Judaism' (p. 68). While the law in Judaism constitutes the bond between people, it is the newly instituted fellowship with God in Christianity 'that gives the idea of Agape

[26] For a discussion of the biblical terminology of love see above, chapter 2.

its meaning' (p. 67). Nygren acknowledges that Jesus took over the commandment to love God from the Old Testament, 'but He fills it with new content by setting it in relation to the new fellowship with God which He has brought' (p. 92). The same applies to the second commandment: neighbourly love springs from the same source as love for God (p. 96). Hence, Nygren sees in the struggle of the Pharisees against Jesus 'the protest of the religion of law against the religion of love' (p. 70). Christian universal love transcends the boundaries of Jewish legal righteousness in two ways: it now includes all human beings and it includes even the sinner.[27]

Nygren distances himself from any theological attention to self-love. He understands eros as 'essentially and in principle *self-love*' (p. 216). 'Self-love is man's natural condition, and also the reason for the perversity of his will' (p. 101)[28] Hence, agape excludes all forms of self-love (p. 217). Self-love is the chief enemy of agape. Concerns for the human self, for subjectivity and for their development are thus eclipsed from any legitimate theological focus.

Agape, God's way to human beings is spontaneous and unmotivated, indifferent to value, creative, and the initiator of fellowship with God (pp. 75–81); it is unlimited and unconditional (p. 91); it naturally includes love for one's enemies (p. 101) and the judgement on all that is not love (p. 104). Agape is 'an outflow from God's own life' (p. 141).

While this Christian love is understood as 'completely revolutionary' (p. 80) and 'entirely new' (p. 53), the eros-motif is shown to be old. It can be traced more or less everywhere, even within Christianity itself. And it is this presence of the self-seeking eros-motif that Nygren wishes to expose and overcome. In other words, he wants to identify and reject all love-discourses that do not build on God's absolute sovereignty. 'Christian love is something other than ordinary human love' (p. 93).

Here we can sense Nygren's implicit, though therefore no less forceful, contribution to the debate on love in Sweden and Europe between both World Wars. 'Neighbourly love loses its specifically Christian character if it is taken out of context of fellowship with God' (p. 95). Merely human forms of love do not stand in any relation

[27] 'We must remember that for the traditional Jewish outlook there could not be a more unacceptable and shocking idea than that of God's love for sinners' (pp. 82–3).

[28] See also Nygren, p. 130.

to God's emerging reign on earth. The split between any general human experience of love and a Christian understanding of love is total.

> Even though the 'humane' ideals of altruism and the ethic of sympathy may present on the surface certain similarities to Christian neighbourly love, they nevertheless have entirely different spiritual roots, and Christian love has really nothing at all to do with such modern ideas. (P. 95)

To be sure, Nygren's point is not to establish a dichotomy between eros as a merely sensual power and agape as a purely spiritual power. 'Deep as the sensual roots of Platonic love may be, its whole tendency is to seek deliverance from the merely sensual' (pp. 50–1). Nygren's concern is not to differentiate between what he calls 'vulgar eros' and agape; he is not at all interested in this vulgar form of eros. Rather he urges us to separate what he calls 'heavenly eros' and agape (p. 51). 'The Agape motif lost its purity' (p. 54). Hence it must be purified from the pollution of the eros-motif that had occurred throughout different periods of Christian history. The agape motif emerges from the 'new and specifically Christian way of fellowship with God, as this is depicted in the Gospels'; it finds 'its highest expression in Paul, in the union of his theology of the Cross with the thought of Divine love and in his preaching of the Agape of the Cross'. The supreme formulation of this motif is found in 1 John 4.8 and 16: 'God is Agape' (p. 57).

Nygren's effort to restore Christian love by purifying it from all eros-ingredients leads him first to an in-depth discussion of New Testament texts, in particular the Synoptic Gospels, Paul's theology of the cross, and the identification of God and agape in 1 John. In Paul's 'supreme expression' of the agape motif (p. 146) he finds the source of renewal for all subsequent theology of love (p. 145), and in 1 John 4.8, 16 Nygren sees the 'supreme formal statement' of the motif: '*God is love, and love, Agape, is God*' (p. 147). In both Paul and John there is a strong connection between agape and the significance of the cross, yet Paul is credited with deeper insight into the agape motif's essential meaning and content (p. 150) and with guarding the purity of the motif much better than John.[29]

Nygren's rehabilitation of the agape motif culminates in his insight into the achievement of the Reformation. Here the agape motif was

[29] Nygren, p. 155, rightly notes the restriction of the scope in John's understanding of Christian love to the members of the Johannine community and to the exclusion of outsiders and enemies. See also above, chapter 2.

renewed; from here the inspiration for the continuing renewal of Christian love in our time must come. In the thought of Augustine the issue between eros and agape, now interpreted in terms of *caritas*, was decided in favour of a synthesis. Nygren argues that the conception of love as caritas in Augustine was not simply a translation of agape. Rather Augustine's caritas represented a significant transformation of agape into something new and different (p. 55). In Augustine as well as in his medieval followers caritas contains elements both of agape and eros. Thus, caritas needs to be exposed as a polluted manifestation of the original Christian idea of love.

Luther's insistence on a purely theocentric relation to God (p. 681) marks for Nygren the necessary separation of perspectives: God's love comes to us from outside; in us there is only selfish or acquisitive love. God's love has been revealed to us in Christ; it is a love that gives. '*The very same thing which made him* [Luther] *a reformer in the matter of justification, made him also the reformer of the Christian idea of love*' (p. 683). Nygren's treatment of Luther's theology of love is firmly based on the Swedish scholar's passionate restatement of Luther's reformational insight into justification by faith alone. Nygren does not offer a detailed discussion of Luther's understanding of love; rather he deducts from Luther's overall theocentric approach the relevant and desired conclusions. Thus, Luther's attack on all human ways to God, i.e. the different heavenly ladders, and his insight that there is no way by which we human beings ever could reach God, provide the framework for Nygren's own rejection of the eros motif. 'In Augustine, the issue between Eros and Agape is decided in favour of synthesis; in Luther, in favour of reformation. Augustine unites the two motifs in the Caritas-synthesis; Luther shatters that synthesis' (p. 692).

Nygren does not discuss material aspects of this Christian love or of the fellowship in which this love is to unfold its transformative qualities. Rather he concentrates on the formal aspects provided by Luther's reformation of theology: God comes to us from outside; only God and the neighbour can be loved with the love that comes from God; any self-love is ruled out (p. 710). Thus, the love promoted by Nygren with the help of Luther is God's love, and this love is strongly distinguished from all forms of human love.

When Luther discusses the double love commandment, Nygren reminds us, he holds that love of one's neighbour 'has the task of completely dispossessing and annihilating self-love' (p. 713). And Nygren approves very much of the close connection in Luther's theology between love and sin: 'Luther's idea of sin is thus governed by his idea of love. "Love seeketh not its own." As the opposite of this, the essence of sin is that man does seek his own' (p. 713).

The only parameters for Christian love offered by Nygren with the help of Luther are: love is spontaneous, to be given freely and to please God. It 'springs forth out of its own source, fellowship with God' (p. 730) and attends to the neighbour without regard of persons, i.e. without being blinded or dismayed by the other's value or lack of value. It is an outpouring love, unmotivated and sacrificial in nature. It 'gives and sacrifices' (p. 726). It is free from all desires,[30] it is divine, it is pure Agape.

Since Christian love has not been produced by us human beings, but has come to us from above, the human being cannot be the subject of this love. God is the only conceivable subject of this love (p. 733). The human being is a mere object of this divine love that 'employs man as its instrument and organ' (p. 734). The Christian is 'set between God and his neighbour. In faith he receives God's love, in love he passes it on to his neighbour. Christian love is, so to speak, the extension of God's love' (p. 734).

Nygren concludes his magnum opus with the following praise of God's love:

> God's love has made a new way for itself down to lost humanity. Once for all, and in a decisive manner, this has come to pass through Christ. He came to us in the form of a servant and in humiliation, yet His majesty has not thereby grown less. He has rather revealed it in still greater glory. His majesty is the sacrificial, self-giving majesty of love. (P. 741)

Clearly, Nygren's book on what he considered to be authentic Christian love can also be read as a most engaged contribution to the debates on the nature of love in Swedish and European cultures during the first half of last century. By denouncing all human desire as in direct opposition to the divine gift of love, Nygren presented a radical dichotomy to his readers: either one accepts Luther's understanding of love or one has already departed from Christian love altogether. Either one participates in the debates on what human beings can achieve through love or one follows authentic Christian love.

However, Nygren's attack on Platonic eros and Augustinian desire should not be misunderstood as in principle anti-erotic in the sense of anti-sexual. Nygren's point is neither to discuss nor to denounce

[30] Nygren, p. 735, praises Luther 'who has overcome the dualism of sensible and supersensible and has delivered Christian love from the category of desire'.

sexuality, marriage or sexual expression in love.[31] Rather his argument is directed against the delusions of human desire and in favour of the acceptance of love as a divine gift. Yet, exactly here lies one of the great problems of Nygren's approach to love: he separates between divine love, on the one hand, and human expressions of love, on the other. God is the sovereign subject of love; the human being is a mere 'channel of God's down-pouring love' (p. 733).

In spite of Nygren's radical critique of Augustine's theology of love (*caritas*) as an unholy mixture between agape and eros, Nygren remains highly indebted to crucial aspects of the Augustinian heritage. Like Augustine and Luther, Nygren approaches love from anthropological and theological presuppositions that consider the human being first of all in terms of original sin, guilt and damnation, i.e. as radically alienated from God and therefore at best as a channel of God's love. The human being is not a divinely empowered agent of love, but a mere instrument of God's own love. It does make a difference whether or not one approaches love from the experience of original sin, guilt and damnation or from the perspective of God's good creation and the, of course always ambiguous, human potential for further development and relationship. It does make a difference whether one approaches love from a coordinated view of human and Christian spheres or from a view that stresses the total hiatus between human and Christian spheres of life.[32]

Nygren's theology of 'Christian love', continuing and enlarging Luther's emphasis on the uniquely Christian nature of this love, does not pay attention to any kind of phenomenology of love, since its chief interest was to rehabilitate the Lutheran doctrine of justification as the only legitimate framework for a Christian understanding of love.

## Karl Barth's Doctrine of Love

In his great work, the *Church Dogmatics*, Karl Barth (1886–1968) treats of love in the context of the doctrine of reconciliation (Vol. IV) which

[31] Konrad Stock draws attention to the strange exclusion of sexual love in Nygren's overall approach to love. Stock, *Gottes wahre Liebe*, p. 83: 'Die Unbedingtheit des Sittlichen, der die Gesinnung der durch Gott selbst begründeten Liebe gerecht zu werden vermag, duldet nach Nygren weder eine Psychologie des Strebens noch eine Güterlehre, die Ziele und Ordnungen des sittlichen Handelns reflektiert.'

[32] Cf. Gert Nilsson, 'Värdelös eller värdefull? Skapelse och frälsning som problem i teologisk etik', in *Modern svensk teologi – strömningar och perspektivskiften under 1900–talet*, Stockholm: Verbum, 1999, 187–238, here p. 199.

first appeared in German in 1953. Hence, for the later Barth, love springs forth from the new freedom made possible by Jesus Christ. In the first part of Vol. IV, Barth offers the following christological foundation for love:

> In Jesus Christ God has demonstrated, He has made it visible and audible and perceptible, that He loved the world, that He did not will to be God without it, without all men, without each individual man in particular. And in the same Jesus Christ He has demonstrated, He has made it visible and audible and perceptible, that the world and all men and each individual man in particular cannot be without Him. The demonstration that He belongs to the world and the world to Him is the choice and work of His love in Jesus Christ, 'the kingdom of the son of his love.' In general terms Christian love is the active human recognition of this proof of the love of God.[33]

Christian love comes from God through Christ. In these introductory comments on love, Barth does not refer at all to God's history of love with Israel or to the presence of love in God's creation. However, unlike Nygren, Barth affirms the human potential to love, i.e. human subjectivity in love, as the work of the Holy Spirit.[34]

Barth distinguishes two dimensions in love: (1) The community which God wishes to have with all human beings and which therefore embraces '*realiter* both the world and the community, non-Christians and Christians. But the knowledge and proclamation of it is a matter only for the Christian community. Those who know it are marked off from all other men as Christians.'[35] In addition to this vertical dimension of love between God and humanity in Jesus Christ, there is also (2) the horizontal dimension of community between human beings, i.e. Christian neighbourly and brotherly love.[36] Neither the love of God nor the love of the neighbour has anything whatsoever to contribute to the justification of the human being.[37] Rather, Christian love is performed in obedience and faithful action in this world.

While love was understood by Nygren in terms of God's action over against human passivity, Barth introduces love as a human response to God's love of humanity in Christ. Both theologians acknowledge fellowship with God as the horizon of Christian love.

[33] Karl Barth, *Church Dogmatics*, vol. IV: The Doctrine of Reconciliation, Part One, ed. G. W. Bromiley and T. F. Torrance, trans. G. W. Bromiley, Edinburgh: T. & T. Clark 1956 (German original 1953), p. 102–3.

[34] Ibid: 'That he can love is the work of the Holy Spirit which makes man a Christian.'

[35] Ibid.

[36] Ibid., p. 104.

[37] Ibid.

However, for Barth this fellowship is more clearly identified as the concrete Christian Church, whereas Nygren cannot draw ecclesiological conclusions from his understanding of love as divine.

At the end of the second part of vol. IV of his *Church Dogmatics*, first published in German in 1955, Barth offers a much more elaborate and, to some extent also different, discussion of the theology of love.[38] Barth's treatment of Christian love immediately follows his discussion of ecclesiology. Thus, like Paul in his First Letter to the Corinthians, Barth considers the features and challenges of Christian community life before letting this discussion culminate in the praise of love.[39]

Like Anders Nygren, Barth distinguishes sharply between eros and agape, yet he presents a rather different framework for his consideration of agape-love. This love is characterized by self-giving (*Hingabe*), by a movement in which the human being turns away from him- or herself, 'wholly to another, to one who is wholly different from the loving subject' (p. 733). Barth's concept of agape-love calls for self-sacrifice for the sake of the other. Strangely, Barth speaks of this other as an 'object of love' (pp. 733ff.), which excludes the other's subjectivity or any mutuality of love between the other and my own self from entering into the spectrum of this particular agape-concept.

Christian love is different from the other 'love' which is characterized by 'a grasping, taking, possessive love – self-love' (p. 734f.). Barth adds that the objects of this other kind of love do not need to be sensual. 'It may be directed to the good, the true and the beautiful. Even in its sexual form, it may have reference (perhaps wholly and utterly) to the soul and not merely to the body' (p. 734). It may even include God as its object. However, while Barth distinguishes clearly between both concepts of love, he acknowledges the ongoing mixture of both loves in the one human being. 'It is always man who encounters us in the two forms' (p. 741). In other words, Barth acknowledges the ambiguity of Christian love.

Criticizing Nygren for believing that the synthesis between eros-love and agape-love should have come to an end with Luther, Barth asks rhetorically: 'Is it not of the very essence of this history that the

[38] '§ 68. The Holy Spirit and Christian Love', in Karl Barth, *Church Dogmatics*, vol. IV: The Doctrine of Reconciliation, Part Two, ed. G. W. Bromiley and T. F. Torrance, trans. G. W. Bromiley, Edinburgh: T. & T. Clark 1958 (German original 1955), pp. 727–840. Numbers in the text refer to this English edition.

[39] For Paul's theology of love in 1 Corinthians see above, chapter 2.

opposition can never be fully overcome?' (p. 738).[40] Thus, while Nygren separates these two forms of love, Barth distinguishes them in terms of assessing which one reflects the true human nature as created by God. '*Agape*-love takes place in affinity, *eros*-love in opposition, to human nature' (p. 743). Barth's verdict on erotic love culminates in his judgement: 'Erotic love is a denial of humanity' (p. 746).

Barth's later theology of love is rooted in his theology of creation and election (p. 743f.), whereas Nygren's was firmly anchored in his understanding of the theology of justification. Moreover, Barth considers the human being able to love God and his or her neigbours (p. 752), whereas for Nygren God alone can be the loving subject. For Barth, God's love is the origin (*der Grund*) of human love and as such always precedes it. God's being and nature is love (pp. 753–4). Both theologians, however, are united in rejecting any form of human self-love. Barth's argument is this: 'If the love of man, as his response to the fact that God loves him in this way, itself consists in his self-giving [*Hingabe*], this certainly means that there can be no more self-love, no more desiring and seeking the freedom and glory of the self' (p. 750). It is interesting to note that self-love is interpreted here in purely negative terms as that desire to enhance human autonomy and glory. Self-love in terms of longing for the possibility of respecting and accepting one's finite humanity and its relational capacity does not enter into consideration here.

Barth argues that God's love and human love need to be understood as related acts. God's love moves us human beings to act accordingly (pp. 759–60). Love is act (*Tat*) and not feeling. More concretely, in reviewing biblical witnesses, Barth identifies three crucial aspects of God's love as the basis of human love: God's love is electing love, purifying love, and creative love, i.e. 'a love which causes those who are loved by Him to love' (p. 776). Barth's approach to love is firmly based on his biblical interpretation. However, Barth wishes to affirm the continuity between the witness of the New Testament to the love of God and that of the Old Testament (p. 769), while, at the same time, stressing the newness of love in Christ as understood by Christian witnesses.

Christian love must not be seen as 'a kind of prolongation of the divine love itself, its overflowing into human life which man with his

[40] For Barth, ibid., p. 751, the Christian is always both a Christian lover and an erotically loving person. This is *simul iustus et peccator* applied to the human person as a loving person.

activity has to serve as a kind of channel, being merely present and not at bottom an acting subject' (p. 785). Here Barth, distancing himself very clearly from Nygren,[41] affirms the loving human being as a genuine subject that loves in response to God's prior love. However, like Nygren, Barth is at pains to demonstrate the originality of Christian love although he, unlike Nygren, also wishes to defend the connection between the Old and the New Testament with regard to God's own love. This tension between God's love and God's love in Christ, on the one hand, and human love in response to this divine love before and after Christ, on the other, is not resolved in Barth's later theology. Clearly, God's love has not changed over the years; rather in Christ we Christians have seen yet another manifestation of this love. Does this imply that human love in response to God's love has been motivated to change as a result of the Christ event?

Barth attempts to show both the continuity and the discontinuity between human love for God in the Old and the New Testament. On the one hand, he formulates in general terms: 'To love God is to give oneself to Him, to put oneself at His disposal. And when man does this, his freedom for love becomes and is his freedom for obedience' (p. 798f.). On the other hand, Barth adds his particular Christian focus on love: 'That in the obedience of love it is a matter of obedience to the living God, or – and this is the same thing – to the living Jesus Christ. It is Him as such that he loves. It is to Him as such that he gives himself' (p. 801). 'Christian love is the response of love based on the electing, purifying and creative love of God. It is thus love for God as the One by whom the Christian is first loved' (p. 790). Is there a specific *Christian* love, e.g. related to the purifying dimension in Barth's concept? Or is there a general call to love in response to the manifestation of God's love? Barth identifies the reconciliation between God and humankind achieved in Jesus Christ as the qualitative difference between Christian love and other love. However, the manifestation of God's love in Jesus Christ does not change God's love as such, but demonstrates God's determination to love humankind totally. Therefore, in Barth's theology, the qualitative difference between pre-Christian or non-Christian love and Christian love would need to be located elsewhere.

Wishing to maintain both the continuity of Christian love with Jewish love and the discontinuity, Barth remains rather vague in his treatment of divine love as to the exact difference between

[41] Cf. Nygren, op. cit., p. 733.

both attempts to love God. However, the theological context of his theology of Christian love, i.e. the doctrine of reconciliation, points clearly in the direction of his underlying approach to the particularity of Christian love (see p. 790). Already in *Church Dogmatics* IV/1, he had declared that any consideration of faith, love and hope must be rooted firmly in christological reflection. Hence, his approach to love does not seem to be motivated by an interest in the theology of love as such, but by an interest in explicating Christian existence from its centre, i.e. Jesus Christ.

> Faith lives by its object, love by its basis, hope by its surety. Jesus Christ by the Holy Spirit is this object and basis and surety. And faith and love and hope in this relation to Jesus Christ are all primarily His work, and His work first in the community of God, and only then His work in individual Christians.[42]

Thus, Barth's treatment of love is a function of his christology and soteriology; and this focus does not really allow him to be attentive to the continuity of love both to God and to other human beings within Jewish and Christian faith praxis.

The christological determination of his understanding of love was already sufficiently manifest in *Church Dogmatics* I/2 (published in German in 1940), where Barth had suggested to replace the word love in 1 Corinthians 13 with the name of Jesus Christ.[43]

The remainder of Barth's explication of his theology of love is dedicated to the love of the fellow human being. Again, Barth presents his arguments both with reference to the continuity of the biblical witness and to the particular challenge of Christian love for the other:

> [N]either the Old Testament nor the New speaks of a love for man as such and therefore for all men; of a universal love of humanity. As the Bible understands it, love both for God and for man has the character of an action. The universal love of humanity can be thought of, if at all, only as an idea which dominates man or an attitude of mind which fills him. But Christian love, as we have seen, is an act of obedience which as such, even if we think of a sequence of such acts, takes place somewhere in time and space, which does not, therefore, take place always and everywhere, but in which there is always a demarcation and limitation of its object or objects. It is the concrete and not the abstract loving of someone who is concrete and not abstract. In correspondence to the love of God, it is a loving which chooses and differentiates. (Pp. 802–3)

Here, Barth parts company with Kierkegaard, who rejected any form of preferential love and instead, with reference to the parable

[42] Barth, *Church Dogmatics* IV/1, pp. 153–4.

[43] Barth, *Church Dogmatics* I/2, trans. G. T. Thomson and Harold Knight, Edinburgh: T. & T. Clark, 1956, p. 330.

of the Good Samarian in Luke 10, demanded from the Christian that he or she should be willing to become a neighbour of anybody requiring so.[44] Moreover, Barth insists on the concrete historical context. 'The proximity in which the act of Christian love takes place between man and man is that of a historical relationship in which the one who loves and the one who is loved both exist' (p. 803).[45] Barth sums up:

> [T]he neighbour [*der 'Nächste'*] as the one who in Christian love is loved apart from and side by side and together with God is the fellow-man [*Mitmensch*] who stands to the one who loves in the historical context of the existence of Israel or the existence of the community of Jesus Christ. He is not the fellow-man as such, but this particular fellow-man. (P. 805)

This historical relationship is the particular Christian history of salvation. Thus, Barth once more firmly locates Christian love within the soteriological drama whose centre is Jesus Christ. Christian love is at home in the Christian community. However, Barth again speaks of both Israel and the Church when considering the people of God and the spectrum of salvation history (p. 806), but quickly advances to its centre, Jesus Christ, and his community when assessing the space of Christian love for the neighbour. Barth does admit that the 'circle of brothers' as the horizon for Christian love may need to be extended beyond what we can see just now (p. 808). Nevertheless, he identifies a significant difference between Old Testament love and New Testament love: 'the emphasis on love for the neighbour, and its express connection with love for God after all corresponds to New Testament insight and witness and not yet Old Testament insight and witness' (p. 810) .[46] Here, as we have seen above in chapter 2, Barth is factually wrong.

Barth affirms the inner connectedness between love for God and love for neighbour, but stresses that both must never be identified. 'The two planes are distinct and must not be confused. But they are also inseparable' (p. 810).

Having established this (false) difference between Israel and Christianity, Barth again hastens to show the interconnectedness of Israel and the Church. What both of these members of the

[44] Cf. Kierkegaard, *Works of Love*, p. 22.

[45] However, Barth would be in agreement with Kierkegaard that even a dead person could thus be loved: 'The one who loves and the one who is loved may be contemporaries, but this is not essential, for a man alive to-day may love someone long since dead' (p. 803).

[46] Translation partially corrected.

people of God have mutually to attest and guarantee is 'simply that God loves them, and that they may love Him in return, as the first-fruits and precursors of the whole of the human race, typically and representatively for all men' (p. 814). Still, Christian love of neighbour and brother is a ministry of witness in response to 'the self-giving of God to man, and the event of man's liberation to give himself to God' (p. 820). And this divine self-giving is attested in the Gospel of Jesus Christ: 'The mystery of Christian love for the neighbour is finally and decisively, because originally, His mystery' (p. 821). The man Jesus is at once this mystery and its revelation: 'He who is the new thing in the New Testament beside which all other things we can think of may only be called relatively new' (p. 822).

In his effort to ground genuinely Christian love in Jesus Christ, Barth now links salvation history, Jesus Christ, and God's love. Jesus is the one Christian 'from whom all others receive their name and in whom the community of Jews and Gentiles has its Lord. In the true sense this One who is the Head of the whole body is the man who is loved by God and loves Him in return and as such the One who loves His fellow-man [*Mitmensch*]' (p. 823).

Barth concludes his reflections on Christian love with an interpretation of Paul's praise of love in 1 Corinthians 13 according to which it is love alone that counts, love alone that triumphs, and love alone that endures (p. 825). Barth sees in this hymn to Christian love a parallel to 'the Song of Songs in the Old Testament with its magnifying of marital love' (p. 825). The Holy Spirit is introduced as the life-giving power behind the act of the individual believer in the Christian community and thus as the mover behind any act of love. Barth's entire discussion of Christian love stands under the heading 'The Holy Spirit and Christian Love', thus underlining both Paul's approach to love in the Spirit and the Trinitarian foundation of Christian love.

Once more Barth rejects Nygren's reservation of loving agency exclusively to God, now in terms of its irreconcilability with Paul's theology of love in 1 Corinthians 13 (p. 827). Love is a human act made possible by the Holy Spirit. Love is an eschatological act, it is 'the connecting link between now and then, between here and hereafter' (p. 837), it is 'the eternal activity of the Christian' (p. 840). Its essence is self-giving (p. 831). For Barth, Christian love is and remains *Hingabe*.

## Eberhard Jüngel's Christology of Love

Self-giving (*Hingabe*) is also the central aspect in Eberhard Jüngel's (b. 1933) reflections on God as love. In his major work *God as the Mystery of the World: On the Foundation of the Theology of the Crucified One in the Dispute between Theism and Atheism*, Jüngel approaches love from a christological and a Trinitarian perspective.[47] He takes his point of departure in the terminology and understanding of the Johannine community. The insight and subsequent confession that 'God is love' is intimately linked to the interpretation of the cross of Jesus as the event of God's self-giving in love. As a result, Jüngel can say that it is the task of theology to think God as love (p. 315).

It is important to see that Jüngel does not present a theology of love. Rather his intention, emphasized in the subtitle of this book, was to reflect on the foundations of the theology of the Crucified in the dispute between theism and atheism. This explains also Jüngel's recurring discussion of Ludwig Feuerbach's inversion of 'God is love' into 'love is god'[48] and the effort to establish theological criteria for distinguishing between God and love, on the one hand, and for maintaining the Johannine identification (i.e. God is love), on the other. Nevertheless, Jüngel does present here a significant outline for a theology of love that needs to be considered in this chapter in which I am examining those theologies of love that are inspired by a clear separation between human desire for love and the divine gift of love. However, Jüngel's approach to love belongs literally at the very end of this chapter since his argument in favour of a separation between eros and agape, much weaker than Nygren's or Barth's, opens up a new constructive interest for the potential of the encounter of human desire and divine love.

In order to invite his readers into the discourse on the mystery of God who is love, Jüngel begins his discussion by examining the pre-understanding of love. Answering his more general question — what is love? — he takes the human love between an I and a Thou as his point of entry into his phenomenology of love.

> If love is the event of a still greater selflessness within such great self-relatedness, then the loving I experiences both an extreme distancing of himself

[47] Eberhard Jüngel, *God as the Mystery of the World: On the Foundation of the Theology of the Crucified One in the Dispute between Theism and Atheism*, trans. Darrell L. Guder, Edinburgh: T. & T. Clark, 1983. Page numbers in the text refer to this edition.

[48] See Ludwig Feuerbach, *The Essence of Christianity*, trans. George Eliot, Amherst, NY: Prometheus Books, 1989. The German original was first published in 1841.

> from himself and an entirely new kind of nearness to himself. For in love the I gives himself to the loving Thou in such a way that it no longer wants to be that I without this Thou. I do not want to have myself anymore without the beloved Thou. (Pp. 317–8, translation corrected)[49]

Jüngel affirms that the loving I desires to possess the Thou. Thus love includes desire (p. 318). Love is not identical with absolute selflessness. While Jüngel too wishes to distinguish between this kind of need-love and gift-love or between the eros-structure and the agape-structure of love, he warns against establishing these different forms as opposing alternatives and, in the footnotes, rejects the respective endeavour by Nygren, Barth and other theologians (p. 318, n. 13). Jüngel is interested to see how any longing to possess (*Haben*) can be transformed in the process of love itself. He distinguishes three attitudes in the love of a couple: (1) affection (*Zuneigung*); (2) turning to the other person (*Zuwendung*); and (3) self-giving (*Hingabe*).[50] However, he does not understand these attitudes in a moral sense; rather he treats of them as ontological aspects of love. As a result, he can speak of an 'exchange of being between the self-surrendering I and the Thou who gives me myself anew'. In this exchange of being consists '*the true desire* or *lust of love*' which never can be made or produced (p. 322). His ontological approach to love encourages Jüngel to go so far as to claim that the lover is nothing without the beloved:

> The lover does not *exist* on the basis of what he has been until now or has made of himself. Instead, in receiving himself from another, the lover *exists*. Thus he *exists* only because of the existence which is *given* to him, and apart from that he is nothing. The loving and beloved I is then totally related to the beloved Thou, and thus to his own nonbeing: without Thee I am nothing. (P. 323)

Jüngel thus understands love as a totalizing power — hence love's peculiar nearness to death (p. 323) — rather than as a transformative power. I am not merely different when not loved, but nothing at all. The dialectic of being and nonbeing belongs to the essence of love (p. 325). Somewhat cryptically, Jüngel hints at the worldly dimension of love (p. 325), emphasizing that love as a matter of the heart radiates outward:

> As love, it presses to move beyond the lovers themselves. For that reason, love does not lead into an idyllic retreat from the world, nor into a realm beyond, away from all lovelessness, hate, or even inattentiveness and boredom. Rather, it leads into all of these, engages in struggle with them, and moves more deeply into them. True love squanders itself. (P. 325)

[49] Here the English edition strangely translates 'liebendes Ich' with 'the loving ego'.
[50] The English edition translates 'Hingabe' with 'surrender' (p. 321).

These rather brief reflections on the essence of love lead Jüngel now back to the Johannine dictum that God is love (p. 326). His subsequent considerations are inspired by 1 John; other relevant biblical texts on love play no prominent role here. 'We are to read the statement "God is love" as an exposition of the self-identification of God with the crucified man Jesus' (p. 326). Love springs from God. He alone can begin, and has begun, to love without any reason or purpose. God's identification with love shows itself most clearly in His giving of His son: 'God is the one and living God *in that he* as the loving father gives up his beloved son and thus turns to those others, those people who are marked by death, and draws the death of these people into his eternal life' (p. 328). In this theology of the cross, i.e. the self-identification of God with the crucified Jesus, and in the Spirit understood as link between Father and Son that includes human beings in this divine relationship, Jüngel recognizes the Trinitarian explanation of the statement that God is love (p. 328).[51] 'To speak of the transforming power of the fire of love, which is requested together with the prayer for the coming of the Holy Spirit, is both the critical and soteriological point of the statement "God is love"' (p. 329). Jüngel both affirms this identification and confirms, following Martin Luther, the essential difference between human love and divine love. God makes the 'object of his love' first of all worthy of His love. The love flowing from the cross makes the ugly person beautiful in the eyes of God.

At this point Jüngel returns to the distinction between eros and agape. Although he rejects Nygren's separation between both aspects of human love, he recognizes a difference in intention between agape and eros. While agape loves eros, eros does not love agape (p. 338). Crucial to this distinction is the term *Hingabe* (surrender/self-giving). *Hingabe* is 'the precise opposite of that self-realization which exhausts all the possibilities worthy of striving after' (p. 339), whereas the emancipated, abstract eros does not love any kind of selfless *Hingabe* (p. 338). Hence, Jüngel wishes to integrate desire and love, thus recognizing the erotic dimension in all genuine love. But he warns against a form of the erotic where the erotic has become

[51] Cf. George M. Newlands' critical reflections on Jüngel's approach to love in Newlands, *Theology of the Love of God*, Atlanta: John Knox Press, 1980, pp. 102–4. See also Markus Mühling-Schlapkohl, *Gott ist Liebe: Studien zum Verständnis der Liebe als Modell des trinitarischen Redens von Gott*, Marburg: N. G. Elwert Verlag, 2000, pp. 127–42.

independent, emancipated, totally self-centred. Love that does not exclude, but integrates eros, does not exhaust itself. It is the epitome of the creative (p. 339). Jüngel's point then is not to reject eros, but to integrate the proper eros in the right way into the understanding of human love. God's love is agape, our love is both desire and *Hingabe*. This distinction, however, is a distinction made in faith. 'Faith alone experiences and knows God as the event, the subject, and the object of love at once, that is, as one who loves, is loved, and is the process of love in indissoluble unity' (p. 339). Thus, Jüngel concludes, the 'erotic and caritative activities of love done by men are, for their part, correspondences of the divine being which is love. But they correspond to it on the basis of faith' (p. 339). Love is our best correspondence to God: 'In the event of love man corresponds to the God who has come to the world in both the most intensive and most extensive ways' (p. 392).

God is love, but no human being *is* love. But faith trusts in the identity between God and love and, thus, distinguishes sharply between God and the human being (pp. 342–3). In Jesus Christ God's love has been made visible. 'Faith in the humanity of God is *the evidence* of the identity of God and love' (p. 343). And this identity, which is the genuine mystery of the world, must be explicated in Trinitarian fashion (pp. 376–96). The victory of love cannot be produced, but only believed. 'One can believe in the victory of love only in the sense that one believes in the identity of God and love' (p. 340).

Jüngel's approach to love does not cover the broader and pluralistic spectrum of biblical reflections on love. Rather it centres around the Johannine community's identification of God and love without any reflection on this particular community's motivation of praising Christ's self-giving (*kenosis*) as the ultimate qualification of love (p. 358). Moreover, Jüngel never problematizes his understanding of selfhood and subjectivity. Who is this self that is to grow into self-giving or self-surrender? How do self-relationality and self-giving relate?[52] Why does Jüngel not discuss the concept of mutuality in human love? Is the ideal of human love to correspond to divine love in terms of a full self-giving (*kenosis*)?

[52] Jüngel describes love in a more formal sense 'as the event of a still greater selflessness within a great, and justifiably very great self-relatedness' (p. 317). Cf. also Konrad Stock's critical comments on Jüngel's approach in Stock, *Gottes wahre Liebe*, pp. 9 and 86.

Although Jüngel needs to be saluted for his insight into the necessary connection between eros and agape in human love, his understanding of the loving self remains deeply problematic. The reduction of his focus on human analogies to divine love to the love of the couple misses the fuller challenge of the love commandment: loving God, the other human being, and the self. The role of the human body and the possible extension of this body into the body of Christ are not explored here. Although Jüngel points to the close relationship between love and death, he does not explore the challenge of otherness and of radical otherness to any theology of love. The different forms and expressions of love are not examined in this approach. Rather the sole focus remains on how to understand love as God's own identity and, in a highly abstract fashion, how human beings can correspond to this divine love in faith.

Finally, it is interesting to observe that Jüngel's theology of Trinitarian love does not open up any kind of social, ecclesial or communal space. God's creation of love is understood exclusively through God's own *kenosis* (self-emptying) in Jesus Christ. Hence, love becomes an exclusively Christian concern. Unlike in Barth's reflections on love, here the Jewish roots of the Christian understanding of love are completely ignored. Approaches to love in other religious traditions never enter Jüngel's theological focus. The love of enemies is not present here either. The created universe does not emerge as an arena of love in this theology. Jüngel's references to the radiation of love and its potential worldly dimension remain highly abstract (p. 325).

## Christian Doctrines of Love

In this chapter we have seen four attempts to develop a Christian doctrine of love. In spite of varying references to biblical foundations and somewhat different doctrinal horizons, all four thinkers have been concerned to distinguish between Christian love and other loves. In all cases divine love is the measure through which human love is assessed. God's self-giving love manifest in Jesus Christ and the Spirit defines love once and for all. The resulting dichotomy between God's love manifest in creation and God's love in Christ and the Church is not resolved. Moreover, no connection is made between God's creative and reconciling love and the universe.

Christian love is right; romantic love, self-love, human desire and longings are wrong. All human forms of love need to be submitted to and properly purified by Christian doctrine. The human being is a sinner, and thus requires first salvation before his or her love can flourish. All four thinkers thus stand firmly in the tradition of Martin Luther's doctrinal approach to love. In this tradition love has become a function of Christian teaching on sin and corruption. Or put the other way round: sin and corruption form the horizon through which love is approached. Thus, love does not represent any challenge to existing or possible Christian convictions, but merely confirms them. It poses thus no threat to Christian confession. So far the commonality of these four approaches.

The differences between these approaches are no less significant for any reflection on adequate theologies of love. Only Barth recognizes the necessary link between Jewish and Christian traditions of love, whereas Nygren and Kierkegaard question any such link, and Jüngel is silent in this respect. But Barth remains unable to solve the tension between both traditions. His christological determination of love does not facilitate a proper consideration of Jewish (or any other tradition) of love. Love is not so much a universal gift from the Creator than a concern for Christian self-understanding and proclamation. Moreover, Barth reflects on love within his overall ecclesiological project, thus never losing sight of the communal horizon of loving action in spite of his constant attention to the vertical nature of God's gift of love.

Barth, Jüngel and Kierkegaard affirm human subjectivity in love. Human beings are co-workers with God. However, their selfhood is given in order to be given away in perfect sacrificial *Hingabe.* Nygren does not affirm much subjective agency in love beyond his understanding of Christian passivity. Rather, God loves through the human being. At best, the human being can be said to be a channel of God's love. Barth and Jüngel affirm the action-character of human love, but not as strongly as Kierkegaard, who insists on the total work-nature of human love.

The Danish philosopher universalizes the horizon of love to include potentially everybody. I have a duty to my neighbour to become his or her neighbour. Moreover, he introduces God as the middle term in any consideration of adequate human love. The eternal nature of love arises from those works of love that are performed in openness to God. For Kierkegaard only proper love of God makes proper love of human beings possible. Thus, there is a hierarchy of loves: only through the link with the love of God can human love genuinely become eternal. Once again, we see that human love is nothing if not endowed by God's redemptive action.

Finally, while Kierkegaard and Nygren denounce human eros in love, Barth and Jüngel shift the debate away from the brutal dichotomy to an acknowledgement of the ambiguity of all human love. For Jüngel, the crucial issue at stake concerns the transformation of the self's possessive desires in the process of self-giving love in as much correspondence with Christ's self-giving as possible.

In the following chapter I shall continue my critical review of modern theologies of love, now focusing on proposals to understand love in a somewhat different key of human desire and divine vocation.

## Chapter 6

# *THE UNITY OF LOVE AND DESIRE*

### Rediscovering Human Love

In this chapter I wish to explore the potential of human love. While the four theologians discussed in the previous chapter have placed great emphasis on the separation between divine and human love and, in spite of differences in detail, recommended the practice of divine love to individual Christians, other theologians instead have chosen to focus more on the potential of human love within the overall network of divine and human love. They too affirm that genuine love originates in God, yet they acknowledge the divine vocation of women, men and children to develop loving relationships with the respective others in their own right. Moreover, these constructive theological projects appreciate desire as a divine gift that is able to draw us human beings more deeply into the divine and human mystery of love.

### Paul Tillich's Ontology of Love

The German-American theologian Paul Tillich (1886–1965) repeatedly treated of love within the framework of his ontological thinking. His more systematic approaches to love can be found in his magnum opus *Systematic Theology* (1951–63) and in his book *Love, Power, and Justice* (1954). Moreover, significant reflections on love are present throughout his work, both in his early career,[1] and, following

[1] Already in his work 'Systematische Theologie von 1913', printed now in Paul Tillich, *Frühe Werke*, ed. Gert Hummel and Doris Lax, *Ergänzungs- und Nachlassbände zu den Gesammelten Werken von Paul Tillich*, vol. IX, Berlin and New York: de Gruyter, 1998, pp. 273–434, Tillich reflects on important dimensions of love, e.g. the connection between love and freedom, the love of God and the loving nature of God, love and

his forced departure from Germany in 1933, in his American period of writing.

In *Love, Power, and Justice* Tillich reflects on the fact that love concerns both human emotion and human action.[2] Moreover, its ethical and its ontological nature are interdependent. Ontology, the understanding of being, is for him the way to discern the 'root meaning' of all principles and concepts, here of the three concepts love, power, and justice.[3] He ascribes to love a uniting power: we human beings experience a strong desire to overcome our alienation from one another, but also from our own self. 'Love is the drive towards the unity of the separated' (p. 25). Love is more than emotion. However, as an emotion it anticipates the reunion which takes place in every love-relation (p. 26). Love is more than passion and pleasure; rather it is the union 'with that which fulfils the desire' (p. 29).[4] Thus, Tillich follows the understanding of love presented in Plato's *Symposium* as that which draws us human beings to union (see above, chapter 1). Moreover, he vehemently rejects the attacks on eros by those theologians 'who depreciate culture' and by those 'who deny a mystical element in man's relation to God' (p. 30).

Although he does not mention Anders Nygren by name here, Tillich clearly argues against Nygren's rejection of eros when he writes that the consequence of 'this rejection is that love towards God becomes an impossible concept to be replaced by obedience to God. But obedience is not love. It can be the opposite of love' (p. 31). For Tillich, *eros* and *philia* overlap (p. 31). Both contain an element of desire (*epithymia*) (p. 32). Both are related to *agape* as their divine depth, but not separated from this depth (p. 33). Thus he can say that in agape 'ultimate reality manifests itself and transforms life and love' (p. 33).[5] Love ultimately links every human being to the ground

---

transcendence, the concrete forms of love, the unity between educating and forgiving love, friendship and love. See ibid., pp. 335–413.

[2] Paul Tillich, *Love, Power, and Justice: Ontological Analyses and Ethical Applications*, Oxford: Oxford University Press, 1960. Numbers in the text refer to this edition.

[3] Ibid., p. 2.

[4] In his book *Dynamics of Faith*, New York, Evanston and London: Harper & Row (Harper Torchbooks), 1958, pp. 114–15, Tillich states most succinctly:

> No love is real without a unity of *eros* and *agape*. *Agape* without *eros* is obedience to a moral law, without warmth, without longing, without reunion. *Eros* without *agape* is chaotic desire, denying the validity of the claim of the other one to be acknowledged as an independent self, able to love and to be loved. Love as the unity of *eros* and *agape* is an implication of faith.

[5] Paul Tillich, *Systematic Theology*, vol. 1, Chicago: University of Chicago Press, 1951, p. 281: 'If *erōs* and *agapē* cannot be united, *agapē* toward God is impossible.' Cf. also Tillich, *Systematic Theology*, vol. 3, Chicago: University of Chicago Press, 1963, p. 137.

of his or her being, God. That is why faith and love must never be separated.[6] Elsewhere, Tillich describes the human being as that being 'that is capable of loving God'[7] and links this understanding to the ecclesial vocation of the human being as that being that is 'justified only in Christ, as a member of the church'.[8]

In the third and last volume of his *Systematic Theology* Tillich offers the following argument for his understanding of the unity of love:

> In spite of the many kinds of love, which in Greek are designated as *philia* (friendship), *eros* (aspiration toward value), and *epithymia* (desire), in addition to *agape*, which is the creation of the Spirit, there is one point of identity in all these qualities of love which justifies the translation of them all by 'love'; and that identity is the 'urge toward the reunion of the separated,' which is the inner dynamics of life. Love in this sense is one and indivisible.[9]

In *Love, Power, and Justice* Tillich understands self-love not as a concept, but as a metaphor. He regrets the semantic confusion that surrounds this term and recommends a clarification in terms of distinguishing between self-affirmation, selfishness, and self-acceptance (p. 34). This clarification allows him to consider the question of justice towards one's own self. Any love that does not include justice, is 'chaotic self-surrender, destroying him who loves as well as him who accepts such love' (p. 68). Thus, Tillich is very much aware of the need to attend to the self in any love-relation. As self-control highlights the dimension of power in love, so justice towards oneself stresses the necessary dimension of justice in love (p. 69). Tillich recognizes the dangers associated with an estranged view of the self in love. 'Love reunites; justice preserves what is to be united' (p. 71).

In the kenotic approaches to human love discussed in the previous chapter no warning that injustice towards oneself can lead to the distortion of love could be found. In Tillich's approach to love, however, human love is not forced into copying divine love; rather it is explored in its relation to the divine depth of love.

---

Cf. also Paul Tillich, 'Religion und Kultur', in Paul Tillich, *Gesammelte Werke*, vol. 9: *Die religiöse Substanz der Kultur: Schriften zur Theologie der Kultur*, 2nd edn, Stuttgart: Evangelisches Verlagswerk, 1975, pp. 82–93, here p. 86: 'Wenn ich gefragt werde, was der Beweis für den Sündenfall der Welt ist, pflege ich zu antworten: die Religion selber, nämlich eine religiöse Kultur neben einer weltlichen Kultur – ein Tempel neben einem Rathaus, das Abendmahl des Herrn neben einem täglichen Abendessen, das Gebet neben der Arbeit, Meditation neben Forschung, *caritas* neben *eros*.'

[6] Cf. *Dynamics of Faith*, p. 113.

[7] Tillich, 'Systematische Theologie von 1913', p. 336.

[8] Ibid., p. 399.

[9] Tillich, *Systematic Theology*, vol. 3, p. 137.

> Love overcomes the separation, creates the into-each-other in which more comes into being than what is contributed by the individuals. Love is the infinity which is given to the finite. That is why we love in the other whom we love not only the other, but the love which is in the other and which is more than his or our love.[10]

This exploration of human love leads Tillich to pay attention to three functions of transforming or creative justice: listening, giving, and forgiving (p. 84). He understands love as the principle of justice (p. 57) and therefore reflects upon these functions of creative justice from within the horizon of love. Love's first task is to listen (p. 84f.). Giving is the second function of creative justice in personal relations. The spectrum of just giving reaches from a minimum, i.e. to acknowledge the other as a person, to the extremes of self-sacrifice if so demanded by the occasion (p. 85) and of sacrificing the other one in his or her existence, though never in his or her being as a person (p. 86). The third and 'most paradoxical' function of creative justice is forgiving. Here Tillich interprets Paul's and Luther's theologies of justification by grace as, though on the surface contradicting any human understanding of justice, in reality the creative fulfilment of justice[11]: 'For it is the only way of reuniting those who are estranged by guilt. Without reconciliation there is no reunion. Forgiving love is the only way of fulfilling the intrinsic claim in every being, namely its claim to be reaccepted into the unity to which it belongs' (p. 86).

Tillich combines a decidedly Lutheran approach to theology with a broader anthropological starting point than his Protestant colleagues discussed in the previous chapter. Thus, it is not true that Protestant approaches to love by reference to their interpretation of justification by faith must automatically lead to a radical separation between divine and human love and to a repression of *eros* in Christian love.[12]

[10] 'Love is stronger than death', thus the title of Tillich's famous sermon of 1940. 'Liebe ist stärker als der Tod', in Paul Tillich, *Impressionen und Reflexionen: Ein Lebensbild in Aufsätzen, Reden und Stellungnahmen. Gesammelte Werke*, vol. XIII, Stuttgart: Evangelisches Verlagswerk, 1972, pp. 249–52, here pp. 250–1. See also Carter Lindberg, *Love: A Brief History Through Western Christianity*, Malden and Oxford: Blackwell, 2008, pp. 166–7.

[11] See also Tillich, *Systematic Theology*, vol. 1, pp. 282–5.

[12] Already in his lectures on social philosophy and social education of 1929/30 Tillich reflects on the necessary correlation of self and eros. See Paul Tillich, *Vorlesungen über Geschichtsphilosophie und Sozialpädagogik*, Frankfurt 1929/30, ed. Erdmann Sturm; *Ergänzungs- und Nachlassbände zu den Gesammelten Werken von Paul Tillich*, vol. XV, Berlin and New York: de Gruyter and Evangelisches Verlagswerk, 2007, p. 300.

With many fellow theologians Tillich shares a deep conviction that love makes Christianity superior to any other religious tradition. However, he sees this superiority not in the imposition of divine love on human beings, but manifested in 'the loving person-to-person relationship' (p. 27). Yet, like so many Christian theologians, he fails to appreciate that in Judaism the law is considered to be a gift from God. Hence, his simplistic contrasting between law and obedience, on the one hand, and love as a gift of the Spirit, on the other hand, does not render justice to the Jewish understanding of the Torah.[13] Instead the interdependence between law and love would need to be explored more fully than is made possible by an attitude of Christian superiority to other religions.[14] However, in another context Tillich does underline the identity of the great commandment in the Old Testament and in Jesus' teaching.[15] In both instances, human love is firmly rooted in God's creative and redemptive love.

Tillich concludes his treatise on love with a triple reflection on the unity of love, power, and justice in personal relations, in group relations and in the ultimate relation. However, unity does not mean identity. Rather, Tillich perceives an element of separation between the application of these three concepts to God with resulting tensions. One such tension exists between God's love and power in creation. Tillich reminds us that the power of God is not to prevent estrangement, but to overcome it — in respect of our human freedom (p. 112f.). The tension between love and justice touches on God's forgiveness and salvation. 'Since God is love and His love is one with His power, He has not the power to force somebody into His salvation' (p. 114).

Once more Tillich firmly stresses the libido, eros and philia qualities of love. Agape does not replace them or annihilate them. Rather agape lifts all forms of love into God's perspective. '*Agapē* seeks the other one in his centre. *Agapē* sees him as God sees him.

[13] Cf. Tillich, *Systematic Theology*, vol. 3, pp. 271–5.

[14] In his reflections on a Christian–Buddhist dialogue, Tillich stresses the difference between compassion in Buddhism and agape in Christianity: *Christianity and the Encounter of the World Religions* (Number 14, Bampton Lectures in America delivered at Columbia University, 1961), New York and London: Columbia University Press, 1963, pp. 71–2.

[15] *Dynamics of Faith*, p. 112: 'In the great commandment of the Old Testament, confirmed by Jesus, the object of ultimate concern, and the object of unconditional love, is God. From this is derived the love of what is God's, represented by both the neighbour and oneself.'

*Agapē* elevates libido into the divine unity of love, power, and justice' (p. 117). It 'conquers the ambiguities of love' (p. 121). This applies also to our relation to ourselves. This relation too is a function of our relation to God (p. 122).

Tillich emphasizes the divine origin of love ('It is a creation of the Spiritual Presence. It is grace'[16]), defends the unity of all loves and explores human possibilities of loving under the guidance of the Spirit. He thus develops an understanding of love in which God remains God and the human person is called to grow in love. Here we find a critical and constructive appraisal of Greek insights into love, an opening towards mystical experiences of love, and a positive attitude towards the different manifestations of love in human culture. Love is the way given to human beings on their journey towards a new unity between the estranged existence of the person and his or her essence.[17] Thus, Tillich can say that love is 'unconditional in its essence, conditional in its existence'; by its very nature it is 'open to everything particular while remaining universal in its claim'.[18]

Finally, unlike the four thinkers discussed in the previous chapter, Tillich does not limit his theology of love to a consideration of the individual self; rather he is concerned with the churches as communities of love.[19] This is not to lift any existing church beyond the level of ambiguity. Rather Tillich is keen to point to the ongoing struggle between the Spirit of love and the particular manifestations of these communities, their ambiguous character and their often problematic interrelationship. 'As the community of love, the church actualizes the Spiritual Community, which is its dynamic essence.'[20] Tillich is aware that any appeal to acting and judging in the name of love is in danger of becoming always more radical, more fanatical, more destructive and more demonic.[21] Thus, love under the conditions of the ambiguities of life must not be seen as a way out of life, rather it is the most promising approach to the vicissitudes of life in spite of the conditions, precisely when there is faith in the Spirit's presence 'which judges the church's judging and struggles against its distortions'.[22] The intimate relationship between love and faith as well as

[16] Tillich, *Systematic Theology*, vol. 3, p. 275.
[17] Ibid., p. 272.
[18] Ibid., p. 273.
[19] Ibid., pp. 177–82.
[20] Ibid., p. 178.
[21] Ibid., p. 179.
[22] Ibid.

their ultimate goal in the life both of the person and the community of love are thus clear: 'Whereas faith is the state of being grasped by the Spiritual Presence, love is the state of being taken by the Spiritual Presence into the transcendent unity of unambiguous life.'[23]

Not long before his death Tillich returned to the relationship between agape and other aspects of love when considering 'The Absolute and the Relative Element in Moral Decisions'.[24] Here he understands *agape* as the New Testament approach to justice. '*Agape* is the fulfilment of the creative justice of the Old Testament',[25] thus claiming a qualitative difference between Jewish and Christian approaches to love. The highest expression of this agape is 'self-sacrifice for him who is loved and with whom in this way a profound union is created'. Hence, for Tillich, love 'in its character of *agape* is the absolute moral principle, the ethical absolute'.[26] This love contains already the basic principle of justice within itself.

> If people deny justice to others but say that they love them, they miss completely the meaning of *agape*. They combine injustice with sentimentality and call this love. *Agape* also must not be confused with other qualities of love: *libido*, friendship, compassion, pity, *eros*. Certainly *agape* is related to and can be combined with all of them, but it also judges all of them.[27]

*Agape* accepts, tolerates and acknowledges the other, including the enemy, as a person. He remains the other for me, but through agape this other is 'united with me in something that is above him and me, the ultimate ground of the being of each of us'.[28]

Hence, at the end of his life and thinking, Tillich celebrates Christian *agape* as 'the absolute moral principle, the "star" above the chaos of relativism',[29] and lifts this Christian principle above the genuine wisdom of other religions and above any expression of mere legal codes. The praxis of love has, once again, become principle, albeit the highest.

Tillich's approach to love thus differs significantly from that of the four thinkers discussed in the previous chapter. To begin with,

[23] Ibid., p. 134.

[24] In Paul Tillich, *My Search for Absolutes*, New York: Simon & Schuster, 1967, pp. 92–112.

[25] Ibid., pp. 107–8.

[26] Ibid., p. 108.

[27] Ibid.

[28] Ibid.

[29] Ibid., p. 109.

Tillich's starting point is the estranged relationship between God and human beings, on the one hand, and the creative and redemptive love of God, on the other hand. Moreover, he does not denigrate human desire for union with God; rather he begins with this desire for love without, for that matter, ignoring the human condition in all its alienation and estrangement from its true vocation and potential. By concentrating on the unity of love he gains a new and different perspective on the potential and dimensions of actual love between God and human beings. Love rises here somewhat above doctrinal convictions to the full-bodied reality of personal and ecclesial relationships with all their ambiguities. Divine love, agape, is here not the opposite of human forms of love, but the perfecting power of all human love to which it has always already been related. Hence, Tillich's ontological reflection on love has opened a new space for the meeting of divine and human love.

In spite of such new and promising departures, ultimately Tillich's reflections on love remain restricted to a Christian orbit. He acknowledged the power of love to relate to ambiguity and to unite, but he did not yet see the fuller potential of love to relate to otherness.

## Karl Rahner's Defences of the Unity of Love

The German Jesuit Karl Rahner (1904–84) is widely acknowledged as one of the leading Roman Catholic theologians of the twentieth century. His theology proved to be a major influence prior to and during the Second Vatican Council (1962–5) as well as in the reception of the Council in the Church. Through his teaching and writing, Rahner, directly and indirectly, influenced countless Christians and Christian thinkers throughout the world. However, Rahner was not a systematic theologian in the sense of Thomas Aquinas or Karl Barth, who both developed a fully structured and organized Dogmatics in which all central questions of faith were covered. Rather Rahner, not unlike Augustine, addressed emerging questions, problems and issues in Christian faith.

In the 23 volumes of *Theological Investigations* that present his mature theological reflections on a great many themes of Christian thinking, spirituality and praxis, Rahner treats explicitly of Christian love on a number of occasions. Moreover, discussions and references that underline his concern for and approach to love can also be found elsewhere in these *Investigations* as well as in a number of his other theological, encyclopaedic, pastoral, homiletic and spiritual[30] publications, including the *Foundations of Christian Faith* (1976), his one-volume introduction to Christian thinking.[31]

Rahner's approach to love has not yet received the careful attention it deserves, partly because of the absence of any single work on love and partly because his reflections must be gathered first from many major and minor publications. Therefore, the gathering and presentation of the sources for an appropriate assessment of Rahner's reflections and their potential for a contemporary theology of love requires somewhat more space than has been allotted to other thinkers in this and the preceding chapter.

In his article 'The "Commandment" of Love in Relation to the Other Commandments' (1961), Rahner understands love as the fullness of God and the human being.[32] This definition is not to exclude other values from the realm of the moral. Yet, ultimately, only love affirms the fullness of the human person. Therefore Rahner can say that

> every virtue which is not love may be regarded – in so far as it tends towards love – as a moment in the movement towards it, and only in this way can we speak of it as a *moral* virtue; or it may be regarded as a moment in and of love, and only to this extent is it complete in its own nature.[33]

Love is not the sum of all elements that concern the historical self-realization of the human being (*Selbstvollzug des Menschen*). Rather love concerns the whole of this process of human self-realization: 'Where the person completely possesses itself, completely pledges itself and engages itself totally in its freedom, there is found love, for all this can be done only through love.'[34] This process, however, is temporal and it occurs in different stages. A person may be on its way

[30] See, for instance, Rahner's early work *Von der Not und dem Segen des Gebetes*, Freiburg i. B.: Herder, 1958, pp. 42–59, in which he develops a more comprehensive theological analysis of Christian love.

[31] Karl Rahner, *Foundations of Christian Faith: An Introduction to the Idea of Christianity*, trans. William V. Dych, London: Darton, Longman and Todd, 1978.

[32] Karl Rahner, 'The "Commandment" of Love in Relation to the Other Commandments', in Rahner, *Theological Investigations*, vol. 5, trans. Karl-H. Kruger, London: Darton, Longman and Todd, 1966, pp. 439–59, here p. 459. The German original: 'Das 'Gebot' der Liebe unter den anderen Geboten', in Rahner, *Schriften zur Theologie*, vol. 5, Einsiedeln, Zurich and Cologne: Benziger Verlag, 1962, pp. 494–517, here p. 517.

[33] 'The 'Commandment' of Love in Relation to the Other Commandments', pp. 442–3.

[34] Ibid., p. 443.

to love, yet move already within love, although the task of love, of that process of self-transcendence of individual virtues into the whole of human self-realization is not yet completed.[35] Rahner even goes one step further: already the decision to love God in the future is love, since it is already on its way to love.[36]

However, love must not be confused with any kind of intentionality towards some object or person. Rather the love of God is 'the free and (in some way or other) explicit acceptance of that basic movement of freedom as such which is at the root of everything else'.[37] Hence, human love is freedom and development. Following Thomas Aquinas' insight that love is the mother and root of all other virtues,[38] Rahner identifies love as the only virtue that challenges the human being to be fully him- or herself, totally self. All other virtues participate in this nature of the one love.[39] This explains the most radical difference between love and other virtues: 'love cannot be performed or negotiated. It is never simply present but is always on the way to itself.'[40] Through this love, then, the human being accepts the adventurous journey towards her own, still concealed, reality. In love, the human being must risk herself without assurances, without guarantees.[41] The essence of love can thus not be fully grasped; rather it is always already marked by an eschatological dimension to which Rahner alludes with reference to Phil. 3.13.[42]

Rahner goes on to link love of God and love of neighbour in such a way as to recognize that love is always already divine gift and grace. Love of God and of the other human being is 'determined by the degree of depth and absoluteness to which the love of God and of the other person admits us'.[43] Thus, our ability to love is already made possible by God's gracious self-communication. Rahner summarizes: 'Since we must give ourselves and not something else, and must give ourselves as a response to God's own giving of Himself to us, it follows that what we have to give is a pure gift from God.'[44]

[35] Ibid., p. 444.
[36] Ibid., pp. 444–6.
[37] Ibid., p. 447.
[38] Cf. ibid., p. 449. On Thomas Aquinas' theology of love see above, chapter 4.
[39] Ibid., p. 451.
[40] Ibid.
[41] Cf. ibid., p. 453.
[42] Ibid., p. 452. Phil. 3.13: 'Brothers, I do not consider that I have made it my own; but this one thing I do: forgetting what lies behind and straining forward to what lies ahead ...'
[43] Ibid., p. 455.
[44] Ibid., p. 456.

It is interesting to note that Rahner's article begins with a New Testament reflection on the nature and scope of the commandment to love (Matt. 22.40) and on the fulfilment of the law through this commandment (Rom. 13.10). Only one more biblical reference appears in this text (see above on Phil. 3.13). Hence, here Rahner approaches Christian love by identifying one particular biblical (New Testament) challenge and by exploring its philosophical and theological significance for Christian life and ethics today. In this text, written before the Second Vatican Council, he frequently refers to the Council of Trent, but also to the debate with Protestant Christians on the relationship between love and justification by faith. He suggests that love must be part of the process of justification.[45] Faith and love are intimately linked and ought not to be played out against each other. Moreover, even love needs to be considered in its concrete steps of moral existence which, on their own, are not yet love. Only the totality called love means 'the fullness of God and of man' (*die Fülle Gottes und des Menschen*).[46]

In his article 'Reflections on the Unity of the Love of Neighbour and the Love of God' (1965) Rahner continues his discussion of love.[47] First, he emphasizes that genuine love constitutes a radically new community of human beings. This new community allows the reign of God to begin in secret; it is the miracle of the birth of eternity in our midst.[48] However, this miracle of love must not be confused with social planning; love cannot be produced, as it were.

[45] Ibid., p. 457. Here the English translation is not very clear. The German text: 'Zum Ganzen des Rechtfertigungsvollzuges gehört also sicher die Liebe', op. cit., p. 515. Cf. also Rahner, 'Justification and World Development from a Catholic Viewpoint', in Rahner, *Theological Investigations*, vol. 18, trans. Edward Quinn, London: Darton, Longman and Todd, 1984, pp. 259–73, esp. p. 270: 'When it reaches its own fullness of being unreservedly, when the loving subject really breaks out of the prison of its egoism and really surrenders itself unconditionally, love of neighbour is the event and factuality of justification.'

[46] 'The 'Commandment' of Love in Relation to the Other Commandments', p. 459. The German original, op. cit., p. 517.

[47] Karl Rahner, 'Reflections on the Unity of the Love of Neighbour and the Love of God', in Rahner, *Theological Investigations*, vol. 6, trans. Karl-H. and Boniface Kruger, London: Darton, Longman and Todd, 1969, pp. 231–49. The German original: 'Über die Einheit von Nächsten- und Gottesliebe', in Rahner, *Schriften zur Theologie*, vol. 6, Einsiedeln, Zurich and Cologne: Benziger Verlag, 1965, pp. 277–98. See also Anne Carr, *The Theological Method of Karl Rahner*, Missoula, Montana: Scholars Press, 1977, pp. 209–14.

[48] Rahner, 'Reflections on the Unity of the Love of Neighbour and the Love of God', p. 231.

Rahner further explores the New Testament thought that the love of neighbour can be understood as love of God. He reviews the double commandment to love God and the neighbour in the Synoptic Gospels, Paul's radicalization of love of neighbour, and the Johannine argument that God has loved us so that we can love one another. Rahner concludes that the concentration of the Christian relationship to God now to the love of neighbour is not without problems. How are these two loves related?[49]

Within the framework of his transcendental approach to theology[50] Rahner distinguishes between love as a reflected and explicit mode of action, on the one hand, and love as an as yet not conceptualized transcendental horizon of action, on the other hand. Thus, I can love my neighbour as my neighbour — and not as a mere instantiation of my love of God. Here Rahner affirms both the agency and subjectivity of the one who loves and the subjectivity of the one who is loved. However, *that* I can love my neighbour is already a result of God's gift of love, and thus not separated from God's love.

> The act of personal love for another human being is therefore the all-embracing basic act of man which gives meaning, direction and measure to everything else. If this is correct, then the essential *a priori* openness to the other human being which must be undertaken freely belongs as such to the *a priori* and most basic constitution of man and is an essential inner moment of his (knowing and willing) transcendentality.[51]

This basic human act of attention to the neighbour is always already related to the God of eternal life, even though we may not always be aware of this relationship.[52] Thus, this love of the other person is the fulfilment of the total and hence also spiritually transcendental nature of the human being and it opens us human beings to the immediacy of the God who communicates himself under the form of grace.[53] Therefore, Rahner can conclude: the act of love

[49] Ibid., pp. 234–6.

[50] For a discussion of Rahner's transcendental approach to theology see, for instance, Anne Carr, *The Theological Method of Karl Rahner*, and Werner G. Jeanrond, 'Karl Rahner, Theologian', *The Furrow* 35 (1984), pp. 577–81.

[51] Ibid., p. 241. Cf. also Rahner, *Von der Not und dem Segen des Gebetes*, p. 48: 'Ob zwei Menschen, die sich lieben, an dieser Liebe den radikalsten Schmerz oder das letzte Glück erfahren, wird davon abhängen, ob sie verstehen, dass in ihrer Liebe eine ganz andere Liebe noch zum Lichte drängt, ob sie zusammen nach Gott verlangen und auch dort noch sich treffen.'

[52] Ibid.

[53] Ibid., p. 243.

of neighbour is the only categorical and original act, in which the human being attains the whole of the given reality, fulfils his or her own self and *thus* experiences God's transcendental and gracious self-communication.[54]

Rahner points to the christological and eschatological significance of this insight. In the human being Jesus the eternal God reveals Himself. Thus, 'the man Jesus takes on and continues to have an eternal significance for our relationship to God right into the "direct" vision of God'.[55]

The relationship between love of neighbour and love of God thus becomes clearer: the categorical and explicit love of neighbour is the primary act of loving God. It is not the total love of God, but it is the beginning of an opening towards God. This opening contains already the whole of Christian salvation and of Christianity. However, this 'must indeed still be unfolded in that complete fullness and breadth which we know and preserve, but whenever someone loves somebody else truly and "to the end", it is already grasped in its original root'.[56]

In 1969 Rahner offers a first comprehensive treatment of Christian love in his contribution to *Sacramentum Mundi*, a theological lexicon for Christian praxis.[57] Here he stresses love as a key concept of Christian faith. Love is *the* New Testament word to bring to expression 'what God is and what the human being is to be' (p. 236). Moreover in Christian faith, salvation and justification, i.e. the totality of the human being, are thematized in terms of love (p. 235). However, love can only be described; it cannot be defined (p. 235).

Here, Rahner understands love as the total act in which a person gains the right and full relationship to another person through recognizing and affirming the totality of the other in his or her goodness

[54] Ibid., p. 246. Here the English translation is not clear. Cf. the original German text 'Über die Einheit von Nächsten- und Gottesliebe', p. 294: 'Der Akt der Nächstenliebe ist also der einzige kategoriale und ursprüngliche Akt, in dem der Mensch die kategorial gegebene ganze Wirklichkeit erreicht, sich ihr gegenüber selbst total richtig vollzieht und *darin* schon immer die transzendentale und gnadenhaft unmittelbare Erfahrung Gottes macht.'

[55] Rahner, 'Reflections on the Unity of the Love of Neighbour and the Love of God', p. 247.

[56] Ibid., p. 249.

[57] Karl Rahner, 'Liebe', in *Sacramentum Mundi: Theologisches Lexikon für die Praxis*, vol. 3, Freiburg, Basel and Wien: Herder, 1969, pp. 234–52. Numbers in the text refer to this article.

and dignity.[58] Hence, love is properly dialogical in so far as the loving subject and the loved subject are related to each other, always in their respective selfhood, dignity, and irreplaceable otherness. Thus, the other subject is willed and affirmed as the lasting other (p. 237). Otherness is for Rahner an essential aspect of any love relation. Here he differs from Tillich's desire for union without proper respect for the otherness of the other (see above in this chapter).

Moreover, against Anders Nygren, Rahner also affirms the erotic nature of human love (p. 239) as well as the many forms and expressions of love (p. 240). All genuine love is always grace, and genuine grace is love (p. 243).[59] Thus, genuine love does not appear as an egoistic human endeavour. Rather it is always already the consequence of God's creative and redemptive love, in God's loving self-communication in history, especially in his Son (p. 244). However, Rahner knows about the difficulties of proclaiming God's love in our world stigmatized by experiences of God's absence, i.e. horrendous evil, Auschwitz. Only on the basis of an ultimate solidarity with the condemned of this earth (*mit den 'Verdammten dieser Erde'*) may the word of the love of God for us human beings be risked (p. 245). God's love, like God self, remains a radical mystery. Every genuine human love for the neighbour — in truth and action, without any self-deception — is an act of faith in God and God's love for the human being, notwithstanding whether or not this is reflexively known (p. 245). The interconnectedness between love of God and love of neighbour is thus once more underlined. Both loves live of each other, because ultimately they are one ('without separation, without confusion') (p. 250).

Rahner concludes this article with a brief reflection on the love of Jesus Christ which is the culmination of salvation history and the final guarantee of the unity of love of God and love of neighbour. As far as love is concerned, incarnation means that the God-man Jesus Christ is always co-loved in any genuine act of human love (p. 250).

[58] Ibid., p. 237: 'Wenn L. [Liebe] von vornherein verstanden wird als der totale Akt, in dem eine Person das richtige und volle Verhältnis zu einer anderen Person ... gewinnt, indem sie die Totalität des anderen in seiner Güte und Würde 'erkennt' und bejaht, dann sind zwei Aspekte dieses Verhältnisses von vornherein gegeben: die Bezogenheit des einen (liebenden) Subjekts auf das andere (geliebte) Subjekt und die umgekehrte Bezogenheit, die ebenfalls im Akt der L. [Liebe] ergriffen und angenommen wird.'

[59] Cf. also Rahner, *Von der Not und dem Segen des Gebetes*, p. 58: 'Gott ist es, der Beginn, Wachstum und Vollendung der heiligen Liebe in uns wirkt nach seinem Wohlgefallen.'

In his *Foundations of Christian Faith* Rahner is also concerned with this unity of the love of God and the concrete love of neighbour. Here he speaks of God as the ground and mysterious partner in any genuine love of neighbour.[60] 'For without him, interpersonal communication in love among men cannot reach its own radical depths [sic] and its final and definitive validity.'[61] Since Christian faith does not interpret death as the conclusion that ends everything, but as fulfilment, Christian love is not simply corporeal. Rather it does not even reach its radical essence and its human fulfilment 'until it transcends these boundaries in faith and in hope'.[62]

Here too Rahner links the orientation of Christian love with the love of Jesus, 'the most concrete absolute'. One can love him 'as a true man in the most proper and vital meaning of this word. Indeed because of who the God-man is, this love is even the absolute instance of a love in which love for a man and love for God find their most radical unity and mediate each other mutually.'[63] Love is, of course, not a Christian invention or possession. However, Rahner identifies in every genuine act of human love of neighbour, anonymously as it were, the presence of Jesus Christ.[64]

Although always keen to stress the link between love of God and love of neighbour, Rahner also adds a cautionary note: the interconnectedness between both love commandments must not mislead us human beings to think that we are able to grasp God's mystery. While interpersonal love gives us a hint of our relationship to God, it remains true

> that only in the act of resigned and self-forsaking surrender of the subject to the incomprehensibility of God as such (which then ceases to be a limitation and becomes the very content of our relationship to God) does the most

[60] Rahner, *Foundations*, p. 309.

[61] Ibid.

[62] Ibid., p. 310.

[63] Ibid. Cf. also Rahner, 'The Mystery of the God-Man Jesus', in Karl Rahner, *Theological Investigations*, vol. 13, trans. David Bourke, London: Darton, Longman and Todd, 1975, pp. 195–200, esp. pp. 197–8; and also Rahner, 'The One Christ and the Universality of Salvation', in Rahner, *Theological Investigations*, vol. 16, trans. David Morland, OSB, London: Darton, Longman and Todd, 1979, pp. 199–224, here p. 223: 'Love does not find its full realisation out of its own resources but from the radical unity it has with the love of God in Jesus Christ.'

[64] Ibid., p. 311. Cf. also Rahner, 'Liebe', in *Sacramentum Mundi*, p. 249. With regard to Rahner's concept of anonymous Christianity, see Werner G. Jeanrond, 'Anonymes Christentum', in *Religion in Geschichte und Gegenwart*, 4th edn, vol. 1, Tübingen: Mohr Siebeck, 1998, pp. 510–11. Cf. also Rahner, 'The Mystery of the God-Man Jesus', p. 200.

> fundamental nature of love really dawn upon us, of which interpersonal love is merely a creaturely reflection.[65]

In some lectures published shortly before his death in 1984, Rahner returns to the challenge of Christian love. More radically and directly than before, he distinguishes between love of God and love of neighbour: the love of God is profoundly misunderstood if it is taken to be just one commandment among other love commandments. Rather, the love of God is the primary goal of human existence and as such the framework for all other loves. 'The love of God is the totality of the free fulfilment (*freier Vollzug*) of human existence. It is not, in the last analysis, the content of an individual commandment, but is at once the basis and the goal of all individual commandments.'[66] God must be loved for His own sake. And the love of God ultimately requires that we human beings are prepared to lose ourselves in the ineffable mystery. Rahner speaks of the need to surrender to God (*Hingabe an Gott*) and of self-abandonment to God (*Enteignung in Gott hinein*), and he claims that only a person who ultimately loves God can 'manage unconditionally to abandon himself or herself to another person, and not make that person the means of his or her own self-assertion'.[67]

In the light of these clarifications Rahner stresses afresh the interconnectedness of the love of God and the love of neighbour. Both stand in a relationship of mutual conditioning, of mutual inclusion: 'There is no love for God that is not, in itself, already a love for neighbour; and love for God only comes to its own identity through its fulfilment in a love for neighbour.'[68]

Once more, Rahner returns to the importance of loving Jesus Christ. He speaks of the courage needed to throw our arms around Jesus,[69] i.e. of our concrete readiness to enter into a love relationship

[65] Karl Rahner, 'The Human Question of Meaning in Face of the Absolute Mystery of God', in Rahner, *Theological Investigations*, vol. 18, trans. Edward Quinn, London: Darton, Longman and Todd, 1984, pp. 89–121, here p. 101. Already in his article 'Liebe', in Karl Rahner, ed., *Herders Theologisches Taschenlexikon*, vol. 4, Freiburg i. B.: Herder, 1972, pp. 319–33, here p. 330, Rahner speaks of 'unity and difference between love of God and love of neighbour'.

[66] Karl Rahner, *The Love of Jesus and the Love of Neighbour*, trans. Robert Barr, Middlegreen, Slough: St Paul Publications, 1983, p. 70. The second part of this book, 'Who Are Your Brother and Sister?' was originally published separately in German: Karl Rahner, *Wer ist dein Bruder?*, Freiburg i. B.: Herder, 1981, p. 14.

[67] *The Love of Jesus and the Love of Neighbour*, p. 71.

[68] Ibid.

[69] Ibid., pp. 22–3.

with this person Jesus of Nazareth. Rahner affirms that we 'can love Jesus, love him in himself, in true, genuine, immediate love'.[70]

Karl Rahner's approach to the theology of love is inspired by a reading of New Testament passages on the double love commandment and by a constructive retrieval of ideas and concepts of the Christian tradition of love within the horizon of his own transcendental theology and his acute attempt to relate the Christian message to the actual existential questions and problems of his time. Rahner rejects any split of the human being in bodily and spiritual love. Rather he wishes to reflect upon the love of the *whole* person.[71]

As a result, he has also reflected on the significance of the human body in the order of salvation[72] and on human sexuality and its significance for understanding Christian marriage. He welcomes the shift of emphasis in the Second Vatican Council's understanding of marriage towards partnership within marriage and the concomitant positive evaluation of human sexuality.[73] Rahner regrets the Manichean, body-denigrating, Platonist tendencies in the Christian tradition that all too often have bedevilled human sexuality. But he also questions distortions of human sexuality in contemporary culture and calls for a proper approach to the ambiguity of human sexuality in church and society.[74] He stresses that we need both to develop responsible forms for our sexuality and to remember that all human persons bear their own responsibility for their sexual acts within the horizon of 'a radically self-less love of neighbour'.[75]

Rahner's discussion of Christian love is wide ranging and impressive. It combines phenomenological analysis with theological depth. Although deeply concerned with *Christian* love and its foundations in the God-man Jesus Christ, Rahner remains open to the unthematic relatedness of all love to God. Yet he never enters into

[70] Ibid., p. 22.

[71] Karl Rahner, 'Liebe. V. Heutige Problematik', in *Lexikon für Theologie und Kirche*, 2nd edn, vol. 6, Freiburg i. B.: Herder, 1961, pp. 1038–9, here p. 1039: 'Die L. [Liebe] des *einen* Menschen ist dann am "geistigsten", wenn sie den *ganzen* Menschen in sich integriert, also auch die notwendige "Trieb"-Grundlage bewahrt u. verbreitert.'

[72] Karl Rahner, 'The Body in the Order of Salvation', in Rahner, *Theological Investigations*, vol. 17, trans. Margaret Kohl, London: Darton, Longman and Todd, 1981, pp. 71–89.

[73] Karl Rahner, *Politische Dimensionen des Christentums: Ausgewählte Texte zu Fragen der Zeit*, ed. Herbert Vorgrimler, Munich: Kösel, 1986, p. 213.

[74] Cf. ibid., pp. 214–15.

[75] Ibid., p. 218.

a fuller discussion of the relationship between Jewish and Christian traditions of love. His references to Old Testament concepts and developments of love remain surprisingly rare and superficial. As a result, the praxis of love initiated by Jesus Christ is implied to be a radically new departure of love rather than developed in constructive continuity with Jewish tradition.

Rahner's phenomenological approach to otherness and its significance for any praxis of love is echoed and further developed in some contemporary philosophical approaches to love, as we are going to see in the next section of this chapter. His insight into the need for a critical and constructive theology of the body to accompany any responsible theology of love is to be welcomed as a clear affirmation of the potential of love to transform the full humanity of human beings, and not only selected spiritual dimensions.

For Rahner, love is the eternal connecting point between God and human beings. At times Rahner approaches Christian theology through love, at times he subjects his understanding of love to his Christology. Sometimes love is the way towards the fullness of God and of the human being, at other times, love demands a total self-giving and self-forsaking surrender. Elements of mystical theology, phenomenological insights, anthropological reflections and starting points compete with christological convictions in Rahner's lifelong and varying struggle with the theology of love. However, he never loses sight of the unity of love and its mysterious potential to bring God and human beings together without dissolving the one into the other.

## Philosophical Problematizations and Clarifications

Before continuing my exploration of important contemporary theologies of love, I wish to pause for a moment in order to benefit from some conceptual problematizations and clarifications contributed recently by the South African-born Dutch philosopher of religion Vincent Brümmer and by the French philosopher Jean-Luc Marion.[76] Both thinkers have offered in-depth studies on love and paid particular attention to the theology of love.

[76] In this section I make use of some reflections previously published in my article 'Love Enlightened: The Promises and Ambiguities of Love', in Lieven Boeve and others, eds, *Faith in the Enlightenment? The Critique of the Enlightenment Revisited*, Amsterdam and New York: Rodopi, 2006, pp. 268–91, here pp. 280–7.

*Vincent Brümmer's Model of Love*

In his book *The Model of Love*, Vincent Brümmer examines the potential of love to serve Christian discourse as a key model for a relational understanding of faith in God.[77] Brümmer emphasizes the limits of any such model by raising the critical question: 'how is the relation between God and ourselves alike, and how unlike, human relations?' (p. 15). Thus, he is aware that no root metaphor or model can ever fully describe God's relationality. Brümmer confirms our own insights into the ambiguous nature of 'love' in the history of Western thought and our misgivings about exegetical searches for 'the true biblical concept of love' (p. 30). Moreover, he points out that most of the concepts of love in the Christian tradition 'have been attitudinal rather than relational. Love has generally been taken to be an attitude of one person toward another, rather than as a relation between persons' (p. 33). Brümmer wishes to correct this restricted view by examining the potential of a relational view of love.

Although love clearly involves feelings, emotions and different forms of desire, such as sexual desire, it transcends all of them in terms of 'a purposive commitment to adopt a complex pattern of actions and attitudes in relation to the beloved' (p. 153). Love involves long-term commitments, i.e. policies that necessarily issue in actions, which are public. Moreover, 'although we cannot be held responsible for our feelings, we can be held responsible for keeping our commitments' (p. 154). What distinguishes love from most other attitudes, however, is the desire for reciprocation. 'Love wants to be returned, requited, and in this way fulfilled in a relationship of mutual love. Of course this does not exclude the possibility of unrequited love' (p. 155). Love desires community, though it does not logically depend on the fulfilment of its desires. Moreover, love is more than beneficence. Love entails beneficence, but unlike beneficence it also seeks a relationship.

Thus unlike many approaches to love in the Christian tradition, Brümmer understands love not as an attitude which might issue in a relationship, but as 'a relationship which involves the partners adopting a complex set of attitudes toward each other' (p. 156). Therefore, he analyses different models of relationship, including

[77] Vincent Brümmer, *The Model of Love: A Study in Philosophical Theology*, Cambridge, UK: Cambridge University Press, 1993. The numbers in the text refer to pages in this book.

manipulative relations, agreements of rights and duties, and mutual fellowship.

For Augustine, and indeed for Anders Nygren, love is issued in the form of asymmetrical relationship between God and human beings. Here, human beings are not proper agents of love. They 'cannot freely decide to love either God or each other, since their love is the exclusive effect which the divine *agape* has on them ... God *causes* us to love him and each other. This seems to turn God into a Heavenly Conquistador' (p. 159). Brümmer concludes that views such as this 'take love to be a highly impersonal concept and the relationship of love to be a very impersonal manipulative one' (p. 160). Therefore, he stresses the importance of rethinking the entire network of divine–human relationships in terms of a love that centres on mutual fellowship. Such a view of love has significant implications for our understanding of both divine and human agency,[78] for our assessment of love as a source of knowledge, for our understanding of sin as broken relationship, and for our appraisal of the ways in which such a broken relationship might be restored.

Brümmer also emphasizes the need to order our different love relationships. This is important if one is to avoid false reductions of the horizon of love. On the one hand, one particular love relationship does not exclude love for others. On the other hand, no two love relationships are ever identical, since in love 'the beloved is valued as an irreplaceable individual' (p. 209). No desire for union in love can annihilate the actual individuality and otherness of the lovers.

Brümmer's approach to love offers important conceptual clarifications. For him there is no dichotomy between eros and agape. He recognizes the significance of desire for love, while he examines the implications of love for our understanding of human subjectivity and also of divine agency. Moreover, love is a dynamic relationship leading to certain attitudes, views and ethics. Here the actual relationship comes always first. Thus the unconditional nature of love makes a new relational order in life possible. Love shapes relations; it always wants community. Here, community is approached through love, and not love through the doctrines and interests of a particular community. Thus, the dynamics of love are preserved.

Although Brümmer shows so much care for self and subjectivity in the Christian praxis of love, body and gender do not receive

[78] Brümmer, ibid., p. 227: 'Part of the conceptual price of looking on God as a God of love is therefore that we should give up the doctrine of divine impassibility.'

much attention. Moreover, one needs to ask if the Christian praxis of love could not also be understood as an offer of generosity in situations where mutuality is lacking or not (yet) possible or where mutuality is realized in non-symmetrical ways, e.g. in the parent–child relationship.[79]

*Jean-Luc Marion's Phenomenology of Love*

Marion has treated of love in two major works, *Prolegomena to Charity*[80] and *The Erotic Phenomenon.*[81] Here I shall chiefly discuss the latter work in order to assess in what way it might be able to contribute to a critical theology of love.

Marion wishes to overcome an inadequate metaphysical understanding of love by pursuing a phenomenological approach to love. He understands the human being not in the first place as a thinking animal, but as a loving animal. 'In short, it will be necessary to substitute erotic meditations for metaphysical ones' (p. 8).[82] His point of departure is the human flesh which can be affected endlessly by the things of this world. For Marion, then, the crucial question is not to reach an ontological certainty, but rather to answer a different question, namely, the question 'Does anybody love me?' (p. 20) (*'M'aime-t-on?*[83]).

The erotic possibility allows me to discover myself as a given — a given phenomenon — and as such the erotic reduction can get under way. First of all, to be loved or hated is an experience coming to me from elsewhere. Hence, any form of self-production of the ego is disclosed as an impossibility. To be loved and to be able to love constitute a world opposed to the world of self-sufficient thinking (p. 28: 'The lover is thus opposed to the cogitant'). The erotic reduction radically alters our understanding of space, time and identity. Selfhood in the sense of ipseity is given only through my

[79] Cf. George Newlands, *Generosity and the Christian Future*, London: SPCK, 1997, p. 193.

[80] Jean-Luc Marion, *Prolegomena to Charity*, trans. Stephen E. Lewis, New York: Fordham University Press, 2002. French original: *Prolégomènes à la charité*, Paris: La Différence, 1986.

[81] Jean-Luc Marion, *The Erotic Phenomenon*, trans. Stephen E. Lewis, Chicago and London: University of Chicago Press, 2007. The numbers in the text refer to pages in this book. French Original: *Le phénomène érotique*, Paris: Grasset, 2003.

[82] *Le phénomène érotique*, p. 19: 'Bref, il faudra substituer à des méditations métaphysiques des méditations érotiques.'

[83] *Le phénomène érotique*, p. 38.

taking flesh (*prise de chair*). Only this taking of flesh 'assigns me to a *here* (in fact to a *there*) that is irreducible, and only permits me a world that individualizes me as far as the final ipseity' (p. 39). Hence the crucial question is no longer 'to be or not to be', but solely 'Does anyone out there love me?' (p. 40).[84]

This approach to love affirms both the necessity of distance for any act of love as well as the impossibility of an unconditional self-love.[85] Moreover, in order to fight the assault of uncertainty, vanity, threat, hatred, rejection etc., I would need to be able to answer the question 'Does anyone out there love me?' (p. 66) However, as yet, the erotic reduction has not gone far enough. It still appears only as an indication of a lack. For this reason, the recognition that I can love first is so important for my becoming myself. 'My acts as lover belong to me incontestably, without admixture or apportionment' (p. 76). Whenever the loving person decides to love without assurances of being loved in return and decides to love first by risking everything, then she does not only transgress reciprocity, but, most of all, contradicts the form of sufficient reasoning in any kind of economy. Love creates its own way of reasoning. Strictly speaking, the one whom we love, we do not know — or only in so far as we love that person. Marion examines in great detail the concrete circumstances of encountering both the other and oneself as loving persons at that moment of encounter. He speaks of a '*crossed phenomenon*' in order to maintain the respective individuality of the two potential lovers and their respective intuition. But this crossed phenomenon carries a common signification (p. 105).

Marion then analyses the crucial importance of desire for love. 'First, the lover is individualized by *desire*, or rather, by the desire that is *his* and no one else's' (p. 108). Next, the lover individualizes himself through the desired eternity. All genuine love desires eternity, or it is not genuine. And finally, the lover individualizes himself through his passivity. This passivity includes three aspects: the lover's oath, the lover's advance, and the taking of a risk. According to Marion, this triple passivity arises clearly from the phenomenon of the flesh (*la chair*). 'I do not have flesh, I am my flesh and it coincides absolutely with me' (p. 112).

[84] Ibid., p. 68: 'M'aime-t-on – d'ailleurs?' might also be translated: 'Does one love me – after all?' As so often, Marion employs ordinary everyday language in order to incorporate a number of possible references at once.

[85] 'In order to love oneself, it is necessary, more essentially, to persevere in one's *own* being' (pp. 48–9).

It is interesting to note that Marion sees the flesh, and not the body, as the primary phenomenon that allows love to be experienced. The reason for this is his focus on love as an erotic encounter between two people that is unmediated by other aspects of existence. The primary phenomenon of love, according to Marion, is the love of a couple made possible through the encounter of two people in their naked flesh. The flesh can be sensed, but not made visible to the gaze. In Marion's understanding, that visibility to the gaze of the other would change the flesh into a body (pp. 116–17). Therefore he speaks of the eroticization of the flesh, and not of the body. In this process, the other gives to me what I do not possess, namely my own flesh, and I give to him what he does not own, namely his own flesh. Thus, I enjoy not my own pleasure, but the other's (p. 128).[86] This flesh turns into a body when we suddenly become aware that we are naked and begin to look at each other. Moreover, Marion insists that ultimately I do not have a body, except in terms of an unwarranted analogy with bodies of the world. In this sense, '[a]ll flesh is born and dies as flesh, all bodies remain bodies' (p. 138). I shall have to return below to Marion's problematic understanding of body and flesh.

The eroticization of the bodies also affects the language between the lovers. This erotic language is performative and thus reminds Marion of mystical theology and its aim of provoking the excess of the union of the lover and the beloved, yet always maintaining the ultimate distance between both lovers. Moreover, Marion concludes 'that erotic speech cannot be performed without the language of spiritual union of man with God, any more than it can avoid the two other lexicons – the obscene and the childish' (p. 149).

Following an examination of a number of possible threats to love, e.g. lies, jealousy, hatred etc., Marion proceeds to reflect on faithfulness (*fidélité*) as the necessary condition for love. Without faithfulness, the erotic phenomenon will turn again into a simple momentary thing, disappearing as soon as it has appeared, 'a phenomenal intermittence' (p. 185). Faithfulness demands nothing less than eternity. We cannot really be said to love provisionally, he concludes. This in turn implies that all authentic love will be carried on by me eternally. I am stigmatized by the love that has left traces

[86] 'Put another way, I do not enjoy my pleasure, but hers; and if, by chance (which does not go without saying), I also climax, this pleasure gushes forth only from hers, as its undertow; if I climaxed without her climax, I would simply not enjoy, but instead would limit myself to using her anew' (p. 128).

in me. Thus, I am irrevocably marked by my loves — even though I may have failed to honour them. All true love is eternal. Therefore, the erotic phenomenon as such is not subjected to death because love does not belong to the horizon of being. Rather, the lover always already anticipates eternity. He does not desire it; rather he presupposes it (p. 193). Here we are reminded of Kierkegaard's insistence that genuine love must undergo the change of eternity,[87] although in this context, unlike Marion, the Danish philosopher does not reflect upon the erotic nature of love.

The arrival of the third, i.e. the child, is not to be understood here in terms of social continuity or biological laws. Rather in the child the oath of love becomes flesh — notwithstanding the actual faithfulness of the lovers.[88] Moreover, in the crossing of their flesh, the lovers become one single flesh, but this is not really theirs; rather this single flesh is the flesh of another person, of a third.

In this context Marion underlines the eschatological character of love. Love is, as we have seen, eternal. The lovers complete their oath of love in their final 'adieu' to each other, i.e. in their passage to God whom they know to be their ultimate witness. Finally, in the light of the love that comes to me I can discover even myself in terms of being a lover, I can finally even love myself, the most difficult love of all.

Only in the concluding pages of his book does Marion widen the perspective from the loving couple to other forms of love, such as friendship and God's own love for us human beings. While Marion denies any opposition between erotic love and friendship, he approaches friendship through his analysis of erotic love and accords it the status of genuine love, yet a love that does not demand either exclusivity or the eroticization of the flesh of the friends (pp. 219–20). It is, we might say, a shorter form of love, though not a more limited form of love. With regard to God's love, Marion says that God loves infinitely better than we. God's highest transcendence does not concern his power, his wisdom, or even his infinity, but his love. 'God surpasses us as the best lover' (p. 222).

In another context, Marion has further elucidated his approach to God in terms of love and gift, rather than in terms of being. 'God can give himself to be thought without idolatry only starting from

[87] Cf. Søren Kierkegaard, *Works of Love*, trans. Howard V. Hong and Edna H. Hong, Princeton, NJ: Princeton University Press, 1995, p. 38.

[88] 'The child manifests a promise that is always already held, whether the lovers wish it or not' (p. 198).

himself alone: to give himself to be thought as love, hence as gift; to give himself to be thought as a thought of the gift. Or better, as gift for thought, as a gift that gives itself to be thought.'[89] His point, he explains in a more recent conversation, is 'that it is much easier to envision the transcendence of God according to love than according to being, because we know that charity and the Good are far above us, far transcendent to us'.[90] Marion does not believe in a univocity of being, but he does think that 'there is a univocity of love'.[91]

Like Brümmer, Marion rejects any dichotomy between eros and agape. He too has analysed the significance of desire for love. And he has certainly stressed the implications of love for our understanding of human subjectivity. For Marion, love is not only a model for an appropriate relationship between human beings and God. Rather, love is the occasion of truth itself. In love and according to the logic of the erotic phenomenon the human person becomes aware of her own self as a loved and a loving self. This loved and loving self, however, is enfleshed rather than embodied. Moreover, love originates always elsewhere; it comes from outside; it hits me in my passivity. Hence, Marion's primary question: 'Does anyone out there love me?' An alternative to this question could be 'How can I love?' Or in Christian terms: 'How can I love my neighbour whom I am commanded to love?' Marion, it seems, has overburdened his approach to the passivity of love with his phenomenological-theological disclosures and, at the same time, underestimated the potential of a fuller theological exploration of the different forms of the Christian praxis of love.

While Marion does not discuss the dimensions of gender in human love, he does, as we have seen, pay a lot of attention to the difference between flesh and body.[92] The union of the flesh gives rise to a third

[89] Jean-Luc Marion, *God Without Being*, trans. Thomas A. Carlson, Chicago: University of Chicago Press, 1991, p. 49. French original: *Dieu sans l'être* (1982), Paris: Quadrige/PUF, 1991, p. 75.

[90] Marion in conversation with Rupert Shortt, in Rupert Shortt, *God's Advocates: Christian Thinkers in Conversation*, London: Darton, Longman and Todd, 2005, pp. 141–52, here p. 146.

[91] Ibid., p. 150.

[92] Cf. also Marion, *Prolegomena to Charity*, pp. 158–64. Marion's understandable protest against the abstract eroticism of our time leads him to insist on the human flesh as the primary presence to be affected in love. 'Without flesh, no body can accede to love, for it remains unaffected by another person, or even any sort of other. Restricted to bodies without flesh, contemporary eroticism slides inevitably into solipsism, an eroticism without other' (ibid., p. 159).

party. But is there also a loving *community* of the body, e.g. the body of Christ? Do we have access to our flesh outside of our bodies? Does not one of the problems of Marion's approach to love lie precisely in this assumed dichotomy between flesh and body? Marion's attempt to reach an unmediated love as an event of pure givenness seems to be disturbed by the human body.

Moreover, is the erotic phenomenon really adequately described when it is limited to the procreative erotic love between a couple? Does this form of love exhaust the depth of the erotic phenomenon? Furthermore, is Marion's overall analysis of love as necessarily unmediated and unreflective really adequate? Why this dichotomy between loving and thinking? Marion's rejection of a hermeneutics of loving is not convincing.[93] In addition, it appears to be dangerous in view of the ambiguous history of love. Rather than searching for the purity of love, it seems to me to be desirable, on the basis of the ambiguity of all concepts of love, to search for a critical understanding of different forms of love. However, such a task requires a hermeneutical thinking beyond the kind of Eucharistic hermeneutic proposed by Marion in another context.[94] Does Marion's overall philosophical agenda of highlighting the superabundance and gratuity of the gift of God's love weaken his appreciation of the potential of human love?[95] Does his prioritizing of flesh over body lead to new forms of non-embodied love?

As we have seen, Brümmer has called for an ordering of love. He wants to avoid both the reduction of love to exclusivity and the false identification of different loves. Hence, a community of mutual love can emerge in response to different initiatives, and is not limited to the paradigm of the erotic love of a (heterosexual) couple.[96] Both philosophers have stressed the importance of commitment (Brümmer) or faithfulness (Marion) for love's creative development.

[93] On Marion's evasion of the hermeneutical question see also Graham Ward, 'The Theological Project of Jean-Luc Marion', in Phillip Blond, ed., *Post-Secular Philosophy: Between Philosophy and Theology*, London and New York: Routledge, 1998, pp. 229–39, here pp. 234–5.

[94] Marion, *God Without Being*, pp. 149–52 (*Dieu sans l'être*, pp. 210–14).

[95] See also Richard Kearney's critique of Marion's philosophy of the love of God in Kearney, *The God Who May Be: A Hermeneutic of Religion*, Bloomington, IN: Indiana University Press, 2001, pp. 31–3. See also Henrik Vase Frandsen, 'Distance as Abundance: The Thought of Jean-Luc Marion', *Svensk Teologisk Kvartalskrift* 79 (2003), pp. 177–86.

[96] Cf. Kearney's comments – following Emmanuel Lévinas – on any reduction of love and desire to the loving couple, in Kearney, p. 65.

Love is the process in which I can emerge as a self — a self always already related to others and the radical other, God.

Returning to my exploration of theologies of love, I shall now examine the Encyclical Letter on love by Pope Benedict XVI and his approach to the Christian praxis of love.

## Pope Benedict xvi's Encyclical Letter on Christian Love

In his first encyclical letter, Pope Benedict XVI (Joseph Ratzinger, b. 1927) develops interesting, surprising and challenging perspectives on the most central dimension of Christian faith: God's gift of love.[97] The Pope treats of God and of the relationship between human beings and God in rational, clear, non-moralizing and inviting language. Further, unlike some of the texts for which former Cardinal Ratzinger was responsible, this encyclical does not engage in direct attack on any particular theologian or theological movement or in polemics against supposed forms of postmodern relativism. Instead, in a positive tone the Pope offers constructive theological and pastoral thoughts and suggestions.

His reflections on God's gift of love are characterized by an ecumenical and inclusive horizon: 'Christian love' is not developed here in opposition to Jewish love. Rather Benedict draws his readers' attention to the biblical tradition as a whole and attempts to unfold its potential for an understanding of God's creative and redemptive project. The Pope's letter 'On Christian love' is addressed to 'the bishops, priests and deacons, men and women religious and all the lay faithful'.[98]

Theologically speaking there cannot be a more central approach to Christian faith than a reflection on how the loving God invites all human beings to participate in his creative and reconciling project of love. That Pope Benedict has chosen this central topic demonstrates his wish to attend to the depth of faith, and, by implication, his conviction that it is his task as church leader to remind the faithful of their primary vocation, i.e. to love God, their neighbours and themselves. However, this threefold love is only possible thanks to the

[97] In this section I make use of some reflections previously published in my article 'Love at the Centre: The Pope's First Encyclical', *Doctrine and Life* 56:3 (2006), pp. 17–26.

[98] In the German original the Encyclical does not refer to 'lay faithful' in the opening, but addresses 'alle Christgläubigen', i.e. all who believe in Christ.

divine gift of love. Love cannot be made by human beings; it can only be received and lived. In this sense, this encyclical also treats of the most practical aspect of Christian faith.

In view of the dramatic cultural and intellectual developments in the Western world that have affected the practice and theory of love, i.e. the new interest in understanding and shaping the human body, the development of gender theory, and fresh approaches to the human self in philosophy, literature, the arts, psychology, sociology, political thinking and other areas of culture, a constructive contribution by a theologically sophisticated church leader is most welcome. Although the Pope does not enter into the field of gender, he does address issues of body, community and self. Moreover, a *theology* of love differs from moral and philosophical concerns for it involves the consideration of God's self-revelation in history as the context for developing appropriate forms of love. Hence, a theology of love must discuss both the concept of God and the Christian understanding of the kind of relationship to which God has invited all human beings.

That the Pope presents his contribution to a theology of love and that he avoids ethical and philosophical reductions, happily surprised all who had grown tired and dispirited of decades of Vatican obsession with detailed questions of sexual morality and of ecclesiastical romanticizing of the nuclear family. Against this bleak history of moralizing and reductionist pronouncements and of the morbid concern for a catalogue of sins, the Pope's fresh *theological* approach to love frees attention to the God-given potential of love both in personal and social relations.

Here I wish to concentrate on some aspects of the Pope's approach to love. In particular I would like to discuss his methodological and theological choices from within the plurality of possible Christian theologies of love.[99]

As we have seen in the previous chapter, the Swedish theologian Anders Nygren sharply distinguished between the ascending *eros*, an invention of humankind, and the divinely revealed descending *agape*.[100] Agape is God's way to man. Nygren insisted that Christian

[99] Numbers in brackets in the text refer to the numbered paragraphs of the Encyclical Letter *Deus Caritas Est* by Benedict XVI, Vatican City: Libreria Editrice Vaticana, 2005.

[100] Anders Nygren, *Agape and Eros: The Christian Idea of Love*, trans. Philip S. Watson, Chicago: University of Chicago Press, 1982.

love was something other than ordinary human love. Christian love has nothing to do with any human way to the Divine: 'Agape is like a blow in the face to both Jewish legal piety and Hellenistic Eros-piety.'[101] For Nygren, Eros and Agape were 'the characteristic expressions of two different attitudes to life, two fundamentally opposed types of religion and ethics ... They stand for what may be described as the egocentric and the theocentric attitude in religion.'[102]

Although the Pope's encyclical never mentions Nygren by name, the Pope's choice of concepts clearly refers and responds to Nygren and his followers. While Nygren rejected eros-love out of hand, Benedict accepts eros as a necessary ingredient in all love, including God's own love (7).[103] Human eros, however, is always in need of purification. 'Purification and growth in maturity are called for; and these also pass through the path of renunciation. Far from rejecting or "poisoning" *eros*, they heal it and restore its true grandeur' (5). In God alone are eros and agape one: 'God's *eros* for man [sic!] is also totally *agape*' (10).

The Pope presents a theology of love that includes both body and desire, and he develops a framework for their flourishing. Hence, this encyclical engages directly with the human condition and concerns instead of denying their legitimacy. The Pope admits previous Christian tendencies of denigrating the body. At the same time and in the light of the Gospel, he critically assesses contemporary tendencies of divinizing the body.[104] This encyclical thus displays a theological approach well able to combine critique with self-critique.

Moreover, unlike Nygren, Benedict emphasizes the subtle connection between all human love and the divine (5). Love is a gift of God and thus is able to disclose the presence of God, however unconscious people may be of the origin and goal of human love. To borrow a phrase from Karl Rahner (see above in this chapter),

[101] Ibid, p. 200.

[102] Ibid, p. 205.

[103] Eros and agape 'can never be completely separated. The more the two, in their different aspects, find a proper unity in the one reality of love, the more the true nature of love in general is realized' (7).

[104] 'Nowadays Christianity of the past is often criticized as having been opposed to the body; and it is quite true that tendencies of this sort have always existed. Yet the contemporary way of exalting the body is deceptive. *Eros*, reduced to pure "sex", has become a commodity ... ' (5).

one could say that all experience of love bears within it an *unthematic* awareness of God. It would then be the task of Christian preaching and theology to make this experience thematic within the framework of the biblical tradition and the Church.

Following this method, Benedict enters more deeply into a discussion of the biblical understanding of God and of the human being. He stresses God's passion for humankind both in creation and reconciliation. The Pope's approach to christology flows from his insight into the connection between creation and redemption — both integrated aspects of God's loving action. Love is the horizon for understanding the coming of Jesus Christ, his proclamation, passion and resurrection.

> His death on the Cross is the culmination of that turning of God against himself in which he gives himself in order to raise man up and save him. This is love in its most radical form. By contemplating the pierced side of Christ (cf. [John] 19:37), we can understand the starting-point of this Encyclical Letter: 'God is love' (1 Jn 4:8). It is there that this truth can be contemplated. It is from there that our definition of love must begin. In this contemplation the Christian discovers the path along which his life and love must move. (12)[105]

In the context of reflecting both on God's love and on the rootedness of *eros* in human nature, the Pope proposes a logical connection between the monotheistic notion of God and human marriage.

> From the standpoint of creation, *eros* directs man towards marriage, to a bond which is unique and definitive; thus, and only thus, does it fulfil its deepest purpose. Corresponding to the image of a monotheistic God is monogamous marriage. Marriage based on exclusive and definitive love becomes the icon of the relationship between God and his people and vice versa. (11)

However, in biblical tradition such a connection between God and marriage is by no means as evident. Moreover, how we in the West today understand marriage is the result of a complex history, too complex to force it into a simplistic formula linking marriage to God's own nature. Here, more historical discussion and theological distinctions are called for (I shall return to marriage in the following chapter). Nevertheless, the Pope's emphasis on the exclusive and definite nature of human love provides a significant opportunity to reflect further on those forms of human love which can be charac-

[105] The German original here offers a more suggestive and powerful expression by speaking of *Blick* instead of contemplation: 'Der Blick auf die durchbohrte Seite ... ' and 'Von diesem Blick her findet der Christ den Weg seines Lebens und Liebens.'

terized by a comprehensive and lasting union, e.g. marriage, and faithful and lifelong partnership.

Although this intimate connection between God and marriage might be interpreted by readers of the encyclical as an indication that marriage (as we understand it today) was the highest form of love, the encyclical does in fact devote more space to another form, namely social love. Love of the self, or self-love, however, is strangely missing.[106] The Pope pays great attention to the transitive dimension of all love, i.e. to the fact that love (divine and human alike) seeks the other, seeks the other's well-being, always longs for community with others. But the encyclical does not reflect on the potential of love to shape also the loving self.

The Pope follows other theological concerns in this encyclical letter. He discusses (and quotes from) significant and relevant sources — stretching from classical Greek philosophy via the Bible (especially the Johannine tradition) and the Church Fathers to modern thinkers, such as Descartes and Nietzsche, and modern intellectual movements, especially Marxism. His predecessor Pope John Paul II is referred to a number of times, certainly in order to demonstrate some form of continuity of thinking.[107] Yet roughly one thousand years of theological and philosophical developments are not directly discussed or referred to, including the entire Middle Ages and the Reformation. That means the challenges of Humanism and Reformation (and related intellectual and cultural transformations to the self-understanding of the Western person) are not taken up in this text. Rather the intellectual resources for reconstructing a theology of love stem from classical and patristic voices, i.e. from sources not really concerned with the development of the modern and postmodern self. Hence, some caution is in order when discussing and appreciating the second part of the encyclical where the Pope treats of the social and communal dimensions of Christian love.

While the first part of the encyclical stresses the unity of love in creation and in salvation history, the second part is devoted to the practice of love by the Church, understood here as a 'community of love'. Hence having demonstrated the unbreakable bond between

[106] Cf. Janet Martin Soskice, 'Heart of the Matter', in *The Tablet*, 4 February 2006, pp. 4–5.

[107] For pertinent quotes from John Paul II on love and some initial discussion see Brady, *Christian Love*, pp. 226–39.

love of God and love of neighbour in part one, Benedict now moves to the Church's charitable activity.[108] The Pope understands the Church as an agent of love. 'As a community, the Church must practise love' (20). However, 'the true subject of the various Catholic organizations that carry out a ministry of charity is the Church herself – at all levels, from the parishes, through the particular Churches, to the universal Church' (32).

Here, I would like to ask in what way, more precisely, should the Church be understood as an agent of love? Can entire communities and institutions be said to be loving subjects? Of course, a community can organize different works of love. But can the Church love? The Pope holds that the Church is a subject of love. Does this claim further reveal his uneasiness with humanist and modern understandings of the self and subjectivity? Moreover, can we also see his fear of any concepts that might undermine the hierarchical and paternal structure of the Roman Catholic Church (cf. 32)? The overall aim of this part of the encyclical is the explicit desire to control the charitable organizations working under the Church's name.

Within the logic of such institutional thinking the Pope reminds the bishops of their God-given duty to make sure that 'today as in the past, the Church as God's family must be a place where help is given and received, and at the same time, a place where people are also prepared to serve those outside her confines who are in need of help' (32). Every Roman Catholic bishop in today's world is thus made aware that he is accountable for fighting poverty, exploitation, and oppression of any kind. The Pope explicitly rules out any ecclesiological reduction of the Church to merely one or two of its callings. The Church's nature comprises all *three* tasks: proclaiming the word of God, celebrating the sacraments, and exercising the ministry of charity (cf. 25 and 32).

Like Søren Kierkegaard in his *Works of Love,* the Pope is thoroughly influenced by the Johannine tradition of love, though, like the Danish philosopher, Benedict too stresses the universal horizon of love expressed in Luke's parable of the Good Samaritan. This parable 'remains as a standard which imposes universal love towards the

[108] The English text edition misses the implied references of the German headings of chapters 19 and 20 that talk about 'das Liebestun der Kirche' to Søren Kierkegaard's *Works of Love,* translated into German under the title *Der Liebe Tun,* 2 vols, trans. Hayo Gerdes, Gütersloh: Gütersloher Verlagshaus Gerd Mohn (1966), 1983.

needy whom we encounter "by chance" (cf. Lk 10.31), whoever they may be' (25b).[109]

The encyclical is aware of the changing economic and social conditions in our world and summons the Church's leadership to a clearer appreciation of the need for more just social structures (27). Moreover, it offers a number of significant clarifications of the relationship between church and state with regard to their different, though related, duties. The Church sees it as its task 'to contribute to the purification of reason and to the reawakening[110] of those moral forces without which just structures are neither established nor prove effective in the long run' (29).

The just ordering of society and the state is a central responsibility of politics. But even in a truly just society, love will always prove necessary. 'There is no ordering of the State so just that it can eliminate the need for a service of love. Whoever wants to eliminate love is preparing to eliminate man as such' (28b). From a Christian perspective, working for justice and works of love are both required for the humanization of this world. 'Social charity' is called for (29).

In this context the Pope reminds his readers of the significance of Catholic social doctrine (28a). Professional charity workers in the Church need a 'formation of the heart' (31a). Moreover, 'Christian charitable activity must be independent of parties and ideologies' (31b) And it must never be confused with proselytism (31c). 'Love is free; it is not practised as a way of achieving other ends' (31c).

Finally, the Pope recommends prayer as a way towards distinguishing love from activism, secularism, fanaticism and terrorism. Love is more than attending to the other's needs. 'My deep personal sharing in the needs and sufferings of others becomes a sharing of my very self with them: if my gift is not to prove a source of humiliation, I must give to others not only something that is my own, but my very self; I must be personally present in my gift' (34) Here the Pope indicates that for him love is the framework in which the subject might give her true self to others. But how does that self to be offered emerge in the first place? Has self-love a meaning beyond this self-giving imperative?

[109] Cf. Søren Kierkegaard, *Works of Love*, pp. 44–90. On Kierkegaard's approach to love see also above, chapter 5.

[110] The German text speaks here only of '*Weckung*', i.e. 'awakening', not of 'reawakening'.

Although the encyclical does not discuss the role of celibacy and chastity in particular forms of love, in its final pages it does praise the works of love emerging from within the monastic movement. It is interesting to note that the secular priesthood is not explicitly presented here as a form of Christian love or charity, while the deaconate is explicitly identified as a 'ministry of charity' (21) and the local bishop is reminded of his responsibility for charity (32). Already at the outset of his encyclical letter, the Pope emphasizes that he does not intend to present an exhaustive theology of love. Nevertheless his text illustrates his particular approach to this central aspect of Christian faith. Every Christian theology of love draws on a number of biblical, philosophical and theological presuppositions, sources, methods and choices. Every theology of love speaks out of a particular cultural and social location and tradition. All human love, even Christian love, has an ambiguous history to which every theology of love in some way, consciously or subconsciously, relates. Moreover, every theology of love relates to issues and images of body, sexuality, family, friendship, worship, community, the common good, etc.

The theology of love presented in outline by Benedict XVI is no exception in this respect. It is a European theology explicitly inspired by classical and patristic conceptions of love and eager to approach modern and contemporary challenges in the light of these spiritual and cognitive resources. The reflections on social love in contemporary society in the second part of the encyclical are inspired by modern reason and experiences of the encounter between the Church's social doctrine and European (and particularly Germanic) societies. The experiences of non-European local churches are not reflected in this theology of love.

Especially in the more speculative first part of the text the Pope shows his particular debt to the Johannine understanding of Christian love. As we have seen in chapter 2 above, John's Gospel and the letters of John highlight the unity of love, the unity between a community (threatened by many foes) and God in Christ, the unity within the Christian community, and the sacrificial nature of love for the other. Even though Benedict sides with Luke's Gospel as far as the universal horizon of love is concerned (John's horizon of love was limited to the Johannine community itself), his theological pathos remains clearly Johannine. Pauline suggestions that love was a means of dealing with conflict and otherness, even within the Christian community itself (cf. 1 Cor. 13), are not prominently present in Benedict's theology, in spite of scattered references to certain passages in Paul's letters.[111] John always remains a more natural choice for any theology of love that wishes to defend a given church order.

But John is not the only biblical source for a Christian theology of love. A combination of Lukan and Pauline dimensions, for example, could generate a somewhat different approach to love — more inclined to explore otherness within and beyond the Christian community, God's radical otherness, and the otherness of the emerging human subject.

The Pope's analysis of corporeality and desire in Christian love offers a welcome deepening of Christian perspectives on love. However, his readiness to conclude that the Jewish and Christian understanding of God demanded a particular view of marriage seems less supported by the biblical tradition than his insistence that all love comes from God and that love between human beings must therefore always be faithful and open to God's eternity. The absence of any reference to contemporary debates on gender and the absence of inclusive language in the English edition of the encyclical demonstrate that more work must be done in order to relate Christian theology to contemporary experience and thought in a mutually critical way.

In spite of all necessary critique of aspects of this papal text on Christian love, it is important to stress Benedict's insight into the fact that love is not a principle, but praxis. His reflections on this praxis, like all theologies of love, must be judged in terms of how they enable and encourage men, women and children to become more responsible agents of love.

## Approaching Love as Praxis

The theological and philosophical approaches to love examined in this chapter have broadened the horizon of love in different ways. Paul Tillich, determined to rediscover the root meaning of love in human life, saw in the gift of love the potential to reunite what is experienced as separated. For him love is the uniting power as such, while justice preserves what is to be united. Thus, the union brought about in love does not destroy the respective lovers, but invites them to a new and transformative community of love. The human desire for this union is not only not bad, but is a creative force in our lives.

[111] For a more detailed analysis of the differences between John, Paul and Luke on love see above, chapter 2.

Tillich located the depth of human love in *agape*. In *agape* 'ultimate reality manifests itself and transforms life and love'.[112] Hence, *agape* is not the opposite of human love, but is its very depth.

Karl Rahner identified love as the supreme gift of God and the goal of all human existence. In love the human being can become more fully human, fully self. Already the explicit will to love envelops the human self in this process. Rahner sees the experience of radical existential openness to both God and self as co-present in every act of loving attention to the neighbour. However, although all human loves are intrinsically related, not all human loves are identical. The later Rahner, more attracted to mystical theology, distinguishes more sharply between love of God and love of neighbour in order not to compromise in any way God's always prior love for us human beings. God must be loved for God's sake, and out of this love flows proper neighbourly love and self-love. Thus, Rahner always defended the unity of love, but changed the direction of his defence later on in life. The creative presence of human desire, however, was never in question.

Our brief excursion into contemporary philosophical reflections on love has helped us to focus anew on the relational, mutual, though not necessarily symmetrical, nature of love. Desire is an integrated part of love. Moreover, commitment or faithfulness is a necessary feature of any love relationship open to its eternal vocation. We have also seen that there is no way to bypass the ambiguity of love. Pure love as a phenomenon belongs to the realm of God's coming reign, but not to embodied and contextualized life on this side of death.

Our reading of Pope Benedict XVI's approach to love revealed a narrowing of love's horizon to 'Christian love', but also a broadening of the horizon of this love to the spheres of 'social love'. Love is not an object of faith, but a concern for God's creative and redemptive project. Hence, the Christian community must engage in the praxis of love. This move beyond mere ontological, transcendental and phenomenological considerations of love, however important these are, connects the horizon of love with the concrete needs and structures of human life in this universe. The Christian praxis of love in this world must become aware of the structural conditions for and obstacles against any charitable action. Thus, in spite of the shortcomings and problems in the Pope's approach to love discussed above, his encyclical letter encourages us to emphasize the praxis

[112] Tillich, *Love, Power, and Justice*, p. 33.

character of love. Contemplation combined with accompanying critical and self-critical reflection characterize this understanding of praxis.

*En route* towards a deepening of this Christian understanding of love as praxis I wish to turn in the following two chapters to an examination of concrete locations and institutions of love.

## Chapter 7

# *INSTITUTIONS OF LOVE*

### LOVE AND LEARNING

Love can be learned. At various stages of our life we subject ourselves to new learning experiences in the vast field of love. Love is not instinctual behaviour, but a praxis resulting from cultural processes in which each human being passively and actively participates. While only few visit specialized schools of love, all women, men and children can be said to be emerging disciples of love in the different 'schools of life'. Unlike sex, politics, household management, etc., love is not a subject on the school curriculum, yet it relates to all aspects of our lives and it requires learning. The Christian insistence that love ought to be at the centre of all human relationships implies that no specialized approach to one or the other aspect of our relational existence would ever be able to capture the full extent of the potential and praxis of love.

Although love cannot be taught as a special or well-defined academic subject in isolation from our relational existence, all aspects of our lives may be affected by love — God's love, our love, and the love of others. Moreover, the Christian faith expects all baptized children to develop and mature in an active relationship with the ground of all love, God, and to grow in love in their respective family and church environments.

Appreciating the complex process of learning about love in our family life we may speak of the family as an institution of love. However, this expression does not imply that all families everywhere and at all times are the soil in which the seeds of love happily prosper. Nor is this to suggest that all children actually enjoy a happy home in which they can grow up and flourish. Rather, most of us are aware that even the best family life sometimes can be experienced as wanting, oppressive, and, in some instances, even as hell. Yet no child can survive without some measure of love and care. And it is in that connection that the family can be identified and explored as a potential institution of love.

The term 'institution' reminds us of two related dimensions of love: the subjective aspect of love and its social and conventional aspects. Love is never a totally subjective praxis; rather it is shaped in conventional forms and genres handed on to us from previous generations. However, as in the case of language, all these conventions, forms and genres of love are adapted by agents of love to particular occasions and cultural contexts.[1] Normally we have no difficulty in determining whether or not an action, expression or emotion conveys love to us. We recognize the forms of love when we meet them. That we are able to do so is in part the achievement of our first family life: here we have begun the process of learning about love and its many expressions. Whatever our families have taught us about the praxis of love can then in later life be refined, developed, confirmed, negated or sublated. But even these later developments are often interpreted in the light of the primary hermeneutics of love acquired in our earliest years. In that sense, the family — notwithstanding its particular shape and extension — can be appreciated to be the first among the institutions of love that influence and shape our lives.

Friendship, partnership, marriage, church, monasteries and convents, schools, clubs and associations are further institutions of love worth considering in this context. All of these can be named 'institutions' because they help forming love relationships according to particular conventions, rules and expectations. Of course, all of these institutions and the forms and expressions of love they produce have a history. They respond to the challenges of cultural, social and political locations and to the changing awareness of gender. They organize desire and eros both for the loving self and the collective body of loving selves. Institutions of love, at best, facilitate our praxis of love through providing us with conventions, forms, genres and expressions of love from the rich local, regional and global traditions of love. Love is thus not invented anew every day, but it is developed

[1] For a discussion of the relationship between conventional and subjective forms of communication see Werner G. Jeanrond, *Text and Interpretation as Categories of Theological Thinking*, trans. Thomas J. Wilson, Dublin: Gill and Macmillan and New York: Crossroad, 1988; reprint: Eugene, OR: Wipf and Stock, 2005, pp. 73–119.

with the help of the patterns and paradigms inherited that are then adapted, challenged and transformed in the process.

The purpose of this chapter is to explore and assess this combination of institutional and collective patterns of love, on the one hand, and subjective and creative frameworks of love, on the other hand. Given the disproportionate importance of the family as primary among the institutions of love we shall spend some time exploring its natural and metaphorical significance for Christian faith. As will become clear in the course of this chapter, Christian marriage is a function of Christian family and therefore can be adequately understood first after the complexities of the family as an institution of love have come into proper focus. This order of attention will help us to avoid treating of marriage in isolation from all other forms and institutions of love. However, marriage is not the only form of love. Rather, chastity and the forms of love emerging from commitment to a chaste life also deserve recognition and analysis.

## Christian Visions of the Family

The understanding of family life and of its boundaries and extensions has always been subject to cultural development and religious influences. The early Church has been accused of undermining the family structures of the Roman Empire by allowing individual women and men, free citizens as well as slaves, to be baptized into the body of Christ notwithstanding any decision by the family father, who hitherto had been the unchallenged authority in his household.

The New Testament reports of conversions to Christian faith by entire households (e.g. Acts 10; 18.8), but also of the conversion of individuals with the ensuing tension for their respective family or household community (cf. the Letter to Philemon). In common with the surrounding Jewish and Roman models of family organization around a male authority that rules over a unit consisting of the patriarch's biological family as well as slaves, other dependents (employees, clients etc.) and friends, and that decides over their physical and spiritual well-being, the emerging Christian Church increasingly centred around household units. However, it also invited individuals into discipleship of Christ and thus made the boundaries of traditional households more porous. The resulting conflict between family allegiance and Christian discipleship appears in different ways in the Gospels and the New Testament epistles.

Jesus did not challenge the existence of the household structure as such, but he relativized it significantly in the light of his proclamation of the emerging reign of God. For him the crucial unit of faith was the family of God and not any particular household. In other words, Jesus used the household language of his tradition, but he radicalized and extended it to comprise all women and men who do the will of God (Luke 11.27–8; 14.25–6; 18.28–30 and par.). This extension of family is expressed most clearly in this passage of Mark's Gospel:

> Then his mother and his brothers came; and standing outside, they sent to him and called him. A crowd was sitting around him; and they said to him, 'Your mother and your brothers and sisters are outside, asking for you.' And he replied, 'Who are my mother and my brothers?' And looking at those who sat around him, he said, 'Here are my mother and my brothers! Whoever does the will of God is my brother and sister and mother.' (Mark 3.31–5. Cf. also Matt. 12.46–50 and Luke 8.19–21)

The early Christians applied the well-known kinship models to this new family experience when referring to 'brothers (*adelphoi*)' (e.g. Acts 1.15–16). The real head of the Christian household is no longer the *pater familias*, but Christ. Thus, although the family patterns are not abolished, they lose their ultimate significance in God's universal household.

Moreover, the new 'family' bonds in Christ are open to all human beings who are prepared to re-evaluate their traditional patterns of bonding in their respective traditions. The new Christian family is thus not only potentially larger and more inclusive than these conventional patterns of family life, but it also invites the development of new forms of respect, attention and care within the divine–human network of relationships.

The Jesus movement does not do away with family as a basic unit in which love for God, the other and the self is learned and practised. Rather it reinterprets the nature, extension and quality of this new family life. I wish to highlight six of its many features.

First of all, this new family has an eschatological orientation. It expects the fuller emergence of God's reign on earth and accordingly assesses all relationships with respective urgency and commitment.

Secondly, God is identified as the true 'father' of this new family, a father who is known not primarily through his power, but through his love, mercy and compassion, a father who cares for his children and goes out of his way to invite them back to the centre of his love and care (cf. the story of the Prodigal Son in Luke 15). The more personal address of 'Abba', i.e. daddy, adds yet one more expression to this new quality of intimacy between God and his children.

Thirdly, when called upon by Jesus, this father manifests himself in acts of healing, of reconciliation, of affirmation of life, of inclusion of women, sinners, outcasts, the poor and the deprived.

Fourthly, children are given prominence in this family of God. Unlike in the social world of early Christianity where children did not enjoy any great significance or value in their own right, in the Jesus movement children were considered to be of central significance. Jesus welcomes them and challenges his friends who were about to turn them away (cf. Mark 10.13–16 and par.) The Gospels narrate many instances where Jesus demanded from his followers an attitude of childlikeness.

> Childlikeness can symbolize the transformation of priorities and radical countercultural lifestyle required of disciples. Disciples are not to seek status in worldly terms or seek to control others to enhance their own position. Like children, they must accept weakness and social scorn, be obedient and willing to be trained, and comply with the demands placed on them by the community formed around the gospel.[2]

Fifthly, the fatherhood of God does not automatically lead to patriarchal models of authority in this emerging Christian family. Rather, acknowledging God as Father creates space for the Christian community to find new and imaginative ways of inner-family organization that allow the love between all members to become the guiding interest.[3] As we have seen above in chapter 2, Paul offers such an imaginative model of love to the disunited church family in Corinth. God's family is to be characterized by the power of love and not by the exercise of power for the sake of maintaining a patriarchal genre of authority. In this connection it must also be noted that at least some women did in fact function as heads of Christian households (e.g. Lydia, Nympha and Priscilla are always named before their husbands).[4]

Sixthly, the life of both Jesus and Paul unfolded outside of and in contrast to established family structures. They neither married nor built biological families of their own. To be part of God's family, therefore, does not require the establishment of biological families.

[2] Lisa Sowle Cahill, *Family: A Christian Social Perspective*, Minneapolis: Fortress Press, 2000, p. 30.

[3] Cf. ibid., p. 31.

[4] C. J. H. Wright, 'Family', in *The Anchor Bible Dictionary*, vol. 2, New York: Doubleday, 1992, pp. 761–9, here p. 768.

Again, this is not to downgrade or abolish family structures. But it is a clear relativization of the centrality of the institution of family as it was hitherto accepted and practised.

This emerging transformation of ancient family values and its attraction to entire households and individual Jews, Gnostics, and other people in the Roman Empire and neighbouring countries was experienced as a threat to social cohesion by the political and religious authorities of the day, both in Jerusalem and Rome, as well as by regional rulers and in local communities. Christians were accused of disrupting family life, of tearing families apart, of not respecting the traditional patriarchal order of family life and of showing disregard for respective religious and social modes of existence. As a result, Christians were considered a political danger in the Roman Empire.[5] Their understanding of the family was literally going beyond the structures of this world. It represented a massive challenge to traditional family values and patterns of household organization.

It is important to recall this Christian vision of God's always larger family when considering the family as an institution of love. All Christian children should experience love in their immediate surrounding as an encouragement for a lifelong journey into God's always greater family life. God's family is inclusive. It includes not only the biological family, but also the local parish or congregation, the network of Christian communities, and the different interreligious encounters. It also includes the strangers, the others, non-persons, enemies, criminals, losers, and other outcasts.[6] It includes all human persons, for all are bearers of the image of God. It includes the dead and the living members of God's great household. Hence, all Christian family discourse is invited to transcend the narrow limits of the nuclear family, however significant this or any first family experience is for most human beings. 'The Christian family is not the perfect family but one in which fidelity, compassion, forgiveness, and concern for others, even strangers, are known.'[7] In this sense, the Christian family can be seen as a school of intimacy, empathy and love.[8]

Christian family life in its evolving and shifting forms and expressions is, of course, closely linked to the life of the local Christian

[5] See Norbert Brox, *A History of the Early Church*, trans. John Bowden, London: SCM, 1994, pp. 31–46.

[6] Cf. Cahill, *Family*, pp. 130–7.

[7] Ibid., p. 137.

[8] Cf. ibid., p. 130.

community as well as to the larger social and cultural contexts. The one cannot prosper without the other. It is impossible to shape and develop forms of Christian love outside of the interrelated forms and structures of Christian life in this world.[9] Recent attempts in secular Western cultures to demand from one or the other institution of love that it carries the full burden of compensation for the failures of the others have led to a series of implosions. Teachers and school environments will never be able to compensate for the failures of families to be supportive and creative schools of love for their children. Local churches and their leadership cannot compensate for the failures of parents and guardians to provide an initial schooling in love for children. And families cannot properly fulfil this vocation if they are left alone by their local Christian communities and are deprived of necessary spiritual and practical support structures.

It has become a most unfortunate practice to moralize about the ongoing decline in Christian family life and the widespread failure of Christian marriages instead of analysing the interdependence of all institutions of love and their respective requirements for a mutually constructive development. Therefore, it is futile to discuss Christian marriage on its own, i.e. outside of an organic understanding of the praxis of love in Christian community.

## The Potential of Christian Marriage

Most women and men who are entering into marriage today are agreed that marriage ought to be based on the love between both partners.[10] That has not always been so in the past. Marriage is an institution with a long history. When we in the Western world emphasize that the foundation of marriage is love, we often forget that for generations not that long ago marriage was mostly an institution concerning civil law whose purpose was to order property rights and to create a reliable order for the children's legal status and upbringing. Even today, the institution of marriage in our societies includes these legal dimensions; however, their importance has

[9] On the demands on women to combine family and work see Bonnie J. Miller-McLemore, *Also Mother: Work and Family as Theological Dilemma*, Nashville, TN: Abingdon Press, 1994; and Miller-McLemore, 'Family and Work: Can Anyone "Have It All"?', in Anne Carr and Mary Stewart Van Leeuwen, eds, *Religion, Feminism and the Family*, Louisville, KY: Westminster/John Knox Press, 1996, pp. 275–93.

[10] In this section I have used and reworked some of my reflections published earlier in my article 'Det sjunde sakramentet', *Pilgrim* 15:2 (2008), pp. 32–6.

declined while the stress on love has been ever increasing. This shift in awareness has been supported by the fact that today the rights of children are mostly guaranteed independently of marriage laws. Thus, marriage is no longer a legal requirement for the upbringing of children; nor is it needed to order and safeguard property rights. In such a legal sense, marriage has today become dispensable.

Christians might wish to welcome this contemporary concentration of marriage on love. Christian tradition has always claimed that marriage enjoys its origin in God's love for human beings and that the love between a woman and a man has been created by God for the best of both partners (Genesis 1 and 2; Matthew 19; Eph. 5). In Roman Catholic tradition marriage is considered as one of the seven sacraments. Thus it is seen as an instrument of the Holy Spirit, as an integrated part of the efficient reality of divine grace. In marriage, God's gift of love takes shape, becomes visible, embodied, creative and transformative. And although not all Christian traditions consider marriage as a sacrament, all Christians agree that marriage is an integral part of the divine order of creation and reconciliation.

### *An Ambiguous Heritage*

This is not the place for an in-depth study of the complex development of Christian marriage throughout the last twenty centuries. However, some major trends characterizing the changing fortunes of Christian marriage need to be recalled here in order to discern the particular interests and convictions that have been influencing shifting Christian attitudes to marriage.[11] Some form of institution of marriage can be found in almost all cultures past and present.

Often marriage has been associated with religious, sacred or cultic convictions and practices in addition to its usual social, economic, legal and personal function. In Ancient Israel no such concept of 'Sacred Marriage' or 'Holy Wedding' was known, otherwise the constitution and operation of marriage was similar to other cultures in Antiquity.

> Marriage was contractual, not so much between the partners as between their families – in effect, arranged marriages. Ordinarily, personal love and mutual choice were therefore not that which brought about marriage, so that if mutual

[11] I am grateful to my colleague Ian Hazlett for important insights into the complex development of the institution of Christian marriage. See also his, 'Marriage and Heterosexuality in History and Christian Traditions: Some Signposts', in The Church of Scotland, *Reports to the General Assembly 1993*, Edinburgh and London: Pillans & Wilson, 1993, pp. 196–215.

> attraction and a fond relationship occurred, this was in all likelihood an additional bonus, as in the case of Rachel and Jacob.[12]

Marriage has been understood, however differently, within the framework of belief in God's good creation. Whereas Genesis 1 stresses the equality of men and women but does not say anything about institutional forms of partnership, Genesis 2 and 3 subordinates women to men, thereby dissolving marital mutuality in favour of male supremacy and patriarchal rule for centuries to come.[13] In Hosea and Malachi, however, marriage is understood as a covenant between man and woman ratified by God. Moreover, there is a mutual analogy between God's relationship to Israel and between the relationship between man and woman. Erotic images can be found in the descriptions of both kinds of relationships: The Song of Solomon, Ecclesiastes and Proverbs affirm and celebrate erotic love between a man and a woman; the Prophets speak of God's intimate attachment to his bride Israel, though never prompting God to engage in sexual relations with Israel. Here faith in Yahweh differed from surrounding other religions, where the deities were at times portrayed as explicitly sexual.[14]

Although marriage is referred to many times in the Old Testament, no coherent theology of marriage can be distilled. 'Most Jewish marriages, however, were monogamous and as time went on they became more exclusively so.'[15] Nor does the New Testament offer any coherent or consistent approach to marriage. In some passages Jesus is portrayed as linking the institution of marriage to God's will and creation (Gen. 1) and approaching marriage as a fusion of the couple into one flesh (Matt. 19.3–12 and Mark 10.2–12). Other passages question the ultimate significance of marriage in the emerging kingdom of God (Luke 20.27–36) or condemn adultery (Matt. 5.27–32) and divorce (Mark 10.11–12). Interestingly enough, procreation is not a theme in Gospel references to marriage. Moreover, both marriage and celibacy are affirmed as genuine options for the disciples of Christ (Matt. 19.10–12). Although Paul values celibacy somewhat higher than marriage (1 Cor. 7), he still recognizes marriage as divine gift (1 Cor. 7.7) in which the

[12] Ibid., p. 198.

[13] See Victor P. Hamilton, 'Marriage (OT and ANE)', in *The Anchor Bible Dictionary*, vol. 4, New York: Doubleday, 1992, pp. 559–69, here p. 568.

[14] Ibid., p. 566.

[15] Hazlett, p. 199.

God-given bodies of the couple are fused and sanctified (1 Cor. 6.12–20). Nevertheless marriage appears in 1 Corinthians as only the second-best approach to body management:

> To the unmarried and the widows I say that it is well for them to remain unmarried as I am. But if they are not practising self-control, they should marry. For it is better to marry than to be aflame with passion. (1 Cor. 7.8–9; cf. also 7.32–40)

Followers of Paul in subsequent generations of Christians, and further New Testament epistles, adopted a very different line and developed strong defences of married life (Eph. 4.21–5.9; 1 Peter 3.17). Against negative views of marriage among some Gnostic groups, we find in the Pastoral Epistles a clear affirmation of marriage, even for the clergy. Bishops and deacons are to be married, though only once (1 Tim. 3.2, 12).[16] Marriage, not considered as a primary form of Christian discipleship by Paul, has now become an institution of supreme witness to Christ.[17] Moreover, as the love between man and woman could be used by the Prophets in order to characterize the relationship between God and Israel, so Ephesians uses the marriage metaphor in order to describe the relationship between Christ and the Church (5.31–3). In this post-Pauline period of the early Church, patriarchy returned in full power to the household and marriage codes, dominating up to our times Christian approaches to the institution of marriage.[18] Equality between man and woman in the Lord Jesus Christ (Gal. 3.28) did not influence the Christian theology of marriage in practice.[19]

The early Church thus inherited an ambiguous theology of marriage: both marriage and chastity were significant options for Christian discipleship — depending on whom and when one asks. Parallel with the canonization of the New Testament texts that inspire this double legacy, a shift can be observed towards 'the notion that chastity, virginity, celibacy, abstinence etc. were the marks of truly dedicated religion, superior spirituality, and apostolic living. The shunning of eros became therefore a *de facto* Christian duty or goal, even in marriage.'[20]

[16] Cf. Raymond F. Collins, 'Marriage (NT)', in *The Anchor Bible Dictionary*, vol. 4, New York: Doubleday, 1992, pp. 569–72, here p. 572. See also Risto Saarinen, *The Pastoral Epistles with Philemon & Jude*, Grand Rapids: Brazos Press, 2008, p. 67.

[17] Hazlett, p. 201.

[18] Cf. Saarinen, *The Pastoral Epistles with Philemon & Jude*, pp. 54–60.

[19] Hazlett, p. 201.

[20] Ibid., p. 203.

What is left for Christian marriage are the procreation of the human race and, as we have seen already in our discussion of Augustine's view of marriage in chapter 3 above, the containment of sexual concupiscence. A theological discourse on the development of a mutually affective relationship of the Christian couple does not take place in this climate of fusion between Christian and neo-Platonist attitudes to the spiritual vocation of humankind. The progressive spiritualization of love and the increasing upgrading of celibacy and monastic existence as superior forms of discipleship blocked any constructive theological approach to marriage.[21] Instead we find occasional considerations of marriage management with regard to divorce, separation, and remarriage in situations of adultery, but also in the case of putative widows.[22]

Until the High Middle Ages marriage remained largely a matter for families and clans to organize and was not yet subjected to an all-embracing church order.[23] Rather it was often handled in a pragmatic and pastoral spirit in spite of a general agreement among Church Fathers that marriage is a lifelong commitment.[24] It is interesting to note that love did not seem to be of any concern in marriage in the early Middle Ages.[25]

The spiritual, theological, social and cultural changes in Western Europe during the twelfth and thirteenth century (see chapter 4 above) led to a radically new approach to love in Christian thought and practice and also deeply affected the institution of marriage in the Christian Church.[26] Marriage was being rehabilitated as a genuinely Christian option besides the previously higher valued forms of celibate life. Against the Cathars and other marriage-renouncing ascetic movements of the time the Church defended marriage as a divinely instituted form of life. Moreover, under the influence of the

[21] Hazlett, p. 204, discusses one exception to this, namely Christian 'spiritual marriage', i.e. the Platonic cohabitation between men and women. John Chrysostom 'denounced such a practice as unnatural, naïve, irreligious and socially disruptive, since it led to a confusion of typically male and female roles'. Cf. Blake Leyerle, *Theatrical Shows and Ascetic Lives: John Chrysostom's Attack on Spiritual Marriage*, Berkeley, Los Angeles and London: University of California Press, 2001.

[22] For a more detailed discussion of significant sources, see Hazlett, p. 205.

[23] Cf. Hans-Werner Goetz, *Leben im Mittelalter vom 7. bis zum 13. Jahrhundert*, Munich: Beck, 1986, pp. 39–43.

[24] Cf. Hazlett, p. 206.

[25] Cf. Arnold Angenendt, *Geschichte der Religiosität im Mittelalter*, Darmstadt: Wissenschaftliche Buchgesellschaft, 1997, p. 279.

[26] Cf. ibid., p. 285.

Church, marriage was increasingly based on the consent of both the man and the woman, although the influence of the families and clans remained very powerful.[27]

In 1206, in a letter to Archbishop Andreas of Lund, Pope Innocent III confirmed that since a marriage is first consummated in actual intercourse, one of the partners in a marriage may still enter religious life (even without asking the other) so long as no intercourse had occurred.[28] Thus, at the beginning of the thirteenth century the papal emphasis is still on the spiritual lifestyle over against the form of life in marriage involving sexual union. However, at a time when marriages were organized by families and clans, the monastic life remained one of the two other options for men (besides priesthood), but the only other option for women.

The upgrading of marriage to an authentic institution of Christian life further progressed throughout the thirteenth century.[29] Usually three reasons for the goodness of marriage were pronounced: marriage served procreation; marriage supported the growth of love between the partners — unlike today when this love is considered to be the foundation for marriage; and, following the Apostle Paul's view, marriage helps to avoid fornication.[30]

In 1274 the Second Council of Lyons affirmed marriage as one of the Church's seven sacraments.[31] However, the increasing institutionalization and the sacramentalization of marriage must also be seen as aspects in the comprehensive effort of the institutional Church to organize and dominate the entire culture of Europe. Like any other dimension of life, marriage was brought into line with the larger project of building a unified Christian society in Europe through a concerted action of Canon Law and Christian secular authorities.[32] In 1302 Pope Boniface VII published his papal bull *Unam Sanctam* in which he decreed that every human being must necessarily be subjected to the Pontiff in order to attain salvation.[33]

[27] Cf. Goetz, p. 41.

[28] Heinrich Denzinger and Peter Hünermann, eds, *Enchiridion symbolarum definitionum et declarationum de rebus fidei et morum*, 41st edn, Freiburg: Herder, 2007, no. 786, p. 349.

[29] See also W. Knoch, 'Ehe. A.I. Biblisch-Theologisch-Sakramentale Eheauffassung', *Lexikon des Mittelalters*, vol. 3, Munich and Zurich: Artemis Verlag, 1986, pp. 1616–18.

[30] Goetz, p. 44.

[31] Denzinger and Hünermann, eds, *Enchiridion*, no. 860, p. 382.

[32] Cf. Hazlett, p. 206.

[33] Denzinger and Hünermann, eds, *Enchiridion*, no. 875, p. 387.

The Church's official influence on and interference in married life was further strengthened by its effective means of pastoral, confessional and penitential care, so that one can speak of a 'deprivatization' of marital sexual life.[34] However, the actual management of sexuality in and outside marriage has remained a battleground between ecclesial authorities and individual Christians ever since. Also the debate on the relationship between a celibate and a married life within the larger understanding of Christian vocation has continued.

In the Reformation period the institutions of marriage and of celibate life received a new theological assessment. While celibate life was considered to be a gift only for very few Christians, married life was proclaimed to be the most appropriate form of life for most Christians.

Martin Luther went so far as to see marriage as a divine command: all human beings should get married.[35] He conceded only three exceptions to this rule: people who were born unable to get married, people who have been made incapable for marriage by human beings (e.g. eunuchs), and those who renounce marriage for the sake of the kingdom of God.[36] For all others marriage was a God-given and natural form of life. 'One should not consider any other form of life better before God than marriage.'[37] Christian marriage must be lived in respect for the will of God, and not following our feelings.[38] However, even the Christian marriage does not exclude sin: original sin is present and implies 'that no marital duty is discharged without sin'.[39] But God's grace and blessings are present in marriage because it is God's will and good institution.

Luther also considered reasons for divorce, such as incapacity to be married, infidelity, and the refusal of sexual intercourse. In the latter cases he suggested that the civic courts should persecute and judge the culprits and, if applicable, even administer capital punishment.[40] Procreation is a prime task of married life. Luther concluded from this belief that it was perfectly normal and acceptable if women

[34] Cf. Hazlett, p. 207.

[35] Martin Luther, *Vom ehelichen Leben (1522)*, in Martin Luther, *Gesammelte Werke*, ed. Kurt Aland, vol. 7, Digitale Bibliothek 63, Berlin: Direct Media, 2002, pp. 284–306, here pp. 284–5. – *D. Martin Luthers Werke*. Kritische Gesamtausgabe (= *WA*), vol. 10.II, Weimar: Hermann Böhlaus Nachfolger, 1907, pp. 275–304, here p. 276.

[36] Ibid., pp. 285–7. *WA* 10.II, pp. 277–9.

[37] Ibid., p. 304. *WA* 10.II, p. 302.

[38] Ibid., p. 296. *WA* 10.II, p. 295.

[39] Ibid., p. 306. *WA* 10.II, p. 304.

[40] Ibid., pp. 290–1. *WA* 10.II, p. 289.

may die as a result of giving birth to too many children. 'Even if they ultimately become tired or die because of giving birth to children, that does not matter, they are there for this. It is better to live healthily for a short time than unhealthily for a long time.'[41]

In accordance with his theology of the Two Kingdoms Luther did not favour direct church intervention in actual matrimonial questions, but suggested that this was part of the tasks of the civil authorities. Of course, even the civil order is under God's rule; thus, for Luther, marriage is both willed by God and ordered according to God's rule for society. The churches in the Reformed tradition, i.e. those influenced by Bucer, Zwingli, Calvin, Knox etc., differed from Luther by favouring direct pastoral intervention in matrimonial breakdowns in the name of church discipline.[42]

In line with their biblical hermeneutics the Reformers did not consider marriage as a sacrament. It did not fulfil the criteria for a legitimate sacrament, i.e. the institution by Jesus Christ himself and the accompanying signs specified by him.[43] But this desacramentalization of marriage did not diminish its increasingly high status in the theology of the Reformers. They did not always question or alter the classical reasons for marriage, i.e. procreation, avoidance of fornication, and divine institution,[44] although the reformed theologians appealed increasingly to notions of partnership and covenant.[45]

While love was not a predominant part of the Reformation theology of marriage,[46] some new developments can be identified in Luther's approach to marriage and human sexuality. Marriage is a gift of God,

[41] Ibid., p. 303. *WA* 10.II, p. 301. Heiko Oberman's praise for Luther's new evaluation of the vocation of women beyond the usual reduction to childbearing is somewhat challenged by this quote from Luther. Cf. Heiko Oberman, *Luther: Man between God and the Devil,* trans. Eileen Walliser-Schwarzbart, New Haven and London: Yale University Press, 1989, p. 277.

[42] Cf. Hazlett, pp. 209–10.

[43] Hazlett, p. 208. Hazlett discusses also aspects of Calvin's, Bucer's and Zwingli's approaches to marriage. See also Maurice Schild, 'Ehe/Eherecht/Ehescheidung VII', in *Theologische Realenzyklopädie,* vol. 9, Berlin: de Gruyter, 1982, pp. 342–3.

[44] Cf. Rolf Schäfer, 'Ehe. IV. Kirchengeschichtlich', in *Religion in Geschichte und Gegenwart,* vol. 2, Tübingen: Mohr Siebeck, 1999, pp. 1075–7.

[45] Cf. Donald K. McKine, ed., *Encyclopedia of the Reformed Faith,* Louisville, KY: Westminster/John Knox Press and Edinburgh: St Andrew Press, 1992, pp. 235–6.

[46] A notable exception was Martin Bucer. See Hazlett, p. 209; and Herman J. Selderhuis, *Marriage and Divorce in the Thought of Martin Bucer,* trans. John Vriend and Lyle D. Bierma, Sixteenth Century Essays and Studies, vol. 48, Kirksville: Truman State University Press, 1999, pp. 180, 185, 239–40, 243–4.

and sexuality is a healthy elemental force of desire.[47] Luther cannot imagine that a woman or man to whom the high and rare grace of chastity is not given might be able to live without sex. He explains:

> [B]egetting children is as deeply rooted in nature as eating and drinking. That is why God provided the body with limbs, arteries, ejaculation, and everything that goes along with them. Now if someone wants to stop this and not permit what nature wants and must do, what is he doing but preventing nature from being nature, fire from burning, water from being wet, and man [*Mensch*] from either drinking, eating, or sleeping?[48]

However, these convictions did not become prominent in the wider reception of Luther's theology, nor in reformed theology in general. In 1519 — that is, early in the process of Reformation — Luther had published a sermon on marriage in which he still considered marriage to be a sacrament.[49] It is interesting to note how much Luther here emphasizes the divine context of any Christian marriage and the purity of married or 'bridal love'.

> If God himself does not give the wife or the husband, anything can happen. For the truth indicated here is that Adam found no marriageable partner for himself, but as soon as God had created Eve and brought her to him, he felt a real married love toward her and recognized that she was his wife. Those who want to enter into the estate of marriage should learn from this that they should earnestly pray to God for a spouse.[50]

Luther distinguishes between false love (e.g. the love of money, possessions etc.), natural love (e.g. between parents and children and between siblings etc.), and 'a bride's love, which glows like a fire and desires nothing but the husband'.[51] However, as a result of the Fall, 'this love is not pure either, for admittedly a married partner desires to have the other, yet each seeks to satisfy his desire with the other, and it is this desire which corrupts this kind of love'.[52] He therefore likens marriage 'to a hospital for incurables which prevents inmates from falling into graver sin'.[53] The later Luther has, as we have

[47] Cf. Oberman, *Luther*, p. 272–6.

[48] Quoted in Oberman, *Luther*, pp. 275–6, from Luther's *Wider den falsch genannten geistlichen Stand (1522). WA* 10 II, p. 156.

[49] Martin Luther, *A Sermon on the Estate of Marriage*, in *Luther's Works*, vol. 44, ed. and trans. James Atkinson, Philadelphia: Fortress Press, 1966, pp. 7–14, here p. 10. – *Ein Sermon von dem ehelichen Stand. 1519.* In *D. Martin Luthers Werke.* Kritische Gesamtausgabe (= *WA*), vol. 2, Weimar: Hermann Böhlau, 1884, pp. 166–71, here p. 168.

[50] Ibid., p. 8. *WA* 2, pp. 166–7.

[51] Ibid., p. 9. *WA* 2, p. 167.

[52] Ibid.

[53] Ibid.

seen already, developed a more positive approach to marriage and sexuality.

Already in this relatively early text Luther stresses the vocation of parents to bring up their children well. He wanted all married people to know that they 'can do no better work and do nothing more valuable either for God, for Christendom, for all the world, for themselves, and for their children than to bring up their children well'. Bringing up their children properly is 'their shortest road to heaven'.[54]

In a text of 1529 on marriage (printed first in 1530), Luther, who himself had entered marriage with Catherine von Bora in 1525, speaks out against forced engagements, thus adding his voice on behalf of the freedom of the couple to enter into marriage: 'Therefore parents sin against God and nature when they force their children into marriage or to take a spouse for whom they have no desire.'[55]

For Luther, and for Calvin, married life was more than the mere legitimation of sexual fulfilment. It concerned partnership between man and woman, education of the children, and the proper conduct of a household community. This included, most certainly for Luther, also a new appreciation of women as marital companions.[56] Although the theology of the Reformers thus contributed to the further liberation of marriage from its lower spiritual status and introduced some new perspectives, it also tended to make marriage compulsory and 'reinforced general patriarchy, since it virtually extinguished the option of non-marriage for women, with the abolition of female monasticism'.[57] The Reformation theology of marriage has thus not been good news for women overall. Traditional gender roles have been continued and in some instances even reinforced: the man is forcefully propagated as the head of the household. Nor has this theology significantly altered the view of sexuality in Christian faith.[58] '[A]t the end of the day, eros continues to be seen as somehow – or at least potentially – subversive of God, and so something which even married couples ought best to approach with prayer.'[59]

[54] Ibid., p. 12. *WA* 2, p. 170.

[55] Martin Luther, *On Marriage Matters*, trans. Frederick Ahrens, in *Luther's Works*, vol. 46, ed. Robert C. Schultz, Philadelphia: Fortress Press, 1967, 265–320, here p. 304. – *Von Ehesachen. 1530.* In *D. Martin Luthers Werke.* Kritische Gesamtausgabe, vol. 30.III, Weimar: Hermann Böhlaus Nachfolger, 1910, pp. 205–48, here p. 236.

[56] Cf. Carter Lindberg, *The European Reformations*, Oxford: Blackwell, 1996, p. 364.

[57] Hazlett, p. 208.

[58] See Lindberg, *The European Reformations*, pp. 363–6.

[59] Hazlett, p. 209.

The Council of Trent affirmed and explained the sacramental character of marriage in its session of 1563. The indissolubility of marriage is confirmed with reference to the will of both the creator and the redeemer. Moreover, the Council prescribes the form of ecclesial marriage in the presence of the priest and of two or three witnesses as legally binding.[60] It is interesting to note that the doctrinal statements contain a reference to the grace of Christ that 'is to perfect the natural love, to strengthen the indissoluble unity, and to sanctify the marriage partners'.[61] This passage that links the grace of Christ with the love of the couple follows directly to a reference to Matt. 19.6: 'So they are no longer two, but one flesh. Therefore what God has joined together, let no one separate.'[62]

Sixteenth-century approaches to marriage in the Western churches, on the whole, move in established furrows. However, there is a difference between Roman Catholic and Protestant doctrine with regard to the sacramental character of marriage. Whereas Protestants recognize the place of marriage in the order of creation, Catholics confirm the place of marriage in the order of salvation. In the latter order, marriage is grace; in the former, it lives off grace.[63] Yet in both approaches marriage is clearly linked to God's creative and reconciling project. While in Luther, a new appreciation of sexuality eventually emerges, both in his thinking and in the Council of Trent references to the love of the couple appear, however cautiously. Hence, even in matters concerning Christian marriage and love, the sixteenth century represents an important departure towards new developments. However, these developments were eventually overtaken by the more rapid shift to a new evaluation of the human being and his or her rationality in the Enlightenment.

David Hume (1711–76) describes marriage as 'an engagement entered into by mutual consent' whose end is 'the propagation of the species'. It must be 'susceptible of all the variety of conditions, which consent establishes, provided they be not contrary to this end'.[64] Hume discusses advantages and disadvantages for divorce

[60] Denzinger and Hünermann, eds, *Enchiridion*, nos 1797–816, pp. 572–7.

[61] Ibid., no. 1799, p. 573.

[62] Ibid., no. 1798, p. 573.

[63] Cf. Horst G. Pöhlmann, 'Ehe, Ehesakrament. XIV. Im protestantischen Verständnis', in *Lexikon für Theologie und Kirche*, 3rd edn, vol. 3, Freiburg: Herder, 1995, pp. 489–91.

[64] David Hume, 'Of Polygamy and Divorces', in David Hume, *Essays: Moral, Political and Literary*, ed. Eugene F. Miller, Indianapolis: Liberty Fund, 1987, pp. 181–90, here p. 181.

and stresses the male need for freedom ('The heart of man delights in liberty'[65]). However, he argues that the conditions in Europe have ruled out polygamy and divorce and favoured monogamy. He lists three reasons in favour of lifelong marriage or, rather, against divorce: the needs of the children; marital friendship needs external constraints for its development; and finally, the need for security: 'nothing is more dangerous than to unite two persons so closely in all their interests and concerns, as man and wife, without rendering the union entire and total. The least possibility of a separate interest must be the source of endless quarrels and suspicions.'[66]

Immanuel Kant (1724–1804) is in agreement with Hume with regard to male liberty ('Marriage makes the woman free; but the man thus loses his liberty'[67]) and generally shares the patriarchal convictions of the men of his time: men contribute reason to marriage, women taste.[68] In cold legal language Kant defines marriage as 'the union of two persons of different sex for the purpose of lifelong mutual possession of their genital properties'.[69] Unlike Hume, Kant sees the sexual relationship through procreation as fundamental for marriage, 'because otherwise marriage would dissolve itself automatically when producing children stops'.[70] Thus, according to the positive laws of pure reason it is necessary for a man and a woman to get married if they wish to enjoy each other's genital properties.[71] Love does not enter into Kant's understanding of marriage.

Much debate centred on this contractual nature of marriage, its legal requirements and protection and its possible dissolution in law, a debate not directly relevant to our theological exploration of marriage as an institution of love. However, attention to the shifting motivation for marriage does have a major impact on our discussion. As a result of the emergence of an understanding of the self as an autonomous subject, marriage increasingly gained significance for

[65] Ibid., p. 187.

[66] Ibid., p. 189.

[67] Immanuel Kant, *Anthropologie in pragmatischer Hinsicht*, in Kant, *Werke in zehn Bänden*, ed. Wilhelm Weischedel, vol. 10, Darmstadt: Wissenschaftliche Buchgesellschaft, 1983, p. 656.

[68] Kant, *Beobachtungen über das Gefühl des Schönen und Erhabenen*, Kant, *Werke*, vol. 2, p. 867; and *Anthropologie in pragmatischer Hinsicht*, p. 657.

[69] Kant, *Die Metaphysik der Sitten*, in Kant, *Werke*, vol. 7, p. 390.

[70] Ibid.

[71] Ibid.

the promotion of the new self's personal life project. In the context of Romanticism, love resumes prominence as the emerging platform on which a lifelong partnership could be entered. 'Now the stress was on "feelings", "friendship", and "relationship" as the basis of marriage. That is to say, marriage for "love" and "partnership"; love subsists autonomously.'[72]

The emancipation of love and its new linkage to marriage have not automatically led to the emancipation of women; rather the new bourgeois ideal of marriage, favoured widely in Victorian and related Western societies of the nineteenth century, remained 'massively patriarchal: women "need" marriage, since they have a "dependent" nature. Men do a favour by obliging. And, of course, generally speaking, this way of thinking was characterized as "Christian", or at least "pious" and God-fearing'.[73]

Thus, linking marriage with love is as such not yet a promising way forward for Christian men and women to build a common life. The future of Christian marriage as an institution of love needs more than a confession of mutual love and more than a mutual appreciation of the potential bliss of the sexual expression and sharing of such love. Reflecting on 1 Corinthians 7.32, Jean Calvin warned against any glorification of marriage:

> It is a great advantage to those intending to be married that they be warned in advance about the troubles, so that if they later unexpectedly encounter them, they may not fall into despair. We see that happening to a great many. They promised themselves pure honey, but when that hope does not materialise in reality, the slightest mishap is enough to depress them. Therefore, let them know in good time what they should expect, so that they may be prepared to put up with everything ... anxieties, which are in contrast to wedding receptions, hilarity, and other joyful circumstances.[74]

### *A Future for Christian Marriage?*

Although marriage is by no means the only institution for the ordering of love in our societies and although its conditions and shapes are always changing, it still enjoys a great attraction even among secularized contemporaries. Weddings are celebrated with ever-increasing pomp and splendour in our societies. Service indus-

[72] Hazlett, p. 213.

[73] Ibid., p. 214.

[74] Jean Calvin, *Commentary on the Epistles of Paul the Apostle to the Corinthians*, trans. from the original Latin and collated with the author's French version by John Pringle, vol. 1, Edinburgh: T. Constaple for the Calvin Translation Society, 1848, p. 259 (adapted). Cf. Hazlett, p. 209.

tries have long recognized the financial potential of weddings and, as a result, developed all-inclusive packages for the preparation, organization, and celebration of weddings as well as, more recently, for the legal and ritual dissolution of marriages. Various media and TV shows give endless support to this buoyant wedding and divorce industry. Even among those women and men who have experienced marriage as a disappointment, if not as a terrible tragedy, many would wish to enter afresh into marriage with a new partner.[75] Marriage is in fact so attractive an institution that groups hitherto excluded from it, such as homosexuals and lesbians, have now demonstrated their interest in this traditionally heterosexual institution as an ideal and publicly recognized form of organizing human love.

Do these cultural trends really confirm or support any traditional Christian marriage ideal? I do not think so. For not only the understanding of marriage in secular society has changed, but also the Christian understanding of marriage and love has undergone radical transformations. As we have seen already above and in chapter 3, marriage was understood for a very long time as a kind of necessary management for sinful human sexuality. Augustine argued that sexual intercourse in marriage was not sinful as long as it was serving human procreation. Yet it remained sinful if it was serving merely the satisfaction of human lust. This view of marriage has changed dramatically even in Christian praxis. Today, marriage is defined less in terms of organizing the external framework of the Christian love life or the rationality of sexual intercourse; rather marriage is approached as an institution of love.

At times it is argued that Christian love ought to be distinguished radically from other forms of human love. I consider such an approach wrong and dangerous. Instead I would like to argue that the difference between a Christian marriage and other forms of marriage cannot be found in a difference of love, but in a difference of love's basic orientation or horizon. A Christian couple celebrates their love as a transformative gift of God, a gift that always transcends the mutual attraction, attention and enjoyment of both partners towards God's universal family.

The Christian couple is thus never alone or isolated in its love. Rather, through love it opens itself to God and God's emerging

[75] Cf. Ulrich Beck and Elisabeth Beck-Gernsheim, *The Normal Chaos of Love,* trans. Mark Ritter and Jane Wiebel, Cambridge, UK: Polity Press, 1995, pp. 172–3.

reign in this universe. Hence, it would be wrong to argue for a separate Christian love, since, according to Christian faith, all genuine love originates in God. In this faith all love implies a vocation to a mature development of the self and its openness to other selves, including God and God's creative and reconciling project.

A sacramental understanding of marriage thus does not result from any particular sacred form of Christian love that would differ from so-called worldly forms of love. Genuine love will always seek the well-being of the other and the transformation of the self in this meeting with the other, and possibly even with God, the radical other. Yet Christian marriage implies an attempt to love not only from the energy of love which both partners contribute to their common life, but also from the loving encounter with God's love which plays an active part throughout Christian marriage as a creative, reconciling and transformative spirit.

This loving encounter necessarily also has an ecclesial dimension. In theological thinking we must avoid separating the Christian couple from the church community. Instead it is important to recall that a Christian couple is married in the midst of the Christian community because it is precisely here that it intends to open itself to God's gracious gift of love and in this way to share in the body of Christ. Christian marriage therefore is a body-building activity, not beyond or apart from the union of the couple; rather the couple's union occurs within the emerging body of Christ, i.e. in the Church. Christian marriage receives its sacramental spirit from this participation and transformation within Christ's eschatological body. Marriage is an integral part of the divine project of creation and reconciliation.

This understanding of marriage might also offer an appropriate starting point for a theological discussion of a possible broadening of the concept of marriage beyond the traditionally heterosexual framework. In Christian homosexual and lesbian partnership, as in heterosexual partnership, the point is the faithful and committed opening towards God's gift of love. Therefore, the consideration of the appropriateness in any given church of just offering a mere blessing to this or that form of lifelong partnership will never suffice either to do justice to the depth of the ecclesial interconnectedness between all forms and institutions of love in Christ or to stress the obligation to relate a couple's praxis of love intimately to the mystery of Christ's emerging body.[76]

Unfortunately, the full impact of such an understanding of the sacramental spirit of love has often been repressed in ordinary church life. Instead of deepening insights into this mystery attempts have been made to define *Christian* love as something totally different and unique. As we have seen in chapter 3, Augustine considered God as the only real subject of love whereas human beings were not able to love in the fuller sense of the word. Sexuality, i.e. the physical possibility to express and form human love, was considered sinful and shameful by this Church Father and his many followers. He imagined Christian body-building rather in Platonic forms: the body of Christ without any real human embodiment. For Augustine, marriage had nothing essential to contribute to the advent and quality of God's reign.

Against this background it must be considered a great step forward when the medieval Church defined marriage as a sacrament. Now the relationship between a man and a woman was appreciated as a natural part of God's ongoing project of creation and healing. Moreover, in more recent times, this sacrament has been increasingly based on the free will and unconditional commitment of the woman and the man to love each other. Neither God nor the Church administers the sacrament of marriage; rather the partners themselves administer this sacrament to each other in the presence of the Christian community, represented by the priest and the witnesses. Against the power and interest of families, dynasties and clans, the free choice of partners is thus confirmed. Moreover, the connection between God and human beings receives a suitable expression in this sacramental approach to marriage. Now, the institution of Christian marriage appears as an efficient sign of God's grace, as a sacrament within the covenant between Christ and his Church.

Even though Martin Luther and the other great Reformers did not readily speak of marriage in terms of an ecclesiastical or canonical sacrament, as we have seen above, they all share the conviction that Christian marriage is willed by God. However, Paul's suggestion that marriage was God's remedy against human weakness (1 Cor. 7.2)

[76] See also Werner G. Jeanrond, 'The Concept of Love in Christian Tradition', in The Theological Committee of the Church of Sweden, *Love, Cohabitation and Marriage: Report from a Public Hearing September 6–9, 2004*, trans. John Toy, Uppsala: The Church of Sweden 2006, pp. 183–93.

continues to haunt Christian tradition.[77] The fact that God has called some human beings to renounce married life for the sake of God's reign is appreciated both in the Roman Catholic tradition and by Martin Luther, although he thought, as shown above, that only very few human beings were called to a celibate life.

A sacramental understanding of marriage underlines the perspective of eternity for human love. Through the marriage vows the Christian couple demonstrate their openness to God's eternal love. In this context eternity does not mean unending time; rather it refers to the quality of God's presence. Participating in God's love links the couple to a transcendent source of energy, an energy in which the partners can both enjoy and explore each other's difference and otherness. Moreover, in this love both partners can open themselves to God's radical otherness and to God's transformative presence in the Church, i.e. the Christian fellowship of love. The vocation of love is not to harmonize all differences; rather it is the vocation of love to allow every human being ultimately to shine in her particular uniqueness and otherness. The body of Christ is radically pluralist precisely because of its body-building potential. This body is never uniform, but united in the mysterious pluriformity of love.

The unconditional mutual commitment in love implies for the Christian couple openness to God's eternity and a willingness to love eternally. Loving the other as other can never come to a conclusion; it involves the lover always more deeply in the other's life as well as in God's — the radical other's — eternal life. Only in this multidimensional eternal process of love can I become truly myself. In this sense Christian marriage implies a radicalization of love: in getting married I open up a pathway (to be sure, not the only possible one) to be transformed by God's grace. By this grace the couple participates in the community of the saints. And it is in this horizon that the couple's possible act of conceiving children could be theologically assessed. If God is acknowledged as present in marriage, then the possible gift of children in such a marriage is linked to God's creative presence, and the children themselves are from their beginning seen as welcome, respected and loved participants in Christ's body.

[77] Cf., for example, *Confessio Augustana* XXIII, in Jaroslav Pelikan and Valerie Hotchkiss, eds, *Creeds and Confessions of Faith in the Christian Tradition*, vol. 2, Part Four: *Creeds and Confessions of the Reformation Era*, New Haven and London: Yale University Press, 2003, p. 79.

The Second Vatican Council has contributed richly to a new appreciation of the sacrament of marriage and related theologies of marriage. 'This shift can be summarized as one which moved from viewing marriage primarily as a biological and juridical union to one which is more interpersonal, spiritual and existential.'[78] Love is now at the centre of marriage. And sexual intimacy is not only acknowledged, but praised as one important aspect of human dignity. Married love is understood as 'an eminently human love'.[79] Thus, the particularity of human love is both recognized and emphasized — no longer as a more or less defective copy of divine love, but as a form of love *sui generis* and willed by God. '[T]he acts in marriage by which the intimate and chaste union of the spouses takes place are noble and honorable; the truly human performance of these acts fosters the self-giving they signify and enriches the spouses in joy and gratitude' (*Gaudium et Spes* 49).[80]

The procreation and education of children are rooted in married love (*Gaudium et Spes* 50).[81] Family life is considered much more multidimensional than in the previous history of the Christian Church. The understanding of marriage is now firmly linked to an appreciation of the human self and its development in human love.

> Without intending to underestimate the other ends of marriage, it must be said that true married love and the whole structure of family life which results from it is directed to disposing the spouses to cooperate valiantly with the love of the Creator and Saviour, who through them will increase and enrich his family from day to day. (*Gaudium et Spes* 50)[82]

The Council unambiguously stresses that marriage is valuable in itself as an institution of love.

> But marriage is not merely for the procreation of children; its nature as an indissoluble compact between two people and the good of the children demand that the mutual love of the partners be properly shown, that it should grow and mature. Even in cases where despite the intense desire of the spouses there are no children, marriage still retains its character of being a whole

[78] David M. Thomas, 'Marriage', in Joseph Komonchak, Mary Collins and Demot A. Lane, eds, *The New Dictionary of Theology*, Dublin: Gill and Macmillan, 1987, pp. 624–8, here p. 624.

[79] *Pastoral Constitution on the Church in the Modern World* (*Gaudium et Spes*) (1965) 49, in Austin Flannery, OP, ed., *Vatican Council II: The Conciliar and Post Conciliar Documents*, Northport, NY: Costello Publishing Company, 1988, pp. 903–1014, here p. 952.

[80] Ibid.

[81] Ibid., p. 953.

[82] Ibid.

manner and communion of life and preserves its value and indissolubility. (*Gaudium et Spes* 50)[83]

It is important once more to recall that Christian marriage does not differ from other forms of marriage or partnership because of any specific *Christian* love, but through its theological radicalization of human love. Naturally, a Christian couple like any other couple undergoes love's different stages: beginning with a first intensive encounter, through the different phases of falling in love including mutual attraction and desire after physical union, to an ever deeper friendship and respect for one another and to an always more mature, more subtle erotic expression of love. Emotions and imagination play their respective part in this intense participation of the lovers in the great building of a new body. Hence, it is urgent to overcome any fear for the human body if Christian work on the great body of love is to succeed.

At the same time, Christian 'body builders' ought not to be blind to existing and emerging obstacles, disturbances, distortions, conflicts and wrong orientations. The interpersonal quality of fidelity requires the accompanying quality of forgiveness.

Marital forgiveness is that special virtue of marriage where one forgives the hurts inflicted upon oneself by one's spouse either intended or unintended. Given the nature of interpersonal development, it inevitably happens that each will experience the other's sinful nature and the narrowness which comes with human limitation. Acceptance and forgiveness are demanded to support an on-going relationship.[84]

In our individualized, Western culture marriage is often approached in terms of a project that only concerns two individuals, a twofold project that is nobody else's business. Even Christian lovers suffer at times from such an individualistic approach to marriage or partnership. If they reflect on what they may get out of their marriage, they have already completely misunderstood the vocation of Christian marriage.

Christian marriage does not demand anything less from me than the investment of my whole self in the dynamic structure of relationship where my self will be transformed in the encounter with my partner's otherness, with God as the radical other, and with God's community of the saints — the living and the dead. Outside of this comprehensive relational horizon marriage runs the risk of

[83] Ibid., p. 954.

[84] Thomas, 'Marriage', p. 626.

implosion. The Church as God's own institution of love, therefore, has the task to support, facilitate and integrate every Christian marriage or partnership covenant. Today, the mutual responsibility of Christian marriage and of the overall project of Christ's Church must be emphasized more clearly.[85] Moreover, new and better forms of Christian networking must be developed in order more adequately to support Christian marriage in its different phases and stages.[86]

The failure of a marriage is always also a fiasco for the entire Church and not only for the separating couple itself. Therefore it is so crucial to reflect anew on how the Church as the body of Christ can take on more responsibility for the support of marriages and not be content with administering well-tuned wedding ceremonies.

When we consider marriage in sacramental terms we signal that we wish to shoulder greater responsibility for the ecclesial climate in which human love projects are becoming open to God's eternal horizon of love; a greater responsibility not only for the beauty of the wedding ceremony, but for the complex everyday life and challenges of the marriage. At the same time, a sacramental understanding of marriage demands a renewed and deepened understanding of the Church: Christian marriage has its home in the Christian community and therefore has the right to expect encouragement and support for its contribution to the emergence of Christ's body. Seeing marriage as a sacrament means to believe in God's creative, reconciling and transformative presence in all dimensions and phases of the life of a marriage.

Marriage is not the only institution of love. The Christian Church has had a shifting appreciation of alternative institutional forms of love. While the early Church ranked a celibate existence, alone or in a monastic community, as the better form of love, since the Reformation marriage has increasingly developed into the standard form for living Christian love while forms of a chaste life have become more exotic in our Western understanding.

[85] See here also Göran Bexell, *Etiken, bibeln och samlevnaden: Utformningen av en nutida kristen etik, tillämpad på samlevnadsetiska frågor,* Stockhom: Verbum (1988), 1991, p. 174: Therefore I cannot really agree with David M. Thomas, who argues that in view of 'the general lack of external support for preserving marriage provided by society, it is necessary that marriage be held together by values within' (ibid., p. 626). A marriage cannot live solely from its own inner resources.

[86] 'The Church should not only propagate certain values, but ought to contribute to their realization, in the first place through actively following the love commandment when it meets with individual women and men.'

Before examining further forms and institutions of love in our changing world in the next chapter, it might be appropriate here to discuss the provocative nature of chastity more generally in the light of love. Is chastity necessarily opposed to the fuller expression of love or has it a potential role to play in all forms of love?

## Love and Chastity

For many of our contemporaries chastity and love do not go well together.[87] Some reject chastity as the opposite of love; others raise chastity to the level of an elitist form of love. Both interpretations are the result of a distorted understanding of chastity and its potential to strengthen love.

Until the Reformation, Christian traditions, as we have seen, valued married life (and sexual expressions of love generally) less than virginity and celibacy. The early Fathers usually equated chastity with celibacy and virginity, rather than marital fidelity. And Thomas Aquinas confirmed the usual hierarchy of perfection according to which virgins came first, followed by the sexually continent widowed persons; and married persons take the last place.[88] The Council of Trent in 1563 stressed this order once again when it stated that it was wrong to claim that marriage was equal to virginity and celibacy.[89] Marriage and human sexuality belonged to the lower states of Christian existence and aspiration. The Second Vatican Council upgraded Christian marriage. However, the fact that the Roman Catholic Church still links priesthood with celibacy underlines both the continuing dominance of this hierarchy of perfection and the continuing intermingling of monastic values and aspirations with a Christian understanding of forms of love. Against this background I would like to reflect on the potential of chastity for a non-monastic, creation-affirming Christian praxis of love.

The point of this reflection, however, is in no way anti-monastic. I fully support religious life as one form of the Christian praxis of love and I firmly defend the need for celibacy in monastic life. But I also recognize the duty of Christian theology to reflect on other equally

[87] In this section I have reworked some reflections published earlier in my article 'Kärlekens sanna samvete', *Pilgrim* 13:1 (2006), pp. 20–3.

[88] See Fiona Bowie, 'Chastity', in Adrian Hastings, Alistair Mason and Hugh Pyper, eds, *The Oxford Companion to Christian Thought*, Oxford: Oxford University Press, 2000, pp. 108–9, here p. 109.

[89] Denzinger and Hünermann, eds, *Enchiridion*, no. 1810, p. 575.

important forms of love which affirm human sexuality as a gift and a blessing. And it is in this context that I wish to consider the potential of chastity for love.

If chastity is reduced to an attitude against the body it misses the necessary embodiment of human love. No human being is able to love outside of her or his body. Thanks to my body I can relate to other persons, to God, to the created universe, and even to my own emerging self. I am a bodily unit, or, as the Christian tradition used to express it, I am both body and soul. Any attempt to separate both dimensions would lead to illness and eventually to death. However, as a human being I am endowed with the possibility to build 'bodies'; I am able to love and thus to become part of larger 'bodies', such as friendship, marriage, family, monastic communities, church communities, and the body of Christ. There are many forms for expressing and shaping love.

Reducing love to only sexuality or even to mere genital acts would imply a catastrophic reduction of human possibilities for love in our lives. To remain meaningful for love, chastity needs to be approached in terms of a bodily relationship to the body. Chastity and body belong together. How can I grasp the meaning of both?

An analysis of the complex history of chastity in Christian tradition points to many efforts of upgrading renunciation to a human achievement on the way to sacred perfection. In all epochs of church history we can observe attempts to reach, or even to force, holiness through different forms of castigating the body, asceticism, renunciation, and even maltreatment of or contempt for the body. Masters of asceticism can be found in all religious movements. However, motives behind asceticism vary significantly. Renunciation might be one way of protesting against a certain religious, social, political or cultural regime.

Peter Brown has shown that the forms that such renunciation took in the early Church varied greatly. 'In each area, sexual renunciation carried a significantly different message, and led to the formation of different patterns of life within the local churches. In the Latin West, "holiness and continence of the flesh" tended to gravitate around the clergy of the Catholic church.'[90]

[90] Peter Brown, *The Body and Society: Men, Women and Sexual Renunciation in Early Christianity*, London: Faber & Faber, 1990, pp. 202–3. See also Margaret A. Farley, *Just Love: A Framework for Christian Sexual Ethics*, New York and London: Continuum, 2006, pp. 252–9.

Certain representatives for Gnostic forms of religion, that developed roughly at the same time as the Christian movement, considered any sexual act as a naïve affirmation of the ruling cosmic order, an order deemed evil by all Gnostics. The really good order exists outside of this cosmos. The good God must be clearly distinguished from the demiurge, i.e. the creator of this bad cosmos. This dualistic faith demands renunciation of every aspect of this creation which tries to capture our souls. Thus, one must try to remain clean, pure, unaffected by the physical order for the sake of the only true universe which lies beyond our embodied reality.[91] Gnosticism has left traces even in the Christian movement, not least through those Church Fathers, such as Augustine, who considered sexuality as impure, as the carrier of original sin from one generation to the next. Here, as always, sexuality and sexual renunciation are approached from very distinctive perspectives.

Even though we today assess love, chastity and sexuality in often radically different ways, even we approach these phenomena from a distinct perspective. What hermeneutics of body, love, chastity and sexuality do we favour?

In our Western culture we are rightly proud of our perspective of freedom. Humanism, Reformation, Enlightenment and many postmodern analyses have conveyed to us a sense of freedom from all sorts of external, foreign and unreasonable coercion as well as from a culture of murky purity laws and prescriptions. At least theoretically, we feel free from contempt of our body, from religious taboos, from the power of priests prescribing ways of expressing love, and from the distorted symbolic world of the chastity belt. We know that love is embodied and that it demands freedom.[92]

I am happy about any progress in this regard. Yet I often wonder *to what* I am actually liberated. How shall I invest my great freedom in my different love projects? What kind of constructive relationship do I have to my body now that this relationship has been liberated from all forms of oppression?

Looking around and exploring myself in any depth I recognize that I am not fully able to reach my body all on my own. My relationship

[91] See Norbert Brox, *Erleuchtung und Wiedergeburt: Zur Aktualität der Gnosis,* Munich: Kösel, 1989; and Brox, 'Selbst und Selbstentfremdung in der Gnosis. Heilsaussicht durch Erkenntnis. Die Religion Gnosis', in Brox, *Das Frühchristentum: Schriften zur Historischen Theologie,* Freiburg i. B.: Herder, 2000, pp. 255–70.

[92] For a discussion of different approaches to the relationship between love and freedom see Björn Larsson, *Besoin de liberté,* Paris: Seuil, 2006, pp. 110–13.

to my body remains problematic. Confronted with a massive media approach to body and bodies, I am not so sure whether or not my body will do. Does this fragile body really support my desires and advances on the terrain of love? Or should I first plan for some necessary improvements of my body — invest in a better, slimmer, younger, stronger, and more attractive body? Would I be more loveable if I were to look different — given that there is no love without the body? How should I interpret this insight? How do I harmonize my deficient at-oneness with my body with my knowledge of my body's significance for love?

Ultimately, I realize that I do not *have* a body — I do not possess my body, but I am an embodied being on the way to becoming human with other human beings. How shall I understand my body's limitations and possibilities to love?

It is becoming clear that my body on its own is not in a position to provide me with a large enough perspective to contemplate love, chastity and sexuality on any deeper level. None of my attempts to control my body, either through expensive interventions or through radical forms of renunciation, automatically leads to love. I cannot make myself loveable. Nor do I reach love through intense efforts of renunciation or asceticism. Neither body nor chastity offers me sufficient perspectives on love. Does love provide me with a perspective on chastity and body?

Biblical faith praises love as God's gift to us human beings. Love is the centre of Christian discipleship: we are invited to love God, our neighbours, and ourselves. Israel received this gift from God; Jesus confirmed it through his life, proclamation, death and resurrection; and the Holy Spirit continues to inspire us to love within the Body of Christ, the Church.

Love comes to me from outside and draws me into the deeper context made possible by God's creative and reconciling process. I am free to say yes or no to the gift and vocation of love. I have to make up my mind: will I, can I, dare I accept the gift of love? Do I really wish to share in the 'body-building' dynamics of love? Do I want to relate to everybody and everything in the horizon of love? Do I want to love God, God's creation, my neighbour and myself? Do I want to belong to Christ and with Christ to God (1 Cor. 3.23)?

If I say yes to the gift of love, I am drawn into a revolutionary horizon. Love embraces me and I can begin to contemplate the question to which of love's projects and forms I feel called. All of love's projects share an orientation to the well-being of the other: God, the partner, the neighbour, the fellow religious, my own emerging self. All manifestations of love are interconnected. Notwithstanding which of the loves I desire, the others will also be present within love's horizon. Love is one, it embraces all, but its forms are many.

In this horizon of love the potential of both body and chastity emerges anew. The horizon of love reveals the body's ultimate vocation to become part of larger 'bodies'. It reveals also the potential of chastity to enable me to consider and decide in which of the 'body-building' projects I should be engaged. In the horizon of love chastity turns into a virtue — the virtue to assess the right relationship to my body, to my corporality in all projects of love.

Hence, chastity is not the way towards love, but the way in love to explore love's wider horizon within Christian discipleship. In that sense it may well be meaningful to speak of 'chaste love' and to continue our exploration of chastity's potential.

In the horizon of love, chastity means much more than renunciation or asceticism. Love looks for the other, desires to be with the other, to build relationship and community, to become one body with the other and the others. Chastity in the horizon of love therefore is something radically different than individual ascetic exercises, subtle psychological processes of sublimation or physical exercises aiming at reaching God and holiness via the 'perfect' speedway.

A Christian praxis of love has nothing to do with self-centred body tactics or with renunciation for renunciation's sake. God's love does not demand ascetic exercises, contempt of body, or obsession with the body. Rather, God's love longs for the corporeal presence of the whole human person and its transformation into the body of Christ. Chastity understood as a hunt for holiness has nothing whatsoever to do with love.

Chastity as a virtue of love is something different. This sort of chastity wishes to test the body's love potential in depth. This might imply that one abstains from certain foods, from sexual intimacy, from talking, from being silent, from asceticism, from everything that involves my physical self, but now *for the sake of love.*

Moreover, chastity in the horizon of love opens space for testing my particular vocation within God's larger community of love. Am I called to marriage, to family life, to partnership, to monastic life, to a hermit's life, to a solitary life among people? Chastity is necessary for determining whether or not I am called to live in such forms of life that require lifelong celibacy, e.g. monastic life, the life of a hermit, or a single life among people. But there is also a need for a time of chastity while I am determining whether or not I should enter into married life, partnership, or family life.

Chastity as a virtue of love leads me to self-examination: am I able to live in a community of love or am I still too much limited by or even obsessed with my own ephemeral bodiliness, individuality, sexuality, identity and piety? Chastity allows me to test my ability for bodily relationship and my eroticism. Do I genuinely long to relate to the other and the other's well-being? Or am I first and foremost concerned about consuming, about incorporating the other into my own ego? Do I want to meet the other as other, make myself vulnerable for the other's otherness? Or am I on the way to instrumentalize the other according to my own assumed needs and desires?

The point of chastity in the Christian praxis of love is not to become world champion in renunciation; rather the point is to learn to see the other, i.e. God, God's universe, my neighbour and myself in the horizon of love. This kind of chastity, then, has nothing to do with body acrobatics or a dualistic contempt for the body, but with the insight into the fact that the Christian praxis of love requires full bodily presence.

Chastity in Christian tradition then is not necessarily the opposite of love or an elitist exercise in love. Rather, chastity thus understood is the true conscience of Christian love. The Christian self is called to love. Chastity helps the self to examine and purify love's intentions. When I am uncertain about my real intentions in my relations and relational networks, I need chastity. When I am uncertain about my partner's intentions, I need chastity. Chastity thus is an opportunity for me to test the depth of my love — and, of course, the degree of my openness to the divine dynamics of love.

Chastity in Christian praxis, therefore, must not be limited to sexual abstinence. Its radius is much greater: it examines, exposes and challenges all bonds that slow down the free and dynamic development of love. I need to be freed from everything that hinders me from loving my loved ones for their sake, God for God's sake, my neighbours for their sake, and my own self for my own self's sake.

Chastity thus is a virtue that requires training as long as I live. It grows through prayer and attention. It develops through concentrating on the other and others in love. Chastity and love go hand in hand.

In the next chapter we shall continue our explorations of institutions and horizons of love.

## Chapter 8

# *THE POLITICS OF LOVE*

### FRIENDSHIP: PERSONAL LOVE AND ETERNAL HORIZON

In the previous chapter we considered family, marriage, partnership and chastity as primary coordinates for our own human development as loving subjects. We learn to cultivate the gift of love in community, and we encounter the different forms of love and desire for love both in the concrete praxis of different communities, but, of course, also through the evocations produced and disseminated by our globalizing networking technologies. Becoming a responsible subject of love is a lifelong learning process of encountering and exploring relational possibilities and limitations and of managing respective desires.

Christian as well as secular thinkers have always paid attention to friendship as that form of love that exists at the intersection between personal and public realms of life. In every culture we seem to be able to find some concept of friendship. In our Western cultures we can observe a broad spectrum of intensity associated with the experience of friendship. We can read or hear about extraordinary friendships that have saved lives under tyrannies and we can hear our contemporaries refer to their hundreds or even thousands of friends on Facebook. Thus, minimally, we understand friendship to consist of some bond, some shared aspect of life, and, maximally, we appreciate friends as lifelong fellow travellers. Moreover, friendship is not restricted to some religious realm; rather it can be experienced in every segment of society.

Today friendship is widely valued as a stabilizing factor in a rapidly changing environment: in times of need, of persecution, of chaos, of disintegration of social patterns or of rapid globalization, close friends may provide security, orientation and reliability. Reliable personal relationships offer human subjects a stable network in which they can live and develop. Moreover, today friendships are valued sometimes even more highly than forms of marital or partnership love because they do not seem to call for this exclusive and demanding lifelong commitment to one person. Hence, the attraction of friendship might increase in times such as ours when marital love is seen to be making very demanding claims on the human person.

Like all the other forms of love, even friendship has a history. For most parts of the development of Western culture, true friendship has been seen as the domain of men. Only in recent centuries have women been publicly acknowledged as equal subjects in friendship, although in fact friendship among women has of course always existed.[1]

In his much-acclaimed book *The Four Loves* (1960) C. S. Lewis described friendship as 'unnecessary': 'Friendship is unnecessary, like philosophy, like art, like the universe itself (for God did not need to create). It has no survival value; rather it is one of those things which give value to survival.'[2]

This assessment would not make much sense today to youngsters troubled by a rapidly changing society, to politicians needing the support of friends for their political careers and ambitions, or to business people that know to value essential networks of friends. These groups of people are all agreed upon the need to have friends for survival — albeit different forms of survival.[3]

In her recent study of friendship, the Swedish historian Eva Österberg argues that 'friendship is part of those conditions without which human beings cannot live'.[4] Thus, for her, friendship is eminently necessary. Our human individuality is shaped through meetings with other human beings, and especially with those people we call friends. Friendship can be found in the private sphere, in the half-private sphere, and in public life.[5]

Friendship functions as a summary term for forms of free relationships built on respect, trust, honesty, obligation and mutuality. Of course, such a wide definition of friendship could also apply

[1] Cf. Eva Österberg, *Vänskap – en lång historia*, Stockholm: Atlantis, 2007, pp. 160 and 287.

[2] C. S. Lewis, *The Four Loves*, Glasgow: Collins Paperback, 1981, p. 67.

[3] For a more extensive critique of Lewis' approach to friendship see Janet Martin Soskice, *The Kindness of God: Metaphor, Gender, and Religious Language*, Oxford: Oxford University Press, 2007, pp. 157–80, esp. pp. 162–6.

[4] Österberg, *Vänskap – en lång historia*, p. 43.

[5] Cf. ibid., p. 38.

to many contemporary experiences of marriage and lifelong partnership. However, in spite of this actual overlap between marital love and friendship, this wider understanding of friendship does not presuppose or require intimate expressions of love. Moreover, friendships can grow with people, and they cease to develop or to exist altogether when circumstances in life change and when friendships no longer receive the necessary attention and care. Friendships need not be symmetrical: older people can be friends with younger people and vice versa. Teachers and students can develop friendships. In classical Greek culture, these teacher–student friendships were considered the highest manifestation of male friendship.

Like all other human phenomena, friendship can also have negative or problematic features: friendship, even the most genuine, devoted and honest friendship, can prove to be dangerous for the lives of the friends when it puts these very lives at risk. Such was the case with Jesus who, in the interpretation of John's Gospel, sacrificed his life for his friends. This Gospel portrays Jesus addressing his friends at the Passover meal after having washed their feet in a lengthy discourse (John 13–17), to which the following well-known passage belongs:

> This is my commandment, that you love one another as I have loved you. No one has greater love than this, to lay down one's life for one's friends. You are my friends if you do what I command you. I do not call you slaves any longer, because the slave does not know what the master is doing; but I have called you friends, because I have made known to you everything that I have heard from my Father. You did not choose me but I chose you. And I appointed you to go and bear fruit, fruit that will last, so that the Father will give you whatever you ask him in my name. I am giving you these commands so that you may love one another. (John 15.12–17)

In this model of friendship shared knowledge and insight as well as dominical election and definite expectations are prominent features. The Johannine Jesus goes on to alert his friends that the world will hate them for his sake. Thus, there can be no doubt about it: friendship with Jesus is a dangerous gift. Moreover, as we have seen already above in chapter 2, this Gospel establishes a direct link between the divine love commandment and the friendship within the inner circle of Christ's followers. Against a hostile world, the Johannine disciples find reassurance in the bond of mutual friendship.

The Synoptic Gospels report how friendship among Jesus' followers can be perverted, can become disingenuous and life-threatening: Judas, one of Jesus' close friends, betrays him to the authorities with a kiss, i.e. the sign of love, in public (Mark 14.43–6; Matt. 26.47–50; Luke 22.47–8). The tragedy about Judas was thus not only that he had broken his friendship with Jesus and his disciples, but also that he misused the kiss, i.e. the sign of closeness, friendship, love and equality, in order to betray Jesus. Here a friend's love turned into hatred and destruction. Expressions of love became destructive.

The Gospel of Mark paints a rather dark picture of the quality of the friendship that exists between the disciples of Jesus and their master. At crucial moments in Mark's story, Jesus' friends either misunderstand him or betray him. Christian friendship thus is not as original or prevalent a theme as an isolated reading of the Johannine texts in the New Testament might suggest. Rather the Christian praxis of friendship is as demanding a task as any aspect of the praxis of love commanded by God and confirmed in the proclamation, death and resurrection of Jesus Christ.

There is a long list of philosophers from Plato, Aristotle and Cicero to Jacques Derrida that have written on friendship, on its true nature, on its significance for the moral fabric of society, on its importance for the growth of the human person, and on its position between private and public life.[6] A number of theologians have considered the spiritual and theological significance of friendship and debated its difference from and identity or overlap with intimate love.[7] Thomas Aquinas, as indicated above in chapter 4, understood friendship (*amicitia*) with God as the supreme form of love, whereas some modern theologians, as we have seen above in chapter 5, have singled out divine *agape* as the supreme form of Christian love. More recently, friendship is being rediscovered and interpreted as the form of love to which God has called human beings in Jesus Christ. In her recent study of friendship, theologian Liz Carmichael has propagated a friendship model of Christian love:

> The love revealed in Jesus Christ is God's love, given to us to practise in the power of the holy Spirit. The love of Christ on the cross is that of a friend who wills to draw all, through forgiveness and reconciliation, into friendship. Hence divine love can be described in terms of the love of friendship, and is creative of friendship.[8]

[6] See Österberg's discussion in *Vänskap – en lång historia*; 'Freundschaft', in *Historisches Wörterbuch der Philosophie*, vol. 2, Basel and Stuttgart: Schwabe, 1972, pp. 1105–14; and Janet Martin Soskice, pp. 157–80.

[7] See E. D. H. (Liz) Carmichael, *Friendship: Interpreting Christian Love*, London: T&T Clark, 2004. See also Mark Pryce, 'Friendship', in Philip Sheldrake, ed., *The New SCM Dictionary of Christian Spirituality*, London: SCM, 2005, pp. 316–17.

[8] Carmichael, *Friendship*, p. 6.

One of the chief mediators of this friendship-love in Christian faith has been the monastic tradition. The emerging Christian subjectivity since the High Middle Ages owes much to this monastic tradition of developing models of friendship in Christ.

In her study Carmichael first discusses prominent Greek and Roman approaches to friendship, points to the central place that John's Gospel gives to the love of friendship, and argues that friendship language ought to be included when we seek to understand the fuller heritage of references to love in patristic writers where aspects of the classical philosophical tradition on friendship had merged with biblical insights. Thus, according to Ambrose of Milan (c. 339–97), 'Christians should display the virtue of friendship and be par excellence potential friends to all.'[9] However, Ambrose's spiritual son, Augustine, links genuine friendship most directly to God. For the African Church Father, as explained above in chapter 3, only God is worthy of love. Therefore, true friendship can only exist in Christ, in whom alone the truth about divine things can be found.[10] Hence, it must not surprise us that Augustine does not explore human reciprocal friendship with God.[11] Although friendship played an important role in Augustine's own life and development as a Christian believer, he does not make it an important theological theme as such.[12]

The real flowering of friendship in Christian literature, prayer and praxis was not to begin until the Middle Ages. 'A whole spectrum of "friendship", ranging from the political to the personal and spiritual, and sometimes combining all these, can be traced in the lives and correspondence of monks, nuns and ecclesiastical figures throughout the Middle Ages.'[13] The monasteries not only offered access to the classical writings on friendship, but also provided the spiritual, intellectual and social framework in which a new awareness of the potential of human friendship with and under Christ could develop. Friendship became an ideal form of Christian love under the particular conditions of the quickly growing monastic movement in Europe.

Monastic theologians such as Anselm of Canterbury (c. 1033–1109), Bernard of Clairvaux (see above, chapter 4), and the

[9] Ibid., p. 50.

[10] Cf. ibid., p. 58.

[11] Ibid., p. 62.

[12] Ibid., p. 66.

[13] Ibid., p. 70.

English Cistercian monk Aelred of Rievaulx (c. 1110–67) explored spiritual love, its joys, its passion, its transcendence and its blessings in the Christian journey on earth towards complete union with Christ in heaven. Aelred's works on love, in particular *Mirror of Charity* and *Spiritual Friendship*, have received renewed attention in our time for their particular emphasis on lived love and on friendship as an interpersonal journey of love with Christ.[14] The abstract love of God in Augustine now makes way for the personal discovery of love in human friendship — the Christian praxis of love explores agency, subjectivity and relationship in new monastic circumstances.

Aelred's theology of love stands firmly in the tradition of the Johannine, Augustinian, and Cistercian thinking on love. Love comes from God; it is grace that allows our restoration to the full humanity originally willed by God prior to the Fall. What distinguishes Aelred's approach to love from that of his predecessors and Cistercian colleagues, however, is his appraisal that both feeling (*affectus*) and reason (*ratio*) are necessary elements of perfect love (*amor perfectus*).[15] Rather than a spiritualization of love that leaves our physical and emotional nature behind on our way to God, Aelred propagates a maturing of love that includes both. Reason 'must sometimes compel choice when *affectus* is lacking or opposed. It is also why we are bid love all people, even our enemies, although we cannot be expected to enter into friendship with all until the eschatological fulfilment of our restoration in heaven.'[16] Human experience is thus not split in this approach to love, but united in its eschatological orientation towards ultimate fulfilment in divine love. Aelred's monastic praxis of love begins where human beings factually are. He does not regret or look down on either the bodily and affective condition of human beings or the human enjoyment of close relationship. Of course, like Bernard of Clairvaux, he considers the attainment of spiritual love to be the particular vocation of monastic life, but he affirms friendship to be the road of this vocation.

Aelred's *Spiritual Friendship* takes the dialogical form and philosophical starting point from Cicero's *De amicitia* (20): 'friendship is

[14] Cf. Janet Martin Soskice, pp. 158–66.

[15] Cf. Bernard McGinn, *The Growth of Mysticism: Gregory the Great through the 12th Century*, The Presence of God: A History of Western Christian Mysticism, vol. 2, New York: Crossroad, 1994, p. 312.

[16] Ibid., p. 314.

mutual harmony (*consensio*) in affairs human and divine, coupled with benevolence and charity (*caritas*)'.[17] Aelred then develops his theology of friendship in conversation with Scripture and tradition, with three of his monastic friends, and in reflecting on his own personal experiences of friendship. In that sense, Aelred's work can be seen as an emblem of the new optimism of his time: the spectrum of reliable sources for his theological thinking has become very wide indeed, so wide that even we today find it relatively easy to relate to this expression of an educated, cultured, and experiential theological discourse.[18] Aelred's theology of love has become social and relational; it culminates in friendship.

For Aelred, friendship originates in the nature of God which he defines in book I of *Spiritual Friendship* as 'friendship' — altering the words in 1 John 4.16 accordingly: 'God is friendship' (*Deus amicitia est*) and 'He who abides in friendship abides in God and God in him'.[19]

> Woe unto him who is alone, for when he falls he has none to lift him up! [Ecc. 4.10] The man without a friend is a man utterly alone. But what happiness, security and joy to have another self to talk with! One to whom you can confess a failure without fear and reveal unblushingly some progress that you may have made in the spiritual life; someone to whom you dare entrust all the secrets of your heart and in whose advice you can have confidence. But better still by far is the fact that friendship is at one remove from the perfection that is rooted in the knowledge and love of God; for our Saviour says in the Gospel, 'I do not call you servants, but friends' [John 15.15], showing that human friendship leads to that of God. (*Spiritual Friendship*, Book II)[20]

The growth of friendship requires discernment: 'Although affection often precedes friendship, one should never give rein to it unless it is led by reason, tempered by integrity and ruled by righteousness.'[21] Moreover, it needs to be tested. Four things are important in this regard: loyalty, intent, discretion, and patience.[22] The test of one's intention in friendship discloses one's expectations: one should 'expect nothing from the relationship excepting God and the benefits

[17] *Spiritual Friendship*, I.11, quoted in Carmichael, *Friendship*, p. 81. Cf. also McGinn, p. 558, n. 235.

[18] On the reception of Aelred's theology of friendship see Carmichael, *Friendship*, pp. 96–100.

[19] *The Cistercian World: Monastic Writings of the Twelfth Century*, trans. and ed. Pauline Matarasso, London: Penguin, 1993, p. 171. Cf. also Carmichael, *Friendship*, p. 85.

[20] *The Cistercian World*, pp. 173–4.

[21] Ibid., p. 177.

[22] Cf. ibid., p. 183.

naturally inherent' (Book III).[23] True spiritual friendship is to be sought for God and for itself.[24]

Progress in spiritual friendship must be the concern of the friends, and not only one's own. Aelred recommends mutual caring, prayer for one another, co-suffering for each other's failures and lapses, shared joy over each other's progress. Friends should offer one another sound advice in a confident, candid and free spirit. 'One owes a friend the truth; without it the word friendship has no meaning.'[25]

Aelred concludes his reflections by reminding his dialogue partners that friendship proceeds from love. Love of neighbour requires the development of proper self-love, by which the abbot understands purification from immorality and concentration on what serves God's purpose. Choosing a friend, however, calls for discernment as to whom one wishes to admit 'to the fullness of one's affection, to whom one will lay oneself open, baring one's heart and the very marrow of one's bones, one's inmost thoughts and purposes'.[26] One cannot be friends with everybody. However, the affinity between true friends opens them to the presence of Christ:

> And on top of all this, reciprocal prayer, which gains in efficacy with the depth of the affection that inspires it, accompanied by the tears precipitated by anxiety, released by emotion or called forth by grief. And while one is entreating Christ in one's friend's favour and seeking to be heard, one is stretching out towards Christ himself in love and longing, and comes the moment when suddenly one's affection passes from one object to another without one's being aware; and as though one were experiencing at close quarters the sweetness of Christ in person, one begins to taste for oneself the delights of his presence. So it is that we ascend from that love, already holy, with which we embrace our friend, to the love with which we embrace Christ, thus savouring joyfully and freely the fruit of spiritual friendship. (*Spiritual Friendship*, Book III)[27]

Here friendship among monks properly purified and cultivated is the way of a mutual opening to Christ's presence. Aelred knows and accepts, as we have seen, that on earth such intense and erotic human friendship must necessarily be selective. But he hopes for the eternal joy of universal friendship when 'friendship to which here we can admit but few be poured out upon all, and thence back into God who shall be all in all'.[28]

[23] Ibid.
[24] Cf. ibid.
[25] Ibid., p. 187.
[26] Ibid., p. 189.
[27] Ibid., p. 190.
[28] Ibid.

Aelred affirms the conditions, possibilities and limitations of human love within his monastic reflections on friendship. He is not saddened about the fact that he cannot love universally; rather he is content that even a selective love and friendship can lead to a deeper union with Christ and be inspired by the hope that God will grant universal friendship at the end of time.

Can this medieval monastic and male approach to friendship as the supreme Christian praxis of love still serve as an inspiration for a Christian theology of love at the beginning of the twenty-first century beyond the confines of a monastic community?

Aelred appreciated the relational character of love in friendship and affirmed what I have identified above in chapter 1 as the erotic-transcendent nature of human love that focuses on God's love. In this spirit he could confront jealousy and related attacks and experiences of suffering.[29] Moreover, his emphasis on the necessary cooperation between feeling and reason in friendship represents a genuine development in any theology of desire. Finally, here love and friendship are not mere objects of faith but concrete relationships, at times painful, that open the path to a deeper understanding of God's love. Thus, the Christian praxis of love can never be private. Rather it is personal and it aims at the larger horizon in which personal love relationships can flourish.

Obviously, a community of celibate human beings appreciating these deeper levels of the praxis of human love will unavoidably have to confront the threat of being undermined by sexual expressions emerging from such deeper forms of relationship. The close connection between an intensifying spiritual relationship and the accompanying hunger for sexual expression will always be a challenge to celibate communities. However, as we have seen in the previous chapter, chastity is best approached from the horizon of love rather than from a denial of sexuality. Aelred was optimistic about the potential of concrete friendship as a form of monastic love. However, this optimism does not seem to have been shared by his contemporaries and successors. His thoughts and visions played no major role until the rediscovery of his works in recent theology.[30]

[29] See Brian Patrick McGuire, *Friendship and Faith: Cistercian Men, Women, and their Stories, 1100–1250,* Aldershot and Burlington: Ashgate, 2002, VI, pp. 255–6. It is interesting to note that Aelred, when physically attacked by a jealous fellow monk, is said to have welcomed, as a follower of Christ, the opportunity for further suffering. Cf. ibid., p. 255.

[30] Cf. Carmichael, pp. 96–100.

Contrasting Aelred's monastic approach to friendship with approaches in our time might help us to challenge any inward-looking, private understanding of friendship as a form of love.[31] The point is not to question that friendship relations also have a stabilizing role to play in one's personal life;[32] rather the point is to widen the horizon of all friendship relation to include its potential of transcendence — not only in terms of offering space for God, but also in terms of locating friendship in the horizon of larger global concerns. Friendships — as much as marital love or partnership love or other forms of love — are endowed with this complex potential of transcendence. All praxis of love is personal and all praxis of love may invite the persons to look beyond themselves. In that sense, inward-looking or 'private' friendships may pose a real danger — not only in monastic communities, because they lose sight of the common good and God. The Christian praxis of love fosters real relationships pregnant with transcendence and thus, far from regretting intense friendships, it welcomes their development within the always larger horizon of love. And this horizon always includes critique and self-critique. In David Tracy's words, a friendship 'that never includes critique and even, when appropriate, suspicion is a friendship barely removed from the polite and wary communication of strangers'.[33] Finally, in the horizon of love, friendship appears as an eschatological relationship: it affects the developments of the friends, what they are in the process of becoming, not individually in isolation from each other, but precisely because of their relationship and its inherent transcendence.[34]

Friendship outside the wider horizon of love is in danger of manipulating the surrounding community and society. As a purely private network, friendship might give rise to distortions of justice, seek immoral privileges in business and academia, and develop secretive instead of transparent structures in public life. Eva Österberg points to two ways in which friendship can be perceived as a threat: private friendships, as we have seen already, can threaten society through non-transparent structures of power and corrupt plots. Publicly,

[31] Eva Österberg, p. 286, refers to private visions of friendship in contemporary Western culture.

[32] Cf. 'Freundschaft', in *Historisches Wörterbuch der Philosophie*, vol. 2, pp. 1113–14.

[33] David Tracy, *Plurality and Ambiguity: Hermeneutics, Religion, Hope*, San Francisco: Harper & Row, 1987, p. 112.

[34] Cf. Janet Martin Soskice, p. 176.

known close and intimate friendships may be experienced as a threat by any political or ecclesiastical totalitarian regime fearing any challenge to its assumed monopoly of organizing and limiting all human relations.[35]

Friendship is a form of love at the interface of the personal and the wider realm of life. After the discussion of the forms and institutions of love that affect our relational development more intimately, I turn now to the institutions of love that invite us to become part of even larger bodies and thus offer us orientation and growth in love beyond the immediate and personal spheres of life.

## The Church as Institution of Love

For Christians, the Church as the body of Christ is the central institution of love. No disciple of Christ can practise love without some form of relationship to this emerging body. Christian faith always calls for community. The Church is the community of disciples who are determined to follow Christ in loving God and in doing the will of God.[36] Thus, the Church is characterized primarily by its response to God's gift of love in creation, in Jesus Christ and in the Holy Spirit.

The New Testament employs a number of terms that illustrate the aim of Christian discipleship. John's Gospel speaks repeatedly of 'eternal life', whereas the Synoptic Gospels, i.e. Mark, Luke and Matthew, often refer to the emerging 'kingdom of God' or 'reign of God'. These are eschatological terms; they point to a state of divine–human interrelatedness which God wishes to promote through the gift of love. The proper relationship between God and God's creation is not yet achieved. Rather the repeated breakdown of relationships, often referred to as sin, characterizes our existence in this universe. In this situation of broken relationships the community of Christians, the Church, is called to help to establish God's kingdom through the pluriform praxis of love.

It is crucial not to confuse the Church with God's emerging kingdom itself. The Church is not the kingdom of God; rather it proclaims the good news of the arrival of God's reign and through its praxis of love in prayer, worship, liturgy, the sacraments, and charity

[35] Cf. Österberg, pp. 289–90.

[36] Cf. Werner G. Jeanrond, *Call and Response: The Challenge of Christian Life*, Dublin: Gill and Macmillan and New York: Crossroad, 1995, pp. 10–15.

it helps to establish God's reign of love here and now.[37] The Church is therefore not so much concerned with any world to come than with the transformation and renewal of this world in love.

Moreover, Christian faith must never be reduced to individual salvation projects. Christian faith is engaged with God's creative and reconciling love project. Christian faith thus pursues a much larger agenda than the saving of souls. It is concerned with the emerging body of Christ. It is always contemplating the whole and how each individual can participate in this project of universal tranformation. If one were to insist on using salvation terminology, one would at least need to admit that no person can ever be saved alone. However, any narrow reference to salvation misses the larger horizon of God's emerging reign of love and runs the risk of fragmenting God's creative and healing project into a series of egocentric concerns.[38]

If God loves this universe, any consideration of God's reign must include such matters as the environment, economics, communication, culture, society, and politics.[39] The environment is the physical context of God's emerging reign. Economics offers reflections on one crucial aspect on how we human beings relate to each other and on how justly we cultivate and distribute the fruits of God's earth. Communication, culture, society and politics are important in terms of how we are organizing human life in this universe and which structures of participation and authority we are setting up in order to enable human beings to relate properly to each other, to nature, to God, and to their own emerging selves.

While it seems relatively easy to include the environment in our treatment of God's reign, economics and politics complicate the case significantly. Christian tradition has much to say about the world as God's creation and hence also about how we ought to treat this gift of God. But this same tradition has many things — and even contradictory things — to say about how to organize authority and communal organizations both in the Church and in the public social realm. No simple reference to tradition will therefore suffice here. Instead we need to contemplate our overall visions of the world and then assess again and again what strategies of love may be called for

[37] Ola Sigurdson has examined the different, but related dimensions of the ecclesial body in *Himmelska kroppar: Inkarnation, blick, kroppslighet.* Logos – Pathos 6, Gothenburg: Glänta, 2006, pp. 288–590.

[38] I shall resume the discussion of love and salvation in chapter 9 below.

[39] Cf. Jeanrond, *Call and Response*, pp. 32–6.

in order to work towards the realization of these visions. However, since we are by now well aware of the dynamics of love, no vision will ever do that is not open to this transformative dynamics.

## Christian Visions for Global Community

Christians have always been praying for the transformation of this universe.[40] In the *Nicene Creed* we confess our belief 'in one God the Father All-sovereign, maker of heaven and earth, and of all things visible and unvisible'. We express our hope that the crucified and resurrected Lord who ascended into heaven 'cometh again with glory to judge living and dead, of whose kingdom there shall be no end'. Moreover, we 'look for a resurrection of the dead, and the life of the age to come'.[41] Hence, according to the long-professed faith of the Church, Christians have always supported a positive and transformative vision for this world. This world is part of God's created universe, a universe to be renewed, judged and sustained by the eternal God. The ultimate quality of the future longed for by Christians is neither unending time nor the fulfilment of all our particular hopes for the future, but the transformation of this universe and of our particular visions and hopes into God's eternity. Accordingly, one might expect us Christians to welcome any process of commending this universe to the transformative action of God's love.

The ongoing process of globalization could therefore be affirmed and welcomed by Christians. Increasing possibilities of global communication, always easier means of travel (at least for some) throughout this universe, progressive intercultural encounter in this world, these and other aspects of globalization clearly enhance our awareness that we live in this one world and share the potential, but also the difficulties and responsibilities of life on this one globe in our immense universe.

There is no way back from this intensifying fact of global existence. No group of people, no nation, no church, nobody can ever live again in a non-global world. Of course, we could choose to become

[40] In this section I make use of some reflections published in my article 'Christian Visions for Global Community', in Sturla J. Stålsett, ed., *Religion in a Globalised Age: Transfers & Transformations, Integration & Resistance*, Oslo: Novus Press, 2008, pp. 157–69.

[41] *The Documents of the Christian Church*, ed. Henry Bettenson, 2nd edn, Oxford: Oxford University Press, 1979, p. 26.

hermits, we might wish to construct a happy ghetto for our own group or we might wish to dream about the merely national benefits of clean air and thus move backwards in time to nationalist ecologies — a contradiction in terms. However, even such paradoxical actions are actions *within* a globalizing world, and not ways of undoing the fact of globalization. We surely can and must react to the ongoing process of globalization, we can try and detect its inherent problems and dangers, but we cannot renegotiate the fact of globalization itself.

Although everybody in this world is affected by this process of globalization, not everybody benefits from it. Many individuals, groups of people and entire countries and cultures have been heavily affected by a rapidly globalizing economy and related powers of cultural hegemonization.[42] Moreover, economic ideologies wishing to capture and steer this process of globalization for the benefit of a capitalist elite, e.g. the ideology of economism, need to be challenged by a convincing Christian praxis of love, hope, justice and resistance. However, the tension between an unjust economic system and a religious praxis of just relations between all people and God cannot be resolved either by simply ignoring the fact of globalization, or by merely accusing existing economic and cultural theories or systems without presenting convincing alternatives. Therefore, from a Christian perspective, the question must be raised: What are Christian visions for a global community in a globalizing world? What ways of living in this universe are promoted by Christians today? Where can these Christian paradigms for global community today not only be studied, but actually witnessed and experienced?

Here I wish to explore the potential contribution of Christian faith to the shaping of this global world. Therefore, I shall first examine some of the overarching conditions and dimensions of Christian faith in this global world and, secondly, turn to particular visions of community building within our global world, in order, thirdly, to bring both levels together in an attempt to develop Christian visions for global community in a globalizing world.

### *Christian Faith and the One World*

Christian churches have always developed theoretical and pragmatic attitudes towards the world in accordance with the faith that this world

[42] Cf. Zygmunt Bauman, *Globalization: The Human Consequences*, Cambridge, UK: Polity Press, 1998.

is God's good creation. However, they have not always developed specific models of concern and care for this world. Rather they have often subordinated their proclamation — that this world is the God-given space for the peaceful and constructive coexistence and development of all people — to particularly narrow visions of global Christianity.

At times, God's call in Christ to transform this world was interpreted as support for dominating Christian projects of establishing order, harmony and uniformity in this world. Ever since the promotion of Christianity to the level of a state religion in the fourth century, Christians have attempted to formulate political visions of the whole and then expected the state to act according to these programmes.[43] Today, developments in some Islamic countries offer parallels to the many church struggles for power in and over the state. During a rather long period of time Christianity had expected to be able to conquer and shape the world with the help of the state and its militant instruments. From emperor Theodosius I via the Crusades to the religious wars of modern times, there is a long history of Christian efforts to dominate the world with the help of the state and its instruments of power.

Once this model had proved questionable and unworkable, Christians replaced it with the vehicle of the one Western Christian culture as an alternative means of promoting Christian mission, often in tandem with diverse forms of colonization. This model was devastating for many peoples selected to be transformed into so-called Christian nations. As is well known, this one-culture model has been and continues to be rather ineffective in those parts of the world where firm religious traditions had already been flourishing. Hence Christian mission has been largely ineffective in Muslim, Hindu and Buddhist cultures.

We know today that the project of creating the one uniform Christian world has failed. The very disunity among Christians themselves, but also the increasing insight into inner-Christian doctrinal pluralism and the pluriformity of Christian praxis, helped to discredit the establishment of a uniform global Christian vision. Looking back over two thousand years of Christianity, one might be inclined to be grateful for the inner-Christian diversity that has hindered the emergence of one single powerful Christian vision for

[43] See Norbert Brox, *A History of the Early Church,* trans. John Bowden, London: SCM, 1994, pp. 53–66.

this world. Thus, particular versions of Christian uniformity did not succeed in imposing their vision on this world, although some are still trying.[44] The struggle to identify the so-called Christian soul of Europe is a good example for the unreconstructed effort to subject Europe to one particular Christian vision.[45]

Since neither militant nor cultural intervention has been able to shape the world according to Christian views and visions, we Christians have to rethink our faith in terms of how it could inspire Christian visions (*note the plural form*) for this globalizing world. As we have seen already, on the one hand, we Christians believe in the sacredness of this world as God's good creation; thus we have to think about this world as the place where our faith takes shape. On the other hand, we Christians have a record of problematic and failed relationships and attitudes to this world and its pluralist religious, political and cultural heritage. Hence it is quite obvious that a new set of relationships to the one world needs to be developed today.

### *Movements of Transformation*

Our globalizing world makes such a new theological initiative necessary, and a number of important movements surrounding and supporting specific aspects of such a new initiative are already well under way. Here I wish to name at least some of them, however sketchily, and point to their central problems and ambiguities.

The ecumenical movement has demonstrated that closer understanding and cooperation between different Christian traditions is possible and promising. The ecumenical movement has also made the painful discovery that an initial understanding of unity in terms of uniformity cannot really enhance Christian oneness. To be one in God's spirit does not require a uniform way of being Christian. Hence, Christians today are discovering that their spiritual and structural pluralism is not a curse. Instead, the variety of Christian traditions can be interpreted as a blessing and a reservoir of creativity in a multicultural and polycentric world.

[44] Cf. Werner G. Jeanrond, 'European Perspectives on Ethics and Religion', in Göran Bexell and Dan-Erik Andersson, eds, *Universal Ethics: Perspectives from Scandinavian Scholars*, The Hague, London and New York: Martinus Nijhoff, 2002, pp. 129–39.

[45] For a more detailed discussion of the ongoing struggle for a Christian Europe see Werner G. Jeanrond, 'Europa och den religiösa utvecklingen', in Svein Aage Christoffersen and others, eds, *Menneskeverd: Festskrift til Inge Lønning*, Oslo: Forlaget Press, 2008, pp. 319–38.

Interreligious encounter and dialogue have shown that people from different religious and cultural backgrounds can explore the richness of each other's traditions and approaches towards the ultimate meaning and vocation of life on this globe. Any concept of God, the one and only, must be tested in such multireligious encounter and dialogue. No religious tradition can claim to grasp all aspects either of God's mysterious presence or of spiritual existence in this world. God must never be reduced to the size of either my church or my faith. However, this does not mean that we would need to embrace a religious pluralism of the sort that would level or transcend all differences between particular religious traditions and movements.[46] As I have argued elsewhere, not one of the theological approaches identified in terms of religious pluralism, exclusivism and inclusivism offers a fully convincing programme for a critical, self-critical and constructive hermeneutics of religion.[47] What we need instead is a constructive way of learning how to respect difference, to nurture the desire to explore each other's otherness, and to be prepared to be transformed by the living God. In Christian faith this way is known as the way of love. Love is thus not the result of any interreligious process, but 'the social miracle' of mutual recognition that is always prior to any exploration of differences and common experiences, interests, orientations, etc.[48]

The feminist movement and increasing gender awareness have promoted a radically renewed emphasis on equality between women and men in all spheres of human life on this globe. Radical equality has always been identified as one of the central criteria of God's coming reign, although Christian movements have found it hard to live up to this criterion. Even today, large Christian Churches, e.g. the Roman Catholic Church, still do not yet mirror such equality in their particular forms of ecclesial organization. However, everywhere on this globe the desire for structures that promote radical equality is increasing.

The peace movement has engaged individuals, Christian groups and entire denominations since the early years of the nineteenth century. Not only the traditional Reformation Churches committed

[46] For some alternative approaches see Werner G. Jeanrond and Aasulv Lande, eds, *The Concept of God in Global Dialogue*, Maryknoll: Orbis, 2005.

[47] Werner G. Jeanrond, 'Att tänka om Gud idag', *Tidskrift for Teologi och Kirke* 75 (2004), pp. 172–82.

[48] Cf. Rowan Williams, *Lost Icons: Reflections on Cultural Bereavement*, London and New York: Continuum, 2003, p. 98.

to peace (e.g. the Quakers, the Mennonites, and the Brethren movement), but (following the terrible trauma of two world wars and unending warfare — hot and cold — during the twentieth century) even wider sections of mainstream Churches have become increasingly committed to working for peace in the world. However, the term 'peace' was used and misused by political propagandists during the cold war period. Hence, any work for peace must include an ongoing discernment on how peace, truth, justice and the integrity of creation are interrelated.[49] Moreover, the intimate connection between love and peace, stressed already by Thomas Aquinas (see above, chapter 4), needs to be explored in greater detail.

Political cooperation is intensifying on all continents and between continents. Never before in human history has there been such a high level of international contact, communication and cooperation. In view of the rapid process of globalization, the need for an equally rapid development of transnational institutions of cooperation is pressing. The nation state and its traditional means of structuring and ordering resources have become insufficient in terms of tackling today's global problems and opportunities.[50] However, not all forms of transnational cooperation are necessarily promoting peace, justice and equality in this world. Hence, they need to be critically examined. Can Christian traditions contribute to this examination or are they still firmly bound by defending the unholy alliance between the nation state and a particular (established) church? In other words, what are the critical resources in Christian tradition that can disclose unjust structures and offer resistance on a global scale?

The movement towards political inclusion and participation through democratic procedures and processes, whilst in practice often flawed, is a movement that will not go away and one that is slowly transforming ecclesial structures and institutions to better reflect the 'body-politic' of love. Participation requires transparency and trust, but also the task of mutual motivation beyond the apathy to an active involvement in the creation of a transformed world together.

The emerging world culture manifests its particular effectiveness today not only in the realms of music, film, and information technology networks, but also in economic-political ventures that wish to secure international markets often without regard for the

[49] Cf. Andrew Shanks, 'Peace', in Adrian Hastings and others, eds, *The Oxford Companion to Christian Thought*, Oxford: Oxford University Press, 2000, pp. 524–6.

[50] Baumann, *Globalization*, pp. 55–76.

integrity of individuals or groups and for the cultural plurality in our world. Johann Baptist Metz has therefore raised the question

> whether the macrocultural variety in our world is invisibly disappearing, whether this variety – slowly, but surely – is being broken down and leveled by that secular westernizing of the whole world that we call 'science' and 'technology,' or even 'technological civilization.' This process with its information and culture industries rumbles like a bulldozer across the planet. It affects not simply the praxis but clearly also the mentalities of peoples.[51]

This form of 'civilization' leads to a new colonization, this time of the spirit, and is 'so much harder to resist because it appears as a sugar-coated poison, and because the gentle terror of this Western culture industry operates not as an alienation but as a narcotic drug'.[52] Metz points to the irony that right at the time when Christianity seems ready to understand itself as World Christianity, affirming cultural polycentrism and diversity, Western culture threatens to destroy the very possibility of such a polycentric world. 'Thus, is what we call cultural polycentrism in World Christianity ultimately anything more than the continuation of a monocultural colonization of the souls of foreign peoples and cultures, only now carried out with less drastic means than used previously in the history of the church?'[53] Although Christian faith can never be developed in isolation or purely, i.e. apart from culture, the relationship between faith and culture must be critically discussed for the benefit of both.

A new global ecological consciousness has been developing since the 1960s. No spirituality can meaningfully claim authority if it is not rooted in respect for the earth on which all life depends. Insight into the rapidly declining ecological balance of our globe has promoted human cooperation on many levels, including the economic and the spiritual level. How we use the material resources of the universe is never only a question of economics; rather it always already involves our particular relationship with God, nature, each other and our own emerging selves.[54] Are these relationships characterized by a mere will to power and resulting attempts to subjugate the other and nature or

[51] Johann Baptist Metz, 'The "One World": A Challenge to Western Christianity', in Werner G. Jeanrond and Jennifer Rike, eds, *Radical Pluralism and Truth: David Tracy and the Hermeneutics of Religion*, New York: Crossroad, 1991, pp. 203–14, here pp. 203–4.

[52] Ibid., p. 204.

[53] Ibid., p. 206.

[54] Cf. Bo Brander, 'Ecotheology', in John Bowden, ed., *Christianity: The Complete Guide*, London: Continuum, 2005, pp. 360–3.

by a genuine desire to grow both with the respective other and with nature in a culture of acknowledgement, respect and love?[55]

Educational cooperation in the world is on the increase. International evaluations of educational and research institutions are common practice in many wealthier countries. International standards of education and international educational exchanges are promoted everywhere. This raises the question of whether religious movements should participate in this process without, at the same time, stressing their particular views on what human formation really ought to entail. The conflict between an education aiming at producing well-attuned global citizens, predictable consumers, reliable voters, and movable workers, on the one hand, and a formation that supports the emergence of subjects within 'communities of memories',[56] love, forgiveness and resistance cannot be avoided. It is the task of religious traditions to articulate deeper levels of humanity that promote love, hope, faith, and resistance to all forms of oppression, inequality and uncritical forms of competitiveness,[57] and to contribute to the development of just institutions.[58]

The need for a global ethics has been powerfully presented by Hans Küng, Karl-Josef Kuschel and other contemporary thinkers.[59] Küng is aware that every ethics grows out of an ethos, i.e. a concrete praxis of life in particular communities, movements and traditions. Moreover, he favours a constructive, open and critical relationship between different ethics-developing contexts. How far should a global ethics go? Is the genuine will to a public, critical and self-critical conversation between the different agents and agencies in the world already the ultimate goal of global ethics? Or should global ethics go further by promoting agreement on how to tackle specific global concerns,

[55] It is interesting to note that Johann Baptist Metz does not mention love in the context of his otherwise pertinent reflection on the ambiguity of the emerging world culture and the potential of Christian faith and thinking in this changing context.

[56] Metz, 'The "One World": A Challenge to Western Christianity', p. 213.

[57] Cf. Rowan Williams, *Lost Icons*, pp. 108–9.

[58] Cf. Paul Ricœur, *Réflexion faite: Autobiographie intellectuelle*, Paris: Éditions Esprit, 1995, p. 80: 'Pour l'éthique, que je tiens pour plus fondamentale que toute norme, je proposai la définition suivante: souhait de vivre bien avec et pour les autres dans des institutions justes.'

[59] Cf. Hans Küng, *Projekt Weltethos*, Munich and Zurich: Piper, 1990; English edition: *Global Responsibility: In Search of a New World Ethic*, trans. John Bowden, London: SCM, 1991; Hans Küng and Karl-Josef Kuschel, eds, *A Global Ethic: The Declaration of the Parliament of the World's Religions*, London: SCM, 1993; Hans Küng and Karl-Josef Kuschel, eds, *Wissenschaft und Weltethos*, Munich and Zurich: Piper, 1998.

such as ecological, economic, interreligious, cultural, educational issues and problems? Whatever the answer to these questions might be, it is clear that only such a form of global ethics will ultimately be convincing that is covered by a supporting praxis in a concrete tradition, movement, church or religious community. However, the postmodern ease of changing commitment, of refusing to belong, and of reducing relationships to either virtual or pure relations, i.e. relations that do not demand lasting commitment or obligation,[60] offers cause for suspicion and further critical reflection. Where does an ethical formation today take place that publicly promotes the care of lasting commitment and obligation as a condition for transformative relationships and communities of love?

A number of philosophers and theologians have pointed to the recognition of conversation as the primary place of human encounter.[61] Rowan Williams, inspired by Charles Taylor, has further sharpened this attention to conversation by introducing the concept of 'conversations of charity'. These conversations help us discover 'that what we have in common is, in one sense, simply the conversation itself; or rather, that my interest is bound up, not with the "out there" we may both be referring to, not with the common defence of what we share, but with the continuance of the conversational relationship'.[62] Such a conversation does not require anything other than the recognition of the other 'as like me simply in respect of being a speaker and listener in this shared act of conversing'.[63]

Obviously, not all of our conversations are conversations of charity. But the point is that conversations of charity always are a human possibility. The 'sharing of speech'[64] is one opening of a relationship. John's Gospel is right when it begins by confirming that 'In the beginning was the Word [*logos*]'. Moreover, this Logos 'was in the beginning with God', and 'the Logos was God' (John 1.1–2). The connection between the Johannine concepts of God as Word and God as love is well expressed in the concept of a conversation of charity.

[60] Zygmunt Bauman, *Liquid Love: On the Frailty of Human Bonds*, Cambridge, UK: Polity Press, 2003, p. 89.

[61] For a critical discussion of the concept of conversation and for references to the respective literature see David Tracy, *Plurality and Ambiguity*, pp. 1–30.

[62] Williams, *Lost Icons*, p. 99.

[63] Ibid.

[64] Ibid., p. 100.

*A Community of Love*

Even such an incomplete list of existing global initiatives demonstrates, I hope, that although globalization is a fact, not all features and forms of globalization are promising, self-evident or compelling. Rather, it seems clear that deeper reflection and a wide public debate on global community are urgently needed. What are Christian visions for such a world community?

Approaching these questions requires some methodological considerations. Under the impression of urgent global issues and promising interreligious encounters on many levels (i.e. dialogue of life, experiential dialogue, theological dialogue, and social cooperation) some theologians have stated that all religions ought to be understood as united by one and the same spiritual quest, as different ways to the same goal, as expressions of 'the fact that we have been on a single spiritual journey from the very outset'.[65] Yet, I must ask, how could we ever know about an implicit singularity or unity of all spiritualities? I cannot share such sweeping claims to interreligious communality.

We human beings do not possess a universal hermeneutical viewpoint from which we could objectively survey all religious journeys and spiritual pilgrimages. Rather such universal perspectives often imply an attempt to subject other cultures to one superior Western (Christian) perspective. Critical hermeneutical thinking has demonstrated that we always already are embedded in particular horizons and related pre-understandings and, although we of course might be able to widen them, we can never completely free ourselves either from our horizon or from our shadow. Hence, we are, have been and will be limited by space, time and language as long as we are alive. Since we cannot own a universal perspective to begin with, any universalistic approach to human spirituality seems problematic and dangerous. Moreover, in view of the now fashionable postmodern choice not to be committed firmly to any one tradition for any length of time, a measure of caution might be in place when confronting claims that the increasing global awareness automatically will radiate back into each and every religious tradition. Instead it would seem wise to unmask global religious players that will never come back to any concrete tradition or church,[66] yet happily continue to float around

[65] Ewert H. Cousins, 'Global Spirituality', in Philip Sheldrake, ed., *The New SCM Dictionary of Christian Spirituality*, London: SCM Press, 2005, pp. 321–3, here p. 323.

[66] See the discussion of the phenomenon of 'passing over' from one culture to another, ibid., p. 321.

different ad hoc forms of spiritual *bricolage*. There is a widening gap between forms of grassroots spirituality and forms of de-traditionalized spirituality, i.e. between individualized spiritual projects and communal efforts to contribute to the constructive development of spiritual traditions — in short: spirituality yes, commitment to local religious communities no.

Spirituality without belonging is a new form of religious existence in the West. Religious commitment with multiple belonging is new only for the formerly homogeneous religious imagination and culture of the West, yet well known in other parts of the world, for instance in Japan.[67] In the midst of a dramatic change in the understanding and appreciation of the role of tradition it is important to reflect anew upon patterns of community formation.

In the light of these observations I see no possibility of offering any straightforward answer in response to the question of how Christian faith might be able to contribute to a global spirituality. Moreover, I am afraid that such proposals often are not covered by actual realities on the ground. Rather than approaching global spiritual perspectives 'from above' I wish to approach the quest for global visions 'from below', i.e. from the experience of and the desire for a convincing Christian praxis. If our political theologies are not covered by an existing spiritual praxis they are like cheques drawn against a non-existing bank. This is, however, not to deny the dialectics between a tradition's global and local dimensions. But for a dialectics properly to unfold its dynamics, both parts first need to exist. Therefore I feel compelled to stress the significance of local communities for global spirituality.

The different Christian communities to which the New Testament bears witness have all, though to a different extent, expressed their faith in God's power to renew this earth and in the demands which this faith in renewal makes on Christian men, women and children. The texts proclaim the *new* covenant, the *new* life, the *new* wine, the *new* creation, the *new* way, the *new* self, the *new* Jerusalem, the *new* heaven and the *new* earth. Early Christians, it seems, have experienced and expressed a strong faith in the renewal process that God has initiated in the incarnation, proclamation, crucifixion and resurrection of Jesus Christ and through the sending of the Spirit at Pentecost.

[67] See Catherine Cornille, ed., *Many Mansions? Multiple Religious Belonging and Christian Identity*, Maryknoll: Orbis, 2002.

However much committed to this newness in the Lord, the eschatological visions of the different early Christian communities were not all inspired by the Pentecost model of one Spirit encountered and understood in different languages across a wide cultural spectrum. While all early churches witnessed to the divine origin of love and the divine call to transform this world through love, i.e. they all experienced love as the primary motor of eschatological dynamics, they approached the particular praxis of love rather differently.

As we have seen above in chapter 2, many New Testament documents bear witness to the intimate relationship between Christian eschatology, on the one hand, and community building through a praxis of love, on the other hand. Within the limits of the Graeco-Roman world early Christians developed a number of eschatological visions. These Christian communities were inspired by a global vision and a global mission and they have engaged, in varying degree, with other political, religious and cultural forces of their time and world.

As we have seen, the Christian development of a praxis of love is firmly rooted in Jewish religious tradition. According to both Christian and Jewish praxis, love of God, love of neighbour (including foreigners and enemies), love of self, and love of God's creation all are closely related. The different forms of love must, of course, be distinguished, but never separated. Ultimately, the divine love command concerns the development of right relationships between persons, families and communities and the various *others*: God as the radically other, the human other, God's mysterious creation project, and the otherness within my own self. Moreover, the Christian praxis of love has been shown to be a pluriform phenomenon. We have seen both tensions and shifts in emphasis between different Christian conceptualizations of love, even if these have not always been admitted or explored.

## The Dialectics of Eschatology and Ecclesiology

In the shadow of the military and missionary paradigms of the past, i.e. the militant establishment of Christian society on earth and the objectifying and instrumentalizing cultural packaging of Christian mission to the world, we Christians have to contemplate afresh our most precious gift and vocation in our globalizing world, namely our praxis of love. This praxis of love builds on three crucial ingredients of Christian faith, i.e. eschatological expectation, the pluriform ecclesial development of tradition, and the transformative politics of love. I wish to consider, however briefly, each of these and their common significance for a Christian vision for global community.

Eschatological expectation is the backbone of all genuine Christian faith.[68] However, eschatological thinking can be conducted in different ways. It can either be done by projecting present images into God's future, i.e. by way of idolatry, or it can be done by opening oneself and one's community to God's creative and reconciling presence. In the past, Christian eschatology has not only suffered from fundamentalist efforts to reduce Christian hope to apocalyptic horror visions, but also from modernist reductions of global visions to mere individual salvation projects. What contemporary theology has to achieve is a more adequate vision of God's comprehensive renewal project in this universe. The entire network of human relations is to be transformed by God, but only if we human beings are willing to open ourselves to this transformative action. If God relates in love to this world, then human freedom to respond in love to God is a *sine qua non* for any praxis of love. Eschatological expectation must thus be tested against the background of both divine and human freedom.[69]

Calling for a pluriform ecclesial development of tradition implies that all divine–human love relationships in response to Jesus Christ's proclamation of God's Spirit acknowledge the transcendent and community-building nature of love. There is no *Christian* praxis of love or eschatology outside of Christian community. Here lies the crux of all Christian visions for global community: Christian visions for global community will have authority in the concert of visionary contributions in our world only if they are supported by a concrete and visible ecclesial praxis. However, stressing the necessity of church in Christian faith and spirituality does not imply any uncritical justification of existing church structures, identities or developments. Rather, I wish to acknowledge the mutually critical relationship between Christian ecclesiology and Christian spirituality, a relationship that fully respects the eschatological difference between the Church, on the one hand, and the coming reign of God, on the other hand.

[68] See Karl Barth, *The Epistle to the Romans*, trans. (from the 6th edn) Edwyn C. Hoskyns, Oxford: Oxford University Press, 1968, p. 314: 'If Christianity be not altogether thoroughgoing eschatology, there remains in it no relationship whatever with Christ. Spirit which does not at every moment point from death to the new life is not the Holy Spirit'.

[69] Cf. Werner G. Jeanrond, *Gudstro: Teologiska reflexioner II*, Lund: Arcus, 2001, pp. 13–31.

Love is always transitive, it always seeks the other — not in order to subjugate, assimilate, outwit, kill or ultimately ignore the other, but in order to acknowledge, respect and encounter both the other and the loving self as genuinely other. The nature of love as a transitive, transcendent and transformative relationship between human beings and between human beings and God defies any church model that does not grant space to this relational nature of love. As most people know from different church traditions, churches have at times a tendency to kill love in pursuit of order and to raise obstacles against the potentially anarchic flow of divine–human and human–human encounters in the spirit of Christ.[70] They often try to avoid any challenge to existing order and to a uniformly interpreted tradition. However, no model of uniformity will ever be able to do justice to the dynamics of love. Love is and remains pluriform by nature, and so is any Christian church truly engaged in the praxis of love.

According to Christian faith the transformative politics of love is the salt of the earth. Any creative Christian development can only come about through works of love — and, as we have seen in chapter 5 above, Kierkegaard includes here even the work of love in honouring the dead.[71] Love respects the otherness of the other including the radical otherness of God while desiring a union with the other. Hence, all works of love are by nature opposed to any form of coercion, use, instrumentalization or objectification of self and other. Only through love and love's 'body-building' capacity are human beings enabled to develop as loving agents within emerging communities. According to Paul, the building up of the body of Christ is the supreme task of Christians (1 Cor. 12).

This careful attention to otherness — without swallowing up the other in the act of reaching out to her or him — provides also the model for the emergence of loving relationships between Christians and non-Christian others. From such a perspective, no interreligious dialogue or encounter is of real interest if it is not carried out in a spirit of love. A praxis of love, accompanied by a critical hermeneutics of love, opens the way for the emergence of new bodies of love. All love extends the body and thus shapes and renews community.

Moreover, this Christian vision of a body-building love is both emancipatory and political by nature. The Church as such does not

[70] Cf. Jeanrond, *Call and Response*, p. 23.

[71] Søren Kierkegaard, *Works of Love*, ed. and trans. Howard V. Hong and Edna H. Hong, Princeton, NJ: Princeton University Press, 1995, p. 349.

love. Movements or institutions are never agents or subjects of love. Only free persons can love. The politics of love thus shifts the question of agency from the global level to the local level which is constitutive of human community, namely to the transitive, transcendent and transformative potential of interpersonal encounter. The politics of love emerges from conversations of charity[72] — inner human conversations and God's conversation with humankind.

While the original agents of a politics of love are always persons, i.e. persons in relationship, they together can form communities of justice. Love and justice are dialectically related in this way. Paul Ricoeur, like Kierkegaard, stressed the commandment character of Jewish and Christian approaches to love: we may not just choose to love; rather we are commanded to love the different others. Moreover, Ricoeur emphasized the superabundant nature of love, love's generosity and gift character, and he located the origin of both love and justice in the same economy of the gift.[73] Hence, all Christian work for emancipation, for peace, for justice and for the establishment of always more just institutions flows from this dialectics of love and justice, a dialectics firmly rooted in faith in the gracious God of love, and always manifest in concrete efforts of building just and transformative communities of love. Ecclesiology and eschatology critically belong together.

The Christian vision for global community developed so far in this chapter is firmly rooted in the transitive, transcendent and transformative praxis of love. This praxis is always local by nature and global in outlook. It is open for otherness and inspired by the creative and reconciling presence of God in Christ. Moreover, it is involved in the building of related bodies of love. Therefore Christian communities can be exclusivist only at the cost of limiting or killing love. Communities of love will always attend to the concrete other and to the conditions of the concrete encounter of the other.

Conditions for a flourishing praxis of love have been developed by the Jesus of the Gospels: they include the freedom to love, radical equality, and the freedom from all forms of oppression.[74] Oppression

[72] Cf. Williams, *Lost Icons*, p. 106.

[73] Paul Ricœur, 'Love and Justice', trans. David Pellauer, in Werner G. Jeanrond and Jennifer Rike, eds, *Radical Pluralism and Truth: David Tracy and the Hermeneutics of Religion*, New York: Crossroad, 1991, pp. 187–202, here p. 197.

[74] Cf. Jeanrond, *Call and Response*, p. 14.

on the level of the individual person could mean physical, social, psychological and political oppression, and on the level of the world it includes all forms of systemic, political, social, economic and cultural oppression as well as ecological corruption of the universe. The universal horizon of Christian love defended in Luke's Gospel identifies all human beings as potential neighbours, i.e. as persons in God's creative and reconciling realm. Moreover, this horizon includes even the dead persons that have lived on this earth before us and those that will come after us, the entire community of saints — living and dead.

The Christian community of love with all its shortcomings, failures, conflicts, sins and new beginnings, congregates around Jesus Christ. To use Paul's words, it wishes to become his body (1 Cor. 12.12). It has in the past chosen different paths of love: a more inward-looking Johannine praxis, a universalistic Lukan path, a path that is inclined to avoid conflict, and a path that confronts conflict. But even the most inward-looking text on love, i.e. the Gospel of John, in its prologue (John 1.1–18) acknowledges God's universal horizon.

It is this horizon that summons all Christians to a relationship with God's creative and healing project through the praxis of love accompanied by a critical hermeneutics of love. This hermeneutics helps Christians to shape communities, to build bodies (1 Cor. 8.1), and to challenge all forms of injustice, oppression, war, and colonization. Christian resistance is born from this hermeneutics of love that desires global community as the form of the most elaborate love on earth.

The ongoing process of globalization in our world has increased this desire for global community, yet at the same time it has intensified the need for a hermeneutics of suspicion[75] and for resistance to all old and new forms of oppression of women, men and children as well as of our global context as a whole. If we wish to participate in the transformative praxis of love, we cannot produce blueprints for the shape of global community. However, if we really believe in global community and therefore wish to resist all forms of globalized community, then our concrete attempts to love seem the only way forward. This way will become more attractive, the more we practise it wherever we live.

[75] See Werner G. Jeanrond, *Theological Hermeneutics: Development and Significance*, London: SCM, 1994, p. 74.

## Love and Global Charity

The needs of our globalized world and its inhabitants are related to us constantly through technological means which have made possible a compression of space and time in our perception of reality. If we so choose we can be exhaustively informed about an unending list of miseries in our world that in theory would all be more or less deserving of my immediate attention. Warfare, hunger, global warming, child pornography, rape, clerical paedophilia, systemic oppression of women and children, ethnic, racial and sexual discrimination, loneliness in old age, severe forms of illness, cruelty to animals — to name just a few of the structural and concrete instances of threatened and unreconciled existence in this universe. Do not all of these predicaments call for our loving attention, for our acts of charity, for our solidarity with and political engagement on behalf of the victims of sin, oppression, discrimination and marginalization? Is not our personal praxis of love in relationships an obstacle to our concern for the many needs of the world?

The Gospels report on the woman who poured costly ointment on Jesus' head and on the reaction of Jesus' disciples, who constructed a contrast between the manifestation of the relationship between the nameless woman and Jesus, on the one hand, and the demands of universal charity, on the other (Matthew 16.6–13; Mark 14.3–9; John 12.1–8, and, with a slightly different angle, Luke 7.36–50). The Gospels reject this contrast: loving attention to Jesus and loving attention to the poor are not matters of calculation, however important both forms of attention are.

Similarly we could say that there is no inherent conflict between personal love relationships and attention to the worthy and pressing concerns of the world. If the human horizon of love is open to God's transcendence and God's acts of reconciliation and transformation then there is no conflict in love since all forms of love are intimately related within this horizon. It has been one of the tragic misunderstandings in Christian tradition that the Christian praxis of love would require sacrificing close loving relationships and friendships for the greater love of God. If God's gift of love is one, it does not take away from love when we human beings combine personal love relationships with our loving attention to the many needs of the world. Moreover, it is in the network of loving relationships, i.e. in family, marriage, partnership, friendship, and church, that we are introduced and challenged to discern the real needs of others and of ourselves. Persons thus holistically educated and supported are likely to be appropriately attentive to the greater needs of society.

The English word 'charity', derived from the Latin *caritas*, means love.[76] While love and charity convey identical meanings, in recent times charity has been used more restrictively for works of love in response to all kinds of need. In a secularized context, charity refers to benevolent actions and attitudes in general, i.e. to philanthropy, compassion, care, almsgiving, solidarity, aid to the developing world etc. In a Christian context, 'Christian charity' is also used as a summary term for the complex network of individual and corporate social services within Christian churches and groups and for Christian participation in aid work with other government or non-government organizations, movements and groups. Charity work can be directed towards meeting individual, social and structural needs throughout our universe. All these needs are also calls for Christians to respond in love.

We encounter a number of questions when we wish to attend to the needs of others: are persons in need identified through their particular needs, reduced to the levels of their perceived needs? For example, are we attending in love to an HIV-sufferer or to a fellow human being that suffers from HIV? Is it enough to attend to the needs of individual persons or does Christian charity demand a critical and self-critical involvement in processes of changing wrong or unjust structures that are co-responsible for the emergence of individual needs? In other words, should we concentrate on helping particular victims or should we also try to alleviate unjust structures? Moreover, does the Christian praxis of love call for ad hoc solutions or for an establishment of bureaucratic structures to meet present needs, to help identify and avoid future needs, and to eradicate as many present and future needs as possible? Finally, should we prioritize needs in view of the fact that we do not seem to be able to meet all the pressing needs at once? How should we handle conflicting needs? The Christian praxis of love commits us to critical and self-critical attention on many levels at once.

The concept of solidarity has become an important point of reference for social-ethical orientation in our globalized age and consciousness. Solidarity stresses our constitutional connection with

[76] Cf. Werner G. Jeanrond, 'Charity', in Adrian Hastings and others, eds, *The Oxford Companion to Christian Thought*, Oxford: Oxford University Press, 2000, p. 108.

others, emphasizes common action of subjects united by common interest and concern, and refers to identification with and action on behalf of the weaker members of a community.[77] All three dimensions of solidarity thus express the wish to act in support of the well-being of others. Hence, the significance of the concept also for a Christian praxis of love. An attitude of solidarity with human beings that have become victims of what has been identified as 'social sin' has been a major inspiration for the development of Christian and similar social programmes and initiatives. Theologically speaking, Jesus' relationship to and actions on behalf of the poor, the sick, the marginalized, women and children have been identified as a manifestation of God's solidarity experienced so richly also in the history of Israel and perceived so clearly by the prophets.[78] This divine revelation of forms of solidarity offers a challenge to structure human life — personal and institutional — in church and society according to egalitarian principles of serving one another and of brotherly and sisterly love rather than according to hierarchical principles of master–slave relations or the relationship between a father and his immature children.[79] The danger of paternalism, however, will always be looming in programmes and acts of solidarity, especially when we decide with whom we wish to be in solidarity and try to impose our solidarity on others whose needs and wishes we did not care to consult and whose subjectivity and integrity we thus did not care to affirm. Voicing solidarity does not automatically contribute to a critical and self-critical Christian praxis of love. All claims to solidarity require a careful hermeneutics of suspicion.

The self-critical struggle with motivation and effect of Christian charity also concerns the question of whether or not distinct Christian strings ought to be attached to specific Christian works of love. Why do we love the other in need: because of some need in us to be needed,[80] because of our concern for Christ's presence in the other (cf. Matt. 25.31–46), because of some missionary call (Matt. 28.18–20), or simply out of love for the other (cf. Luke 10.25–37)?

[77] Cf. Konrad Hilpert, 'Solidarität', in Peter Eicher, ed., *Neues Handbuch theologischer Grundbegriffe*, Neuausgabe 2005, vol. 4, Munich: Kösel, 2005, pp. 152–60, here pp. 152–3.

[78] Cf. ibid., p. 157.

[79] Cf. ibid., pp. 158–9.

[80] See Arne Jarrick, *Behovet att behövas: En tänkebok om människan, kulturen och världshistorien*, Stockholm: SNS Förlag, 2005.

This question brings us back to the issue of '*Christian* love'. Do we love because we are Christians or do we love because as Christians we are called to love? Do we love because of secondary motivations, i.e. for reasons of mission or church order, or do we love because we have received God's gift of love?

One test of motivation and attitude in the Christian praxis of love is the concern for the personal integrity of the recipients of love to become themselves afresh free subjects and agents of love. Thus, the aim of love is to enable more free and creative love, not mere copies of our acts of love. Moreover, it is important to remind ourselves that every opportunity to meet the needs of others, individually or structurally, is itself a gift of God. Hence, charity as part of the Christian praxis of love must be seen and developed within the framework of faith in God's grace and of hope for God's emerging reign on earth, as indicated above in this chapter. The ultimate criterion for judging expressions of Christian works of charity is the willingness to serve human beings while respecting their dignity as God's creatures, and not one's ego and its intricate desires and projects. Therefore, works of charity constantly require both spiritual nourishment and self-critical examination.

Finally, it is important to link works of charity with work for just institutions. Charity must not be a way of bypassing justice. Rather, as already mentioned above in this chapter, love and justice need each other, and a life inspired by love requires a commitment to just institutions. Therefore, the development of a natural and social environment which safeguards justice, in terms both of equal respect for individuals and of the fair distribution of available goods and services, is better than mere 'acts of charity', especially if these are expressions of technocracy and paternalism. The Christian praxis of love must face its ambiguities, dangers and challenges — on the personal as well as on the structural level — if it wants to become a praxis of 'just love'.

In the context of discussing Christian sexual ethics and love, Margaret A. Farley defines 'just love' in a way that also applies to the larger perspective on love pursued in this chapter: 'A love is right and good insofar as it aims to affirm truthfully the concrete reality of the beloved.' However, Farley continues, 'it must also be "true" to the *one loving* and to the *nature of the relationship* between lover and loved. A love will not be true or just if there is an affirmation of the beloved that involves destruction of the one who loves.'[81] Her point is not to rule out specific occasions for self-sacrificial love but 'a letting oneself be destroyed as a person because of the way in which one loves another'.[82]

Part of the confusion between just love and destructive love has to do with the occasional confusion in Christian tradition of divine and human love, to which we must return now in the final chapter of this book.

[81] Margaret A. Farley, *Just Love: A Framework for Christian Sexual Ethics*, New York and London: Continuum, 2006, p. 200.
[82] Ibid., pp. 200–1.

# Chapter 9

# *THE LOVE OF GOD*

## God is Love

One of the richest theological statements in the Bible is the Johannine dictum that God is love (1 John 4.8 and 16). This expression has given rise to much thought. As we have seen above in chapter 3, Augustine interpreted this dictum within his Neo-Platonist horizon of thinking and concluded that only God could love. Hence, whenever I love my neighbour, it is in fact God who through me loves the other human being. As already indicated, Augustine's understanding of love cannot be reconciled with our contemporary understanding of human agency and subjectivity, nor for that matter with our reading of the biblical texts. We read the Bible also as a witness to the network of love to which all human beings have been invited. Moreover, many Christians see in the Gospels a strong witness to Jesus' confirmation of the human capacity to love, affirmed in Jewish tradition.

While all the theologies explored in this book emphasize the divine origin of love, there is no agreement as far as the human potential of love is concerned. The Augustinian heritage has imposed a heavy burden on Christian theologies of love. While it has encouraged human desire for God and God's love, at the same time it has crossed out any suggestion that human beings could be involved directly as subjects in God's creative and reconciling project. Moreover, it has located the ideal nature of human life in the mythical past and not in a universally envisaged human future with God. Instead of eschatological desire and enthusiasm, we meet here a large measure of cosmological and anthropological nostalgia combined with a negative view of this world. Only late, though not very well developed, do we hear Augustine affirm the resurrection of the body.[1] Augustinian anthropology has not been good news for a theology of love.

The rediscovery of human agency in love since the High Middle Ages is an ongoing process. Although, as we have seen above in chapter 4, men and women in monastic, apostolic, lay and emerging secular walks of life have worked towards rehabilitating human subjectivity in love, ultimately the Augustinian inheritance proved difficult to handle. The negative view of the human being, of its sinful nature, its corrupted body and distorted desires that has broken through time and again in theology allowed only for more or less paralysing approaches to the divine gift of love, its networks, its creativity and its transformative potential in this universe. It seems that at times it was more important for theologians to explore human sinfulness than the potential of love.

The invention of 'Christian' love, the confessionalization of love since the Reformation, the reduction of love to an object of belief in both Roman Catholic and Protestant Orthodoxy, and the reduction of salvation to a mere concern for individualist immortality, have further added to the subordination of love to doctrinal interests and confessional controls of faith. Once more, the interdependent network of loving relationships was split by Anders Nygren into divine and human love, and the commandment to love God, one's neighbour and oneself was divided into two loves, God's good love (agape) and human corrupt love (eros). And since we cannot love with God's love and our human love is not to be trusted, all that is left is God's own agape which needs to be funnelled directly into our hearts. 'Nygren's rejection of the human desire for self-fulfilment turns Christianity into a form of quietism which seeks to renounce all human self-esteem.'[2]

An additional difficulty on the way to retrieving human love within the divinely gifted network of love relates to the Platonic heritage which defined the aim of love in terms of reuniting formerly divided parts. Is the goal of human life to be reunited with what has been split as a result of some original sin or cosmological accident? Or is the human aim in life to love and be loved and thus to join the creative network of mutually loving relations? In other words, is the goal of

[1] Cf. Christoph Horn, 'C.II.6. Anthropologie', in Volker Henning Drecoll, *Augustin Handbuch*, Tübingen: Mohr Siebeck, 2007, pp. 479–87, here p. 482.

[2] Vincent Brümmer, *The Model of Love: A Study in Philosophical Theology*, Cambridge, UK: Cambridge University Press, 1993, p. 242.

life located in a mythical past in which the future is pre-ordained or in an eschatological future opened for us by God who is love? Does this love respect and welcome difference and otherness or is it supposed to annihilate both? Can we welcome and adopt Augustine's existential desire for union with God without risking the annihilation of human subjectivity and without accepting the Church Father's location of human destiny in the restoration of a vision of a paradise lost? Can we long for God's future and open ourselves for the transformation of subjects and communities towards this future in the praxis of love?

Hence, the classical statement that God is love requires a generous amount of critical and self-critical attention.[3] This applies also to efforts in recent theology, some more desperate than others, to identify the inner-Trinitarian love-dynamics as the ultimate experience, criterion and authority of genuine love. While in response to the Johannine formula (God is love) it makes good sense to contemplate the mystery of God as love and to reflect on the grace emerging from the triune God, it seems to me to be a dangerous move to draw concrete conclusions from such contemplation in terms of actual patterns, forms and genres of human love.[4] As we have seen above, God loves divinely, and we human beings are invited to love humanly. Moreover, the praxis of love is the most intimate way to respect and get to know the beloved other and the radical other, God. Therefore it would seem unwise to approach the loving God with any firm expectations to deduce a set of divine paradigms or blueprints for the formation of human love. Rather than trying to decode inner-Trinitarian love, we could explore

[3] Kevin J. Vanhoozer, *First Theology: God, Scripture and Hermeneutics*, Downers Grove, IL: InterVarsity Press, 2002, p. 81, is right: 'The concept of the love of God is both fundamental to the doctrine of God and, oddly, disruptive of it. There seems to be no one place in a systematics in which the notion of the love of God neatly fits.' See also the critical clarifications in this respect in Markus Mühling-Schlapkohl, *Gott ist Liebe: Studien zum Verständnis der Liebe als Modell des trinitarischen Redens von Gott*, Marburg: N. G. Elwert Verlag, 2000.

[4] See Gavin D'Costa, 'Queer Trinity', in Gerard Loughlin, ed., *Queer Theology: Rethinking the Western Body*, Oxford: Blackwell, 2007, pp. 269–80. D'Costa examines Hans Urs von Balthasar's theology of the Trinity, whose exclusion of female imagery he regrets: If von Balthasar

> had questioned the Aristotelian identification of the male with activity/generation, and not written this into the Godhead, we might have been shown how the Trinity is capable of leading us to envisage a society without patriarchy, without the driving of holes into bellies of women, and without their eradication from the symbolic order. Instead we might have had a divine symbolic which allowed for a richer hermeneutics of the Bible and for women to be included within ministerial priesthood. (Ibid., p. 279)

the divinely gifted network of loves for which human beings believe they have been created and invited to contribute to through their human praxis of love.

Hence, I find it problematic to speak of the human praxis of love in terms of 'icons of godly love'.[5] Moreover, any identification between human forms and projects of love and divine love, however well intended, are in danger of not respecting and not loving God as God and the human being as human being. As I attempted to demonstrate in chapter 7 above, human love needs to be assessed as human love. Therefore, for example, arguments in favour of same-sex relationships must emerge from an understanding of human love as divinely endowed and graced rather than from any sort of Trinitarian deduction that claims that the Holy Trinity was 'a paradigm for "same-sex" friendship'.[6] Social, political or communitarian models of the Trinity pre-empt the Christian praxis of love.[7]

## Divine and Human Love

The dynamics of love opens always new insights into self and other. This interdependence of knowledge and love is especially pertinent for any human approach to God. Human love for God is a wonderful gift from God. However, it is, as we have seen, a gift that always draws us more deeply into the entire network of loving relations. Whenever we love God, we are at the same time directed towards God's creative and reconciling project, we are directed to the larger body of love which in Christian experience is desired as the body of Christ. Even the most intense experience and expression of our love of God thus involves the entire love story between God and God's creation.

This holistic approach to love that affirms the unity of love, however, does not confuse the different agencies of love. God's love

[5] Marilyn McCord Adams, 'Trinitarian Friendship: Same-gender Models of Godly Love in Richard of St. Victor and Aelred of Rievaulx', in Eugene F. Rogers, Jr, ed., *Theology and Sexuality: Classic and Contemporary Readings*, Oxford: Blackwell, 2002, pp. 322–40, here p. 323.

[6] Ibid., p. 325, with reference to Richard of St. Victor.

[7] For a more detailed discussion of recent problematic approaches to Trinitarian arguments see Werner G. Jeanrond, 'Thinking about God Today', in Werner G. Jeanrond and Aasulv Lande, eds, *The Concept of God in Global Dialogue*, Maryknoll: Orbis, 2005, pp. 89–97; and Werner G. Jeanrond, 'Revelation and the Trinitarian Concept of God: Are they Key Concepts for Theological Thought?', trans. John Bowden, in Werner Jeanrond and Christoph Theobald, eds, *God: Experience and Mystery*, *Concilium* 2001/1, London: SCM, 2001, pp. 120–30.

is and remains divine, and our love is and remains human. Christian faith sees God's loving self-revelation and self-communication at work in God's creative, intimate and stormy love relationship with Israel, in Jesus Christ's confirmation of the centrality of love as reconciling and transformative praxis here and now, in God's incarnation in Jesus, in Jesus' ministry of love including his total self-giving (*kenosis*) at the cross and his divine glorification through his resurrection, in God's sending of the Spirit of love, and in the dynamics of love which God's Spirit has unfolded in and beyond the Christian praxis of love.

God's love for human beings and for this universe remains faithful in spite of all human failures and breakdowns in love. The triune God's creativity flows from this self-giving, self-engaging love of God. 'To give oneself leads always to new life.'[8] God is thus intimately present in our lives as creator, reconciler and inspirer. God is engaged in the process of humanization of men, women and children through love. God wills and respects the freedom of human beings to say yes or no to the invitation to participating in the dynamics of love.

Although God has invited women, men and children to take part in her eternal love project and thus expresses her will to establish a union in love with her creatures, this invitation never wishes to dissolve our humanity. The opposite is the case: our humanity is best affirmed, enhanced and consummated in this network of loving relationships.

As we have seen, such a theological approach to the dynamics and interconnectedness of divine and human love faces many risks, dangers, distortions and pitfalls. As one of the foremost challenges to a Christian theology of love we have identified the question of agency. Notwithstanding shifting philosophical underpinnings, any human praxis of love witnesses to the vocation of the subject to open herself to the transcendence offered in love. Yet it also witnesses to the limitations of the human subject. Moreover, the perspective of love first of all enables a proper view and assessment of failure, breakdown and sinfulness in human efforts to engage in relationships. Love provides the most appropriate measure for assessing failure and sin, because it wishes to explore, respect and relate to the other subject's subjectivity and otherness as well as to the self's subjectivity and otherness. Love explores the truth in every relationship.

[8] Wilfrid Stinissen, *Störst av allt är kärleken*, Skellefteå: Artos and Örebro: Libris, 2008, p. 114.

A crucial question for any theology of love concerns its starting point: does the praxis of love require preliminary steps and appropriate preparation or can anyone at any time and without preconditions accept being loved and beginning to love? As we have seen, a host of objections have been raised against such spontaneity in love. What limitations are experienced by human subjects pursuing the praxis of love?

A first group of objections concern *the subject's ability to love.* Am I able to love God and my neighbour? Can I love enough, and for the long-haul? Is my body perfect enough to love? In what way do my physical, psychological and social handicaps impinge on my capacity to love? Is my motivation for love pure enough? Can I consider myself to be a fully capable agent of love? Is my character too selfish to truly love another? Is my family, educational, psychological, social, political, cultural and religious background suitable for the praxis of love? Can I love one person without hurting others? Should I first relinquish my own self before I can properly love God and God's creation? Is self-giving a precondition for love?

A second group of objections concern *the subject's dignity to be loved.* Why should anybody love me? There is so much problematic with me, my character, background, history, sexual desires and sexual orientation that I consider myself unworthy of love. I am not beautiful enough to be desired and enjoyed in love. My attempts to love have failed in the past, I do not dare to love or be loved anymore. Perhaps I am afraid of hurting or being hurt in love.

A third group of objections concern *the hopelessness of the situation.* There is so much conflict, evil, sin and division in our world that any human effort to practise love against this background seems futile. What can I do with my little love against a massive amount of evil in the world? I am a victim of all kinds of external powers which make my limited potential to love appear to be ridiculous. I might lack faith about the power of love in the face of overwhelming evil.

A fourth group of objections concern *the difference between divine and human love.* Since God's love alone is perfect I want to love like God or not at all. Since God has shown us in his Son that true love requires total sacrifice and the aim of Christian love therefore ought to be total self-surrender, I, like Jesus, would need to practise *kenosis* in my praxis of love. But how? Can I love and love 'purely' enough?

In addressing these and other sceptical assessments of the human capacity to love and be loved we are confronted with the basic challenge of Christian faith: do we trust in the God-given dynamics of love or not? Do we accept the gift of love to participate in this divine dynamics of love as human subjects, created, pardoned, affirmed, invited and encouraged by God? When we approach our human predicament in the light of love, we arrive at radically different conclusions about our human potential to love than when we approach love in view of assumed or real human capacities or incapacities to love.

Taking love as our starting point frees our horizon for the dynamics of love, for transcendence and for personal and communal transformation. It allows us to live more fully in the larger network of interconnected relations. This praxis of love will provide us with appropriate criteria for assessing our failures and those of our ancestors, while it will at the same time relocate us in the presence of God's forgiveness, reconciliation, transformation and new creation in the Body of Christ.

Approaching love through doctrines of sin and original sin cripples our imagination, because it views our finitude and flaws as the insurmountable barriers to the work of love, and reduces our attention to our own ontology of failure. It blocks eros, spontaneity and community development and locates us in negative and self-centred spiritual reckoning.

Hence, the choice whether we wish to approach our human condition through the gift of love or to approach the gift of love through lamenting over past and possible breakdowns of love proves crucial for any Christian praxis of love. Either we allow ourselves to be drawn into the incalculable flow of love or we hold love at bay in the name of efforts to correspond to fixed norms of selfhood assumed to be required prior to any concrete praxis of love.[9]

This dilemma was not Augustine's since he did not attribute subject status to human beings with regard to love. But once we acknowledge that women, men and children are able to love, are able to give themselves, the question of the starting point receives great significance.

As we have seen in the preceding chapters of this book, the Christian insight into the mystery of love does not lead to any new

[9] Cf. here Beverly Wildung Harrison, *Making the Connections: Essays in Feminist Social Ethics*, ed. Carol S. Robb, Boston: Beacon Press, 1985, p. 11:

> I believe that an adequate feminist moral theology must call the tradition of Christian ethics to accountability for minimizing the deep power of human action in the work of or the denial of love. Because we do not understand love as the power to act-each-other-into-well-being we also do not understand the depth of our power to thwart life and to maim each other. The fateful choice is ours, either to set free the power of God's love in the world or to deprive each other of the very basis of personhood and community.

commandment over and above the double love commandment in the Torah (Deut. 6.4–9). Rather, all the Gospels report Jesus' affirmation of this central commandment in Jewish tradition and his powerful call to everybody to enter into this multidirectional praxis of love without delay and without conditions. Moreover, the fullness of God's gift of presence in God's universe (the 'kingdom of God' or 'eternal life') is bound to this transformative praxis of love.[10] None of the above-listed objections, therefore, carries any weight with Jesus' insistence on love as praxis. Love is neither theory, nor principle nor an object of belief. Rather, love is praxis requiring critical and self-critical reflection, wisdom and judgement, yet not perfect bodies, divine attitudes, and angelic intentions. Rather the very praxis of love first reveals what needs to be done from within the perspective of the dynamics of the network of relationships. No level of prior strategy and planning can ever reach the type of love's own knowledge. Rather, participation in the transformative praxis of love gives rise to appropriate ways of tackling the personal, communal and structural needs in our world.[11] Jesus did not proclaim a new theory of love nor did he initiate a particular 'Christian' form of love. Rather, in his life, ministry, death and resurrection he confirmed the praxis character of all genuine human love in response to divine love. Love meets the other where the other is right now and not where we would ideally prefer the other to be. This applies both to God's love and to our human love.

By stretching out his hand to all the people alienated in one way or another from either or both God and/or fellow humans, Jesus initiated a relational process of reconciliation between people and God, between people, and between people and their own inner selves. The point of this multilayered process of reconciliation, however, is not to restore real or assumed forms of harmony in

[10] For an insightful discussion of Jesus' preaching of the kingdom of God see John Riches, *Jesus and the Transformation of Judaism*, London: Darton, Longman & Todd, 1980, pp. 87–111.

[11] Robert J. Schreiter, CPPS, *The Ministry of Reconciliation: Spirituality & Strategies*, Maryknoll: Orbis, 1998, p. vi, is right to connect spirituality and strategy. It is important to note that he does not demand a strategy that would lead to spirituality; rather he stresses the need for strategy resulting from Christian praxis. He argues that 'strategies cannot be dispensed with. Concrete experiences of struggling to achieve some measure of reconciliation require decisions, and those decisions must have some grounding. I still believe that reconciliation requires a certain spiritual orientation if it is to be successful.'

a distant or mythical past. Rather, the process of reconciliation confirmed by Jesus opens people for a radical transformation of their understanding of God, of God's people, of God's universe, and of their own selves.

One of the great misunderstandings of this process has been the urge of Christians to copy Jesus himself rather than to accept his invitation to participate in the transformative dynamics of humanity thus reconciled with God. It seems that some Christians are more concerned with reinventing Christianity than with following Jesus as respected and free subjects in the praxis of love. The point of Christian discipleship is not to copy Jesus, but to accept his proclamation and self-sacrifice so that we can live life fully in God's loving presence. Hence, Christian discipleship does not call for the prior surrender of the human self (*kenosis*), but for the surrender of the human ego in love so that the loving self can emerge and grow in the relational and creative praxis of love.[12]

## Love and Salvation

The connection of love and salvation has not always been very clear in Christian faith. Does salvation mean deliverance from the conditions of Adam's Fall including sin, death, suffering, illness and alienation? Or does salvation mean participation in the divine project of creation and new creation? The first meaning relates salvation to an ordered exit from this world and its fallenness, whereas the second meaning refers to the eschatological dynamics of love.[13]

Although the outcome of each of these visions of salvation is life in loving relationship with God,[14] the process differs radically. In the first instance, this world and this universe are not part of the horizon of salvation, whereas in the second instance, they are. Moreover, in this latter case, salvation leading to the fullness of life always desires inclusion of the respective others, since in the network of love it does

[12] For an attempt at a critical retrieval of the potential of *kenosis* for Christian discipleship see Sarah Coakley, *Powers and Submissions: Spirituality, Philosophy and Gender*, Oxford: Blackwell, 2002, pp. 3–39.

[13] George M. Newlands, *Theology of the Love of God*, Atlanta: John Knox Press, 1980, p. 166, defines this second type of salvation in its most comprehensive sense as 'the final goal to which God wills to bring his creatures in relationship with himself in the eschatological future'.

[14] Cf. Trevor Williams, 'Salvation', in John Bowden, ed., *Christianity: The Complete Guide*, London: Continuum, 2005, pp. 1078–9, here p. 1078.

not make any sense to be 'saved' alone. Moreover, seen from within the horizon of love any attempt to be 'saved' alone must appear as a double betrayal: it neglects this universe as created and willed by God, and it neglects the interrelationship of all human beings — dead and alive — with God, each other, and God's creation.

In his Letter to the Romans, the Apostle Paul offers a moving expression of this anguish not to be cut off from his own people in the eschatological community. He is concerned about the ultimate communion with his Jewish brethren (Rom. 9.2–4) and then broadens his concern for God's ultimate mercy to all people (Rom. 11.32) and creation of everything (Rom. 11.36). Romans 11 closes with a praise of God's inexhaustible mystery.[15] Here we find a passionate expression of the desire for ultimate community with all others with whom we are related in the God who is love. Surely, God's ultimate community with Israel in the Covenant and with the Church in Christ will be open for all who participate however mysteriously in the God-given dynamics of love.

Even though the story of the Fall and the doctrine of original sin must be reinterpreted in order to disclose their insights into human freedom to do good and evil and into the nature of structural and social sin (see my discussion of Paul Ricœur's proposal above in chapter 3), the fact of broken relationships, suffering, pain and social death cannot be denied. We human beings need God's salvation. Moreover, we also need to renew our perspective of the implications of God's gift of love for this creative and healing process into which we are called to participate through our own human praxis of love. Christian faith, I wish to argue, awaits divine salvation not besides love but in love, not apart from God's universe but in and with God's universe.

This relocation of salvation within God's creative and reconciling project of love does not imply any human power or control over the eschatological process. Rather, it implies human participation. Thus, it opens this process of love for human praxis. God's love is not to be funnelled into human souls, but human beings are invited to become responsible agents of love in the network of loving relationships. This

[15] See the instructive discussion of Rom. 9–11 in E. P. Sanders, *Paul*, Oxford: Oxford University Press, 1991, pp. 117–28; and in Eckart Reinmuth, *Paulus: Gott neu denken*, Leipzig: Evangelische Verlagsanstalt, 2004, pp. 170–81. Reinmuth, p. 179: 'Es ist erschütternd, wie sehr seit der Alten Kirche die Antwort, die Paulus in den Kapiteln 9–11 des Römerbriefes zu geben versucht, übersehen, umgedeutet oder verfälscht worden ist.'

participation is not a denial of grace, but the consequence of grace. Human love thus need not be played out against divine grace.[16]

Becoming a full and fulfilled subject with others and with God in and through love is an essential aspect of this salvific process. However, this insight must result in a critical and self-critical assessment of the structures of evil, sin and distortion that continue to permeate our roads towards subjectivity and transcendence. Neo-orthodox thinkers such as Paul Tillich and Karl Rahner devoted much of their energy to uncover personal and systemic distortions that hinder human love. Liberation theologians have carried this work further: beyond a mere contemplation of individual existence and its fragility and estrangement towards a thorough analysis of structural evils and of distorted socio-political, communicative and economic conditions. Poverty, exclusion, denial of personhood, and injustice need to be overcome if the human being is to retrieve her divine gift of agency in and for love and solidarity. Feminist theologians have examined the structural oppression of women in the Christian tradition of patriarchy and *kyriarchy*.[17] The critical and self-critical Christian praxis of love thus always already implies an acute awareness of the need for confession, conversion, forgiveness, reconciliation and healing in love.

However, this awareness does not put a condition on love in terms of doing this or that in order to begin to love. Rather, the Christian praxis of love begins with love in order then to review the personal, structural, social, political, economic, cultural etc. context in which love is taking place.

## Love and Sexuality

Many of our contemporaries believe that sexual acts not only fulfil a deep human need and desire, but that they also open an alley to

[16] Newlands, p. 169:

> Salvation through Christ remains, as I see it, from whatever theological perspective it is considered, God's permanent invitation to participation in his new creation, which includes the humanization of mankind. This humanization is to be completed, perhaps not in the deification of man, but in the humanization of man in God for ever.

[17] Elisabeth Schüssler Fiorenza, 'Prophet of Divine Wisdom-Sophia', in Patrick Gnanapragasam and Elisabeth Schüssler Firoenza, eds, *Negotiating Borders: Theological Explorations in the Global Era – Essays in Honour of Prof. Felix Wilfred*, Delhi: ISPCK, 2008, pp. 59–76, here pp. 62–3: 'The neologism *kyriarchy* which connotes the rule and domination of the emperor/lord/master/father/husband is a more apt analytical tool than patriarchy, which in white feminist theory has been understood as the domination of all men over all wo/men equally.'

love. Sexual desire is celebrated today, and — at times — confused with love, although nobody would deny the deep connection between human sexuality and love. Against the ambivalence in Christian tradition about sexuality, reaching from the recommendation of total abstinence to the affirmation that sexual desire is a gracious gift of God, secular prophets of sexual liberation have promised utter fulfilment on the basis of a return to a 'natural' attitude towards sex.[18] However, as the history of human sexuality has demonstrated, a natural attitude towards sex has never existed. Rather, sexuality has been feared, praised and understood as a complex, revolutionary, ambiguous force in human life that demanded some form of discipline and order — social, political, religious, philosophical, cosmological, cultural, aesthetic, ritual, etc.[19]

It is true that Enlightenment and bourgeois ideals of sexual relationships were, on the whole, not emancipatory and, in connection with ancient theological suspicion of sexuality, led to many forms of distortion, repression, patriarchal domination, hypocrisy and debilitating moralizing.[20] It is also true that the Christian churches in today's Western cultures have lost the battle for control over the sexuality of believers. Thus, between the secular prophets of total sexual liberation, on the one hand, and the clerical administrators of total sexual control, on the other hand, a vacuum has emerged in which many young adults often feel rather lost. How should we approach our sexuality today?

From a Christian perspective sexuality may be approached in the creative and constructive light of love. Sexuality can be appreciated as an integral dimension of human life, as created by God to be a source of desire, of physical, emotional and spiritual pleasure, and a force for human development in love. Thus, the ultimate home for the many expressions of sexuality is the network of loving relationships. Sexuality is more than what comes to expression in genital activity; it concerns our whole personality, our intimate as well as our public relationality in this universe.

[18] For a critical analysis of appeals to nature in contemporary approaches to sexuality see Regina Ammicht Quinn, *Körper – Religion – Sexualität: Theologische Reflexionen zur Ethik der Geschlechter*, Mainz: Grünewald, 1999, pp. 58–66.

[19] See in this context Michel Foucault, *A History of Sexuality* (1976–84), trans. Robert Hurley, 3 vols, London: Penguin, 1990–8.

[20] A good illustration of the modern treatment of sexuality can be found in the shifting approaches to solitary sex or masturbation in recent centuries. See Thomas W. Laqueur, *Solitary Sex: A Cultural History of Masturbation*, New York: Zone Books, 2003.

In this book I am not pursuing questions of ethics or sexual morality; rather I am interested in the theological reflection on the connection between love and sexuality. However, it seems important to me to raise the issue of growth and human development towards becoming a conscious and responsible sexual being. As we have seen above in chapter 7, the development of love benefits from institutions of love. In what way can these same institutions provide orientation for the sexual development of children, young adults, and adults? Family, marriage, chastity, church, friendship and monastic life are important institutions in which the intimate connection between love and sexuality may be explored and learned, provided these institutions do not see their vocation in policing sexual orientation and expression. Of course, sexuality is and remains ambiguous — like all other phenomena of our human existence. But it would be more helpful exposing and reflecting on these ambiguities than repressing sexual pleasure in the name of contrasting divine love with sinful sexual desire in the aftermath of the mythical Fall of Adam and Eve. Moreover, it is a genuine act of sexual liberation to free human beings from the reduction of sexual acts to the sole goal of procreation.

Sexual acts receive their dignity from love and its network of relationships that are open to transcendence. This network includes, of course, also my sexual relationship to my own emerging self.[21] All sexual acts can be assessed in the light of love. If love is the home in which sexuality can flourish, all sexual acts taking place within this matrix of love are blessed by grace. However, not all sexual activity takes place within a framework of love; and many forces in society and religion wish to assert control over human sexuality. Demonizing and repressing sexuality, on the one hand, and idolizing it and becoming obsessed with it, on the other hand, lead to harmful distortions of human life and relationships.[22] In this situation it seems to me to be important to analyse and cultivate the intimate connection between sexuality and love in order to respect and develop the framework in

[21] See also Rowan Williams, 'The Body's Grace', in Eugene F. Rogers, Jr, ed., *Theology and Sexuality: Classical and Contemporary Readings*, Oxford: Blackwell, 2002, pp. 309–21, here p. 313; and Laqueur, *Solitary Sex*, p. 420: 'Potentially autarkic solitary sexual pleasure touches the inner lives of modern humanity in ways we still do not understand. It remains poised between self-discovery and self-absorption, desire and excess, privacy and loneliness, innocence and guilt as does no other sexuality in our era.'

[22] Cf. also Konrad Hilpert, 'Sexualethik', in Peter Eicher, ed., *Neues Handbuch theologischer Grundbegriffe*. Neuausgabe 2005, vol. 4, Munich: Kösel, 2005, pp. 139–52.

which, according to Christian faith, the sexual energy present in all human beings can unfold its joyful, playful, imaginative, disturbing, interruptive, creative and procreative potential. In this framework of love the interplay of God and human subjectivity can overcome both the contempt of the body in parts of Christian tradition and transform the institutions of love (family, marriage, partnership, chastity, friendship, church, etc.) into always more responsive eschatological forces.

### Love and Forgiveness

Forgiveness is not a necessary precondition of love, but certainly a necessary dimension of all loving relationships. All human relationships in the network of love are threatened by failure, by disturbed communication, by intended and unintended hurt, and by sin. 'Sin' refers here both to the wilful disrespect for the other, for the self, for God and for God's creation, and to the intended or unintended participation in structures of disrespect, injustice, oppression and exploitation. Structural sins include participation in racist, sexist, ageist, patriarchal, kyriarchal and other forms of oppression. The horizon for forgiveness thus transcends the merely interpersonal level, however important forgiveness is also on this level. Love is not only endangered by personal failure, but also by structural failure. Pope Benedict XVI's attention to social love, as we have seen above in chapter 6, is pertinent for this reflection.

This is not the place for an in-depth analysis of the power and potential of forgiveness in our relationships, lives and communities. I only wish to emphasize the close relationship between love and forgiveness. It has been said that giving ourselves over to the passion of love is to suffer 'a sometimes demanding discipline, which reaches its climax in the practise of forgiveness: the decision, made out of compassion and for the sake of a fruitful future, to absorb injury rather than retaliate'.[23] This kind of forgiveness originating in love is amply demonstrated in the Gospels. In Luke's Gospel Jesus is reported to have shown forgiveness to sinners of all sorts and asking God for forgiveness, even for the ones who were about to take his own life, literally up to the last moments of his life (Luke 23.34). No sin is too big to be forgiven. When the apostle Peter asked how often he

[23] Nigel Biggar, *Good Life: Reflections on What We Value Today*, London: SPCK, 1997, p. 70.

should forgive, Matthew's Gospel reports Jesus answering: 'Not seven times, but I tell you, seventy-seven times' (Matt. 18.21–2).

Forgiveness in all of these biblical instances implies the facilitation or rehabilitation of authentic relationship — with other human beings, with God, and with one's own self. The biblical understanding of forgiveness always includes all of these aspects. To forgive and to pray to God for forgiveness even for those who do not care about any relationship with their victims are asymmetrical expressions of love that will not by necessity lead to mutuality. Recognizing God's image in the other and re-inviting the other into the network of loving relationships are dramatic and transformative actions notwithstanding the other's factual response to these actions. It is important, however, not to identify this loving outreach to the other with any form of condoning the other's misdeed, crimes or participation in structural evil. Respecting the other as a fellow human being and offering inclusion of the other into the various bodies of community appreciates the other as always more than his or her actions. Forgiving thus also means to see wider, further, deeper than the pain or harm afflicted on me, anybody else, God and God's creation. Forgiving implies the desire for a new and creative relationship, for transcendence and transformation of the other — and of my own self.

> Those who refuse to forgive, cease to live. They cease to live in the sense that they become unfree. They become immured in the past, chained to their loss, irrationally imagining that suffering inflicted on the one who injured them will somehow bring release. They become embittered, turned in upon themselves, twisted and darkened. They become barren, incapable of creating new life. They die because they repudiate the claims of love.[24]

As we have seen above in chapter 4, Thomas Aquinas acknowledges the close connection between love and peace. Love can bring about peace; he understands peace as an act of love. Thus, he also stresses the praxis character of peace. Peace flows from the praxis of love, and not simply from a belief in love. Love is praxis, not an object of belief or a principle of reason. Love requires engagement and self-investment. Peace requires the acts of forgiveness demanded by love.

At the beginning of my examination of love in chapter 1, I defined love as a relationship, a relationship that affirms some subject (or object), acknowledges its value and is motivated further to explore the subject (or object) of one's attention. This kind of relationship

[24] Ibid., p. 78.

is often inspired by an intense desire to seek some sort of union with the other, to enter into community with the other, to form a common body, to become one. The discussion of love and forgiveness and any reference to the love of enemies problematize and challenge the relational understanding of the Christian praxis of love. If the other and others refuse God's and our offer of relationship, is that not the end of a relational understanding of love? Was it therefore not more appropriate to speak of love as an attitude to others and otherness? I do not think so. If we were to reduce love to the level of mere attitude we would forget about its erotic nature. Love desires the other. Even the love of enemies is erotic.[25]

Love desires relationship; it desires community; it may even desire union. Thus, love is more than mere attitude. We may develop, cultivate and display attitudes of mercy, compassion, altruism,[26] solidarity and sympathy. But love aims at more: love desires to be in relationship with the other and others. Hence, even when love remains unrequited, when the perpetrator does not even ask me to forgive him or her, my desire for loving relationship can still be developed, nurtured and sharpened. The failure of love is not a good argument either against love understood as God's gift or against the understanding of the network of loving relationships. What Karl Rahner (see above, chapter 6) said about loving God holds true also for the Christian praxis of love in general: already the decision to love in future is love, since it is already on its way to love. We can always begin to love by wanting to love — without any other condition than to be ready for change and transformation.

## Love in Creation

All love, as we have seen, includes the experience of otherness — our love of God, of God's universe, of each other and of our own selves.

[25] Cf. Stinissen, p. 122.

[26] For a discussion of altruism and altruistic love in view of current scientific trajectories see Stephen G. Post and others, eds, *Altruism & Altruistic Love: Science, Philosophy, and Religion in Dialogue*, Oxford: Oxford University Press, 2002. Cf. 'General Introduction', ibid., p. 4:

> Altruistic love, which is uniquely human however much certain of its building blocks might be found in nonhuman species, is an intentional affirmation of our very being grounded in biologically given emotional capacities that are elevated by world view (including principles, symbol, and myth) and imitation into the sphere of consistency and abiding loyalty.

See also Stephen G. Post, *Unlimited Love: Altruism, Compassion, and Service*, Philadelphia and London: Templeton Foundation Press, 2003.

And all love affects our entire personality — body, emotions, soul. Relating in love to others and ourselves opens a dynamics of mysterious encounters: we do not possess a total concept of our body, of our sexuality, of our subjectivity, of our self, or of the other to whom we relate in love. Hence, it is true to say that the dynamics of love opens ways of knowing, the ends of which are not, and cannot, be known to us. To some extent love always remains uncharted territory. However, all cultures tend to develop forms, genres, taboos, starting points and institutions of love in order to help structuring the path of love, to offer directions in love, to present us with a kind of compass for navigating through the complexity of the act of loving other human beings, God, the universe, and the emerging self.

Moreover, in most cultures there is a certain consensus that love needs to be learned, first of all at home, then in school, church, temple, synagogue etc., in friendship, chastity, marriage, partnership, in training courses for parenting, caring for the elderly and handicapped. However, the social, educational and religious support structures in which such institutions of love can emerge today have changed radically from previous cultures. I would like to identify and briefly consider six among the contemporary challenges to the praxis of love.

First, as a consequence of the ongoing process of globalization, all cultural forms and patterns have undergone a certain amount of relativization, on the one hand, and of homogenization, on the other hand. More than previous generations we are aware of alternative and different forms and patterns of love. At the same time we are exposed to the global force of the contemporary media which leads to a levelling of such cultural differences.

Second, unlike in medieval Europe, few people today are supported by firmly structured guilds, associations and groups. Rather, the power of the social group into which one is born has diminished if not disappeared altogether in Western culture. As a result of humanism, Renaissance, Reformation, Enlightenment and postmodernism the individual human being has emerged as the primary agent of life, of emancipation towards autonomy, of choice and happiness. Thus, while the burden on individuals to shape their own life has grown, the support of social and religious groups and structures has weakened. The individual is widely considered to be the prime mover of love.

Third, love is seen by many contemporaries as the only escape from loneliness. Hence, love has become a carrier of many new weights on her increasingly unsupported wings. For many people love has become a project related to status, success and security rather than an adventure; a scheme to design and shape one's own life, one's own children, one's own religion, one's own god, one's own relations, one's own destiny.

As we have seen above in chapter 7, sociologists have alerted us to the fact that although the divorce rate among married couples is constantly increasing, trust in marriage as an institution is therefore not necessarily decreasing. Hence, we seem to be longing for ordered and structured forms of love even though we have lost many of the traditional means to sustain and develop them. Today, love relationships are threatened not so much by assaults from outside as by implosion. Zygmunt Bauman characterizes contemporary escapes into love: 'People seek partners and "enter relationships" in order to escape the vexation of frailty, only to find that frailty yet more vexing and painful than before. What was meant/hoped/expected to be a shelter (perhaps *the* shelter) against fragility proves time and again to be its hothouse …'[27]

Fourth, more than previous generations in the West our generation often considers children as the ultimate and purest projects of love.[28] We no longer need children to look after us when we are old; we no longer need to fear the unplanned arrival of children when we have sex; we no longer are condemned to childlessness when we are single or engaged in previously outlawed love relationships such as gay and lesbian partnerships; we no longer need to give birth to a child when we do not like his or her sex, shape, handicap or colour. Hence, children have become objects of our personal designs and lifestyles.

Nevertheless, every child, however much designed and planned, however purely desired, adopted, accepted and loved, will eventually need to develop into his or her own self. Every love of a child will sooner or later become aware of its asymmetrical character: children demand to be loved for their own sake, loved away from their parents and guardians. They will resist being mere objects of our love, care and possession. They will demand to be respected as emerging subjects in their own rights. Thus they have to disrupt and disappoint our project planning, our hopes and desires. Eventually, they will test

[27] Zygmunt Bauman, *Liquid Love: On the Frailty of Human Bonds*, Cambridge, UK: Polity Press, 2003, p. 25.

[28] Ulrich Beck and Elisabeth Beck-Gernsheim, *The Normal Chaos of Love*, trans. Mark Ritter and Jane Wiebel, Cambridge, UK: Polity Press, 1995, pp. 102–39.

the true extent of our love. They demand from us sacrifices in love. Hence, even the 'purest' projects of our love confront us with their otherness. There is no love without otherness.

Fifth, in our cultures we can observe trends to instrumentalize and compartmentalize relationships into the specific needs they are hoped to fulfil. I sleep with one partner, I play tennis with a second, I learn Japanese with a third, and I spend my holidays with a fourth. Moreover, all of these engagements may have a time-limit imposed on them. My relationships are limited and follow the implicit motto of 'limited love'. Anthony Giddens and Zygmunt Bauman have explored the contemporary desire for what they have identified as 'pure relationship'.

> It is a feature of the pure relationship that it can be terminated, more or less at will, by either partner at any particular point. For a relationship to stand a chance of lasting, commitment is necessary; yet anyone who commits herself without reservations risks great hurt in the future, should the relationship become dissolved.[29]

And the 'widely shared, indeed commonplace awareness that all relationships are "pure" (that is frail, fissiparous, unlikely to last longer than the convenience they bring and so always "until further notice") is hardly a soil in which trust may take root and blossom'.[30] That is why so many of our contemporaries would wish to keep their love uncommitted, i.e. 'liquid': they are prepared to invest some of their energies for a shorter period of time without any lasting commitment to a relationship with the other. However, the other's real otherness, and indeed one's own fuller otherness, can never come into full play in such short-cut relationships. Love cannot be unleashed without allowing the full otherness of both partners to come into play. Hence, 'pure relationships' in this sense are not really about love; rather they desire to taste a bit of love without ever wanting to be transformed by love. Therefore they cannot be creative or transcendent.

Sixth, the desire for 'pure relationships' shares an important feature with what we normally call romantic love. In both instances, love is reduced to a myth, amputated of its full force of otherness, sentimentalized, and elevated to an object of desire, projection and fetishism. In one sentence, love has been objectified. Here love has become an idea or an ideal. Romantic love objectifies

[29] Anthony Giddens, *The Transformation of Intimacy: Sexuality, Love and Eroticism in Modern Societies*, Cambridge, UK: Polity Press, 1993, p. 137.

[30] Bauman, *Liquid Love*, p. 90.

and fetishizes an idea of love. That is why in a well-known German pop song one hears the confession 'I am in love with love' (*Ich bin verliebt in die Liebe*). Gustave Flaubert's *Madame Bovary* escapes from her everyday tristesse into the projections of romantic love in order then to suffer under the painful realization of the difference between dream and reality. Moreover, Emma Bovary escapes from her *ennui* into her dream world with the help of books. Her love of books was motivated by her desire to escape the power of otherness through reading books of love. Hence, love of books and books of love do not offer us any straightforward mode of coping with the challenges of otherness in love. The sweet and threatening otherness of both the other and the self as well as the radical otherness of God can only be more fully explored in the actual praxis of love itself. However, this exploration will unavoidably transform all subjects involved. Thus, it makes no sense both to desire to love and to wish to remain unchanged. Romantic love is an illusion that changes nothing, a desire that, ultimately, does not want to be fulfilled.

Since love is not principle but praxis, it makes no sense to demand from ourselves and others that a number of requirements would need to be met before beginning the adventure of love: for instance, to meet certain physical expectations, to have a clearly developed project outline, to know already in advance how exactly love will transform the respective self and other. Since love is a transformative power, no advance plan can ever correspond to its genuine dynamics. In that sense, love knows no presuppositions other than our will to encounter otherness, even radical otherness, and our readiness to be transformed in the process.

Assessing the history of love in our Western culture, then, does not help us to love better, but it might help us to free ourselves from false expectations, to recognize reductions of love to egoistic desires, and to disclose possible context-specific distortions. Although, ultimately, the dynamics of love cannot be planned and orchestrated in advance, institutional structures need to be developed in order better to support and promote this dynamics in our families, churches, cultures and societies. Love needs space and imagination. It benefits from critical and self-critical reflection. And it calls for creative and adaptable structures in which its transformative spirit can unfold her blessings.

If we are to grow in love with our loved ones, our respective commitment to these others requires lifelong support. While nobody can love in my place, much grace and help is needed so that I can remain faithful in committed and mutual love to my partner, my family members, my friends, my communities, and to the body of Christ and through this body to God. My love is always already part of the universal love story initiated by God. It is dialectically related to this larger development. It requires much prayer and contemplation to stay on course. The love that makes our love possible has inspired the development of structures for the purpose of supporting love. My love both benefits from these structures and, at the same time, contributes to their ongoing transformation. Every occasion of love thus has both an individual and a communal dimension. Our postmodern culture has concentrated on the love of the individual and neglected the communal dimension of love, the larger work of 'body-building'.[31] This imbalance must be corrected, and more adequate Christian approaches to a culture of love need be developed. However, the dialectics between individual expressions of love and communal forms of love must be respected in this process.

Finally, love most of all needs courage: the courage to respect and explore the other and the self as other, and to let both be seen, judged, desired, nurtured and transformed by the loving eye of the radical and eternal other, God. In God's creative space, time and language, our love can prosper and mature and explore always more adequate and more rewarding forms, structures and expressions.

[31] For important recent theological contributions to this work of building bodies of love see Graham Ward, *Cities of God*, London and New York: Routledge, 2000; and Ola Sigurdson, *Himmelska Kroppar: Inkarnation, Blick, Kroppslighet*, Logos – Pathos 6, Gothenburg: Glänta, 2006.

# *SELECT BIBLIOGRAPHY*


Adams, Marilyn McCord, 'Trinitarian Friendship: Same-gender Models of Godly Love in Richard of St. Victor and Aelred of Rievaulx', in Eugene F. Rogers, Jr, ed., *Theology and Sexuality: Classic and Contemporary Readings*, Oxford: Blackwell, 2002, pp. 322–40.

Ammicht Quinn, Regina, *Körper – Religion – Sexualität: Theologische Reflexionen zur Ethik der Geschlechter*, Mainz: Grünewald, 1999.

——, 'Erotik/Eros', in Peter Eicher, ed., *Neues Handbuch theologischer Grundbegriffe*, vol. 1, Neuausgabe 2005, Munich: Kösel, 2005, pp. 253–9.

Ammicht Quinn, Regina and Elsa Tamez, eds, *Body and Religion*, *Concilium* 2002:2, London: SCM, 2002.

Anderson, Pamela Sue, 'Unselfing in Love: A Contradiction in Terms', in Lieven Boeve, Joeri Schrijvers, Wessel Stoker and Hendrik M. Vroom, eds, *Faith in the Enlightenment? The Critique of Enlightenment Revisited*, Amsterdam and New York: Rodopi, 2006, pp. 243–67.

Angenendt, Arnold, *Geschichte der Religiosität im Mittelalter*, Darmstadt: Wissenschaftliche Buchgesellschaft, 1997.

Aquinas, Thomas, *Summa Theologiæ*, vol. 19: *The Emotions*, trans. Eric d'Arcy, London: Eyre & Spottiswoode, 1967.

——, *Summa Theologiæ*, vol. 34: *Charity*, trans. R. J. Batten, OP, London: Eyre & Spottiswoode, 1975.

——, *On Charity* (De Caritate), trans. Lottie H. Kendzierski, Milwaukee: Marquette University Press, 1997.

Arendt, Hannah, *Der Liebesbegriff bei Augustin: Versuch einer philosophischen Interpretation*, Berlin: Julius Springer, 1929.

——, *Love and Saint Augustine*, ed. Joanna Vecchiarelli Scott and Judith Chelius Stark, Chicago: University of Chicago Press, 1996.

Aristotle, *The Nicomachean Ethics*, trans. Hippocrates G. Apostle, Dordrecht and Boston: D. Reidel, 1975.

Augustine, *On Christian Doctrine*, trans. D. W. Robertson, Jr, New York: Macmillan, 1958.

——, *Concerning the City of God against the Pagans*, trans. Henry Bettenson, London: Penguin, 2003.

——, *Confessions*, trans. Henry Chadwick, Oxford: Oxford University Press, 1992.

——, *Enarrationes in Psalmos*, Avrelii Avgvstini, *Opera* X, 1, Corpus Christianorum, Series Latina 38, Turnhout: Brepols, 1956.

——, *Enarrationes in Psalmos*, Avrelii Avgvstini, *Opera* X, 2, Corpus Christianorum, Series Latina 39, Turnhout: Brepols, 1956.

——, *The Good of Marriage*, trans. David G. Hunter, in Eugene F. Rogers, Jr, ed., *Theology and Sexuality: Classic and Contemporary Readings*, Oxford: Blackwell, 2002, pp. 71–86.

——, *Later Works*, trans. and ed. John Burnaby, The Library of Christian Classics, Ichthus Edition, Philadelphia: Westminster Press, 1955.

——, *On the Morals of the Catholic Church*, trans. Richard Stothert and Albert Newman, in *St. Augustine: The Writings against Manicheans and against the Donatists: The Nicene and Post-Nicene Fathers of the Christian Church*, vol. 4, ed. Philip Schaff, Edinburgh: T&T Clark, (1887) 1996, pp. 37–63.

——, *Ten Homilies on the First Epistle General of St. John*, in Augustine, *Later Works*, trans. and ed. John Burnaby, The Library of Christian Classics, Ichthus Edition, Philadelphia: Westminster Press, 1955, pp. 251–348.

——, *The Trinity*, in Augustine, *Later Works*, trans. and ed. John Burnaby, The Library of Christian Classics, Ichthus Edition, Philadelphia: Westminster Press, 1955, pp. 37–181.

——, *De vera religione*, in Avrelii Avgvstini, *Opera* IV, 1, Corpus Christianorum, Series Latina 32, Turnhout: Brepols, 1962, pp. 169–260.

Badinter, Elisabeth, *L'amour en plus: Histoire de l'amour maternel (XVIIe–XXe siècle)*, Paris: Flammarion, 1980.

Balthasar, Hans Urs von, *Love Alone Is Credible* (1963), trans. D. C. Schindler, San Francisco: Ignatius Press, 2004.

Barr, James, 'Words for Love in Biblical Greek', in L. D. Hurst and N. T. Wright, eds, *The Glory of Christ in the New Testament: Studies in Christology in Memory of George Bradford Caird*, Oxford: Clarendon Press, 1987, pp. 3–18.

Barth, Karl, *Church Dogmatics*, vol. IV: The Doctrine of Reconciliation, Part One, ed. G. W. Bromiley and T. F. Torrance, trans. G. W. Bromiley, Edinburgh: T&T Clark 1956 (German original 1953).

——, *Church Dogmatics*, vol. IV: The Doctrine of Reconciliation, Part Two, ed. G. W. Bromiley and T. F. Torrance, trans. G. W. Bromiley, Edinburgh: T&T Clark 1958 (German original 1955).

——, *The Epistle to the Romans,* trans. Edwyn C. Hoskyns, Oxford: Oxford University Press, 1968.

Bauman, Zygmunt, *Globalization: The Human Consequences,* Cambridge, UK: Polity Press, 1998.

——, *Liquid Love: On the Frailty of Human Bonds,* Cambridge, UK: Polity Press, 2003.

Bayer, Owald, Robert W. Jenson and Simo Knuuttila, eds, *Caritas Dei: Beiträge zum Verständnis Luthers und der gegenwärtigen Ökumene. Festschrift für Tuomo Mannermaa zum 60. Geburtstag,* Helsinki: Luther-Agricola-Gesellschaft, 1997.

Beck, Ulrich and Elisabeth Beck-Gernsheim, *The Normal Chaos of Love,* trans. Mark Ritter and Jane Wiebel, Cambridge, UK: Polity Press, 1995.

Bein, Thomas, *Liebe und Erotik im Mittelalter,* Darmstadt: Wissenschaftliche Buchgesellschaft, 2003.

Benedict XVI, *Deus Caritas Est,* Encyclical Letter, Vatican City: Libreria Editrice Vaticana, 2005.

Bernard of Clairvaux, *Song of Songs,* 4 vols, Kalamazoo: Cistercian Publications, 1971–80.

——, *Selected Works,* trans. G. R. Evans, The Classics of Western Spirituality, New York and Mahwah: Paulist Press, 1987.

Bernhardt, Reinhold, 'Die Polarität von Freiheit und Liebe. Überlegungen zur interreligiösen Urteilsbildung aus dogmatischer Perspektive', in Reinhold Bernhardt and Perry Schmidt-Leukel, eds, *Kriterien religiöser Urteilsbildung,* Beiträge zu einer Theologie der Religionen 1, Zurich: Theologischer Verlag, 2005, pp. 71–101.

Bexell, Göran, *Etiken, bibeln och samlevnaden: Utformningen av en nutida kristen etik, tillämpad på samlevnadsetiska frågor,* Stockholm: Verbum (1988), 1991.

Biggar, Nigel, *Good Life: Reflections on What We Value Today,* London: SPCK, 1997.

Bovon, François, *Das Evangelium nach Lukas: 2. Teilband: Lk 9,51–14,35,* EKK III/2, Zurich and Düsseldorf: Benziger and Neukirchen-Vluyn: Neukirchener Verlag, 1996.

Brady, Bernard V., *Christian Love,* Washington, DC: Georgetown University Press, 2003.

Brander, Bo, 'Ecotheology', in John Bowden, ed., *Christianity: The Complete Guide,* London: Continuum, 2005, pp. 360–3.

Braaten, Carl E. and Robert W. Jenson, eds, *Union with Christ: The New Finnish Interpretation of Luther,* Grand Rapids: Eerdmans, 1998.

Brown, Peter, *Augustine of Hippo: A Biography*, London: Faber & Faber, 1967.

——, *The Body and Society: Men, Women and Sexual Renunciation in Early Christianity*, London and Boston: Faber & Faber, 1990.

Brox, Norbert, *Erleuchtung und Wiedergeburt: Zur Aktualität der Gnosis*, Munich: Kösel, 1989.

——, *A History of the Early Church*, trans. John Bowden, London: SCM, 1994.

——, 'Selbst und Selbstentfremdung in der Gnosis. Heilsaussicht durch Erkenntnis. Die Religion Gnosis', in Brox, *Das Frühchristentum: Schriften zur Historischen Theologie*, ed. Franz Dünzl, Alfons Fürst and Ferdinand R. Prostmeier, Freiburg i. B.: Herder, 2000, pp. 255–70.

Brümmer, Vincent, *The Model of Love: A Study in Philosophical Theology*, Cambridge, UK: Cambridge University Press, 1993.

Bynum, Caroline Walker, *Jesus as Mother: Studies in the Spirituality of the High Middle Ages*, Berkeley, Los Angeles and London: University of California Press, 1982.

Cahill, Lisa Sowle, *Family: A Christian Social Perspective*, Minneapolis: Fortress Press, 2000.

Calvin, Jean, *Commentary on the Epistles of Paul the Apostle to the Corinthians*, trans. from the original Latin and collated with the author's French version by John Pringle, vol. 1, Edinburgh: T. Constaple for the Calvin Translation Society, 1848.

Capellanus, Andreas, *The Art of Courtly Love*, trans. and ed. John Jay Parry, New York: Columbia University Press, 1990.

Capps, Walter H, 'Lundensian Theology in the United States', *Svensk Teologisk Kvartalskrift* 72 (1996), pp. 59–63.

Carmichael, E. D. H. (Liz), *Friendship: Interpreting Christian Love*, London: T&T Clark, 2004.

Carr, Anne, *The Theological Method of Karl Rahner*, Missoula, MT: Scholars Press, 1977.

Chadwick, Henry, *Augustine*, Past Masters, Oxford and New York: Oxford University Press, 1986.

Chenu, M.-D., OP, *Nature, Man, and Society in the Twelfth Century: Essays on New Theological Perspectives in the Latin West*, selected, ed. and trans. Jerome Taylor and Lester K. Little, Chicago and London: University of Chicago Press, 1979.

*The Cistercian World: Monastic Writings of the Twelfth Century*, trans. and ed. Pauline Matarasso, London: Penguin, 1993.

Clack, Beverley, *Sex and Death: A Reappraisal of Human Mortality*, Cambridge, UK: Polity Press, 2002.

Coakley, Sarah, *Powers and Submissions: Spirituality, Philosophy and Gender*, Oxford: Blackwell, 2002.

——, ed. *Religion and the Body*, Cambridge Studies in Religious Traditions 8, Cambridge, UK: Cambridge University Press, 1997.

Collins, Raymond F., 'Marriage (NT)', in *The Anchor Bible Dictionary*, vol. 4, New York: Doubleday, 1992, pp. 569–72.

Cornille, Catherine, ed., *Many Mansions? Multiple Religious Belonging and Christian Identity*, Maryknoll: Orbis, 2002.

Cousins, Ewert H., 'Global Spirituality', in Philip Sheldrake, ed., *The New SCM Dictionary of Christian Spirituality*, London: SCM, 2005, pp. 321–3.

D'Costa, Gavin, 'Queer Trinity', in Gerard Loughlin, ed., *Queer Theology: Rethinking the Western Body*, Oxford: Blackwell, 2007, pp. 269–80.

de la Croix, Arnaud, *Lebenskunst und Lebenslust: Sinnlichkeit im Mittelalter*, trans. Gritje Hartmann, Darmstadt: Wissenschaftliche Buchgesellschaft, 2003.

Dalferth, Ingolf U., ed., *Ethik der Liebe: Studien zu Kierkegaards 'Taten der Liebe'*, Tübingen: Mohr Siebeck, 2002.

Davies, Oliver, *A Theology of Compassion: Metaphysics of Difference and the Renewal of Tradition*, London: SCM, 2001.

de Rougemont, Denis, *Love in the Western World*, trans. Montgomery Belgion, Princeton, NJ: Princeton University Press, 1983; French Original: *L'amour et l'occident*, Paris: Plon, 1972.

Denzinger, Heinrich, *Enchiridion symbolorum definitionum et declarationum de rebus fidei et morum*, 41st edn, ed. and trans. Peter Hünermann, Freiburg i.b.: Herder, 2007.

Dinzelbacher, Peter, *Bernhard von Clairvaux: Leben und Werk des berühmten Zisterziensers*, Darmstadt: Wissenschaftliche Buchgesellschaft, 1998.

Doob Sakenfeld, Katherine, 'Love (OT)', in *The Anchor Bible Dictionary*, vol. 4, New York: Doubleday, 1992.

Drecoll, Volker Henning, *Augustin Handbuch*, Tübingen: Mohr Siebeck, 2007.

Dumoulié, Camille, *Le désir*, Collection Cursus, Paris: Armand Colin, 1999.

Dunn, James D. G., *The Theology of Paul the Apostle*, Grand Rapids: Eerdmans (1998), 2006.

Dünzl, Franz, *Braut und Bräutigam: Die Auslegung des Canticum durch Gregor von Nyssa*, Tübingen: J.C.B. Mohr (Paul Siebeck), 1993.

Eberl, Immo, *Die Zisterzienser: Geschichte eines europäischen Ordens*, Darmstadt: Wissenschaftliche Buchgesellschaft, 2002.

Engberg-Pedersen, Troels, 'Fra 'Eros och Agape' til Venskab: Antikkens forestilling om kærlighed i forhold til kroppen, selvet og det gode (frelsen)', in Henrik Rydell Johnsén and Per Rönnegård, eds, *Eros and Agape: Barmhärtighet, kärlek och mystik i den tidiga kyrkan*, Skellefteå: Artos & Norma, 2009, pp. 11–27.

Erling, Bernard, 'Motif Theology, a Neglected Option', *Svensk Teologisk Kvartalskrift* 77 (2001), pp. 126–35.

Esler, Philip, 'Jesus and the Reduction of Intergroup Conflict: The Parable of the Good Samaritan in the Light of Social Identity Theory', *Biblical Interpretation* 8 (2000), pp. 325–57.

Fabris, Adriano, *I paradossi dell'amore fra grecità, ebraismo e cristianismo*, Brescia: Morcelliana, 2001.

Farley, Margaret A., *Just Love: A Framework for Christian Sexual Ethics*, New York and London: Continuum, 2006.

Ferreira, M. Jamie, *Love's Grateful Striving: A Commentary on Kierkegaard's* Works of Love, Oxford and New York: Oxford University Press, 2001.

——, 'The Glory of a Long Desire: Need and Commandment in *Works of Love*', in Ingolf U. Dalferth, ed., *Ethik der* Liebe: *Studien zu Kierkegaards 'Taten der Liebe'*, Tübingen: Mohr Siebeck, 2002, pp. 139–53.

Feuerbach, Ludwig, *The Essence of Christianity*, trans. George Eliot, Amherst, NY: Prometheus Books, 1989.

Foucault, Michel, *A History of Sexuality*, 3 vols (1976–84), trans. Robert Hurley, London: Penguin, 1990–8.

Frandsen, Henrik Vase, 'Distance as Abundance: The Thought of Jean-Luc Marion', *Svensk Teologisk Kvartalskrift* 79 (2003), pp. 177–86.

Frankfurt, Harry G., *The Reasons of Love*, Princeton, NJ: Princeton University Press, 2004.

Freymann, Jean-Richard, *L'Amer amour*, Strasbourg: Arcane, 2002.

Fromm, Erich, *The Art of Loving*, London: Allen & Unwin (1957), 1975.

Geels, Antoon, *Kristen mystik: Ur psykologisk synvinkel*, Part I, Skellefteå: Norma, 2000.

Gerhardsson, Birger, *The Schema in the New Testament*, Lund: Novapress, 1996.

Gerrish, Brian A., *Grace and Reason: A Study in the Theology of Luther*, Chicago and London: University of Chicago Press (1962), 1979.

Giddens, Anthony, *The Transformation of Intimacy: Sexuality, Love and Eroticism in Modern Societies*, Cambridge, UK: Polity Press, 1993.

Gilson, Etienne, *History of Christian Philosophy in the Middle Ages*, London: Sheed and Ward, 1980.

Goetz, Hans-Werner, *Leben im Mittelalter vom 7. bis zum 13. Jahrhundert*, Munich: Beck, 1986.

Goulder, Michael, *St. Paul versus St. Peter: A Tale of Two Missions*, Louisville, KY: Westminster/John Knox Press, 1995.

Gregory, Eric, *Politics and the Order of Love: An Augustinian Ethic of Democratic Citizenship*, Chicago and London: University of Chicago Press, 2008.

Grenholm, Cristina, *Moderskap och kärlek: Schabloner och tankeutrymme i feministteologisk livsåskådningsreflektion*, Nora: Nya Doxa, 2005.

Grøn, Arne, 'Kærlighedens gerninger og anerkendelsens dialektik', *Dansk Teologisk Tidsskrift* 54 (1991), pp. 261–70.

——, 'Kierkegaards zweite Ethik', trans. Hermann Schmid, in Niels Jørgen Cappelørn and Hermann Deuser, eds, *Kierkegaard Studies: Yearbook 1998*, Berlin and New York: de Gruyter, 1998, pp. 358–68.

——, 'Ethics of Vision', in Ingolf U. Dalferth, ed., *Ethik der* Liebe: *Studien zu Kierkegaards 'Taten der Liebe'*, Tübingen: Mohr Siebeck, 2002, pp. 111–22.

Hadewijch, The *Complete Works*, trans. Mother Columba Hart, OSB, The Classics of Western Spirituality, New York: Paulist Press, 1980.

Hägglund, Bengt, *De Homine: Människouppfattningen i äldre luthersk tradition*, Lund: Gleerup, 1959.

Hamilton, Victor P., 'Marriage (OT and ANE)', in *The Anchor Bible Dictionary*, vol. 4, New York: Doubleday, 1992, pp. 559–69.

Harrison, Beverly Wildung, *Making the Connections: Essays in Feminist Social Ethics*, ed. Carol S. Robb, Boston: Beacon Press, 1985.

Hazlett, Ian, 'Marriage and Heterosexuality in History and Christian Traditions: Some Signposts', in The Church of Scotland, *Reports to the General Assembly 1993*, Edinburgh and London: Pillans & Wilson, 1993, pp. 196–215.

Heine, Susanne, 'Leben=Lieben / Lieben=Leben', in Gregor Maria Hoff, ed., *Lieben. Provokationen*, Salzburger Hochschulwochen, Innsbruck and Wien: Tyrolia, 2008, pp. 106–23.

Hilpert, Konrad, 'Sexualethik', in Peter Eicher, ed., *Neues Handbuch theologischer Grundbegriffe*, Neuausgabe 2005, vol. 4, Munich: Kösel, 2005, pp. 139–52.

——, 'Solidarität', in Peter Eicher, ed., *Neues Handbuch theologischer Grundbegriffe*, Neuausgabe 2005, vol. 4, Munich: Kösel, 2005, pp. 152–60.

Huizinga, Johan, *The Waning of the Middle Ages,* trans. F. Hopman, London: Penguin, 2001.

Hume, David, *Essays: Moral, Political and Literary,* ed. Eugene F. Miller, Indianapolis: Liberty Fund, 1987.

Jarrick, Arne, *Kärlekens makt och tårar: En evig historia,* Stockholm: Pan – Norstedts Förlag, 1997.

——, *Behovet att behövas: En tänkebok om människan, kulturen och världshistorien,* Stockholm: SNS Förlag, 2005.

Jaschke, Helmut, *Heilende Berührungen: Körpertherapeutische Aspekte des Wirkens Jesu,* Mainz: Grünewald, 2004.

Jasper, Alison, 'Recollecting Religion in the Realm of the Body (or Body ©)', in Pamela Sue Anderson and Beverley Clack, eds, *Feminist Philosophy of Religion: Critical Readings,* London: Routledge, 2004, pp. 170–82.

Jasper, David, *The Sacred Desert: Religion, Literature, Art, and Culture,* Oxford: Blackwell, 2004.

Jeanrond, Werner G., *Text and Interpretation as Categories of Theological Thinking,* trans. Thomas J. Wilson, Dublin: Gill and Macmillan and New York: Crossroad, 1988; reprint, Eugene, OR: Wipf and Stock, 2005.

——, *Theological Hermeneutics: Development and Significance,* London: SCM, 1994.

——, *Call and Response: The Challenge of Christian Life,* Dublin: Gill and Macmillan and New York: Crossroad, 1995.

——, 'Revelation and the Trinitarian Concept of God: Are they Key Concepts for Theological Thought?', in Werner G. Jeanrond and Christoph Theobald, eds, *God: Experience and Mystery, Concilium* 2001:1, London: SCM, 2001, pp. 120–30.

——, *Gudstro: Teologiska reflexioner II,* Lund: Arcus, 2001.

——, 'Text/Textuality', in Kevin J. Vanhoozer, ed., *Dictionary for Theological Interpretation of the Bible,* Grand Rapids: Baker Academics, 2005, pp. 782–4.

——, 'The Concept of Love in Christian Tradition', in The Theological Committee of the Church of Sweden, *Love, Cohabitation and Marriage: Report from a public hearing September 6–9, 2004,* trans. John Toy, Uppsala: The Church of Sweden, 2006, pp. 183–93.

——, *Guds närvaro: Teologiska reflexioner I,* 2nd edn, Lund Arcus, 2006.

——, 'Der Gott der Liebe: Entwicklungen des theologischen Liebesbegriffs bei Plutarch und in der frühen Kirche', in Plutarch, *Dialog über die Liebe,* SAPERE X, trans. and ed. Herwig Görgemanns, Tübingen: Mohr Siebeck, 2006, pp. 274–93.

——, 'Europa och den religiösa utvecklingen', in Svein Aage Christoffersen and others, eds, *Menneskeverd: Festskrift til Inge Lønning*, Oslo: Forlaget Press, 2008.

——, 'Liebe in Schweden: Per Olov Enquists "Gestürzter Engel"', in Christoph Gellner and Georg Langenhorst, eds, *Herzstücke: Texte, die das Leben ändern. Ein Lesebuch zu Ehren von Karl-Josef Kuschel zum 60. Geburtstag*, Düsseldorf: Patmos, 2008, pp. 193–202.

Jeanrond, Werner G. and Aasulv Lande, eds, *The Concept of God in Global Dialogue*, Maryknoll: Orbis, 2005.

Jeanrond, Werner G. and Andrew D. H. Mayes, eds, *Recognising the Margins: Developments in Biblical and Theological Studies – Essays in Honour of Seán Freyne*, Dublin: Columba Press, 2006.

Johnson, Elizabeth A., *She Who Is: The Mystery of God in Feminist Theological Discourse*, New York: Crossroad, 1993.

Jüngel, Eberhard, *God as the Mystery of the World: On the Foundation of the Theology of the Crucified One in the Dispute between Theism and Atheism*, trans. Darrell L. Guder, Edinburgh: T&T Clark, 1983.

Kärkkäinen, Veli-Matti, '"The Christian as Christ to the Neighbour": On Luther's Theology of Love', *International Journal of Systematic Theology* 6 (2004), pp. 101–17.

Kant, Immanuel, *Anthropologie in pragmatischer Hinsicht*, in Kant, *Werke in zehn Bänden*, ed. Wilhelm Weischedel, vol. 10, Sonderausgabe, Darmstadt: Wissenschaftliche Buchgesellschaft, 1983.

——, *Beobachtungen über das Gefühl des Schönen und Erhabenen*, in Kant, *Werke in zehn Bänden*, ed. Wilhelm Weischedel, vol. 2, Sonderausgabe, Darmstadt: Wissenschaftliche Buchgesellschaft, 1983, pp. 821–84.

——, *Die Metaphysik der Sitten*, in Kant, *Werke in zehn Bänden*, ed. Wilhelm Weischedel, vol. 7, Sonderausgabe, Darmstadt: Wissenschaftliche Buchgesellschaft, 1983, pp. 305–634.

Kearney, Richard, *The God Who May Be: A Hermeneutic of Religion*, Bloomington, IN: Indiana University Press, 2001.

Keel, Othmar, 'Erotisches im Ersten Testament', *Meditation: Zeitschrift für christliche Spiritualität und Lebensgestaltung* 26:2 (2000), pp. 6–11.

Kegley, Charles W., ed. *The Philosophy and Theology of Anders Nygren*, Carbondale, IL: Southern Illinois University Press, 1970.

Kern, Udo, *Liebe als Erkenntnis und Konstruktion von Wirklichkeit: 'Erinnerung' an ein stets aktuales Erkenntnispotential*, Berlin and New York: de Gruyter, 2001.

Kierkegaard, Søren, *Works of Love*, ed. and trans. Howard V. Hong and Edna H. Hong, Princeton, NJ: Princeton University Press, 1995.

King, Martin Luther, Jr *Strength to Love*, New York, Evanston and London: Harper & Row, 1963.

Klassen, William, 'Love (NT and Early Jewish)', in *The Anchor Bible Dictionary*, vol. 4, New York: Doubleday, 1992, pp. 381–96.

Klauck, Hans-Josef, *Der erste Johannesbrief*, EKK XXIII/1, Zurich: Benziger and Neukirchen-Vluyn: Neukirchener Verlag, 1991.

Knauber, Bernt, *Liebe und Sein: Die Agape als fundamentalontologische Kategorie*, Theologische Bibliothek Töpelmann, Berlin and New York: de Gruyter, 2006.

Kobusch, Theo, *Christliche Philosophie: Die Entdeckung der Subjektivität*, Darmstadt: Wissenschaftliche Buchgesellschaft, 2006.

Köpf, Ulrich, 'Hoheliedauslegung als Quelle einer Theologie der Mystik', in Margot Schmidt together with Dieter R. Bauer, eds, *Grundfragen christlicher Mystik*, Stuttgart-Bad Cannstatt: Frommann-Holzboog, 1987, pp. 50–72.

Küng, Hans, *Global Responsibility: In Search of a New World Ethic*, trans. John Bowden, London: SCM, 1991; German original: *Projekt Weltethos*, Munich and Zurich: Piper, 1990.

Küng, Hans and Karl-Josef Kuschel, eds, *A Global Ethic: The Declaration of the Parliament of the World's Religions*, London: SCM, 1993.

Küng, Hans and Karl-Josef Kuschel, eds, *Wissenschaft und Weltethos*, Munich and Zurich: Piper, 1998.

Kuhn, Helmut, *'Liebe': Geschichte eines Begriffs*, Munich: Kösel, 1975.

Kuhn, Hugo 'Liebe und Gesellschaft in der Literatur', in Kuhn, *Liebe und Gesellschaft*, ed. Wolfgang Walliczek, Stuttgart: J. B. Metzlersche Verlagsbuchhandlung, 1980, pp. 60–8.

Lamberigts, Mathijs, 'A Critical Evaluation of Critiques of Augustine's View of Sexuality', in Robert Dodaro and George Lawless, eds, *Augustine and His Critics: Essays in Honour of Gerald Bonner*, London and New York: Routledge, 2002, pp. 176–97.

Laqueur, Thomas, *Making Sex: Body and Gender from the Greeks to Freud*, Cambridge, MA and London: Harvard University Press (1990), 1992.

——, *Solitary Sex: A Cultural History of Masturbation*, New York: Zone Books, 2003.

Larsson, Björn, *Besoin de liberté*, Paris: Seuil, 2006.

——, 'À quoi ça sert de lire des romans d'amour … et de les écrire?', in Centre des Écrivains du Sud – Jean Giono, *Comment j'ai lu des romans d'amour*, Marseille: Transbordeurs, 2008, pp. 14–44.

Lawless, George, OSA, *Augustine of Hippo and His Monastic Rule*, Oxford: Clarendon, 1987.

Lewis, C. S., *The Four Loves*, Glasgow: Collins (1960), 1977.

Lexutt, Athina, *Luther*, UTB Profile, Cologne, Weimar and Vienna: Böhlau, 2008.

Leyerle, Blake, *Theatrical Shows and Ascetic Lives: John Chrysostom's Attack on Spiritual Marriage*, Berkeley, Los Angeles and London: University of California Press, 2001.

Lienhard, Marc, 'Luther and the Beginnings of the Reformation', in Jill Raitt, ed., *Christian Spirituality*, vol. 2: *High Middle Ages and Reformation*, New York: Crossroad, 1989, pp. 268–99.

Lindberg, Carter *The European Reformations*, Oxford: Blackwell, 1996.

——, *Love: A Brief History through Western Christianity*, Malden, MA and Oxford: Blackwell, 2008.

Long, J. Bruce, 'Love', in Mircea Eliade, ed., *The Encyclopedia of Religion*, vol. 9, New York: Macmillan, 1987, pp. 31–40.

Loughlin, Gerard, ed., *Queer Theology: Rethinking the Western Body*, Oxford: Blackwell, 2007.

Louth, Andrew, 'The Body in Western Catholic Christianity', in Sarah Coakley, ed., *Religion and the Body*, Cambridge Studies in Religious Traditions 8, Cambridge, UK: Cambridge University Press, 1997, pp. 111–30.

Lunceford, Brett, 'The Body and the Sacred in the Digital Age: Thoughts on Posthuman Sexuality', *Theology & Sexuality* 15:1 (2009), pp. 77–96.

Luther, Martin, *Disputatio Heidelbergae habita. 1518*, in *D. Martin Luthers Werke*, Kritische Gesamtausgabe, vol. 1, Weimar: Hermann Böhlau, 1883, pp. 353–74.

——, *Decum praecepta Wittenbergensi praedicata populo. 1518*, in *D. Martin Luthers Werke*, Kritische Gesamtausgabe, vol. 1, Weimar: Hermann Böhlau, 1883, pp. 394–521.

——, *De captivitate Babylonica ecclesiae praeludium. 1520*, in *D. Martin Luthers Werke*, Kritische Gesamtausgabe, vol. 6, Weimar: Hermann Böhlau, 1888, pp. 497–573.

——, *Adventspostille. 1525*, in *D. Martin Luthers Werke*, Kritische Gesamtausgabe, vol. 10.I.2, Weimar: Hermann Böhlaus Nachfolger, 1925, pp. 1–208.

——, *Der Brief an die Römer*, in *D. Martin Luthers Werke*, Kritische Gesamtausgabe, vol. 56, Weimar: Hermann Böhlaus Nachfolger, 1938.

——, *A Sermon on the Estate of Marriage*, in *Luther's Works*, vol. 44, ed. and trans. James Atkinson, Philadelphia: Fortress Press, 1966, pp. 7–14. See also *Ein Sermon von dem ehelichen Stand. 1519*, in *D.*

*Martin Luthers Werke*, Kritische Gesamtausgabe, vol. 2, Weimar: Hermann Böhlau, 1884, pp. 166–71.

——, *On Marriage Matters*, trans. Frederick Ahrens, in *Luther's Works*, vol. 46, ed. Robert C. Schultz, Philadelphia: Fortress Press, 1967, pp. 265–320. See also *Von Ehesachen. 1530*, in *D. Martin Luthers Werke*, Kritische Gesamtausgabe, vol. 30.III, Weimar: Hermann Böhlaus Nachfolger, 1910, pp. 205–48.

——, *Vom ehelichen Leben (1522)*, in Martin Luther, *Gesammelte Werke*, ed. Kurt Aland, vol. 7, Digitale Bibliothek 63, Berlin: Direct Media, 2002, pp. 284–306. See also *D. Martin Luthers Werke*, Kritische Gesamtausgabe, vol. 10.II, Weimar: Hermann Böhlaus Nachfolger, 1907, pp. 275–304.

Luz, Ulrich, *Das Evangelium nach Matthäus: 3. Teilband: Mt 18–25*, EKK I/3, Zurich and Düsseldorf: Benziger and Neukirchen-Vluyn: Neukirchener Verlag, 1997.

——, *Studies in Matthew*, trans. Rosemary Selle, Grand Rapids: Eerdmans, 2005.

Malone, Mary T., *Women and Christianity*, vol. 1: *The First Thousand Years*, Maryknoll: Orbis, 2000.

Manns, Peter and Rainer Vinke, 'Martin Luther als Theologe der Liebe', in Owald Bayer, Robert W. Jenson and Simo Knuuttila, eds, *Caritas Dei: Beiträge zum Verständnis Luthers und der gegenwärtigen Ökumene. Festschrift für Tuomo Mannermaa zum 60. Geburtstag*, Helsinki: Luther-Agricola-Gesellschaft, 1997, pp. 265–86.

McGinn, Bernard, *The Foundations of Mysticism: Origins to the Fifth Century*, The Presence of God: A History of Western Christian Mysticism vol. 1, London: SCM, 1992.

——, *The Growth of Mysticism: Gregory the Great through the 12th Century*, The Presence of God: A History of Western Christian Mysticism, vol. 2, New York: Crossroad, 1994.

——, *The Flowering of Mysticism: Men and Women in the New Mysticism (1200–1350)*, The Presence of God: A History of Western Christian Mysticism, vol. 3, New York: Crossroad, 1998.

——, ed. *Meistert Eckhart and the Beguine Mystics: Hadewijch of Brabant, Mechthild of Magdeburg, and Marguerite Porete*, New York: Continuum, 1994.

McGuire, Brian Patrick, *Friendship and Faith: Cistercian Men, Women, and their Stories, 1100–1250*, Aldershot and Burlington: Ashgate, 2002.

McIntyre, John, *On the Love of God*, London: Collins, 1962.

Malina, Bruce J. and Richard L. Rohrbaugh, *Social-Science Commentary on the Gospel of John*, Minneapolis: Fortress Press, 1998.

Marion, Jean-Luc, *God Without Being*, trans. Thomas A. Carlson, Chicago: University of Chicago Press, 1991; French original: *Dieu sans l'être*, Paris: Quadrige/PUF (1982), 1991.

——, *Prolegomena to Charity*, trans. Stephen E. Lewis, New York: Fordham University Press, 2002; French original: *Prolégomènes à la charité*, Paris: La Différence, 1986.

——, *The Erotic Phenomenon*, trans. Stephen E. Lewis, Chicago: University of Chicago Press, 2007; French original: *Le phénomène érotique*, Paris: Grasset, 2003.

Mayes, A. D. H., *Deuteronomy*, New Century Bible, London: Oliphants, 1979.

Metz, Johann Baptist, 'The "One World": A Challenge to Western Christianity', in Werner G. Jeanrond and Jennifer Rike, eds, *Radical Pluralism and Truth: David Tracy and the Hermeneutics of Religion*, New York: Crossroad, 1991, pp. 203–14.

Mieth, Dietmar, *Das gläserne Glück der Liebe*, Freiburg i. B.: Herder, 1992.

Miller-McLemore, Bonnie J., *Also Mother: Work and Family as Theological Dilemma*, Nashville, TN: Abingdon Press, 1994.

——, 'Family and Work: Can Anyone "Have It All"?', in Anne Carr and Mary Stewart Van Leeuwen, eds, *Religion, Feminism and the Family*, Louisville, KY: Westminster/John Knox Press, 1996, pp. 275–93.

Mühling-Schlapkohl, Markus, *Gott ist Liebe: Studien zum Verständnis der Liebe als Modell des trinitarischen Redens von Gott*, Marburg: N. G. Elwert Verlag, 2000.

Murk-Jansen, Saskia, *Brides in the Desert: The Spirituality of the Beguines*, London: Darton, Longman and Todd, 1998.

——, 'Beguine Spirituality', in Philip Sheldrake, ed., *The New SCM Dictionary of Christian Spirituality*, London: SCM, 2005, pp. 146–8.

Mussner, Franz, *Was hat Jesus Neues in die Welt gebracht?* Stuttgart: Katholisches Bibelwerk, 2001.

Newlands, George M., *Theology of the Love of God*, Atlanta: John Knox Press, 1980.

——, *Generosity and the Christian Future*, London: SPCK, 1997.

Newman, Barbara, *From Virile Woman to Woman Christ: Studies in Medieval Religion and Literature*, Philadelphia: University of Pennsylvania Press, 1995.

Nilsson, Gert, 'Värdelös eller värdefull? Skapelse och frälsning som problem i teologisk etik', in *Modern svensk teologi – strömningar och perspektivskiften under 1900–talet*, Stockholm: Verbum, 1999, pp. 187–238.

Nørager, Troels, *Hjertets længsel: Kærlighed og Gud religionsfilosofisk belyst*, Copenhagen: Anis, 2003.

Nussbaum, Martha C., *Love's Knowledge: Essays on Philosophy and Literature*, New York and Oxford: Oxford University Press, 1990.

Nygren, Anders, *Agape and Eros: The Christian Idea of Love* (1930–6), trans. Philip S. Watson, Chicago: University of Chicago Press, 1982.

Oberman, Heiko, *Luther: Man between God and the Devil*, trans. Eileen Walliser-Schwarzbart, New Haven and London: Yale University Press, 1989.

O'Donnell, James J., *Augustine, Sinner & Saint: A New Biography*, London: Profile Books, 2005.

O'Donovan, Oliver, *The Problem of Self-Love in St. Augustine*, Eugene, OR: Wipf and Stock (reprint), 1980.

Olsson, Birger, *Johannesbreven*, Kommentar till Nya Testamentet (KNT) 19, Stockholm: ESF-förlaget, 2008.

Österberg, Eva, *Vänskap – en lång historia*, Stockholm: Atlantis, 2007.

Outka, Gene, *AGAPE: An Ethical Analysis*, New Haven and London: Yale University Press, 1972.

Pieper, Josef, *Über die Liebe* (1972), in Pieper, *Werke in acht Bänden*, vol. 4, ed. Berthold Wald, Hamburg: Felix Meiner Verlag, 1996, pp. 296–414.

Plato, *Phaedrus*, trans. R. Heckforth, in *The Collected Dialogues of Plato*, ed. Edith Hamilton and Huntington Cairns, Bollington Series LXXI, Princeton, NJ: Princeton University Press, 1961, pp. 475–525.

——, *The Symposium*, trans. Christopher Gill, London: Penguin, 1999.

Popkes, Enno Edzard, *Die Theologie der Liebe Gottes in den johanneischen Schriften*, Wissenschaftliche Untersuchungen zum Neuen Testament, 2. Reihe 197, Tübingen: Mohr Siebeck, 2005.

Post, Stephen G., Lynn G. Underwood, Jeffrey P. Schloss and William B. Hurlbut, eds, *Altruism & Altruistic Love: Science, Philosophy, & Religion in Dialogue*, Oxford: Oxford University Press, 2002.

Post, Stephen G., *Unlimited Love: Altruism, Compassion, and Service*, Philadelphia and London: Templeton Foundation Press, 2003.

Price, Richard, *Augustine*, Fount Christian Thinkers, London: Fount, 1996.

Rahner, Karl, *Von der Not und dem Segen des Gebetes*, Freiburg i. B.: Herder, 1958.

——, 'The "Commandment" of Love in Relation to the Other Commandments', in Rahner, *Theological Investigations,* vol. 5, trans. Karl-H. Kruger, London: Darton, Longman and Todd, 1966, pp. 439–59.

——, 'Reflections on the Unity of the Love of Neighbour and the Love of God', in Rahner, *Theological Investigations,* vol. 6, trans. Karl-H. and Boniface Kruger, London: Darton, Longman and Todd, 1969, pp. 231–49.

——, 'Liebe', in *Sacramentum Mundi: Theologisches Lexikon für die Praxis,* vol. 3, Freiburg, Basel and Wien: Herder, 1969, pp. 234–52.

——, 'The Mystery of the God-Man Jesus', in Rahner, *Theological Investigations,* vol. 13, trans. David Bourke, London: Darton, Longman and Todd, 1975, pp. 195–200.

——, *Foundations of Christian Faith: An Introduction to the Idea of Christianity,* trans. William V. Dych, London: Darton, Longman and Todd, 1978.

——, 'The One Christ and the Universality of Salvation', in Rahner, *Theological Investigations,* vol. 16, trans. David Morland, OSB, London: Darton, Longman and Todd, 1979, pp. 199–224.

——, 'The Body in the Order of Salvation', in Rahner, *Theological Investigations,* vol. 17, trans. Margaret Kohl, London: Darton, Longman and Todd, 1981, pp. 71–89.

——, *The Love of Jesus and the Love of Neighbour,* trans. Robert Barr, Middlegreen, Slough: St Paul Publications, 1983.

——, 'Justification and World Development from a Catholic Viewpoint', in Rahner, *Theological Investigations,* vol, 18, trans. Edward Quinn, London: Darton, Longman and Todd, 1984, pp. 259–73.

——, 'The Human Question of Meaning in Face of the Absolute Mystery of God', in Rahner, *Theological Investigations,* vol. 18, trans. Edward Quinn, London: Darton, Longman and Todd, 1984, pp. 89–121.

——, *Politische Dimensionen des Christentums: Ausgewählte Texte zu Fragen der Zeit,* ed. Herbert Vorgrimler, Munich: Kösel, 1986.

Raunio, Antti, *Summe des christlichen Lebens: Die 'Goldene Regel' als Gesetz der Liebe in der Theologie Martin Luthers von 1510–1527,* Mainz: Philipp von Zabern, 2001.

Reinmuth, Eckart, *Paulus: Gott neu denken,* Leipzig: Evangelische Verlagsanstalt, 2004.

Riches, John, *Jesus and the Transformation of Judaism,* London: Darton, Longman & Todd, 1980.

Ricœur, Paul, '"Original Sin": A Study in Meaning', trans. Peter McCormick, in Ricœur, *The Conflict of Interpretations*, ed. Don Ihde, Evanston: Northwestern University Press, 1974, pp. 269–86.

——, 'Love and Justice', trans. David Pellauer, in Werner G. Jeanrond and Jennifer L. Rike, eds, *Radical Pluralism and Truth: David Tracy and the Hermeneutics of Religion*, New York: Crossroad, 1991, pp. 187–202.

——, *Figuring the Sacred: Religion, Narrative, and Imagination*, trans. David Pellauer, ed. Mark I. Wallace, Minneapolis: Fortress Press, 1995.

——, *Réflexion faite: Autobiographie intellectuelle*, Paris: Éditions Esprit, 1995.

Rist, John, 'Augustine of Hippo', in G. R. Evans, ed., *The Medieval Theologians*, Oxford: Blackwell, 2001, pp. 3–23.

Rogers, Eugene F., Jr, ed, *Theology and Sexuality: Classic and Contemporary Readings*, Oxford: Blackwell, 2002.

Rubenson, Samuel, 'Himmelsk åtrå: Höga Visan i tidigkristen tolkning', in Henrik Rydell Johnsén and Per Rönnegård, eds, *Eros and Agape: Barmhärtighet, kärlek och mystik i den tidiga kyrkan*, Skellefteå: Artos & Norma, 2009, pp. 105–27.

Saarinen, Risto, *The Pastoral Epistles with Philemon & Jude*, Grand Rapids: Brazos Press, 2008.

Sanders, E. P., *Paul*, Past Masters, Oxford and New York: Oxford University Press, 1991.

Sanner, Inga, *Den segrande eros: Kärleksföreställningar från Emanuel Swedenborg till Poul Bjerre*, Nora: Nya Doxa, 2003.

Schimmel, Annemarie, *Wie universal ist die Mystik: Die Seelenreise in den großen Religionen der Welt*, Freiburg i. B.: Herder, 1996.

Schmidt, Alfred, 'Praxis', in Hermann Krings, Hans Michael Baumgartner and Christoph Wild, eds, *Handbuch philosophischer Grundbegriffe*, vol. 4, Studienausgabe, Munich: Kösel, 1973, pp. 1107–38.

Schrage, Wolfgang, *Der Erste Brief an die Korinther, 3. Teilband: 1 Kor 11,17–14,40*, EKK VII/3, Zurich and Düsseldorf: Benziger and Neukirchen-Vluyn: Neukirchener Verlag, 1999.

Schreiter, Robert J., CPPS, *The Ministry of Reconciliation: Spirituality & Strategies*, Maryknoll: Orbis, 1998.

Schüssler Fiorenza, Elisabeth, *In Memory of Her: A Feminist Theological Reconstruction of Christian Origins*, London: SCM, 1983.

——, 'Prophet of Divine Wisdom-Sophia', in Patrick Gnanapragasam and Elisabeth Schüssler Firoenza, eds, *Negotiating Borders:*

*Theological Explorations in the Global Era – Essays in Honour of Prof. Felix Wilfred*, Delhi: ISPCK, 2008, pp. 59–76.

Selderhuis, Herman J., *Marriage and Divorce in the Thought of Martin Bucer*, trans. John Vriend and Lyle D. Bierma, Sixteenth Century Essays and Studies, vol. 48, Kirksville: Truman State University Press, 1999.

Sheldrake, Philip, ed., *The New SCM Dictionary of Christian Spirituality*, London: SCM, 2005.

Shortt Rupert, *God's Advocates: Christian Thinkers in Conversation*, London: Darton, Longman and Todd, 2005.

Sigurdson, Ola, *Kärlekens skillnad: Att gestalta kristen tro i vår tid*, Stockholm: Verbum, 1998.

——, *Himmelska kroppar: Inkarnation, blick, kroppslighet*, Logos, Pathos Nr 6, Gothenburg: Glänta, 2006.

Singer, Irving, *The Nature of Love*, 3 vols, Chicago and London: University of Chicago Press, 1966–87.

——, *The Pursuit of Love*, Baltimore and London: Johns Hopkins University Press, 1995.

Søltoft, Pia, 'Den Nächsten kennen heißt der Nächste werden: Über Ethik, Intersubjektivität und Gegenseitigkeit in *Taten der Liebe*', in Ingolf U. Dalferth, ed., *Ethik der Liebe: Studien zu Kierkegaards 'Taten der Liebe'*, Tübingen: Mohr Siebeck, 2002, pp. 89–109.

Soskice, Janet Martin, *The Kindness of God: Metaphor, Gender, and Religious Language*, Oxford: Oxford University Press, 2007.

Stinissen, Wilfrid, *Störst av allt är kärleken*, Skellefteå: Artos and Örebro: Libris, 2008.

Stock, Konrad, *Gottes wahre Liebe: Theologische Phänomenologie der Liebe*, Tübingen: Mohr Siebeck, 2000.

Stolt, Birgit, *Martin Luther, människohjärtat och Bibeln*, Stockholm: Verbum, 1994.

Stålsett, Sturla J., ed., *Religion in a Globalised Age: Transfers & Transformations, Integration & Resistance*, Oslo: Novus Press, 2008.

Taylor, Charles, *Sources of the Self: The Making of the Modern Identity*, Cambridge, MA: Harvard University Press, 1989.

Theißen, Gerd, *Die Religion der ersten Christen: Eine Theorie des Urchristentums*, 3rd edn, Darmstadt: Wissenschaftliche Buchgesellschaft, 2003.

Thomas Aquinas – see Aquinas, Thomas.

Thomas, David M., 'Marriage', in Joseph Komonchak, Mary Collins and Demot A. Lane, eds, *The New Dictionary of Theology*, Dublin: Gill and Macmillan, 1987, pp. 624–8.

Tillich, Paul, *Systematic Theology*, 3 vols, Chicago: University of Chicago Press, 1951–63.

——, *Love, Power, and Justice: Ontological Analyses and Ethical Applications*, Oxford: Oxford University Press, 1954.

——, *Dynamics of Faith*, New York, Evanston and London: Harper & Row (Harper Torchbooks), 1958.

——, *Christianity and the Encounter of the World Religions* (Number 14, Bampton Lectures in America delivered at Columbia University, 1961), New York and London: Columbia University Press, 1963.

——, *My Search for Absolutes*, New York: Simon & Schuster, 1967.

——, *Impressionen und Reflexionen: Ein Lebensbild in Aufsätzen, Reden und Stellungnahmen. Gesammelte Werke*, vol. XIII, Stuttgart: Evangelisches Verlagswerk, 1972.

——, 'Religion und Kultur', in Tillich, *Gesammelte Werke*, vol. 9: *Die religiöse Substanz der Kultur: Schriften zur Theologie der Kultur*, 2nd edn, Stuttgart: Evangelisches Verlagswerk, 1975, pp. 82–93.

——, 'Systematische Theologie von 1913', in Tillich, *Frühe Werke*, ed. Gert Hummel and Doris Lax, *Ergänzungs- und Nachlassbände zu den Gesammelten Werken von Paul Tillich*, vol. IX, Berlin and New York: de Gruyter, 1998, pp. 273–434.

——, *Vorlesungen über Geschichtsphilosophie und Sozialpädagogik* (Frankfurt 1929/30), ed. Erdmann Sturm, *Ergänzungs- und Nachlassbände zu den Gesammelten Werken von Paul Tillich*, vol. XV, Berlin and New York: de Gruyter and Evangelisches Verlagswerk, 2007.

Tracy, David, *Plurality and Ambiguity: Hermeneutics, Religion, Hope*, San Francisco: Harper & Row, 1987.

Turner, Denys *The Darkness of God: Negativity in Christian Mysticism*, Cambridge, UK: Cambridge University Press, 1995.

van Bavel, Tarcicius J., 'Love', in Allan D. Fitzgerald, OSA, ed., *Augustine through the Ages*, Grand Rapids and Cambridge: Eerdmans, 1999, pp. 509–16.

Vanhoozer, Kevin J., *First Theology: God, Scripture and Hermeneutics*, Downers Grove, IL: InterVarsity Press, 2002.

Walsh, Carey Ellen, *Exquisite Desire: Religion, the Erotic, and the Song of Songs*, Minneapolis: Fortress Press, 2000.

Ward, Graham, *Cities of God*, London and New York: Routledge, 2000.

Watson, Francis, *Agape, Eros, Gender: Towards a Pauline Sexual Ethic*, Cambridge, UK: Cambridge University Press, 2000.

Wehr, Gerhard, ed., *Martin Luther – der Mystiker: Ausgewählte Texte*, Munich: Kösel, 1999.

Welz, Claudia, *Love's Transcendence and the Problem of Theodicy*, Tübingen: Mohr Siebeck, 2008.

Wilckens, Ulrich, *Der Brief an die Römer. 2. Teilband: Röm 6–11*, EKK VI/2, Zurich, Einsiedeln and Cologne: Benziger and Neukirchen-Vluyn: Neukirchener Verlag, 1980.

Williams, Daniel Day, *The Spirit and the Forms of Love*, Digswell Place: James Nisbet, 1968.

Williams, Rowan, *Lost Icons: Reflections on Cultural Bereavement*, London and New York: Continuum, 2000.

——, 'The Body's Grace', in Eugene F. Rogers, Jr, ed., *Theology and Sexuality: Classical and Contemporary Readings*, Oxford: Blackwell, 2002, pp. 309–21.

Wright, C. J. H., 'Family', in *The Anchor Bible Dictionary*, vol. 2, New York: Doubleday, 1992, pp. 761–9.

# INDEX OF NAMES

# *INDEX OF SUBJECTS*